Toyohiko Kagawa:
Apostle of Love and Social Justice

Toyohiko Kagawa at Takane Gakuin, Gotemba,
during the Farmers' Gospel School, August,
1933. *(Umeko Momii photo.)*

Toyohiko Kagawa

Apostle of Love and Social Justice

Robert Schildgen

CENTENARY BOOKS

© 1988 American Committee for the
Kagawa Centennial Project
Published by Centenary Books
1442-A Walnut Street, Suite 415
Berkeley, California 94709, USA
Printed in the United States of America
All rights reserved
Designed and produced by David Comstock

Library of Congress Cataloging-in-Publication Data

Schildgen, Robert.
Toyohiko Kagawa : apostle of love and social justice.

Includes index.
1. Kagawa, Toyohiko, 1888–1960.
2. Missionaries—Japan—Biography.
3. Christian biography—Japan.
I. Title.
BV3457.K3S26   1988   209'.2'4   [B]   88-20316

ISBN 0-9620537-0-8
ISBN 0-9620537-1-6 (pbk.)

To all people who care—
like Haru Kagawa, his wife

Haru and Toyohiko Kagawa, about 1935.

Contents

Photographs

Acknowledgments

S o MANY DEDICATED PEOPLE volunteered assistance and encouragement in this project that it is impossible to acknowledge them all appropriately in a few paragraphs. However, let me first thank the American Committee for the Kagawa Centennial Project for the grant underwriting the research and writing of this book (funded primarily by the Marjorie Barker F.D.B. Charity), and, more importantly, for the freedom I was allowed to present frankly the problematic aspects of Kagawa's life wherever they occurred rather than replaying the somewhat one-dimensional biographies of earlier years.

Kagawa's daughter, the Reverend Umeko Momii, was especially helpful in providing candid interviews and family data. George Yasukochi patiently edited, challenged and advised me throughout. The Reverend Frank Omi translated Japanese texts that proved valuable in understanding Kagawa. Andrew Kuroda's assistance was indispensible in procuring texts and government documents. Morris Lippman, Robert Neptune and Emil Sekerak aided in explaining Kagawa's influence on the cooperative movement in the United States, the Reverend Thomas Grubbs on American Christian churches, and Koji Murata and David Tatsuno on Japanese Americans.

The Reverend Robert Stieber of the Buraku Liberation Center furnished important background information about Kagawa's relation to the buraku (outcaste) community in Japan. Carl Van Drey, author of the latest Kagawa biography in German, relayed materials in his files not readily available in the United States. Many of the basic references were obtained from the extensive collections of the libraries at the University of California (Berkeley), the Graduate Theological Union (Berkeley) and the University of San Francisco. My research depended heavily on their cooperation.

I am grateful to Yasuo Furuya for inspiring me with confidence at the beginning of this work, when I had expressed doubts to him about being equal to the task of interpreting Kagawa's complex life. In his own essay on Kagawa, written 25 years ago, Furaya had lamented that no critical biography of Kagawa had been written. Perhaps this book will partly fill that need and stimulate further research. To the Reverend Hideo Hashimoto I owe the greatest thanks and respect for his unstinting help in locating and analyzing information, for sharing his personal experiences, and for his warm encouragement.

The time and efforts of these individuals and others who assisted on this book are notable examples of the "Kagawa spirit" of Christianity.

ROBERT SCHILDGEN
Oberlin, Ohio
April 13, 1988

Kagawa and his bride, Haru, as newlyweds in 1914.

The young labor agitator, Kagawa, with Bunji Suzuki, Labor
Fellowship leader, in the 1920s.

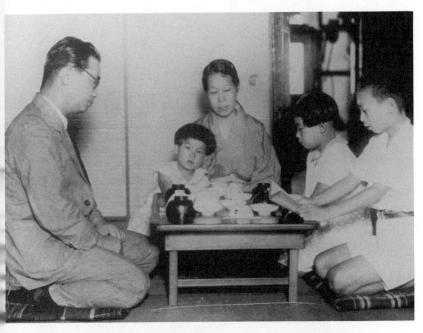

Left to right: Toyohiko, Umeko, Haru, Chiyoko, and Sumimoto
Kagawa observe morning devotion at home in 1932 or 1933.
(Umeko Momii photo.)

Kagawa with Dr. Charles Logan, a Presbyterian missionary who was influential in Kagawa's early life; about 1936.

Kagawa during his
1936 American tour.

Kagawa at tomb of Abraham Lincoln's mother in Gentryville,
Indiana, March 1936. *(Umeko Momii photo.)*

New York, 1953 or 1954. Left to right: Shige Kagawa (his niece), Rev. Giichi Kawa (pastor of the Dutch Reformed Church in New York), Toyohiko, and daughter Umeko (a student at Yale Divinity School). *(Umeko Momii photo.)*

Toyohiko and Haru Kagawa, about 1950, after many years of intense effort for peace, social justice and the Christian faith.

Introduction:
Gandhi—Schweitzer—Kagawa?

O N CHRISTMAS EVE IN 1909, a brilliant 21-year-old student packed some books and clothes into a bamboo box, put it on a hand cart and trudged off to one of Japan's most notorious slums, the Shinkawa district in the city of Kobe. The slender young man checked into a run-down, stucco-covered house with two dark little rooms and a common toilet, a water hydrant and a kitchen in the back shared among a few dozen impoverished neighbors, including ragpickers, pimps, prostitutes, rickshaw pullers and the chronically ill or unemployed.

Among his first roommates were an alcoholic suffering from malnutrition and acute dermatitis, a syphilitic, and a murderer released from prison. The place had been unoccupied for some time because the previous tenant had been murdered, and it was feared that his ghost was lurking about the gloomy premises. As if one evil spirit weren't enough for the cramped quarters, the young student had to hold the hand of the murderer to calm him down when the ghost of his victim paid a visit in the man's nightmares.

Such was the bizarre beginning of the career of Toyohiko Kagawa, who went on to become one of the most influential social reformers and religious leaders in Japan and perhaps the most famous and revered Japanese figure in the rest of the world during the 1930s. A convert to Christianity, he was one of those rare and troublesome Christians who decided to live the Gospel quite literally, dedicating himself to the poor by giving all he owned, whether material or emotional resources. He fed, sheltered, nursed, educated and preached in the slums at tremendous risk to his own health, contracting the painful eye disease, trachoma, which plagued him through his life, and risking a recurrence of tuberculosis which had almost killed him twice before he plunged into the slums.

1

He was heckled, beaten, robbed and menaced by knife-wielding gangsters. When he gave away his last clothing, he was forced to wear a woman's kimono borrowed from a destitute neighbor. But he stayed on, fearless and seemingly invincible, even making converts to the new religion. Those who first thought him insane began to believe he had supernatural powers. Those who laughed would come to call him Kagawa *Sensei*, the Japanese term for teacher which commands considerably more respect than its English counterpart.

Kagawa. The name alone was magic in the West, once evoking the kind of reverence many people now feel at the mention of a Martin Luther King or a Mother Teresa. Like them, this Japanese minister was seen as a Christlike model of selfless dedication to the poor and a peacemaker consumed with a hunger and thirst for justice. He was, in fact, variously hailed as "the Japanese Gandhi," "Japan's Albert Schweitzer," "the Saint Francis of Japan," or more comprehensively canonized as the "Saint of Japan." He was also named "Christ's Samurai" and, in Teutonic fashion, was dubbed by one German writer as an example of "Christian Knighthood."[1] In 1940, when he was jailed on suspicion of publishing articles which violated Japan's military code, the *New York Times* headline announced "GANDHI OF JAPAN PUT UNDER ARREST."[2]

His life and works were chronicled in books with dramatic titles such as *Three Trumpets Sound: Kagawa—Gandhi—Schweitzer*[3] and *Whither Asia?*,[4] while hundreds of articles in many languages detailed his tireless activities as minister to the poor and social activist. His own voluminous essays, fiction and poetry were translated into German, Dutch, Spanish, Czech, Chinese, Hindi, Hebrew, and the Scandinavian tongues, to name a few.[5] The translations were regularly reviewed in major newspapers and journals in the United States and England. In 1936 alone, over 750,000 attended his lectures in the United States and Canada. In reviewing one of Kagawa's novels, *A Grain of Wheat*, the noted critic Alfred Kazin wrote:

> Kagawa is the greatest Christian leader in the Orient today, and being a missionary whose labors are confined to his own country, he makes much the same use of the novel that Bunyan and the later Tolstoy did. . . . It is significant that Kagawa's book

has had a success in Japan comparable to that of *Pilgrim's Progress* in seventeenth-century England and *Resurrection* in late nineteenth-century Russia.[6]

Kagawa's work was not confined to his own land. His admirers among peace activists in the West were deeply moved by the anti-war refrain in his lectures and writings, as well as by pacifist actions like his refusal to participate in school military exercises when he was a mere 15-year-old. Yet many became disenchanted with him after World War II, when reports from Japan accused him of capitulating to the Japanese government and collaborating with the "enemy."[7] These reports may have cost him the Nobel Prize when he was nominated for it in 1955.

These are a few glimpses into one of the most fascinating and complex lives of modern times. Kagawa was a prophet with abundant honor in his own land and abroad, but the way he burst into national prominence forms perhaps the most intriguing chapter in his long life. For a golden period in the early 1920s, Kagawa was a Mother Teresa, Upton Sinclair, Thorstein Veblen, Samuel Gompers and Jane Addams combined into one prodigiously versatile, energetic and disciplined personality. He became almost simultaneously a minister to the slums, the author of a best-selling novel, a trail-blazing sociologist, a leader in Japan's fledgling labor movement, and organizer of farmer and consumer co-ops.

As president of the Kansai Labor Federation in 1919, he captured the nation's attention by leading the largest strike in its history up to that point and heading a demonstration in 1922 of 30,000 workers protesting the policies of the giant Kawasaki and Mitsubishi corporations in the Kobe dockyards. Merely leading marches, negotiating the demands of dispossessed, and making speeches was not enough to satisfy a man of his talents; he also wrote songs to inspire the workers and edited the union's official newspaper.

When his pacifism led to a break with the urban labor movement, whose syndicalist wing was agitating for violent action, he turned his energies to the plight of the rural poor, helping found the Japanese Farmers Union, and organizing a peasantry in many respects more miserable than the urban proletariat. He founded a number of consumer cooperatives, one of which became a billion-dollar-a-year enterprise, and he left a pacifist legacy to the Japanese cooperative movement, now one of the strongest voices for peace in contemporary Japan.

Though the government jailed him for union activities, his organizing skills and reputation were such that it appointed him to a leadership position in relief work after the devastating 1923 Tokyo earthquake. Kagawa maintained a high profile both in Japan and abroad before World War II, making tours of the United States in 1924, 1931, 1935 and 1941 and visiting many countries in Asia and Europe. This international stature and his influence on the Japanese people led to consideration of Kagawa as prime minister of the new government after the war, and he continued to use his reputation to foster the moral and physical reconstruction of Japan. He backed social democratic candidates and encouraged the many reforms which converted Japan into a modern, pluralistic democracy.

His theology linking faith to social action and the fact that his complex life reveals so much about modern Japan are compelling reasons for a reassessment of Kagawa. Yet another reason for reassessment is that Kagawa has been the victim of biographers who portrayed him as such an idealized holy man that the eventual appearance of human flaws led to disillusion. He was transformed into a kind of Protestant saint, only to suffer a fate similar to some of the Catholic saints when their lives were exposed to the cold light of demythologizing research. His strongest admirers diminished his achievements by oversimplification. In venerating him as one of the elect, chosen from above to bear a cross for the suffering poor of Japan, they denied him his other cross, the cross of a complex, often contradictory and tormented personality.

The tragic irony is that the war which darkened his life precipitated the very reforms he had fought for with such dedication. The framers of the postwar Japanese constitution and the Allied Occupation fulfilled some of the fondest dreams of the aging Kagawa. Labor unions were granted full freedom a quarter of a century after he led them in defiance of the government. Women were guaranteed the rights he advocated. Massive land and agrarian reforms were enacted and the oppressive power of the huge business monopolies was diminished, though some may argue not enough nor long enough. Religious freedom was guaranteed, and the famous Article 9 of the new constitution, forbidding the use of war as an instrument of policy, became the law of the land.

Reformers of the prewar era were soon upstaged by the rush of postwar events. A decade after Kagawa's death, a colleague and biographer Shiro Kuroda in 1970 lamented:

> Kagawa was tremendously famous. While I traveled all over Japan as Kagawa's companion for five years, among the numerous people we met, there was only a single person who did not know who he was. However, nowadays virtually no one of the younger generation knows Kagawa's name.[8]

We would paint too solemn a portrait, however, if we ignored the everyday side of his life—his biting humor, his sense of wonder at the slightest things, his eye for details, his personal quirks. Of the immense nuclear problem he could say "We must understand atomic science from the religious standpoint. I am interested in the wonderful construction of the atom."[9] Riding past the United Nations building in 1950, the now-stocky man in the shabby black suit squinted through his thick glasses and remarked: "It is too rectangular and it has no symbolism of what the United Nations should stand for."[10]

He was a sardonic cartoonist who illustrated some of his own works, including satires on environmental pollution in Japan. He was an accomplished calligrapher who bragged to his children about his skill. A compulsive writer, he managed a fair amount of his correspondence by dictating letters while enthroned on the toilet in protracted duels with hemmorhoids. Within the family he insisted with patriarchic authority that the children practice his brand of austerity rather than buy new clothes, and he cajoled his wife into writing a book because of his fervent belief in women's liberation. The upstairs rooms of his house were such a weighty clutter of books that the floors had to be reinforced to prevent their caving in. At times he launched into his favorite hymns in a voice that could be annoyingly loud and off key.[11]

One would not expect to find all these symptoms of reckless vigor in a rather frail man who could spend hours in silent meditation. But then Kagawa was a master of the unexpected, a sort of "miracle," he acknowledged, while rattling off the list of near fatal diseases he had suffered or the perilous situations he had escaped. Kagawa called himself "God's Gambler" and experienced the Biblical injunction that one must lose his life to gain the life abundant. He crossed the death line and was resurrected a hero. The absorbing details of his struggles, their consequences and how they bear upon our own struggles in our time—these we are exploring in 1988, the centennial year of his birth.

Chapter 1
Making of a Mystic Rebel

*T*HE MAN WHOSE WORLD-WIDE REPUTATION was based on Christlike service to the poor was emphatically not born in the poverty of a stable or laid down in a manger. He spent his earliest years in a mansion owned by his father, who was a merchant, politician, and wealthy scion of a prominent samurai family. But when adverse circumstances came, they hit hard. They hammered out a person with an incredible ability to bear suffering and to feel it in others, to be mystical and pragmatic, to attend to the dirtiest details of a suffering beggar and in the same day write ecstatic poems to the God he encountered behind this complex drama.[1]

To begin to understand Kagawa, one must look at his unusual childhood, his ancestry and the social contradictions into which he was born. Somewhat puzzling to a Westerner is that he was not only not a Kagawa, but an illegitimate Kagawa, who nevertheless enjoyed, while they lasted, the privileges of an elite family name.

Kagawa's father, Denjiro, was born March 17, 1847, in Awa, near the eastern tip of Shikoku, the smallest of the four main islands in the hundreds of the Japanese archipelago stretching almost from the tropics to the tundra. Nestled in the southwestern curve of the largest island Honshu, Shikoku is separated from it by the straits known as the Inland Sea. Denjiro, one of nine sons of *sake* manufacturer Yanogoro Isobe, became a Kagawa through the Japanese custom of adoption. In this male-dominated society which placed strong emphasis on the perpetuation of the family name, a clan without a male to carry on the lineage would often adopt a son, bestow the family name on him and marry him to an eligible daughter.

This is precisely what happened to Denjiro, who was adopted at age 15 by Seibei Kagawa, head of one of the most prominent samurai families in the area. The Kagawa family was "nobility" in the Western sense, landholders who had been in the region for centuries. The very name "Kagawa," which means "happy river," derives from their home environs watered by the Yoshino River just a dozen miles from the ocean. By the Genroku period (1688–1703), the family head had become the chief of 19 villages, firmly ensconced in the feudal system. On the plains along the river they raised rice, fruit and silkworms, and were among the first to produce indigo, a major cash crop in the area. Toyohiko himself was eventually dubbed the "fourteenth heir" of the family. Upon adoption, Denjiro was renamed Junichi, and a marriage was promptly arranged with a Kagawa daughter, Michi, seven years younger than he. Further evidence of nobility is the fact that the adoption was arranged at the suggestion of the *daimyo* (feudal lord) of Awa.

Clinging to such traditional customs contrasted sharply with other aspects of the senior Kagawa's career. He was also the product of that turbulent period when Japan leapt from feudalism straight into the "modern" world. By the middle of the 17th century, Japan had sealed itself off from the world by expelling almost all foreigners, forbidding Japanese to travel outside the country, banning the import of books from the West, and limiting contact with China. It was the mysterious land of the samurai and the Tokugawa shoguns.

This meant that the nation had been cut off from the momentous technological and political developments taking place the world over. Two hundred years later, when the United States opened up Japan with "gunboat diplomacy" and Commodore Perry sailed into Edo Bay in 1854, Japan would change forever. The jolt of seeing the power of the West convinced the Japanese that they had to adapt rapidly or be conquered. Thus began that combination, often bewildering to the West, of Japan's eager adoption of Western ways mixed with its thoroughgoing traditionalism.

Rising discontent within the feudal system itself, feeding upon exposure to new ideas, led to a revolution which culminated in the emperor's "restoration" in 1868 and laid the foundations for a constitutional monarchy. What emerged was not a genuine constitutional monarchy, however, because the emperor was considered a god and vested with divine authority. Japan was left with a strange mixture of a theocratic state and a constitution which opened the way for democracy. The emperor served as an anchor of stability, a link with the past, and a focus of unity, backed by a cult of nationalism and compulsory military service, borrowed from French and German models.

Tremendous strains occurred in the attempt to achieve a sudden transformation from a feudal-agrarian to an industrialized society, strains that became a factor in driving Japan to totalitarianism in the period between World Wars I and II. In a single generation, the legendary gowned samurai, swords strapped to their belts, hair in topknots, were replaced by soldiers carrying guns and dressed in western uniform, and sailors piloting state-of-the-art warships. By the end of a second generation, the isolated land which walled out all intruders had begun to set forth on its own imperialist course, entering Korea and engaging in war with China. Millions of peasants moved off the land to the cities which were in the throes of an industrial revolution.

In the end, the nation was unable to reconcile the ancient paternalistic society with the new demands of an urban proletariat, an aroused peasantry and a rising middle class emboldened by adoption of customs and ideas from the West. Modern capitalism, socialism, parliamentary democracy, Christianity, totally new styles of art and literature, and discoveries of modern science, followed by trade-unionism and Marxism created a tornado of change—a kind of hyper-stimulation the likes of which the world has rarely seen. Junichi's career began in this turbulent atmosphere and Toyohiko's entire life can be seen as an effort to cope with such staggering diversity and conflict.

The senior Kagawa was an excellent student, a trait inherited by Toyohiko. He became a partisan in the *Jiyuminken*, a "freedom and rights" movement which agitated for governmental reforms and demanded a broader popular voice. His presidency of the Jidosha (Self-help Society) later caused him political problems. Among his associates were a number of young activists who later achieved national prominence like Yukio Ozaki, the premier elder statesman in Japan, who served in public office well into the post World War II era. Junichi moved to Tokyo in 1875 and was appointed secretary of the senate, the advisory body to the emperor, but when the Jidosha became critical of an imperial rescript, he was exiled back to Awa. The Awa governor Takaaki Tomioka, however, appointed him sub-prefect of Tokushima. Junichi finally wearied of politics, resigned from government, and moved to the port city of Yokohama. Assisted by Heihachi Tanaka, a banker and entrepreneur, he started a brokerage business exchanging dollars, and subsequently founded a shipping company with offices at strategic locations.

Junichi's marriage was unsuccessful, and he was drawn to other women, which was not unusual in a country with a tradition of concubinage in the upper classes. The system amounted to polygamy, an arrangement which the serious and sometimes puritanical young Toyohiko strongly condemned. Finally, Junichi left his childless wife Michi and her mother back on the estate in Awa. He fell in love with a geisha named Kame, who bore him five children, beginning with a son Tanichi born in 1873. A daughter followed, then Toyohiko on July 10, 1888, after Kame had moved to Junichi's mansion in the port and industrial city of Kobe, across the channel from the island home. To legitimize these children of his mistress, the elder Kagawa had them adopted into the family, an acceptable procedure for maintaining the lineage.

Seven days after birth, the baby was named after the god, Toyouke Daijin, the deity of the Osahiko shrine near the estate in Awa. He was undoubtedly given the usual ceremonies for newborn babies. After the first month, he would be dressed in an ornately embroidered black silk kimono and carried into the temple to be blessed. At four months he would receive his first solid food, dressed in a bright kimono and placed in front of an enamelled tray with a small bowl and tiny chopsticks. He would be carried around on the back of his nurse or mother, as was the custom in Japan.

The child's first few years were happy, as he was by all accounts a pampered younger sibling in a culture famed for pampering children. He was said to be bright, gregarious, fun-loving, and privy to all the delights which a wealthy family could furnish. He apparently charmed the apprentices in his father's company, and must have shown flashes of the wit and verbal agility which he later displayed as a speaker and writer.

Then disaster struck, and struck again. Junichi died at age 44 in November 1892 of complications from influenza or dysentery, although drinking and high living may have been contributing factors. While a parent's death can obviously have a shocking effect on a child of four, a chance event made it even more stunning for Kagawa. He had been quarreling with a playmate and, in a fit of anger, ran and grabbed the wooden lock bar from a door to strike the child. Fortunately, he was intercepted by a servant, who told him to put the bar down and follow along. Coming up the steps to the room where Junichi lay, the boy apparently sensed the tension and sorrow in the people around the dying man and began to cry. Kagawa's strong aversion to violence in later life may have resulted from the association of his childhood anger with the passing away of his father.

A few months later on January 10, 1893, Kagawa's mother also died, just eight days after the birth of her fourth son, Masuyoshi. Besides the new born baby, she also left behind a two-year-old boy, Yoshinori and an eight-year-old daughter, Ei.

After a conference of the clan, the 19-year-old Tanichi was designated as head of the family, and little Toyohiko and his older sister Ei were sent back to the family estate in Awa to live with the widowed Michi and her mother, Sei. This traumatic change stamped Kagawa for life, as can be seen from his frequent references to it in his later writings and conversations. He recalled the sadness of departure, of waving to family and friends from the boat as it sailed from Kobe to Awa, heading for what he later called "a big house without love."

Though "without love," it was certainly an interesting piece of real estate. The house was a large structure with thatched roof, big rooms, latticed windows, doors and screens of tissue paper, and soft straw mats on the wooden floor. There were numerous outbuildings for the estate's operations.

While the physical surroundings were comfortable, a harsher and more foolish way to handle children can scarcely be imagined. The neglected wife, clearly bitter over having foisted on her the children of her husband's concubine, made them a target of pent-up anger through scolding, pitiless scorn and in the girl's case, constant beatings. It was impossible for her to find a way to display affection for the little intruders, whom she sometimes even taunted for being the children of her husband's mistress.

Psychologically, this was a tormenting situation for a gifted and sensitive child who already had been devastated by the death of both parents and removal from his secure home. Almost as soon as he became conscious of himself, Kagawa felt like an outsider, an alien, unwanted, unloved. This feeling stayed with him and was the basis for his attraction to Christianity, for both in its ideals and in the friendly Christians he encountered, he found a home for the homeless. It is understandable that a physically and emotionally orphaned person would identify with the child in the Nativity who had no place to stay and the Son of Man who had not a stone on which to rest his head.

The family were members of the Shingon sect of Buddhism, and displayed the typical "god-shelf" in the home as a domestic altar. On this shelf memorial tablets bore the names of various ancestors inscribed on them. From the time he was six or seven, Kagawa had to place an offering of food in front of the tablets every morning before he had his own breakfast. He would enter the dark room, light candles, and strike the little bell. Though the boy's dominant religious emotion at this time was fear, he credited this and other Japanese rituals with helping to develop his sense of piety and spiritual presence.[2]

Learning was an early consolation in his life. The family succeeded in enrolling him in the local primary school at age four years and nine months, when the minimum age was six. This precocious student did extremely well. He was eager to attend school because of a hunger for learning and a desire to escape from the depressing home atmosphere. His teachers were impressed with the little prodigy who, besides being a gifted scholar, had unusual talent in calligraphy and painting. Not surprisingly books became a refuge for him to the end of his life.

Toyohiko spent much time alone and was easily given to

crying and self-pity. The enormous compassion he would later express for the poor and the outcast probably arose from these early feelings and his discovery of "Christian love" as anything but theoretical. Having been wounded as a child, he was able to respond to the suffering of others with a rare intensity. He described the scene this way:

> We had many rooms in the house and many servants. Our ancestors ruled over nineteen villages in the feudal system, and we were the wealthiest family in the village. We owned a factory and manufactured indigo, and we also manufactured some wine and had many fields.
>
> My stepmother and her mother, who also lived with us, did not seem pleased to have me there. They always acted as if I were an intruder, an interloper. I lived in a big house without any love. So I always pretended I wasn't there. I would go out among the flowers and the bamboo trees in the garden, or out to the fields to work with the men, or into the storeroom to study all the relics—suits of armor and swords and shields—that my ancestors used in the feudal system. But I was very lonely as a child.[3]

The treasure room was in a cool, dark building with only a small window to let in the light. Its foot-thick mud walls and tile roof were designed to protect the valuables from fire. It served as an ideal refuge in which to indulge a melancholy sense of the past and present. Toyohiko actually played with the armor of samurai ancestors, toyed with relics like ornate saddles and pored over ancient sagas in books and scrolls.

He found small consolation in his sister, who had little relation to him even as a playmate, much less in the area of emotional support. She was withdrawn and depressed as the result of being beaten often and forced by the stepmother and grandmother to labor at hard tasks on the farm. Later Kagawa portrayed her in his autobiographical fiction as a pathetic and half-insane character, a hapless creature for whom he could only express a mixture of pity and scorn.

This is not to say that Kagawa's character was wholly determined by his early experience. Many people have suffered similar rejection and loss as children. The difference is that for an exceptionally sensitive child, certain incidents cut more deeply than usual and are more vividly recollected and dwelt upon.

Such incidents are also used in later life as emotional referents, as means of explaining one's personality to others. Kagawa never tired of writing and telling about the misery and loneliness of his childhood. It is poured into his big novel *Shisen o koete* (Crossing the Death Line) and appears in other works with titles such as *Attitude toward Affliction* (1924), *Thorns that Remain* (1926), and *God and Victory over Suffering* (1932).

Again and again he refers back to this sense of alienation and melancholy which becomes a metaphor for the human condition. The home, the place to belong for such a youth, could not be in the family, but was found in meditation, in service to others, in participation in the religious community, in Christ.

As if the problems described here were not difficult enough, there were other serious events that emerged as touchstones for an introspective child. When Kagawa was ten years old, he was falsely accused of causing the death of a school custodian's daughter. The little girl had fallen into a ditch, seriously injuring herself, after which she contracted pleurisy and died. Local children accused young Toyohiko of attacking her and pushing her into the ditch. The community believed them, and the girl's father demanded a hundred yen from Kagawa as an obituary gift. In order to make amends, Kagawa took all the money he had earned selling the eggs from chickens he raised himself and gave it to the child's parents. Like other dismal episodes of his childhood, this incident cut deeply enough to affect his emotional life for years to come. He even wrote about it just six months before his death in 1960: "The saddest event in my entire life was confessing to the sins which I had not committed and spending my savings for medical expenses for her."

It was not until much later that Toyohiko found out the girl was injured when she accidently fell while working on an irrigation treadmill, a device that moved water in buckets. The village children may have accused him because the Kagawa family was itself becoming the target of resentment among their increasingly disgruntled tenants. His upper class position was attracting more attention because he had taken on such aristocratic duties as collecting rents, conducting religious ceremonies, and appearing at social functions. There may also have been envy of his ability in school. Village gossip undoubtedly contributed to the resentment, because Kagawa was often taunted by the local children for being the "son of a concubine," according to his brother Masuyoshi.[4]

In addition to books and the ancient storehouse, he found refuge and solace in nature, spending time along the river, in the bamboo groves, under towering pine trees on the family grounds, watching birds as he wandered through mulberry fields. He carried on conversations with the snails and crabs he encountered in sand bars and reeds along the river. An ancient imperial mausoleum about a mile from the house became one of his favorite sites for contemplation.

Young Toyohiko was also immersed in nature because he was expected to work in the field and take responsibilities. He had to stand in mud and transplant the young green rice plants, tend animals, help harvest, weave straw for mats and other household equipment and participate in the operation of the farms. The sense of wonder at creation often expressed in his poetry and meditations is not some romantic affectation, as is too often the case with "nature poets," but a sense of union with nature that was grounded in these childhood experiences. If communication with schoolmates and family was lacking, then one could commune with the universe, losing oneself in the changes of seasons, growth of crops and all the rhythms of nature. From this background also developed his later interest in agriculture and condemnation of the environmental pollution pouring from the factories of Japan's growing industrial cities.

Besides religious ceremonies in the home and temple, another important early influence was the training in Confucianism and Buddhism which Toyohiko began to receive at the age of nine at the Daienji Zen Temple in Ohtsu village. This study of ancient texts would later impel him to write about the synthesis of Asian philosophy and religion with Christianity in works such as *Rethinking Asian Philosophy* (Toyo shiso no saiginmi) and *Christ and Japan*, the latter of which was written specifically for the English-speaking world.

The Confucian and Buddhist texts he studied tended to compound the boy's melancholy, because they held up an ideal of human behavior to which, as far as he could see, no one around him was living up. The ideas of Confucius, Mencius, and the Chinese classics were easy enough to grasp, but he lamented:

> When it comes to putting these ideas into practice it is a truly different matter. And the standards in my home were certainly far different from these ideas. Every room in the house and the storeroom besides was filled with licentious books, and that was true also of the houses of my relatives. The Buddhist temple alone stood out in contrast as a place where the atmosphere was clean and pure.

Later, he expressed exactly the same attitude toward Christianity, refusing to tolerate a gulf between Christian theory and practice, and demanding that human deeds match the sacred text. He created enemies in the church establishment with his scathing criticism of the hypocrisy of Christians who talked mightily of doctrine on Sunday but ignored the poor at the church steps.

Toyohiko's youthful impatience with the corruption of the world sometimes spilled over into self-contempt. He brooded:

> My father had transgressed, and as a result I was born. My older brother too had gotten off the track and ruined the family. Seeing this, my one prayer was that somehow I might escape from this contaminated atmosphere and might not have to follow their wicked ways.

Several times, when family business made it necessary for him to take a message to his brother Tanichi, Toyohiko was appalled to find him drunk and carousing with women in a geisha house.

The women of his house reinforced this fear, often lecturing the child about his father's dissipation, so that the horror of squandering his life became an early fixation. In reaction to this, he set up austere regimens of discipline in school. He puritanically avoided the usual adolescent vulgarity, causing other boys to consider him an eccentric bookworm. When he encountered popular Darwinian ideas about the inheritance of moral traits, his fears of evil were intensified because he thought he had inherited this propensity to vice. His phobia of evil at the tender age of eleven was portrayed rather luridly:

> I realized that if I were the least bit careless, I myself might be easily drawn into the whirlpool of vice, and that I would be led away into a future of which no one could predict the outcome.

But while I felt this keenly, I could not see clearly at that time how I was going to rise victorious over this danger.[5]

After the traumatic incident with the custodian's daughter, it is fair to say that Toyohiko was close to suffering the kind of mental illness which today would be treated by a counselor or therapist. He was depressed, frequently in tears, and he spent more of his time alone reading to escape. He persuaded his brother Tanichi to permit him to attend Tokushima Middle School in Tokushima, the port city at the tip of Shikoku. Tanichi could see that it made sense to get the boy out of his painful situation and into a boarding school. His birthdate was apparently falsified in order to gain admission, because he was a year younger than the minimum age. He passed the entrance exams with distinction and enrolled in April 1900. The prospect of getting away from the village to a new place and a receiving a chance to expand overjoyed him. "There was hardly a happier time in my life, than when I found out I was accepted by the school," he commented years later.[6]

Toyohiko moved into the dormitory at the Katayama-juku, a private school operated by Sokichi Katayama, a Christian and English language teacher who also taught at the middle school. The youth was far more comfortable here than he had ever been at home. Some of his cousins were among the boarders who shared quarters with him. His intense reading gave him a reputation as a bookworm without necessarily isolating him from the others. Following the lead of the boys who were attending church, mainly out of curiosity or the desire to learn English, he made his first contacts with foreign Christians when he attended church with his cousin Itaru Nii.

The school not only led him to Christians, but furnished the troubled boy with two sets of badly-needed surrogate parents. Dr. Charles A. Logan, a 28-year-old Southern Presbyterian missionary from Kentucky, gave weekly lectures on the life of Christ for the students, which Toyohiko attended from the time of Logan's arrival in 1902. He soon met another Southern Presbyterian missionary at Katayama's house, Logan's brother-in-law, Dr. Harry W. Myers from Virginia. Myers was impressed when Toyohiko recited a story in English to show off his proficiency.[7] The bright-eyed, slender student so charmed the

missionary that he was soon invited to enjoy the hospitality of
the minister and his wife, Grace Field Myers. He was heartened
by the kindness of the missionaries and pleased to find people
living up to the prescriptions of their sacred text, in contrast to
the corruption that had so disturbed him. Kagawa movingly
described his admiration for these missionaries:

> It was in the third term of my third year in Middle School that
> Dr. Logan, who had just arrived from America, began a series of
> lectures on the life of Christ for us students. The lectures were
> given in English to help us in our study of that language. It was
> the first time I had ever heard English spoken by a foreigner and
> also the first time I had heard anything like Christian teaching. I
> had seen Dr. and Mrs. Myers, but I had never spoken with
> them.[8]

The student Kagawa was attracted to Logan's "mild and
shining face" and appreciated Logan's careful preparation for
the class, which included lecture outlines mimeographed with
green ink from the missionaries old-fashioned machines. He
later reminisced:

> His careful preparation for the class drew my heart to
> him. . . . It was a time when my thirst for knowledge was deep
> and sometimes I felt as though I could ill spare the time to go to
> Dr. Logan's home, yet because I liked him so well, I was a
> frequent visitor there. To tell the truth, I was the loneliest person
> in the world just at that time and as I was searching for someone
> who would treat me kindly I was naturally drawn to this man,
> who was so gentle and kindly, who taught us English without
> charge and told us the fascinating stories of Genesis with con-
> summate skill.[9]

So excited was Toyohiko about these sessions that he spent far
more time studying Logan's notes than in preparing for the
English classes in the regular school course. He confessed the
extent of his need for this type of person: "I was just fifteen
when I heard Dr. Logan's lecture on Genesis, and for the first
time in my life I really began to awake to a sense of being alive, a
human being.[10]

The American missionaries' examples of Christianity in action
had a lasting impact on the impressionable young man:

> Two homes which have taught me what love means, are the

homes of Dr. Logan and Dr. Myers. It is not the Bible alone which has taught me what Christianity means but the love of these two homes. When tired of the battle and with no place to go, these two homes were open to me and a welcome always awaited me. These people brought me up as one of their own children.[11]

While they recognized his brilliance, they could not have predicted the extent of his future success. Mrs. Logan once remarked, "If we'd known he was going to become so famous, we'd have taught him better pronunciation."[12] Kagawa was extremely well-read in English, but his English speech remained heavily accented throughout his life, which was not necessarily a disadvantage. If anything, it added an exotic touch that captivated audiences in the United States and reinforced confidence in the universality of the Christian faith.

He was fortunate to encounter these Presbyterian ministers. Not only were they dedicated but they possessed the intellectual tools to stimulate Kagawa's eager adolescent mind. They were evangelists—one of Kagawa's early encounters with Logan was at a tent-meeting—but they definitely were not the narrow-minded, Bible-pounding zealots commonly associated with evangelism today. They regarded preaching as a duty rather than a sanctimonious performance for a paying audience. Their evangelizing message was obedience to the Biblical command to go forth and teach all nations, using the apostle Paul as their model.

Sensitive to Japanese culture, they would speak, read and publish in both Japanese and English. Though nurtured in a strictly fundamentalist tradition, they were broad-minded, well-read and unafraid of doctrinal pollution from either avant garde theologians or secular agnostics. This is evident from the variety of texts they fed the intellectually hungry young Kagawa. These teachers were far from the stereotype of the missionary as an ethnocentric alien, ignorant of foreign culture, who inflicted both his religion and an inferiority complex on the natives. Because of the Myers and Logan families, Kagawa experienced intellectual growth while picking up the fervor of evangelism. Myers recalled him as a "slender, precocious boy of fourteen," with a prodigious memory.

Building a fruitful relationship with the missionaries did not eliminate Toyohiko's troubles. When he was twelve or thirteen, he was already experiencing the coughing of blood and other alarming symptoms of tuberculosis—the first of many illnesses that would torment him throughout his life. Worries about health were compounded by serious financial trouble. The ancient Kagawa estate went bankrupt in April, 1903, because of bad investments, poor management and Tanichi's high living, all subsidized by loans against the family property and heirlooms. Much of the property had to be sold to settle debts. Even the family home had to be vacated.

This financial disaster cut off Toyohiko's money for tuition, room and board, forcing him to leave the dormitory. He then moved in with his wealthy uncle, Rokubei Mori, who agreed to pay the tuition. Mori was the president of the Tokushima railway and politically influential. The uncle was willing to help, but he had no intention of spoiling Kagawa with a free ride because he was convinced that pampered male children needed a rather harsh introduction to reality and responsibility when they reach adolescence. In exchange for room and board, the sensitive young scholar was expected to do houshold chores and practice his intellectual skills by tutoring his cousin Kanzo.

Uncle Mori was a thoroughly secular man with little use for religion, much less for the alien Christianity. He objected to Kagawa's spending time with Christians, studying their bible and showing interest in the church. The strained relationship broke down into constant arguments. As is often the case when adolescents are lectured by adults, Mori's harangues had the opposite efffect of driving Toyohiko closer to the dreaded Christians. In the middle of these overwhelming financial and family troubles, he was dealt yet another blow when his brother Tanichi died on a trip to Korea less than a year after the family lost most of its wealth.

Myers and Logan recognized that they had a potential convert, but their interest in Kagawa went beyond collecting a Japanese trophy for the Christian cause. They knew he was brilliant and they saw that he was deeply disturbed by physical, emotional and financial problems. Myers once consoled him, "Dry your tears with the sun." This was the Biblical message of the need to let go of anxiety. Toyohiko continued to be not only welcomed into the missionaries' homes where he could dine at any time, but he had free run of Myers' extensive library.[13]

Intense reader that he was, Toyohiko pillaged the library, and was especially attracted to Tolstoy, Ruskin, and Kant. Myers recalled him dipping into such works as Christlieb's *Modern Doubt and Belief* and Fairbairn's *Philosophy of Religion*.[14] Kagawa began writing for the school paper, and by the time he was seventeen had already published his translation of Ruskin's *Sesame and Lilies* in Tokushima's daily paper. He came under the influence of Tolstoy's pacifism and the Christian socialist ideas of Japanese writers like Isoo Abe (1865–1949) and Naoe Kinoshita (1869–1937). The riot of reading that began at this time and continued through his teen years is portrayed vividly in *Crossing the Death Line*.

But it was the study of the Bible which had the deepest emotional effect on him. The boy who had no father was attracted to and soothed by the idea of a loving father in heaven, a deity with whom one could be intimate, and yet, as the missionaries explained, who permeated the universe. The surrogate parents had introduced him to the cosmic parent.

Devout as they were, Logan and Myers probably didn't realize the grip that the Bible would come to have on Kagawa, because an aptitude for religious experience is somewhat hard to detect. Myers first noticed it late in 1903, when the boy Kagawa came to him sobbing late in 1903, saying that he "read the story of the Cross of Christ, and, like the Apostle Paul, the love of Christ constrained him."[15]

Back in the previous summer, when the missionary went on vacation, he had assigned the students some biblical passages to memorize, one of which was the Sermon on the Mount. While reading and memorizing this passage in Luke, Kagawa had an intense experience. He was struck by the image of the lilies of the field. It seemed to speak from eternity straight to his own misery when Christ said: "Consider the lilies how they grow; they toil not, they spin not; and yet I say unto you, Solomon in all his glory was not arrayed like one of these. if then God so clothes the grass, how much more will he clothe you, oh ye of little faith."

The comfort these lines gave young Kagawa was enormous—an adolescent beset with psychological problems, alienated, at odds with his family, worried about money, and worried about sheer physical survival. He was suddenly gripped by the message not to be concerned, to let his worries go, and to exist as nature exists. He would describe this intense spiritual experience in different ways at different times.

"When I memorized those simple verses," he said in 1931, "it was an inspiration to me. Through Christ I found the truth; I found the Life; I found the way to become holy, to be godly."[16] The episode involved a sense of the presence of God, a feeling of cleansing from care and fear of corruption. Kagawa felt God asking him "If you want to cleanse your corrupt soul, and go into a life of purity, look at heaven and earth again with the spirit of the lilies of the field."[17] In trying to describe this ineffable moment he also said simply: "I discovered my Father in heaven and in me."[18]

Toyohiko began to pray to the Father at this time, pulling the futon (quilt) over his face and saying simple prayers like "O God, make me a good boy! Amen."[19] God was no longer an abstraction or a theological proposition, but experienced as an intimate reality. It was apparently so intimate that paternal imagery wasn't adequate, for he would use maternal references to describe religious experience, saying that his prayer was like a baby sucking at a mother's breast or that people live in God the way a baby lives in its mother's womb.

Kagawa was not totally "born again," as his own writings clearly demonstrate. Despite certain intense religious experiences, he was not transformed overnight. But the consolation of the Bible opened him up to the possibilities of Christianity and of finding a home in this new faith. His spiritual growth was visibly clear to his minister-teachers.

Finally, in late January of 1904, the usually gentle missionary Myers hurled a challenge to Toyohiko, who had stopped by to borrow more books. He began interrogating the young man, asking if he believed in Christ. When Kagawa replied affirmatively and added that he was praying, Myers continued, "Why don't you come to church?" His reply was that his uncle would throw him out of the house if he did. Uncle Mori disliked

Christians partly because Catholic converts were responsible for promoting the 16th century revolts. Myers countered that the early Christians had not seen eye-to-eye with the Roman Empire.

"You're a coward," Myers shouted.

"What?" the stunned disciple asked.

"You're a coward," Myers repeated.

This stung Toyohiko. It was not only a shocking thing to hear from the beloved minister, but a challenge to his manhood. To be called a coward in a land with a samurai history and a strong military cult was a brutal blow, even to a boy as unconventional as Toyohiko. A real man, Myers had implied, would stand up for his beliefs, regardless of the consequences. Young Kagawa accepted the challenge, and began attending church on Sunday.

Toyohiko was baptized on February 14, 1904, by Dr. Myers at the Tokushima Japanese Christian Church.[20] He was 15 years old. This was the official beginning of a religious life that would encompass a variety of religious experiences, from the dark night of the soul when the total absence of God drove him to despair, to mystical experiences when he felt himself immersed in a divine presence. He would suffer many twists and turns in his personal development over the next few years before he became more deeply confirmed in the Christian faith. It was period of rapid intellectual growth, severe illness, and intense soul-searching.

Chapter 2
Ideas Into Action

A PROTEST AGAINST JAPAN'S rising militarism was the first public action taken by Toyohiko Kagawa at the age of 15. That baptism came a few weeks after Japan fired the first shots of the Russo-Japanese war, attacking the Russian fleet with torpedoes in Port Arthur harbor, February 8, 1904. A relatively small number of Japanese Christians and socialists denounced the war, pointing to its waste of natural resources and the loss of lives of the peasant and working classes. More than 20,000 perished in the first six months.

The country had been caught up in a military and nationalistic frenzy fueled by its victory in the 1895 Sino-Japanese war. Even before that, Japan had been moving rapidly towards militarization. Since the dismantling of the feudal system and the promulgation of a monarchy in 1868, the Japanese leaders insisted on the need for a strong military force to defend the new government from threats both within and without. An imperial army of 10,000 was drawn from the warriors of the large feudal domains, and the ministries of the army and navy were established.

A conscription law had been passed in 1873 requiring all able-bodied men, regardless of social status, to undergo three years of military service followed by four years in the reserve. This was a revolutionary reversal of the preceding three centuries when the common people were forbidden to own swords. The peasants, comprising 80 percent of the population, were not at all eager to assume the warrior role, viewing conscription as yet another episode in the long history of their exploitation. When it was first introduced, they cynically called the draft *ketsuzei* (blood tax).[1]

The educational system was revamped to emphasize patriotism and the military. In Kagawa's Tokushima Middle School, the students wore military uniforms. Military drills such as marching and war games were conducted as part of the regular curriculum. One day as students were marching to drill, rifles in hand, young Toyohiko threw down his weapon declaring that he was a pacifist and would not carry a tool used for killing people.[2] When he refused to pick it up at the order of his instructor, he was kicked and beaten, but he would not relent.

This serious breech of discipline brought Kagawa to a hearing before the head of the teacher's association, a man nicknamed "The Blue Devil." Knowing that the man was a Christian, Kagawa astutely sabotaged the interrogation by quoting the Gospel of Matthew: "For all they that take the sword shall perish by the sword." He managed to escape with a mere reprimand.[3] This was a daring attitude for an adolescent in an authoritarian setting. The successsful episode must have strengthened several traits which became hallmarks of his behavior: an absolute sense of the righteousness of his cause, the ability to act on his convictions regardless of personal risk, and the desire to sacrifice himself to redeem others in conscious imitation of Christ.

It was exactly this stubborn adherence to his beliefs that caused Kagawa to reject a promising career at this juncture. He graduated from middle school in March 1905. A perfect candidate for higher education, with his family status he could easily have catapulted into a high position in business or government. His uncle Rokubei Mori knew this and offered to pay Kagawa's way through the prestigious Tokyo Imperial University, an obvious setting for the rising stars of the new Japan. Kagawa flatly rejected the generous offer and instead made plans to study for the Christian ministry at Meiji Gakuin, the Presbyterian college in Tokyo.

His insistence on dedicating himself to an alien religion climaxed the running feud between Kagawa and the uncle, the pragmatic businessman attached to traditional Japanese values. It was one thing to take advantage of the Christians to learn English and explore other aspects of Western culture that would be useful in commerce or diplomacy. Thousands of young

Japanese were doing this. But to join them and to convert to their faith, which Japan had banished from its islands three hundred years earlier—that was a harsh betrayal of family, state and traditional life. It was not unlike the shock modern day parents in traditional religions might feel when a son or daughter drops the family faith and joins a cult.

The disputes which took place between these two strong-headed individuals are chronicled in Kagawa's remarkable auto-biographical novel *Shisen o koete* (Crossing the Death Line), which became a best seller after its publication in 1920. Stern resistance from his elders served only to reinforce Kagawa's Christian resolve. In his case, sternness was even more futile, because it was applied to an adolescent already alienated from family, one who had recently been inspired by a successful defiance of school officials and had learned, as well, to cope with authoritarian oppression by enjoying the bittersweet feelings of rejection. His novels, essays and talks are full of references to such melancholy.

Ordered out of the house, young Kagawa packed his belongings and headed for the Myers home where he had been promised a place to stay until his enrollment at Meiji Gakuin in Tokyo. Dr. Myers believed so strongly in Kagawa's potential that he raised funds to finance his education from the mission congregation. Shortly thereafter, in April 1905, Kagawa journeyed 300 miles northeast to the metropolis of Tokyo and entered the Presbyterian college.

In the dormitory where he lived, Kagawa soon dazzled or disgusted the other students with his prodigious reading, and he was regarded as an eccentric bookworm. Even his friends nicknamed him *chozen* (transcendentalist or outsider). Dr. A. K. Reischauer, who taught there many years, was quoted as saying he was the most brilliant student ever to attend the school.[4] The school library was well-stocked with texts in English, and the energetic 17-year-old plowed through such intimidating works as Kant's *Critique of Pure Reason*, Darwin's *Origin of Species*, Ruskin's *Modern Painters*, Schopenhauer's *The World as Will and Idea*, and Müller's *Sacred Books of the East*. He was stirred by Mommsen's *Rome* and Grote's *Greece*, and he plunged into whatever classical authors were available in translation.

William Axling, a personal friend who authored in 1932 the first major English biography of Kagawa, claims that Kagawa had read almost all the important books in the library during his two-year stay at Meiji.[5] The sheer frenzy of his intellectual activitity is characterized with a healthy dose of irony in *Crossing the Death Line*.

Kagawa would cut classes to spend more time reading, which was just as well for his teachers, because by this time he was capable of embarrassing them with his superior knowledge of particular subjects. He was also turning into a good-looking young man, who could look dandyish either in Western attire or in the kimono worn when relaxing in the dormitory. Close to his adult height of 5 foot 2 inches, the young Kagawa was quite conscious of the bright-eyed, lean and well-groomed figure he cut. He looked very little like the image the world would become familiar with—that slightly stoutish man squinting through glasses and dressed in a rumpled black suit. He read through the night sometimes and skipped meals while finishing a book.[6] Though he learned to moderate the reading habit, it stayed with him even in the near blindness of later life when he was seen in busy stations and airports, oblivious to his surroundings, scanning a text through a magnifying glass with his one good eye.

Kagawa's reading was utterly without specialization or focus, seemingly bent on absorbing the whole range of Western knowledge and culture. He delved into every field: philosophy, science, literature, history, theology, agriculture and art. His one weakness in learning during this period was his neglect of classical Japanese and Chinese works, where he would fall behind in his assignments.[7] The amazing jumble of ideas he assembled over the years would later cause listeners to complain that they were unable to understand Kagawa's lectures, as he jumped from one topic to the next, tying together seemingly unrelated concepts.[8]

Marxism also found a niche in the sprawling museum of the young man's mind. A classmate Shiro Murata, spoke of Kagawa monopolizing the Marx books in the library and recommending to fellow students that they attend to Marx.[9] Kagawa's first encounter with Marx was probably in the *Heimin Shimbun* (Commoner's Newspaper), which was launched in November 1903 but shut down by the government within a year because of its anti-war stance.

Kagawa earnestly agreed with Marx's critique of capitalism, his analysis of its problems, and his passionate concern for the sufferings of the working class. He often cited Marx to prove a point, even while battling the Japanese Marxists years later. Because Japan had begun industrialization a hundred years after Europe, the miserable conditions in England of the 1830s and 1840s described by Marx and Engels were being replicated in Japan at the turn of the century. Such conditions were similarly reported by Kagawa's *Hinmin shinri no kenkyu* (Studies in the Psychology of the Poor) published in 1915. The vivid descriptions of the slums in Kagawa's novels form a Japanese version of the 19th Century urban horrors classically depicted by Charles Dickens.

Although he accepted Marx's diagnosis of capitalism in these teen years, Kagawa as a pacifist refused to accept the Marxist emphasis on violence and class struggle as the cure for the agonies of the working class. His other major disagreement with Marxism was over its definition of man as almost exclusively an economic creature, ignoring the subjective and religious dimensions of human consciousness. To a young man gifted with a capacity for religious ecstasy, the atheism of Marxism and its contempt for religion was unacceptable. Even at this early age, he did not believe that human problems would be solved solely by improving economic conditions, though he was soon to do everything in his power to improve the lives of the poor. He was convinced that there also had to be a change in the inner person, a religious dimension to human activity which Marxist philosophy left out. Without the mystical and ethical dimension of religion, he was convinced that socialism itself would lose reverence for the sanctity of the individual, becoming heartless and dehumanized.

The intellectual developments that were terrifying fundamentalist Christians at the beginning of this century—and are still major issues for them today—were welcomed by this young Japanese convert to Christianity. Rather than being outraged by Darwinism, Kagawa was exhilarated by *Origin of Species*. At various times he studied paleontology to enhance his feeling for the evolutionary process. Yet just as he disputed the Marxian view of class struggle, he challenged the Darwinian emphasis on evolution as a struggle for the survival of the fittest. He regarded evolution more as the result of harmony between creatures, an unfolding of the divine plan, the miracle of the universe striving to be born into a multitude of beautiful forms, and an ever-expanding growth of human freedom and consciousness. Throughout his life, he expressed in his writings and lectures a sense of wonder about the growth of life on the planet, and he enthusiastically studied geology, biology and other sciences.

This feeling for nature was often expressed in autobiographical passages describing his mood when looking at nature. He said of himself that his reading was in the "romance of nature," and in this way his knowledge and love of nature became deeper. His reading helped his meditations and his meditations helped his reading. In his wanderings on Rokko-san (the mountain overlooking Kobe) he collected botanical specimens and observed wild bees. His sense of the immanence of God was developing because of, not in spite of, science. He was moved, as in the words of Gerard Manley Hopkins,

> The world is charged with the grandeur of God.
> It will flame out, like shining from shook foil.

Very early in his career, the precocious Kagawa had projected his ecstatic, poetic grasp of evolution into the world of human activity. His first intellectual work appeared in a six-installment essay on world peace, published in the daily newspaper *Tokushima Mainichi* in summer 1906, when he had come back to Tokushima for school vacation.[10] The ambitious intellectual interwove the thoughts of Kant, Hegel and Marx in interpreting the life of Christ along evolutionary lines. He argued that there has been steady progression towards greater democracy and the liberation of the human spirit, which is the ultimate source of true world peace.

In this early work, Kagawa accepted the Marxist thesis that capitalism is the root of imperialism and colonialism, engendering war and impeding human progress, declaring: "It is socialism that has raised its voice in opposition and dared to face up to autocracy based on money power."[11] He optimistically and

naively predicted that the forces of capitalism and imperialism
would soon be extinguished in the birth of a more just society.[12]
Even at this early date, the young convert had decided that the
proper role of a Christian was to help build such a society. He
had the conviction that a Christian must take the personal peace
found in faith and spread it through the world. "This is what
Christ's words meant when he said, 'The kingdom of God is
within you,' and 'The Kingdom of God is at hand.'. . . World
peace is on the way. It is nigh. It already exists in our hearts."[13]

Young Kagawa was linking social justice, the Gospel, and the
need to free the human spirit from the barriers imposed by an
exploitive economic system. Cataloguing the wrongs of the
capitalistic economy, he attributed much of worldwide warfare
and suffering to colonialism and imperialism. He insisted that
religion must not retreat into self-contained pietism, pompous
ceremony or ecclesiastical bureaucracy. He believed that the
Bible commanded people to take action in order to bring the
Kingdom of God closer to realization.

As Kagawa's brand of "liberation theology" began to take
shape, his critique of imperialism included Japan itself. In this
same Tokushima newspaper he challenged a statement by the
principal of his old school, Kentaro Suzuki, justifying Japan's
position in the war with Russia.[14] The budding young philosopher used Engels' thesis of recurring crises in capitalism to
attack his government's aggression as indiscriminate pandering
to the entrenched wealthy. Writing the essay had afforded him
yet another opportunity to defy authority. The depressed
adolescent was suddenly a published writer wielding the power
of authorship, brandishing his knowledge of Western philosophy and jabbing at an establishment figure.

These fledgling articles weren't the only "firsts" for Kagawa;
they also resulted in a police interrogation—the first of many
times in his career when he came under surveillance. Japan's
Peace Police Law of 1900 had handed the government broad
control of the press, political groups and labor organizations,
whenever they were perceived to pose a threat to the state. This
law was strengthened periodically over the next three decades
as Japan marched relentlessly down the road of militarism. The

flow of public information was monitored and even relatively mild disturbances were suppressed.[15]

Another experience that foreshadowed his later activity was a brief excursion into evangelism. When Logan went on preaching trips into the country on his bicycle, Kagawa, home on vacation, often accompanied him on Mrs. Logan's bicycle. Years later, Kagawa said he could never forget those times.[16]

Kagawa was not nearly as precocious in sexual matters. He was extraordinarily shy with women all through adolescence, placing them on pedestals and venerating them from afar in the manner of a courtly lover. He went through several intense crushes, that are best described with sentimentality and self-irony in his autobiographical novels. His puritanical attitude concealed a fear of sexuality and a powerful libido, which he managed to sublimate with fantasies or writings. In his novel *Taiyo o iru mono* (A Shooter at the Sun), his autobiographical hero Eiichi lies in sickbed fantasizing about selecting a wife from several amours:

> He was almost driven out of his mind. It seemed as if he could never rise again from his sick bed. The God whom he had served, who had hitherto kept his heart pure, had deserted him, he thought. Like Samson he had no longer the spirit of the prophets. If he put aside all ideas of marriage and decided to remain a bachelor, perhaps God would return to him. Yet he wanted to get married; he wanted once in his life to touch the smooth skin of a maiden, to hear her blood throbbing in her veins. Unless he felt the beating of a maiden's heart he thought somehow that he could never be a man.
>
> His veins were filled with the hot blood of youth, which had many times troubled him. Yet he had never pressed a maiden to his heart, so timid was he. Even at the Tamanoya (an inn), when Kohide and Kiyonosuke had made him sleep between them, his timidity had deprived him of all feeling of sex. But he knew that the hot blood of youth could not be restrained.[17]

Kagawa enlisted Greco-Roman goddesses into his fantasies. These fictional accounts square with the attitudes about sex often expressed in lectures and religious writings. His inhibitions and naivete were not simply matters of Christian sexual mores, but also the consequence of his feelings about Japanese society and his own family experience. Even before his conversion to Christianity, he had blamed his family's ruin on the sensuality of his father and brother, and publicly stated on numerous occasions his fear of falling into the same trap.

He attributed other families' problems to dissolute living, combined with prostitution and the type of concubinage fairly common in Japan and practiced by his own father. He was repelled by the pornographic drawings he had found in his family storehouse as a child and by the impurity of those who failed to live up to the Buddhist and Confucian texts he had once studied. The exploration of sex was a frightening prospect for him. His rarified fantasies about women were a strategy to sublimate his obviously strong desires.

Kagawa's religous feelings, however, were not merely a sublimation of repressed sexuality. His sense of religious awe existed long before libido flared. Different individuals have different capacities for religious experience. Kagawa happened to be extremely gifted with this capacity, just as an artist or an athlete is gifted.

Back at Meiji Gakuin after a vacation in 1906, Kagawa's intensive studies continued. He staged another protest, this time against formalistic religion, right in front of the Takanawa Church. He chided the women of the congregation for wearing their Sunday best, telling the faithful that the church was not just a place for social gatherings.[18] This was probably the first of his clashes with the established churches. They disapproved of his intense involvement in secular causes, while he condemned their failure to bring Christian values into the world.

Like any curious youth, he was constantly experimenting. Following Tolstoy's example, he became a vegetarian using the *suichi ryoho* (water therapy) theory of Dr. Kellogg, which maintained that meat was harmful to health.[19] His efforts at practicing charity extended to the animal kingdom. Once he rescued a stray cat and brought it into his room, then later a bedraggled dog. To those who objected to the dog he said, "Anyone will befriend a good-looking dog, but no one will care for an unfortunate cur unless I do it."[20] Worst of all was the beggar he befriended. Fellow students were nauseated by a disgusting odor that they had traced to his room where they found him swabbing this man's sores.[21] Kagawa often passed on his extra pocket money to needier students and his better clothes to beggars, whom he then tried to convert to Christianity.

That did not mean that the young student did not succumb to vanity and temptation. He could be vain, as the self-conscious poses in his early photographs show. Whether in Western military uniform or traditional kimono, the portraits show an image of a meticulously groomed adolescent. Once, instead of using the money sent by Dr. Myers for books as intended, he splurged on a new college uniform of a smart, popular design with white piping around a dark collar. Conscience-stricken, he wrote a letter of apology to Dr. Myers, and apparently never wore the uniform again.[22]

Although he may have been emboldened by his role as a brilliant but eccentric intellectual and a budding activist, he paid for his eccentricities. In a hazing incident a group of twenty students took him to the college baseball field and beat him brutally all the while taunting him for his self-avowed pacifism. Not resisting, he practiced non-violence and openly prayed for their forgiveness.[23] Unwittingly they had played into Kagawa's hands, providing him training for becoming a Christlike martyr, a role that he would play to the fullest in a few years.

After completing the term at Meiji Gakuin in March 1907, Kagawa decided to move to Kobe to attend the Kobe Shingakko, a Southern Presbyterian seminary. Dr. Myers had received an appointment there to teach church history, astronomy, music and other subjects, and it was probably because of this that Kagawa decided to transfer there.[24] The new school was a conservative institution compared to Meiji and did not offer the same quality library as the Tokyo college. Temperamentally, Kagawa was more suited to the latter, but his loyalty to Myers was deep.

Although he had rejected a career in business or politics, Kagawa could easily have found a comfortable niche in the established church. Indeed, he had a brief stint in that position. That summer, prior to his Kobe Shingakko enrollment, he secured employment as an assistant to a pastor of Okazaki Church, Aichi prefecture, midway between Tokyo and Kobe. The pastor had evidently heard about Kagawa's controversial political ideas and warned him not to interject his socialist viewpoint into church work. Although Kagawa maintained a low political profile within the church, his outside activities cost him his job in July.

A meeting on the consequences of the Portsmouth Treaty, which had officially concluded Japan's victory over Russia the previous September, was degenerating into a bitter skirmish between rival political factions because some advertised speakers had failed to appear. Kagawa moved to the platform and calmed the crowd with a speech on pacifism.[25] He further promised to arrange a refund of the admission price to the disappointed, angry spectators. Not all who lined up for refunds had paid, so Kagawa decided to make up the difference from his meager savings. This grand gesture left him broke— and jobless when the church fired him for what it considered imprudent public behavior.[26]

He was fortunate to find a temporary job as an assistant at the Japan Christian Church in Toyohashi City in the same prefecture on the Atami Bay, 25 miles away. An ancient fortress town in the heart of a silk producing region, it was a center of textile manufacturing with the usual squalor that accompanied such development. Unlike many churches in Japan which looked like their neat, spired counterparts in small town America, this new church was the Japanese equivalent of the low-budget storefront operation of American inner cities. The ground floor of an ordinary building had been converted into the church, while the second floor served as the living quarters for the family of the minister, Ken Nagao.

The humble Nagao was an inspiring example of the authentic practice of Christianity, and Kagawa soon developed a reverent regard for him.[27] Poor himself with 10 children to support, Nagao was serving his impoverished neighbors by feeding, counseling and preaching the Gospel to them. Kagawa touchingly described this reverence, writing:

> When I was 19, I discovered in Ken Nagao a life which thrives on poverty and religious action. It is a blessing to have had an evangelist like Ken Nagao in Japan. . . . Though scores of years have passed, the world has not forgotten his name. He was completely immersed in joy. His life was actually the life of God.

> In him I saw the art of life at its ultimate. I studied his life myself
> and recommended it to others. Jesus was a child of God and a
> carpenter. Ken Nagao was like him. . . . I was taught the true
> Christianity of Japan by him.[28]

Kagawa always had a strong capacity for admiring people he
considered to be exemplary Christians, and was lavish with
praise when he found them.

Besides helping Nagao, Kagawa took up street preaching in a
style bordering on fanaticism. The scholar blossomed into a
street orator. Wearing his kimono, wooden sandals on his feet,
the sophisticated author would wander into the poorer section
of Toyohashi in the evening, pounding a drum to attract attention, determined to stand and preach the Gospel to anyone who
would listen. If sacrifice for others was the key to personal
salvation, then he would set out on a path of evangelistic
sacrifice. True believers had to share the good news. Christ
preached, Peter and Paul preached, and so, too, would their
ardent imitator, full of the zeal of his new religion. Despite the
fact that he was feeling weak and experiencing symptoms of
tuberculosis, Kagawa preached like a tent revivalist consecutive-
ly every day for almost six weeks, regardlesss of the late
summer heat and rain. On the last evening, sick and exhausted,
he collapsed unconscious in the rain, gravely ill with tubercular
pneumonia, contracting a fever of 104 degrees.[29] He described it
in his own words:

> After two years at college, when I was nineteen, I spent
> summer preaching in the slums. There I preached continuously
> by myself on the streets every day for forty days.
>
> On the fortieth day, at about nine o'clock in the evening, it
> began to rain while I was still preaching. For a week my voice
> had been getting weaker, and when the rain began falling my
> body was swaying to and fro. At one time I had difficulty getting
> my breath. I began to feel horribly cold, but I was determined,
> whatever happened, to finish my sermon.
>
> In conclusion I cried, "I tell you God is love, and I will affirm
> God's love till I fall. Where there is love, God and life reveal
> themselves."[30]

His condition was diagnosed as critical and he lay close to
death for a week to ten days. During the illness he had a

near-death mystical experience that had a profound and lasting effect on him. This encounter seemed to have given him an immediate sense of God and a feeling that he was indeed "crossing the death line," the title of the novel in which he graphically relates this experience. What happened was so convincing and unforgettable that it changed his life irrevocably, as he described years after:

> On the third day my condition seemed completely hopeless. I could not cough anymore, nor even breathe without effort. For a week I lay there, just praying and waiting. Then the hemorrhages got worse and I got a very high fever. I thought that the time had come for me to die. The doctor said to notify my friends.
>
> The sun was setting in the west. I could see its reflection on my pillow. For four hours I prayed, waiting for my last breath. Then there came a peculiar, mysterious experience—an ecstatic consciousness of God, a feeling that God was inside me and all around me. I felt a great ecstasy and joy. I coughed up a cupful of clotted blood. I could breathe again. The fever was reduced. I forgot to die. The doctor came back at nine-thirty. He was disappointed. He had written a certificate for my cremation and feared that the people would call him a quack.[31]

Kagawa had his narrator convey this experience in his novel, in these words:

> He grasped his own wrist to feel his pulse and was surprised that he could feel nothing. But the duty which God had entrusted to him, which was to realize the spirit of Jesus by work among the poor—for the sake of accomplishing which holy ambition he wished to spend his life in the slums—convinced him that he would not die. He believed that he had leapt over death and thrust himself into that mysterious world.
>
> He concentrated his gaze on the reflection of the electric light fixed on the pillar by the alcove. He gazed at it for one minute, two minutes,—as long as fifteen minutes, and during that time, in some indescribable way, he felt himself absorbed in the unknown wonders of reality. The point of light on which he concentrated his gaze appeared to him like a rainbow, the room in which he lay like Paradise and the common quilt that covered him like cloth of gold. It seemed as if he was being held tight by the hand of God the Father,—nay, that God was something closer than a father,—that God dwelt in him. It was a joyful

feeling that he was immersed in God. No sooner had this joyful feeling come over him than his fever departed and he was surprised to find that his pulse had returned to normal.[32]

Kagawa had now felt the presence of God in a way that he had not known before and in a way that empowered him to carry on his mission. More than ever, God became for Kagawa a direct experience rather than an abstraction or a subject of theological debate. In addition to preaching, like many other mystics he shared this experiences through artistic expression in novels, poems and meditative writings. In some instances, we learn more about Kagawa's theology and his mystical experience from his creative writing than from any other source, which is why the modern Japanese theologian Yoshitaka Kumano refers to Kagawa's faith as "poetic Christianity."[33]

This near fatal illness demonstrated his incredible power to endure and overcome suffering. It challenged his will and endurance and helped him prepare for a life that would be plagued with a litany of ill health, including tuberculosis, trachoma, nephritis, pyorrhea, sinusitus and heart trouble. He was able to turn illness into an opportunity, and he advised others to do likewise. Yet he was highly sensitive to their pain. A substantial portion of his career was dedicated to agititating for adequate medical care and securing the means for providing it. Though ascetic in his own duels with pain, he was unfaltering in his efforts to relieve others.

After partial recovery from his illness, he made the 200-mile trip west to the much larger city of Kobe to begin studies at the Shingakko. He found a different setting from the intellectually free-wheeling Meiji Gakuin where he had ranged through an intriguing library. This new seminary actually had a fundamentalist faculty member opposed to the teaching of evolution. Along with his studies, Kagawa embarked upon another program of street preaching, this time in the Shinkawa slums across the Ikuta River, about a mile from the seminary. Within a week he suffered a serious relapse, prompting Dr. Myers to put him in a local hospital and then transfer him to convalesce at the Minato Hospital in Akashi just east of Kobe, at the Myers' expense.

Probably because he did not wish to be dependent on Dr.

Myers' charity, Kagawa departed four months later to recuperate in the fishing village of Fuso, on Atsumi Bay about five miles
from Toyohashi, where he hoped to benefit from the fresh air
that was believed to cure lung conditions.[34] From January to
September of 1908 he rented a fisherman's shack for one yen (50
cents in U.S. money) per month. He practiced the art of simple
living on which he would insist for the remainder of his life. He
cooked for himself, subsisting on a diet of vegetables, fruits,
eggs and bean curd, although fish must have been plentiful and
cheap. His monthly living expenses amounted to only 15 yen.[35]

The relaxed atmosphere did his health immense good. There
were no slums in which to preach, fewer books to read, and no
required study nor intense discussions of the burning issues of
the day. He got along well with the villagers who were warmly
hospitable to him. He wrote letters for them, played games with
their children, and gave them advice when an educated opinion
was needed. In the spring, he was invited on an all-night fishing
trip with the local fishermen.[36]

Kagawa did not live there in complete isolation. According to
the diary he kept, *Koya nikki* (Hut Diary), he made trips to Kobe,
Tokyo and nearby villages. Still, it was far less hectic than before
and he had the latititude for contemplation—of the natural
environment, of philosophical thoughts and himself.

Perhaps most important for his future was that he had time to
write. It was here that he produced the first draft of *Crossing the
Death Line*, which would make him famous when it was completed 12 years later. Kagawa had so little money during this
time that he wrote the novel on old magazine pages and scrap
paper with *fude* and *sumi* (brush and ink). His original title was
Hato no mane (Like a Dove), taken from the Biblical injunction in
Matthew 10:16: "Behold, I send you forth as sheep in the midst
of wolves: be ye therefore wise as serpents and harmless as
doves."

No other phrase in the Bible could have been more apt for
Kagawa. Intellectually, he was a serpent, well-read and adept at
challenging pretentious authorities with his quick mind. At the
same time, his dedication to the poor and his non-violent
approach made him harmless like a dove. Kagawa had the nerve
to show his novel to the famed Japanese author Toson Shimaza-

ki, a Christian and a graduate of Meiji Gakuin. Shimazaki advised the young author to wait before attempting publication.

In a letter written years later, Kagawa delved into his motives for writing the novel and the fortunate circumstances when it was finally published and became an instant best-seller in 1920:

When I had consumption and moved out of the hospital into a fisherman's outbuilding in Mikawa-ura County, I was alone and so lonely that daily I began work on a novel. . . . The reason I wanted to write a novel was because the sad experiences of my past had so seriously affected my small heart. I also very much wanted to write in novel form how my feelings had changed tremendously as I had become religious. I once had Shimazaki Toson *Sensei* take a look at my completed manuscript. He responded with a thorough letter, saying that I should let it sit for a few years first. Then he told me, after I had come to understand it better I should publish it.

My consumption gradually improved after that, and I moved into the slums. Thirteen years passed. During the thirteenth year Mr. Sanehiko Yamamoto of Kaizo Publishing Co. came to my office in the slums and urged me to publish my novel. So I quickly wrote the last one-third of *Crossing the Death Line, Vol I.* At that time I thought the first two-thirds of my work was too rough and clumsy. Writing is a strange thing, and when you decide to change one section, you end up having to change the entire work. . . . My writing from the period when I was coughing up blood was extremely austere; and since my feelings of that time are most honestly expressed in that writing, I decided my feelings had priority over the quality of my writing. So I decided to overlook the quality of my work and preserve my raw feelings from the period when I was coughing blood. As a result, there are some quite rough sections in the first half, but it is also a fact that a strong tone remains, a tone which did not permit any revisions.

You ask about my models. You should ask the people who surround my life on this matter. Circumstances do not permit me to say anything about my models when I have chosen to write about the life of my heart.

As Mr. Takeo Arishima once said, a novel may be a novel, but it has more truth than pure fact. You'll have to excuse my silence on this matter, as Mr. Arishima was excused.

I do not necessarily think that *Crossing the Death Line* is a successful novel. When it appeared in the magazine *Kaizo,* I felt uneasy because of its clumsy style. When it was published in book form and sold so well, even I was astonished. But when I think of it now, I am thankful because I think my readers overlooked my rough style as I had hoped they would, and instead read and appreciated the history of my heart. In other words, they appreciated the movement of my heart, which I so wanted to write about . . .[37]

This letter is revealing, because it shows Kagawa as a literary man, a critic keenly aware of the limitations of his work. It confirms the idea of "poetic Christianity," where "theology" is expressed through his creative writing rather than through an intellectual system. Kagawa was an artist. This fact tends to get lost among his many other achievements.

His rather frank and humble assessment of the novel's stylistic limitations reflects the reaction of his contemporaries. The famed writer of popular novels and literary critic Kan Kikuchi argued that a polished style was not the only value in literature and that the substance of a story had its own aesthetic weight. Of Kagawa's novel, he confessed,

I set about reading this work with considerable antipathy, as was normal of a member of the *bundan* (the literary establishment), but even though I kept telling myself, "He can't write, he can't write," at quite a few places in the work, I could not hold back the tears that filled my eyes.[38]

Kagawa had little use for the "art for art's sake" type of literature then dominant in Japan. From this early age, his fiction and poetry were both deeply engaged in social problems, even if that meant a sacrifice of elegance. This aesthetic is stated even more emphatically by Kagawa when his autobiographical hero Eiichi reflects upon the death of the emperor in 1912:

Eiichi wondered what the change would produce. What would the transition from the Meiji to the Taisho Era bring forth? Would there be a change in political affairs—in literature? But this did not trouble him much. His business was to succor the poor, and it was all one to him what changes there were in an administration which did not concern itself with such matters. It was the same with literature. The literature which did not concern itself with the poor, who formed eight or nine-tenths of the nation, was to Eiichi of no importance. He did not regard as literature the diversions of the nobility or the pastimes of the rakes, the love affairs of some titled miss or the entanglements of the young son of a house with a geisha. He knew nothing about the principles of art, but he did not think there was any art in the narration of amorous adventures which were like the rutting of cats on the roof.[39]

Kagawa's main mission in his big novel was to portray himself, his inner life and the movements of his heart. The book captivated its audience in the 1920s, because, for all its flaws, it contained vivid descriptions of the sights and sounds of urban Japan and a sense of the intellectual ferment of the times. Despite the fictitious names, many of the characters are identifiable. Their actions and conversations give the reader exactly what Kagawa wanted—a sense of what it felt like to be a bright but confused young intellectual in those times.

In the story he takes literary license with certain historical facts, as novelists do. For example, his uncle is transformed into the hero's father, although the feeling of the antagonistic relationship is conveyed. As a record of his growth, illness, conversion, depression and formation of his character, it is as revealing as any autobiography can hope to be. The book is also instructive for the Western reader, offering a rich, haunting picture of the period with scenes of the poverty that Kagawa knew firsthand. It shows the excitement and confusion arising from the frenzied assimilation of ideas from the West. The teen-aged hero, earnest and ambitious, suffers delusions of grandeur one moment, then follows abruptly with a sense of utter worthlessness. He experiences religious ecstasy and sexual fantasy. The story is not only of young Kagawa but of a new Japan reeling into the 20th century.

When Kagawa was writing the first draft of this novel in the solitude of the hut by the sea in 1908, he reflected upon some of his troubles. He recorded his "emotion recollected in tranquility" in a diary, amplifying his thoughts about religion and the need for a person to develop to full capacity and become immersed in the struggles of life. "The self exists only to the extent that we become engaged in a difficult project," he noted.[40]

This is one of the earliest formulations of his oft-repeated doctrine that suffering, challenge and adversity can be a kind of "crucifixion" which leads to personal resurrection. It is a rejection, so often expressed in his career, of religious quietism, or the search for total release from pain and escape into a world of contemplation. In that solitude by the sea he was starting to develop his theory of redemptive love, an idea that personal growth takes place through intense engagement with that world, and that barriers within the individual soul are torn down through service to others.

By April his health had improved sufficiently to enable him to take the physical examination for conscription. He was placed in class C, or indefinite deferral.[41] That he consented to such an examination indicates that his pacifism was not unconditional even in these early, idealistic years, but linked to the ethics of a given situation.

As Kagawa steadily recovered, he further clarified his thinking. He came to appreciate nature even more, exercising his compassion on other earthly creatures. He fed a stray dog out of his meager supplies and maintained good relations with a snake which lounged around the little Buddhist altar in the hut.[42] He claimed to find a natural purity that clarifies the soul. He claimed that nature had become a new robe for his soul.[43]

Although his health had improved, his bouts with illness were not over. After resuming his studies at the Kobe Shingakko in September, he was soon down with sinusitus. He was placed in Hyogo Hospital the following month, and because his lungs did not recover fully from an operation, his condition worsened to a critical state. Twenty-seven days after he had entered the hospital, his classmates led by Dr. Myers began a deathwatch at his bedside.[44] A fellow student Tatsu Hiratake apparently made arrangments for a funeral service. Once more Kagawa rallied. In November he was able to go to the neighboring city of Kyoto for yet another operation, this time for tubercular hemmorhoids.

During his second near-death crisis Kagawa apparently made a pact with God: "I told God that if he would let me live, I would serve his children in the slums."[45] It is unclear which of the two serious illnesses drove Kagawa to this resolution. In the novel, he fuses the two illnesses together, both the mystical experience and the resolution to serve the poor. In his sermons and lectures he was also vague about which illness occasioned his resolution.

In any event, his resolution was strengthened by reading John Wesley's diary while convalescing at Rev. Honnami's Japanese Christian Church in Kyoto. The action-oriented Wesley furnished a perfect model of a person dedicated to working for the urban poor while ill with tuberculosis. He had organized the Holy Club at Oxford University in England, a group which fasted twice weekly and lived austerely in a Protestant form of monasticism. Kagawa often praised both Wesley's accomplishments and the monastic movements in Catholicism, because they provided an organized method of recreating the life of primitive Christian communities. As a Japanese coming out of a pluralistic religious tradition with its numerous sects and orders, he was already perplexed and sometimes dismayed by the rigid denominational distinctions plaguing Western Christianity. Kagawa had no quarrel with the idea of separate religious groups themselves, but he was a thoroughgoing ecumenist. Though he was baptized as a Presbyterian and remained one all his life, he deplored the sectarian disputes, divisions and intolerance existing within Christendom.

When he had regained sufficient health to resume schooling in the winter of 1908–09, he took up exactly where he had left off in his ferocious reading, delving into the Russian anarchist, Peter Kropotkin, and Tokuzo Fukuda, a Marxist scholar who wrote *Nihon keizaishi ron,* an economic history of Japan. Kagawa clearly derived from Kropotkin his theory of cooperation as the driving force in evolution. Because of the limitations of the Kobe Shingakko library, Kagawa and the more ambitious students often turned to the Kansai Gakuin library for enlightenment. He eagerly borrowed books also from the professors and his fellow students and was noted for finishing each of them in a day or two. Legend had it that he polished off the entire *Encyclopedia Britannica* in several months.

Kagawa taught himself German, working on it day and night, at one point dropping all other reading to focus exclusively on the language, in order to have direct access to the great German philosophers in their original text.[46] He exhibits some of this knowledge by quoting various classical German authors in *Crossing the Death Line.*

Another chapter in his rebellion against authority occurred at the seminary, when with four other students he organized a strike to protest the firing of the Hebrew scholar Seijiro Aoki, one of their favorite professors. Aoki advocated "higher" biblical criticism—the "scientific" approach to biblical studies which sought to explain sources, authorship, and dates of composition as assiduously as any other document from antiquity. Kagawa supported this type of investigation, both because of his increasingly sophisticated knowledge of archaeology and historiography and because his basic faith was existential by now and not threatened by "scientific" research.

The acting head of the school announced the expulsion of the strike organizers at a prayer meeting in the chapel, inviting each student to shake hands with him as they left the chapel. This event was seized upon by the budding activist Kagawa as an invitation to deliver another ringing performance in Christian defiance of authority. He rose weeping (one of his specialties) and lamented the school's actions. His exact phrasing is unknown, but Axling's reconstruction of it is not out of character with Kagawa's growing independence: "Christianity is a religion of love. A theological seminary must be a school of love. A school of love should guide a mistaken student. As God never abandons anyone, so a seminary ought never to drive a student away."[47]

Having once again wielded his Christian logic like a club, Kagawa consciously took on the Christlike role of self-sacrifice for others by adding, "Please forgive and reinstate the other four students, and let the sentence of expulsion fall upon me alone."[48] This was another example of his stubbornly literal attempt to imitate Christ—in this case, by laying down his academic life for others. It also happened to be a brilliant strategy, for Kagawa prevailed and the students were all reinstated, including himself.

There was, however, a grim side to this period. Despite his ecstatic union with God and his silent vow of service to the poor, he was undergoing serious depression. Illness, a sense of hopelessness, inability to make good on his commitments, a feeling of no longer being cradled in the hand of God—all of these preyed upon him and brought him close to a suicidal state. This despair is poignantly expressed in his novel and confirmed in the following diary entries:

> Boycott against tuberculosis patients threatens my residence in the dormitory. *(January 20, 1909.)*
>
> Attended German language class. Interesting. A dream of self-immolation! *(January 22, 1909.)*
>
> A foreign medical doctor told me that I have not recovered from tuberculosis. He does not seem to believe me. I want to commit suicide. Suicide! *(January 23, 1909.)*[49]

He was still tinkering with the novel, but found little consolation in this work:

> Revised chapter seven of the novel, spending half a day. . . . Read up to chapter seventeen. Disgusted at the novel. Dry and uninteresting! *(January 29–30.)*[50]

Even grimmer is the indication that Kagawa came close to losing the faith which had been his support. His entries of a few months later cry out:

> A pathetic story! A pathetic story! Madness? Suicide? . . . Speaking of Christianity! It's a lie! It has no authority on economy! Oh! Pity this oppressed youth! Wept! Wept! For self-preservation! This frail body! *(April 11, 1909.)*
>
> I haven't got an earthly chance! Hopeless! Hopeless! I have totally doubted the values of life! Wept a whole night! *(May 30, 1909.)*
>
> Hopeless! Hopeless! Despair! Despair! Suicide! Human beings are all false! *(May 31, 1909.)*[51]

His brooding and despondency led him to a sort of philosophical breakthrough. It is expressed in an essay, *Mu no tetsugaku* (The Philosphy of Negation), asserting that dealing with death is the greatest task for an individual. Kagawa groped with the idea of suicide as an option putting all values in the perspective of death:

> Do values really exist? Is it possible that God really made a world devoid of values? Is our existence an act of God or is it the result of the mundane acts of men?
>
> In the past I said I will live on and not die, but now the pain is

such I cannot go on living. . . . Ah, the value of life is to be doubted in its essence. Why does man exist? Ah, the solution is only this—to die, die, die, die. . . .

God, too, is struggling desperately. I will also struggle just like God. Ah! God is suffering, too. God. God.[52]

Unlike the idealized portrait of a sudden conversion painted by Kagawa's earlier biographers like Axling, Kagawa's religious faith developed in distinct stages, punctuated by regression into profound doubt.[53] His understanding of death was the latest phase in a very complex development. His soul-shaking revelations were followed by despair just as deep; his moments of delusions of grandeur were followed by the burning desire to sacrifice himself for others.

Kagawa appears to have temporarily turned away from a vital attitude towards life and fully accepted death, seeing it as an escape from excruciating pain and a release into a mysterious beyond. He felt that he had already crossed over into death, just as Christ had on the road to Calvary. He was determined to die bearing the cross, no matter how heavy, just as his Master did. His "enlightenment" lay in the "strenuous effort" of dying in the noblest way he could conceive. He was sacrificing himself as Christ had, while most of the world had little idea of his purpose for bearing the cross—Kagawa would term it "redemptive love."

Because he was an emotional outsider in childhood, Kagawa ultimately fit the role of a misunderstood sufferer better than that of a "normal" teenager. He had learned to cope with the world by weeping over his sense of being abandoned. Yet underneath the cold comfort of weeping was an enormous need to belong, to be validated, and a need for recognition that was never fully satisfied. He was a deeply paradoxical figure who was at once so fond of solitude and yet so hungry for approval.

He had made some daring practice runs at self-sacrifice, for which he had already received a share of recognition. He had come to regard Christ's sacrifice as the highest example of service to others. Still, those who knew him were shocked when Kagawa took his sacrificial plunge and moved into the slums of the Shinkawa district on Christmas Eve in 1909.

Chapter 3
Into the Slums

W HEN KAGAWA WALKED AWAY from the dormitories with his
school friend Teiji Ito pushing his handcart, loaded with a
bamboo box of clothes, books and quilts, across the bridge over
the Ikuta river into Shinkawa, he entered an urban hell as
gruesome as any described in the Dickens novels he read.[1] The
booming industrial city of Kobe was the second busiest port in
all Japan with that chasm between rich and poor, common to all
cities in the early phases of the industrial revolution. Japan was
then "catching up" with the West in a frenzied rush toward
industrialization.

Once a sleepy trading town, Kobe had consisted of just 1000
houses before the Meiji Restoration fully opened Japan to the
outside world in 1868. The Kobe port, later the scene of the
dockyard strikes led by Kagawa, opened in January of that year.
In the next two decades the population climbed to 135,000,
making it worthy of its name "Gate of the Orient," and a major
expansion of the port was begun in 1907.[2] When Kagawa entered the slums on Christmas Eve of 1909, the dwellings numbered 100,000 and the population 388,000.

As in almost every other part of Japan, the impoverished,
tax-burdened, rent-wracked and often famine-plagued peasantry poured into the cities by the millions. Some came voluntarily,
simply seeking excitement or cash. Most came to escape the
excruciating poverty of rural life. Many young women were put
into domestic service or small factories, or sold into prostitution
by their families in order to raise money for sheer survival.[3]
These refugees from the country often landed in the squalor of
places like Shinkawa, where 10,000 people were jammed into
one-story shacks and apartments in an area ten blocks square.

47

Muddy alleys, sometimes only a few feet wide, were full of the
stench of rotting garbage, backed up drainage, and "honey
buckets" used to haul away feces. Flies and mosquitoes
swarmed in the air, while rats and bedbugs bored their way
through the filth. The noise of arguments, gamblers, prostitutes
and thugs created a constant din. Alcoholics and unemployed
slouched outside the buildings by day and the homeless slept
against them at night.

Kagawa's new home was typical of the dwellings in Shinkawa. The size of the quarters was measured in "mats"—that is,
the standard three-by-six-foot straw *tatami* mats for the wood
floors. It was common for a half-dozen people to occupy a
six-mat house or section of a tenement. Kagawa had a three-mat
space in the front and a two-mat area in the rear. Behind this
tiny quarters was a kitchen with a dirt or concrete floor. In the
back yard was a water hydrant and toilet facilities shared by
neighbors from adjacent shacks. Crime and disease were ram-
pant in this environment, with epidemics of cholera, typhoid,
diphtheria and smallpox striking periodically along with tuberculosis, pneumonia and numerous chronic diseases caused by
malnutrition and lack of sanitation. Heat was provided by
portable, charcoal-burning hibachis, which caused frequent
fires. Kerosene lanterns provided light.

The apartment rent was cheap, a mere two yen a month ($1),
with payments due monthly instead of every day, as was
customary in this part of town where neither the solvency nor
life of the tenants was predictable.[4] Having little money, Kagawa
purchased three used mats and settled down to sleep in pitch
darkness because he had not yet acquired a lamp. He soon had
an appropriate guide for his stay in this inferno, the pock-
marked hunchback Kitaro Inagi, who arrived on Christmas
night asking for a place to stay. Kagawa had met him while
street preaching, and rather naively befriended this 24-year-old
who had served a nine-year jail sentence for starting a fire to
distract from a robbery he was committing. More than 200
houses had been incinerated in this caper, according to Kagawa.
Kitaro had learned to read in prison, knew the Bible, and
professed to be a Christian on the road to reform, but he was
mainly using Kagawa for his own purposes. They had a falling

out after he turned into a parasite constantly demanding money and food.

The mere act of moving into this tenement created a supernatural aura around Kagawa that continued to grow during his years in the slums. The uneducated and highly superstitious slum dwellers believed in ghosts and lived in great fear of them. During the year before, the previous tenant of Kagawa's apartment had been murdered in a quarrel over a dog worth 20 sen (about 10 U.S. cents). He had broken into the flophouse where his antagonist lived, and ended up beaten so severely that he died while being carried back to his own house. Because of rumors that the dead man's ghost was haunting the place, it went unoccupied until Kagawa moved in.[5] Anyone so brazen as to invade such quarters would have been considered abnormally courageous, in touch with the higher powers, or insane. The Kagawa legend began with rumors about the strange young man almost as soon as he arrived.

Of course, he had far more to fear from his living neighbors than from any ghost. Some were carrying contagious diseases. Others were outright criminals—thieves, gangsters, gamblers and pimps to whom life was cheap. A man next door kept women captive in his brothel. Nearby were an alcoholic scavenger and his family, and a ricksha puller who slept in the street under the same blanket he used to cover his passengers in the daytime.

No matter how depraved these people were, Kagawa had resolved to bring them into the Christian fold by helping them in the manner of Saint Francis, John Wesley, the British social reformer Canon Barnett and the many others about whom he had read who had dedicated themselves to the least of God's children. Kagawa had made an absolute commitment to follow these examples and the command of the Gospel to lay down one's life for others.

There were many times when he came close to despair and felt he had gotten more than he bargained for. He entered with wildly idealistic hopes about the possibilities of serving the poor and reforming their lives by his example. The realization soon dawned, however, that the mistrust, hardheartedness and dehumanization bred in this poverty would make his mission infinitely more difficult than he had imagined. He learned some very sobering lessons about the depths of total corruption to which human beings could sink in such an environment.

From Kagawa's own account, it appears that some of the local hoods were aware of his naivete and decided to amuse themselves by testing him. One of the best known gamblers Umpei Sonoda came to him and said, "Kagawa, you're a friendly fellow. Do you want to take in a man who drinks, is out of a job and hasn't got anything to eat, and make him your disciple?" Kagawa naturally accepted this challenge and the man Heikichi Maruyama arrived. Kagawa nicknamed him "The Copper Statue" because constant drinking had flushed his face to a copper color and he would stand motionless for hours on end.

Kagawa's reaction to this creature and others in the slums was somewhat complex, combining sheer disgust with compassion, love, self-irony, admiration, scientific detachment and a certain sense of moral superiority. His emotional and intellectual full-ness of response to the poor undoubtedly helped sustain him through many harrowing experiences. Of the Copper Statue he later wrote, "Now I had to take care of this statue. I had to feed it. I felt sorry for myself." Elsewhere, he expresses the frustra-tion followed by a comical mood of scientific detachment:

> Many a time I was on the point of losing patience with such a sluggard. But he was too useful for my study of slum life, for he was so well-trained in its ways that he could dodge all sorts of difficulties that arose from time to time and treat them almost as jokes.[6]

Kagawa also liked the man because he started to take care of the cooking and "he was gentle and prayed to God habitually." He further saw Heikichi as a down-to-earth Sancho Panza of his own quixotic adventure in charity, expressing a fondness for this quality:

> He lived with me under the same roof for about two years, during which time he never failed me. To jump into slum-life with little knowledge of it is just the same as Jutaro Iwami, the celebrated samurai in the days of Taiko Hideyoshi entering upon an adventure. In my own adventure I was always attended by Murayama. It was a great advantage to me to have him, for he was a faithful servant, waiting upon me with the respect suitable

for a lord or a boss of chivalrous spirit, for whom he took me apparently. So I rendered him due sacrifice in return. As there was only one coverlet, I used to sleep with him although he was suffering from the itch, and gave it to me, when we would scratch ourselves in concert.[7]

This "convert" did give Kagawa dermatitis, the first of the infections he contracted in the slums.

Word about Kagawa's generosity in sharing his hole in the wall spread quickly. Next a man with dishevelled hair, a swollen face and trembling hands appeared at the door, begging Kagawa to take him in. He was a bean cake dealer, who had recently spent a year and a half in jail for murdering a drunk. The drunk had bumped him, knocking the bean cakes out of his wicker baskets on his shoulders. In return the enraged bean cake dealer hit the drunk over the head, killing him. Though he was pardoned, the man had become mentally unbalanced, imagining the ghost of the dead man following him. That anxiety often caused him insomnia. He believed that Kagawa had some power over ghosts, because of his boldness in occupying the haunted house. When the man lay down at night, he could not sleep unless Kagawa held his hand. When he did get to sleep, he would loosen the pressure on Kagawa's hand until he had a nightmare in which the victim's ghost appeared. Then he would begin to squeeze Kagawa's hand so hard that Kagawa had to wake him up and allay his panic.[8]

Another tenant was a syphilitic beggar named Jiro Hayashi, who had not eaten in days.[9] Others came, too, including a woman carrying on her back her 40-year-old husband. Disabled with rheumatism, he asked for faith healing. Kagawa soon had a "family" to support on his monthly scholarship of ¥11 ($5.50) for the seminary, which he continued to attend. Not able to count on any revenue from these roommates, Kagawa went to Myers and offered to clean the chimney at the seminary for a few more yen. That and other odd jobs enabled him to keep this grotesque household together, though they often were reduced to two meals a day of only rice gruel.

The young idealist was quickly learning that it was one thing to read about serving the poor and quite another to actually live with them every day, sleep and eat with them, and be swept into their realm of violence, crudity and ignorance. The physical danger was as great as the danger from disease. A few days after Kagawa arrived, a slum dweller drew a knife and demanded money. He was driven out by Hayashi, but the latter made his own demands. Then Sonoda came in brandishing a pistol, demanding 30 yen that Kagawa did not have. He and Hayashi got into a violent argument that finally ended after the faithful Copper Statue mediated. Sonoda returned that evening, punched Kagawa in the face, tossed a pot of burning charcoal on the floor and broke a door. Kagawa fled out the rear of the building and went to the river bank to pray.

Similar violent episodes followed, as the time one assailant fired five shots into the house. When Kagawa returned home later, he was given protection by one of the local thugs, who had his sword drawn. The only problem was that the man wanted Kagawa to pay him for the service. Sometimes Kagawa simply ran away until the danger subsided. On other occasions he was not so fortunate. Once an angry drunk knocked out four of his front teeth.

Kagawa met these difficulties by trying harder to follow the biblical mandate. He had the ability to banish irritation and anger by further acts of charity. He gave away his clothing to the rag-clad beggars who prowled the narrow, dirty streets. The beggars, hustlers and street people grasped Kagawa's Christianity, at least to the extent that they could use it to make demands on him. One beggar came and asked, "Give me your shirt." Kagawa handed it to him. Then he asked for the coat and trousers. Kagawa gave him these, too. That eliminated his Western wardrobe. His own kimono was already gone so he accepted a kimono with a bright red lining from a neighbor woman who had been a prostitute. (It was not unusual for men in the slums to be seen in women's kimonos.) The poverty was so great that people wrapped themselves in whatever they could find. Yet it must have created a stir when he showed up in this outfit at the seminary. No doubt, he was jeered by the more conventional students. The parallel with Christ stripped of his garments and draped in the purple robes of a king for mockery was not lost on a young man steeped in the New Testament. For a person who had learned to turn rejection into a positive experience, it offered emotional consolation during some discouraging times.

Kagawa's "strange" behavior did not shake the faith of Dr. Myers. The missionary had recognized something special in Kagawa and was willing to back him, regardless of how the young man might shock both the Christian community and the local residents. Myers' own streak of primitive Christianity helped him appreciate Kagawa's religious fervor and eventually led to his expulsion from Japan during the war for publicly preaching against the institution of the emperor. Myers viewed the ever changing wardrobe of his disciple with a joking tolerance, "In those days it was an utterly hopeless enterprise to see him sensibly or comfortably dressed. A new shirt, a new kimono, a new suit would be given away the next day. We finally solved the problem by keeping a full suit ready for him in our house. Every Tuesday he came to us for breakfast, changed his clothes, and left them there to be cleaned.[10]

Kagawa began making regular rounds of the slums, visiting sick people, helping them obtain medicine, arranging doctor's visits, washing their bedsores, and cleaning filthy hovels that no respectable person would consider entering. Besides attending to the physical needs of sick and desperately poor people, he spent a considerable time listening to recitations of their overwhelming troubles, acting as a prototype of today's "psychiatric social worker." He was able to add to his stock of odd stories and experiences which would find their way into his novels and sociological studies.

He became fond of some of the miserable people who later appeared in his fiction, such as "Granny of the Cats." This ancient bag lady lived in a section of Shinkawa where individuals and families rented six-by-six foot rooms in large tenement houses. In her room with its stench and sooty ceiling where the plaster had peeled away, she kept bedraggled cats to fend off the ghost of a man who had hanged himself in front of her place. She collected assorted garbage which she sold to make a living: empty tin cans, old pieces of rope, discarded dolls, pots, and any other resaleable junk she scrounged in the streets and garbage heaps. Kagawa periodically cleaned up her place, remarking that it was difficult to extract all the cat litter ground into the filthy mats on the floor. Nevertheless, he would make the attempt, even rearranging her artifacts to make them presentable.

With Granny, he may have been consciously imitating good deeds that he had read or heard about. He knew of the New York Salvation Army's practice called "White Apron Parties," where volunteers went out and cleaned house for people who couldn't help themselves. Once noticing that Granny had no bedding, he asked what had happened to hers. She replied that she had loaned it to a man across the alley who hadn't returned it. Kagawa rushed home and brought her a large quilt.

He wasn't consciously using the old woman and others as material for his fiction or research, though he did often refer to the slum as his "laboratory." He was moved by a strong sense of compassion for their pain, a feeling he often expressed in his poetry. Granny had lost her husband and her daughter many years earlier before she drifted to the slums. She adopted a baby girl whom she raised to adulthood, but the girl ignored her and contributed nothing to her support.

Granny would proudly present him with objects she found on her rounds of scavenging. One day she offered him some garish posters from a steamship company. They weren't works of art—and having read Ruskin, Kagawa had definite ideas about art—but he smiled tolerantly, saying they were very pretty pictures and accepted them. He took them home and pasted them up on the walls of his house, already covered with newspapers to protect against the crumbling plaster.

As he stared at the colors of the posters, he thought about the shades of red, blue, purple and green so much in contrast with the dimness of the slum. He reflected about it in his novel *A Shooter at the Sun:*

> The slums seemed to him to be forgotten while he meditated deeply on color—on the mysterious phenomenon which seemed to envelope the whole world. The humble life of the slums was suddenly illuminated. He was able to think of it as Paradise.[11]

His religious talent was able to turn an encounter with a half-insane bag lady into a mystical experience.

In addition to the compassion he felt for many of the people in the slums, his capacity to admire them was unusual. When

Granny of the Cats showed no resentment toward the man who had taken her bedding, Kagawa was reminded of "Tolstoy's principle of non-resistance," which made him like the woman still more. The level of generosity to which people could rise in the worst of circumstances often amazed him. Always extremely sentimental in his response to pain, he wept openly at the troubles he saw.

In the midst of Shinkawa's filth and chaos, Kagawa established a highly disciplined daily routine that helped him make the most efficient and purposeful use of his time. He arose from his bedding on the floor long before sunrise to pray and meditate while his ragged collection of roommates was still sleeping. This was a spiritual habit he continued throughout his life. An admirer of the disciplined routines of both Buddhist and Catholic monastic orders he became the first member of his own order, and this was his matins duty. Kagawa believed that spiritual growth was not only the result of God's grace, but had to be developed through resolute contemplation.

He was acquiring a reputation for possessing magical healing powers. Though he often sent people to the doctor, some would come simply to have him pray over them, and some would be "cured" on the spot by what they called the Christian faith cure. Kagawa himself did not claim to be a faith healer. He was puzzled because his prayers sometimes seemed to be effective, and after his reputation spread, sick people came from outside the slums to see him. At times he regarded his reputation as a nuisance, because the people seeking cures deprived him of the time he needed for reading, writing and contemplation.

He viewed his fame with typical irony, saying that he "became the fashionable saint. Everyday people were coming to him from all the tenement houses inviting him to say a Christian prayer for them . . . the strange thing was that the prayer was very efficacious."[12] With Japan's pluralistic and pragmatic attitude toward religion, people tended to experiment with a variety of cults, and the popularity of a cult was linked to its effectiveness in dealing with life's problems. New healers and sects constantly appeared, so Kagawa was simply regarded by many as a distinguished representative of the new cult of Christianity. Kagawa himself ascribed his power to autosuggestion rather than to any supernatural intervention, though he did not discount the possibility that some psychic force might be at work.[13]

Day after day he was called upon to arbitrate disputes between gang members or settle domestic violence. Day after day a new horror of slum life was pressed upon him. He vividly describes a concert of woes, such as the time a woman came to tell him about her beating by her husband at the very same moment a loud domestic battle was taking place across the alley, amid torrents of profanity and the sound of smashing furniture. The women showed him a burn on her thigh her husband had inflicted with hot tongs. He had further shoved a towel in her mouth and tormented her by holding a knife at her throat, threatening to kill her, and making a deep gash that required three stitches to close up. Kagawa looked at the wound, bound it back up, and wept, as he often did when overwhelmed by the situation and his growing fear that there was little he could do to change it.

He had gained such respect that the locals began to refer to him as Sensei, a term in Japanese that literally means "teacher," but is more honorific, rather like the word "rabbi." In this respect the teacher is not merely a transmitter of subject matter, but an almost sacred repository of wisdom. Kagawa became a teacher, opening a school in his house offering instructions in reading, mathematics and other basic subjects early in the morning before his students went to work.

When he wasn't attending class at the seminary, he made morning rounds of the slums to help the sick, settle disputes, or bring food to the hungry. A grisly task he assigned himself was arranging funerals for families who couldn't afford to dispose of the bodies. Kagawa washed the corpses with alcohol or hot water sometimes before putting the body in a coffin. On other occasions, he personally hauled the corpse to the crematorium. He managed 14 of these funerals his first year in the slums and 19 the second. Of this activity he said simply, "At first it was a very difficult test, but the Lord blessed me, and I was willing to do his work."[14]

At home he devoted as much time as possible to his voluminous reading and writing, after which he would go out and make the rounds to talk to the alcoholics—trying to catch them while they were still relatively sober. From dinner until about eight o'clock, he conducted another school for adults to bring them along to the point where they could read the Bible, convinced that the ignorance of slum dwellers aggravated their condition.

One of these students, Masaru Takeuchi, later became one of Kagawa's most trusted aides, as his mission among the poor expanded and took on the dimensions of a social movement. Takeuchi worked in an enamel factory and also helped his mother and brothers, moonlighting at home making buttons. He first came into contact with Kagawa through his father, a street-based fortune teller who had heard Kagawa preaching near his booth. Takeuchi took classes from Kagawa in regular school subjects and the Bible, coming in at five in the morning before work. He later became the head of Kagawa's settlement in Kobe, as well as chief of the Employment Bureau there.

Kagawa preached in the streets, assisted by Takeuchi carrying a paper lantern to light the way when it got dark. Kagawa stuck stubbornly to this street preaching routine, although he himself felt it was ineffectual. In his first four years and eight months, he only succeeded in making about 50 genuine converts to Christianity. After preaching, he conducted prayer meetings with local Christians and the handful of converts he had made. Once a week he preached to the longshoremen at the harbor.

When he had free time, he wandered around the city or took long hikes, wearing his wooden clogs, kimono and wielding a bamboo stick through the mountains up Mount Rokko or to Nunobiki Waterfall. He could not fail to observe the contrasts as he climbed into this idyllic setting with its summer houses, gardens and parks. He could look down on temples and the modern, Western-style municipal and office buildings, including the court where he would be on the witness stand more than once in the years to come. To the west was the imperial villa on Tsukimi Yama (Moon Viewing Mountain) and on the north the imposing Butoku-Den (Military Virtue Palace). But down in the flatlands were the homes of the poor, the slums, the dockyards, the crime, and the industrial pollution in the economic heart of the city.

Besides these solitary hikes, his other respite from the slums was the thought of young women who had struck his fancy during his mission work. Kagawa's good looks and charisma clearly appealed to a number of young women, some of whom were more forward in signaling their affection than others. It is likely that more than a few of his Kobe female disciples had a strong crush on Kagawa or the hope that he might be landed as a mate. There was a preponderance of young females in some of the group photographs taken during these years. Kagawa wryly observed that after his marriage in 1913, a number of these young women lost interest in his religious activities.[15]

He candidly portrays his obsession with these women in his autobiographical writings, where he devotes considerable space to describing his affections for several of them and his debates with himself on the desirability of each as a mate. He builds his self-revealing novel, *A Shooter at the Sun*, upon descriptions of the slums alternating with his feminine encounters.

Because of his contacts with Myers, Kagawa was able to secure funds to support his slum work that began in 1909. In addition to contributing some of his own income, Myers mentioned Kagawa's work to potential donors, such as the wife of a Presbyterian pastor in New York, Mrs. Arthur T. Pierson, who had met Kagawa and witnessed his work first hand. She contributed ¥550 ($275) to the cause in the early days.[16] J. Hart Sibley, a businessman from Georgia, was sending $50 per month to help Kagawa, though this funding appears to have dried up in 1913 due to Sibley's business difficulties.

After only a year in Shinkawa, Kagawa had obtained sufficient funding to expand his original quarters. He rented adjacent apartments, knocking down the walls between them and his own quarters, and created a larger hall for his meetings and classes. This new space became Kagawa's study in the daytime, a lecture hall and chapel in the evening, and a shelter for the homeless at night. He launched his sermons from a gray platform and blackened the white plaster wall behind it with soot to make a blackboard. It was at this time that he developed the dazzling technique of writing and drawing at manic speed to illustrate his points. Later, he changed to brush pen and paper since the chalk dust bothered his ailing lungs.

The Sunday 5 a.m. services were attended by about 20 converts from the neighborhood. There would be Granny of the
Cats, a barber and his wife, a bean curd seller, a cleaning lady, a
young ex-gangster, an orphaned girl he had taken in, and others
who squirmed out of their shanties to sing and pray with the
Sensei. Kagawa didn't dress up to preach, but wore an ordinary
working man's black cotton suit. The hugely erudite young man
spoke in the simplest possible language to these uneducated
people, encouraging them to pray out loud to God. He tolerated
their almost childish expressions of worship, like the cleaning
lady's prayer, "Dear Heavenly Father, I thank Thee when the
kettle of boiling water turned over when so many people were
around that no one was hurt."[17]

One of the most dismal social transactions Kagawa observed
was a kind of delayed infanticide, whereby an illegitimate or
unwanted infant was sold down into the slums and gradually
starved to death. Typically, the infant would be turned over to a
middleman, who accepted a fee for taking it off the parents'
hands. In turn he would arrange for payment of about ¥30 ($15)
and ten garments to a second party who turned the baby over to
another for ¥20 and half the garments. The infant would be
passed further down this grim chain with decreasing payments.
Everyone along the line made some money, while the baby was
gradually starved to death on a diet of rice gruel. When it finally
died, the cause would appear to be malnutrition rather than
infanticide. Passing it through so many hands made it difficult
to trace a child back to the mother.[18] It was Kagawa's task at
times to bury the victims of this inhumane practice.

At one point he himself became a "mother" in 1910 or early
1911 while still a theological student.[19] A local woman who had
received a baby girl was jailed for petty theft, and asked the
police to summon Kagawa to take the child. The baby was filthy,
ill and half-starved when he went to pick it up at the police
station.

Despite the sordidness of this situation, he managed to describe his awkward introduction to parenthood with a certain
amount of humor. The baby was in such bad condition that he
was ashamed to take it aboard the street car, so he carried it
through the city to the doctor's office for an examination. The

doctor was not sure the child would be saved, but he gave
careful instructions on how to mix condensed milk, when to
feed the infant, and how to keep its fever under control with ice
on its forehead. Kagawa made a bed for it by facing two bamboo
chairs toward the wall.[20] He became attached to the baby and
was able to sentimentalize while debating whether to keep the
child or send it to an orphanage:

> . . . he thought that as such a priceless work of art had come
> into his hands it would be a pity to part with it. Moreover, if he
> kept the baby he would be able to bring it up as he liked, cuddle
> it all night, kiss it, carry it on his back, in fact make of it a perfect
> toy. There were times when he was tired of everything in the
> slums; a wife was a far away prospect, and now he had a child
> without having had a wife. Nay, tired of being a man he had
> become for the nonce a woman. The mood came over him that
> he and Ishi could wander together through the world.[21]

The first night the child slept well, but the second night
Kagawa was disturbed by its constant crying. His scabrous
collection of roommates on the floor was unanimous in urging
him to get rid of the child, but he kept on, feeding it, putting ice
on its forehead and changing its diaper. His exasperation, and
his early ideas about feminism were expressed like this: "At that
time he realized the hardships endured by a mother. To get up
seven or eight times a night to change the napkin or feed a baby
was a labor, he thought, beyond him. Without the maternal
instinct it would be impossible."[22] He was overjoyed to find a
local woman to take care of it while he attended the seminary in
the day. She was returning the favor for Kagawa's kindness to
her own child. His relief was great, as he "felt as delighted as if
he had met a saint in hell, and went off to school in high spirits.
He felt very glad to be relieved of the baby. That he should be
glad both to have the baby and be relieved of it caused him to
feel amused."[23]

He continued to struggle with it at night, feeding it, weeping
over it, and fondling it. In Biblical comparison he likened the
baby to Ishmael and himself to Hagar. He kept the child for
several months, finally locating the real mother in a *buraku*
(outcaste) village in Hyogo Prefecture, where he negotiated its

return.[24] It is doubtful whether he was able to make any financial contribution to the child's upbringing.

Kagawa also witnessed and documented other transactions in human beings which were common in Japan among the poor. In order to raise money for survival, parents often sold children, especially females, into positions in factories and in geisha or prostitution houses. He blamed the moral degeneration of the slums on the dehumanizing effects of poverty. In a typical case, the husband started gambling and the wife began scavenging to supplement the already meager income. Their 12-year-old son became a pickpocket. Their daughter, whom Kagawa had actually converted and baptized, was sold for ¥300 ($150) in a three-year contract to work in Shinkawa.

Kagawa came close to despair at the plight of the poor and the fact that as an individual he was only able to rescue a few. A visit to Tokyo early in 1912 deepened his pessimism because he found conditions in the capital as dismal as in Kobe. Two years of attempting to patch up the woes in the slums had convinced him that individual acts of charity could never attack the fundamental problems of poverty which were built into the socioeconomic system. Time and time again in his writings he expressed his sense of futility in trying to make a dent in the situation and the burnout he felt from the day-to-day frustrations of living in such degrading conditions.

Sometimes in describing the situation, he took on a strong tone of righteous indignation and penned a bitter satire of the officials. With emotion he wrote of his work in moving impoverished victims of a typhoid epidemic to the hospital's fourth-class ward where they had to sleep in the hallways. He considered that society was both callous and lacking in common sense:

> There was only one water closet for every twenty houses and the cleaning was always delayed till they overflowed and stunk out the alleys. To allow such conditions to remain, and to spend thousands of yen in building infectious disease hospitals and piling up expenses in fighting infectious disease was useless. It was just the same with plague and infectious diseases in the slums. Besides neglecting to destroy the terrible breeding-ground of infectious diseases in the slums, when notice of an infectious case was sent in thirty-six hours passed before an

official arrived, while in the infectious diseases hospital the nurses had to sleep in the badly disinfected passages. Surely there was a tile loose in the heads of city authorities when they regarded this as prevention of infectious diseases? But, this was verging on dangerous thoughts, even if it only referred to the treatment of the attendants on the free patients in the fourth-class ward.[25]

The sarcastic reference to "dangerous thought" shows the degree to which the government was suppressing dissent and criticism under the terms of the Peace Police Law of 1900, and was a portent of the the future, when Kagawa himself and all critics of the government would be muzzled as these laws were tightened in the 1920s and 1930s.

Sometimes his anger turned to despair, as in his gloomy thoughts on the death of the Emperor in 1912:

It was a period of national mourning; no sound of music was heard throughout the land. Eiichi thought that the loss would mean a change in the country, but the slums were indifferent to all outside events. There only the waves of progress did not roll. With a watch for the police set at the crossroads, hundreds of men were gambling in the alleys by the light of candles fastened to clogs. The prostitutes were plying their trade, and every five or ten minutes a victim fell into their net. The dust-pickers went out at their usual time and the beggars showed no concern. The only change noticeable was that the boys and girls of the slums were gathered outside the cheap sweetshops.[26]

Yet there was consolation. In this same passage, he describes his sheer delight in the rain, running barefoot in it, his enjoyment of lightning, and the studies he made of the color of the atmosphere. His description of these times show many flashes of joy and religious ecstasy in the midst of the overwhelming squalor and degradation.

He was reluctant to depend on charity nor did he want to make the residents in the slums dependent. Very early in his social work he was promoting the idea of economic self-sufficiency, and cooperatives attracted his attention. They already existed in Japan and were well established in some European nations, starting with the first successful retail cooperative established in 1844 by striking weavers, who were religious and political revolutionaries in Rochdale, England. Kagawa had learned about cooperatives as early as 1905, when he read a book by Sanjiro Ishikawa. He was deeply impressed by the idea of democratic control of business enterprises and by the way in which co-ops empowered people to take charge of their lives. He saw them as, perhaps, a way out of immediate economic woes and the dependencies created by the paternalism of Japanese society.

From his study of health sciences, Kagawa knew that malnutrition was one of the worst problems in the slums. People there were ignorant of proper diet and often too poor to buy a decent meal; others had no place to cook. With this in mind, Kagawa decided to establish a cooperative eating house in 1912, with sixty percent of the earnings going to the manager Eijiro Nakamura and the rest to the cooperative society. He borrowed ¥120 from Dr. Myers as start-up capital for this venture. Nakamura was a priest turned into a con-man when he embezzled the charitable donations he had collected for renovating his temple and spent the proceeds on himself. He had repented, and Kagawa, with that sometimes naive eagerness to believe in conversion, placed him in full charge. Nakamura astutely rounded up second-hand equipment for the kitchen and eating area. A large banner was hung up in front of the newly-rented space painted with the name *Tengokuya* (Heavenly shop).[27]

The restaurant was an immediate success when it opened on November 18, 1912. Ever the promoter, Kagawa found a man to make the rounds of the slums the day before announcing the new venture. The crier apparently gave the impression that the food was free, so that hungry people were lining up at three-thirty in the morning. There were, however, enough customers willing to pay that by five o'clock the food was gone and the co-op had to cook up another batch. Running this operation was not as simple as its naive young promoter had imagined. Some would eat without paying so that about a tenth of the daily gross of ¥14 or ¥15 had to be written off. Though there was competition from eight other eating places in Shinkawa, the Tengokuya regularly fed 70 or 80 customers, mostly longshoremen and laborers in the early part of the day, followed by women in the afternoons. Kagawa himself occasionally helped serve the customers, who amazed the ascetic vegetarian with their ravenous appetites.

Because he observed that alcoholism was one of the major causes of misery in the slums, the teetotaling Kagawa did not allow sake to be served. Any customer asking for it would be told that as a Christian business they could not sell sake, though the man in charge would then go to a sake shop, purchase the beverage and serve it to the customer. Kagawa rationalized that he could accept this lapse because the quality and freshness of the food was superior to that of the other public eating places.

The venture failed, however. Its closing was precipitated by the vandalism of a drunken gang, apparently with the encouragement of competitors.[28] Kagawa used this episode in a chaotic scene in *A Shooter at the Sun*, also describing how one man left the restaurant and created havoc at Kagawa's own house, smashing pieces of furniture and attacking the mission's organ with an ax. One of the local drunks, "Fighting Yasu" as Kagawa had nicknamed him, rushed in naked to defend Kagawa with a rusty sword, but Kagawa convinced him to stay out of the fray. The angry man then attacked Kagawa, choking him and kicking him in the stomach. Others arrived on the scene and tied the assailant down. By this time the police were summoned and the attacker was hauled off to jail, despite Kagawa's pleas that he be left alone to sleep it off. Kagawa wept when he saw the man's wife grab the hand cart the police used to carry him away.[29]

The failure of this cooperative did not sour him on the co-op concept, but it taught him some sobering lessons about the importance of management. He remained convinced that cooperatives were Christianity in action, because they gave control of business to the common people and distributed the wealth equitably among members rather than letting capital pile up in the coffers of the elite.

The young man who had felt so alienated had now begun to carve out a place for himself, strange though the setting was. He began to express such confidence that some observers accused him of arrogance. But it was the arrogance of a prophet, of a person absolutely convinced of the moral righteousness of his mission. He openly declared that his deeds would be recorded in history, and become a continuation of the Acts of the Apostles. When someone jokingly asked Kagawa who was greater, he or the famed general and political leader Hirobumi Ito, Kagawa replied, "I am the greater; for if I live as long as Prince Ito, I shall do greater works than he."[30]

There was in him a parading ego that reveled in his achievements, but it was combined with a comic self-irony that swiftly undercut the ego. He managed to do this with clever dialectics to project the image of a sage—which in turn enhanced his reputation. For example, when an old woman in his audience complained that she forgot everything he was saying, he replied: "To remember everything, including sorrows, is burdensome. It is sometimes a blessing to forget. Please continue to come."[31]

Kagawa's discipline at the writing table was also beginning to pay off. His fairy tale about David and Jonathan, *Yujo*, was published in December 1912, followed a year later by another little book about the prophet Jeremiah. That he was also able to continue his incessant theological philosophical study is evident by his third publication in December, *Kirisuto den ronsoshi*, a rendition of Albert Schweitzer's *Quest of the Historical Jesus*. He was also receiving recognition from the people he served, a recognition he seems to have needed. He enjoyed the Sensei status and, later, even liked the irony of the term *oyabun*, (gang boss) when he was called "boss of the beggars."

Along with his fiction and theology, he found time to gather data and record observations for his landmark sociological treatise, the 654-page *Hinmin shinri no kenkyu* (The Study of the Psychology of the Poor). This was one of the first books in Japan to trace in detail the plight of the poor. He enjoyed modest success with the small religious group he had founded in January 1911, which he called the Kyurei Dan (The Spirit Salvation Group). This organization composed of Takeuchi and others influenced by Kagawa formed the nucleus of a quasimonastic community, working when they could, sharing their goods, and praying together in the headquarters. It evolved subsequently into the influential Friends of Jesus Group.

Most important of all, Kagawa was falling in love. He was finding himself more and more attracted to Haru Shiba, a bright and practical woman whom he had first met in October 1912 when she began to attend his services. He had also gone to preach in a printing shop where she was employed. She came from a family which had fallen on hard times so Haru was working to help support the family. She had steadily become more involved in his community, to the point where she came to services regularly.

Haru impressed Kagawa with her organization and working ability. At Christmas time in 1912, he erected a big tent for a festival, inviting over a hundred of the poor to come and eat for free, and join in a party for their children. Some slum dwellers came the night before and waited inside the tent. In a gigantic pot outside Kagawa's crew of helpers tended to the boiling rice and red beans. Other treats for the famished crowd were meat stew, fish, soup and salad, and a bag of biscuits and oranges.

What caught Kagawa's eye at this gala event for the poor was Haru's down-to-earth approach in preparing and dishing up the food. It was in sharp contrast to the casual attitude of some of the well-to-do church ladies from the hills who had volunteered to help. He later paid tribute to her by writing that she "worked with all her might,—not chattering in a silver voice like the people from the hill, but carrying on her work, in silence and quickly."[32] The famished beggars ate helping after helping inside the busy tent, some stretching out aprons or sleeves for rice to carry home. Kagawa was concerned with some of the women privately ridiculing the beggars by mimicking their crass eating habits. Kagawa noted that Haru "was superior to the more cultured ladies and did not laugh as she went on with her work, pouring the rice unconcernedly into the beggars" sleeves.[33] He was moved to tears by what he called her "divine compassion."

Kagawa at times debated with himself on whether to remain celibate, but in the end his romantic tendencies won out. He was extravagant in his praise for Haru, sentimentalizing her every action, singing her praises in love poems, an art form in which he indulged throughout their married life. His love prose would gush forth: "How delightful was her gentle ministration! How could he bear to lose her, with her pink freshness, her beautifully curling hair, her rounded cheeks, her clear limpid eyes." In praise of her spirit, he rhapsodized, "How quick she was to read other's wishes, how quiet in her manner, how necessary a part of his life! He thought how great a blank would be caused in his life if she were to get married and go away."

Haru was one of the many young women attracted by Kagawa's good looks, heroism and charisma. They were not much different from today's "groupies" who develop crushes on their favorite stars. Haru herself made no secret of this affection when she described their first encounters with tenderness:

> There was a young man in the notorious slum district of Kobe who proclaimed the love of God on the streets, exposed to the wind and rain. Often I saw him laughed at, scorned and even kicked by the ruffians around him. It was said that he had lung trouble, and that he would give away his clothes and his money, and go hungry himself after feeding some one with his own food. It struck me as strange that those who stood up for him were all Christians. Just as a mist is cleared away by the sun, my spiritual eyes began to see very clearly this young man's courageous spirit, which made him victorious over poverty and persecution. As I was then the head of women laborers in the Kobe Printing Company, I had no time for anything extra, but during the noon rest hour I would hurry off in my work dress to hear him preach, and in my holidays I was privileged to work with him for the poor. The more I knew this young man the better I understood the love of God working through him, till at last I was baptized by Dr. Myers. . . .[34]

The difference Kagawa noted between Haru and the others was her depth, intelligence and practicality. He gradually came to see that this was someone who could be a lover, who could stand unswervingly by him, and who would make a definite contribution to his work. The growing affection was thus cemented by a strong sense of a bond in their sharing a common cause to live the Christian life intensely in the heart of the slums. She did not flinch at the sight of sores on beggars' bodies or the half-starved, filthy and insane spectres who came begging for handouts. She was proving to be a match for Kagawa's social activism, not simply admiring his heroism from afar, but actually assisting him. Here was a woman of great compassion who was also be tough enough to stand by him in his mission. Without these qualities she could never have endured the hardships of Shinkawa. Haru herself wrote:

> In that neighborhood, the weak, the sick and the maimed exist. In five or six blocks more than 10,000 human beings are

huddled together, who have all lost out in the struggle of life. When I learned that the little group of Christians had come to live among these poor people, I was very glad.[35]

She found herself spontaneously imitating the man she admired so much. One night in November 1912, she heard a child screaming as she was walking through Shinkawa. She found the father beating his little girl while the mother lay sick. He was apparently enraged because they were out of kerosene for the lamps. Haru gave them all the money she had, cleaned the house and bathed the child. She had discovered her vocation to help the poor. "From this I received great stimulation," she said. "If by living among them I could help such wretched people, I should be glad to do so. I resolved to enter the slums."[36]

Reminiscing on their romance, Kagawa painted a mocking picture of his flights of fantasy, confessing that he found her rather plain looking and wasn't sexually attracted to her. At first he simply couldn't stir up any of those conventional feelings of "love" for her, no matter how much he appreciated her spiritual growth, her help in his social and religious work, and her obvious admiration. To this disappointing mood he added another confession that "at one time he had thought of falling in love with her younger sister. But although she was a beautiful girl she had not the brightness of her elder sister."

From this romantic nonsense, the ascetic Sensei went straight to the practical, calling her a Joan of Arc—"a strong and yet a womanly woman." He wrote of his alter ego in an autobiographical novel contemplating marriage, "The man would be lucky who had her for a wife. A helpful wife like that must be rare. Sometimes he thought that he would marry her, but then again she was not a beauty . . ." Worse yet, enough of Kagawa's elitism remained that even this fantasy was marred by the thought that this woman would be beneath him because her position in the printing works "made him hesitate to make so low a match."[37] After such musing he proceeds to critique another object of his romantic affections, but concludes that her beauty is entirely too superficial for a seeker of truth like himself. He even notes that the pores in her nose are filled with

dirt and that she is only impressive when her powder is properly applied.[38]

In spite of his fantasies and crushes on attractive young
women who attended Bible classes or helped in the mission
activity, he kept turning back to Haru Shiba with that interesting
mixture of sentiment and practicality that makes for strong
marriages. So reticient was he with women that he appears to
have been waiting for her to intrude on his musings with her
own proposal of marriage.

His fullest reminiscence of these feelings came in the form of
autobiographical fiction:

> Had she come to talk to him about her marriage? Her manner
> during the two years and a half he had known her had not
> changed. Since he had come to live in the slums he had admired
> her for the courage with which she faced the world. He had not
> spoken of marriage, but if she broached the subject he would
> hear her joyfully. She was different from other women. She
> wanted to be independent and such a woman had a strong will.
> She was a woman who would marry of her own free will. If she
> were only better-looking she would be a very fine woman.[39]

Perhaps a measure of the bond between them is that she
could in fact tolerate this kind of criticism of her looks when it
appeared in print! The truth is, that while she was not a
ravishing beauty, she was certainly attractive enough. Though
she was almost 26 years old—dangerously close to the age when
women of that era were relegated to spinsterhood—even this
unconventional fact appealed to Kagawa. She had an integrity
he admired, because she had not rushed into marriage for
romance or economic security. In many respects she was the
prototype of the liberated woman, willing to take charge of her
life and not bow to the conventions of society.

Haru was, in short, both the practical manager and a non-
conformist like himself—the ideal partner for a man with Kagawa's needs. She could help him run his projects without at the
same time questioning their legitimacy, because she enthusiastically shared his religious zeal and the dedication to social
service. In addition, she was a genuinely likeable person. He

could not resist showing off his learning and describing her reliability in terms of Greek goddesses:

> She exhaled a charm which attracted everyone. She left it in the air like a perfume after she had gone. Such a woman could not be judged by her face. She was not a Venus, but she had the dignity of a Juno. She was not a plaything, but a faithful ruler.

Haru knew how close they had been drawn together. Her negotiating strategy showed a cleverness that probably exceeded even Kagawa's high estimation of her. She came to see him, sat down on the mats beside him where he was bundled up with a severe cold, and announced that she was considering a serious marriage offer from another man. Her alternative proposal was to come and live with him in Shinkawa, working as his servant. With a reputation to protect, Kagawa responded that she would have to marry him because of the gossip if she merely moved into his quarters. She blushed, and countered with the sentiment that she was not of a high enough social station to marry the Sensei. He reached out and held her hand which was resting on the fiber mat on the floor, hiding his face in the quilt while he cried.

It was the moment of truth in a romance where strong emotions have not been fully expressed. After a long silence, she replied that she would let him know about her decision in three weeks. She finally sent him a note accepting his proposal, and concluded with her declaration of love. He responded by asking her to meet him on the beach the next morning at six, where they had a sunrise tryst to confirm the engagement. The couple were married on May 27, 1913, at the Kobe Presbyterian Church by Rev. Seijiro Aoki, the instructor whom Kagawa had defended at the seminary.

The slum itself was the setting for the young couple's honeymoon. A few days after the wedding, Kagawa invited a large group of slum dwellers for *sushi* at his house, and introduced his wife as "Jochu San," or "maid." He told them, "I myself would like to be your servant, but I have not the ability. My wife will be your servant.[40] From this time on, she became the person who did more than anyone to hold Kagawa's community together and carry on the work among the poor. She administered everything from finances to swabbing the beggars' sores. Every evening, regardless of the weather, the couple went to their preaching spot at a corner in front of a wine shop, carrying large paper lanterns on long poles to attract attention, with the words "God is Love" and "Only Believe" written on them.

She was experiencing growth through the difficult role she had assumed. As she wrote, "One might think that there was not much difference between me and the slum people themselves. But the work I was going to do made a very great difference.[4] It was not the work alone, but Kagawa's insistence that she be educated and develop her potential. Kagawa wanted a liberated woman, partly because he loved to see people grow and gain control of their lives and partly for his own purposes. He needed a "Juno" to take charge, a mate idealistic enough to live with him in squalor and at the same time practical and skillful enough to cope with it. A wife who failed to meet these exacting demands would have sabotaged his entire project.

In the miserably hot summer of 1913 the drought was so severe that water had to be trucked into the area. Kagawa strung a hammock between the pillars of the building for his wife. Her health had suffered from the round of hard work and the poor diet. Haru had a very strong constitution—she lived to 95—but according to Takeuchi, even she sometimes broke down under such difficult conditions.

Though Kagawa had actually begun to see some tangible improvements in the slums as a result of his work, such as a reduction in gambling, he was still depressed by the magnitude of the problems of the poor in Shinkawa and all of Japan. He knew in his heart that all his sacrifices had but a miniscule effect on the massive evils of poverty, dangerous working conditions, and the grossly uneven distribution of wealth in his nation.

The couple decided it was time to step back from their personal involvement in the slums and gain new perspective. Obtaining loans totalling 200 yen from Myers and Logan, plus 50 yen from Logan for translating Charles A. Oliver's *The Teaching Method for Sunday Schools*, he decided to make his way to the United States to study at Princeton University and the Princeton Theological Seminary, a major intellectual and educational center for Myers' Presbyterian denomination. Having

mended fences with some relatives and maintaining good relations with others, he also received parting gifts in the Japanese
tradition that helped pay his fare. Haru left Shinkawa for further
education at the Kyoritsu Women's Theological School in Yokohama. She had lost weight and may have been suffering from
tuberculosis. The reliable Takeuchi was left in charge of the
growing Shinkawa mission.

In August, 1914, just after the outbreak of World War I,
Kagawa departed for the United States aboard the *Tamba maru*.
There was clearly a lot of unfinished business. He was sailing
into the Western world where his youthful visions of peace were
being shattered in the very land of the mighty Kant. He was
leaving the slum where he had become a revered public figure in
four years, and he was separating from a wife who had given
him physical love. His funds were limited, and his study of the
psychology of poverty, which some modern scholars consider
the best of his writing, was languishing without a publisher. His
first trip across the Pacific could not have been a carefree cruise
in spite of the fact that this 26-year-old already had, by both
Asian and Western standards, a record of accomplishments far
beyond his years.

Chapter 4
American Interlude

K AGAWA LANDED IN SAN FRANCISCO and took a train across
the United States. He went over the Sierras, down into the
desert, up through the Rocky Mountains and across the plains
to Kansas City. Then he headed south, crossing Missouri and
the Mississippi, and rode through the South to Athens, Georgia.
There he visited Sibley, the company director who had sent
funds to support his work.

During his stay of a few days, he marveled at the old colonial
style houses with pillars in front which made them seem like
palaces. After such a trip, he was amazed at the ethnic variety
and vastness of the United States. It was a powerful experience
for a man from an island nation with a homogeneous population, and he gave full expression to this sense of wonder in his
second novel, *Taiyo o iru mono* (A Shooter at the Sun).

His health was improving, and he was relatively free of
money worries because he received $25 monthly from a schol-
arship for his studies at Princeton. He enrolled in courses in
psychology and mathematics, spending a great deal of time
reading wherever his interest took him. Eventually he received
Master of Arts credits for a thesis he wrote on experimental
psychology, but he was not officially awarded that degree
because his class work at Meiji Gakuin was not considered the
equivalent of an American college degree.

Kagawa was so well read and tutored by the Presbyterian
missionaries Drs. Myers and Logan that he found little to
interest him in the theological offerings at the Princeton seminary. He went out of his way to make critical remarks about the
theology department in his novel.[1] He was exempted from the
standard course work required for a theology degree. This
permitted him to spend time studying biology at the university,
with particular attention to evolution.

He took courses in embryology, genetics, comparative ana-
tomy, paleontology, all with the intention of reinforcing his
notion that the theory of evolution was not in conflict with
Christianity, but rather in harmony with it. These studies confirmed his earlier vision that Christianity was a religion of
evolution, because it was oriented toward collective salvation.
With Kropotkin, whom he had already studied in Japan, Kagawa regarded evolution in the universe from lower to higher
forms as an example of the increasing love in the mutual
relationships between things.

More than ever, Kagawa saw the Darwinian "survival of the
fittest" in a constant struggle for life as a one-sided version of
evolution. The ability of members of a species to cooperate with
each other was at least as critical to survival as the ability to do
battle. When he transferred this thinking to the human world, it
became his answer to Social Darwinism and the underpinning
of his philosophy on cooperatives.

Social Darwinism justified a contempt for the underprivi-
leged. It preached that evolutionary competition was nature's
inevitable method of weeding out inferior specimens which
were not strong enough to survive, and backed it up by "scientific" evidence. Kagawa countered by showing that cooperators
were better equipped to survive, and that mutual aid was a far
stronger formula for success than competition. As we shall see,
these studies had a profound effect on his later thinking.[2]

Kagawa plunged into the intense rounds of study for which
he was noted while a student in Japan. He thoroughly enjoyed
this retreat to academia; it was such a relief from the dangerous
and difficult life in the slums. Here was an opportunity to
recuperate and contemplate that he had not enjoyed in years.
He described the intellectual activity and the feeling of freedom
at Princeton, when he wrote about himself as the student in his
autobiographical novel staying:

> . . . in the natural history museum of the University until it
> was dark studying the evolution of the skeleton, and the draw-
> ings of the lion's skull and the sabre-toothed tiger.
>
> He read from before dawn till past midnight. In the library he
> delved into the development of the civilizations of Egypt,
> Greece, Babylon, and Assyria, before the advent of Christianity.

He was thankful to be rid of the threatenings of the Shinkawa bullies and the anxiety over infectious disease. It seemed like a dream that he was able to study quietly in that university.[3]

Kagawa had language problems, as is common to foreign students. Although he probably had read more in English than most native speakers of the language, his use of the spoken word had been limited. Another foreign student, the Dutch-born Jan Van Baalen who sat in the front row with Kagawa, said, "Taking notes in the classroom was an ordeal during those first few months. Except in Doctor Erdman's class. He knew foreigners."[4] Van Baalen complimented Erdman's habit of watching him and Kagawa, and when he could see that they hadn't gotten the point, he would reword his ideas. Van Baalen consoled himself by the fact that sometimes "friend Toyohiko apparently left as many gaps in his notes as I did."[5] Kagawa may not have been able to pronounce the word "door," but his vocabulary was prodigious, a tribute to his remarkable memory.

During his Princeton stay, Kagawa was rather reserved, certainly much more so than the man who was to stir Americans 20 years later on a grand tour of lectures. He was modest about his achievements in Japan and apparently reticent in discussing his work in the slums. Van Baalen lived in the same dormitory, talked often with Kagawa, and moved in the same circle of students, but he was unaware of Kagawa's life in Shinkawa until he read of it years later.

This budding orator, street preacher, author, social worker, self-promoter and egotist from Japan projected quite a different image on his first visit to the United States. He was the reticent and exquisitely polite Oriental. A classmate Harry Richmond cautioned, "We have to be very careful in judging people. Here we always think of the Japanese as proud and arrogant; and yet, what a dandy little chap is Kagawa."[6]

Kagawa quickly realized that the image of a non-threatening, deferential Asian would play better in the States than the relentless warrior or the xenophobic traditionalist. He felt more comfortable representing the mystical Japan of the Buddhists than the military Japan of the samurai. Even the publication of his *Study of the Psychology of the Poor* in November of 1915, did not create a stir on the campus.

Nor was he outspoken in discussing his feelings about the United States at this time. He avoided overt criticism of the racism he had observed and experienced. He played the politest of roles, introducing himself with the instinctive Japanese bow and a smile. If indeed he was Japan's future prophet, he certainly did not attempt to create that impression among his Princeton classmates.

He did, however, immediately take the initiative to work on international relations. Soon after Van Baalen arrived, Kagawa knocked on his door and introduced himself. "Mr. Van Baalen," he said, "I hear you are from Holland. I am from Japan. So I thought I would call on you to tell you how much our country owes your country, and how highly our people think of your people."[7] When Van Baalen answered that he had not learned anything about good relations between the two nations in his home training, Kagawa gave a polite history lesson: "Oh yes. We learned many things from you: our medicine, our science. Our ports were closed in those days to every European country except Holland. We became almost scared of all that was not Dutch."[8]

It is a historical fact that among Europeans, only the Dutch were allowed at Japan's foreign port of Nagasaki during the 250 years of the Tokugawa Shogunate. Kagawa was not, however, merely making small talk with a foreigner. He regarded himself as Japanese, a representative of his nation, and he was relating to foreigners in these terms. Though already "westernized" in much of his thinking and considered an eccentric in Japan, he remained thoroughly Japanese in his concern to avoid bringing "shame" upon his people. The Japanese culture makes the individual far more sensitive to his role in the family and the social group than does the European and American.

He got along well with the other students at Princeton and enjoyed outings with them like canoe trips and hikes. During the first summer vacation he went into New York City to find temporary work. After some searching he obtained a position as a servant in a large summer resort home 20 miles outside the city. Here he worked for a month before returning to Princeton in September.[9]

The next year passed quickly in quiet study at Princeton. He

finished his thesis and received a Bachelor of Divinity degree in
May 1916. With sixty-five other graduates, he stood on the
platform to received his diploma, singing the class hymn in a
loud voice:

> When I survey the wondrous Cross
>   On which the Prince of Glory died,
> My richest gain I count but loss,
>   And pour contempt on all my pride.
>
> Forbid it, Lord, that I should boast
>   Save in the death of Christ, my Lord;
> All the vain things that charm me most,
>   I sacrifice them to his blood.
>
> Were the whole realm of nature mine,
>   That were a present far too small:
> Love so amazing, so divine,
>   Demands my soul, my life, my all.

He planned to enroll at the University of Chicago in the fall,
but needed work for the summer. Again he went to New York,
where he roamed around the slums much as he had done in
Japan. He described his reaction to the New York slums with a
mixture of anger and ironic detachment similar to that of his
biting analysis of poverty in Japan:

> There being no work to be had he took the opportunity to
> investigate New York's slums. He wandered about them, from
> Chinatown to the Bowery, and was astonished to find that
> Manhattan, between the Hudson and East rivers, from First
> Street to Third Street, a distance of ten miles, was all covered
> with slums. In the Bowery, young prostitutes called to him in the
> street and even caught hold of his coat. Of churches for the
> workers there were any number in Fourteenth Street, but the
> prostitutes were walking the street in search of customers. Some
> of them looked thin and ill, while some were unhealthily fat.
> Sometimes, as in Shinkawa, they were followed by bullies and
> pimps. In the shops at night were sold picture postcards of nude
> figures. At the offices of specialists in veneral disease crowds of
> sufferers waited.
>
> There were negro slums and Jewish slums. Immigrants from
> all the countries of the world took refuge in the slums before
> drifting all over America in inextricable confusion. . . . The
> slums of the celebrated Bowery lie just behind Wall Street, where

the wealth of the world is accumulated. The iniquity of capitalism is here too plainly seen. . . . He studied New York's slums in the light of his experiences in the slums of Shinkawa, and he discovered that the lot of the poor was the same whether in the East or West.[10]

Like so many other Japanese revolutionaries and reformers who visited the United States both before and after him, the experience convinced Kagawa that Japan's problems were not unique, but reflected the injustices of the whole world's economy. Like them, he learned also from the organizations for social change in the United States. Kagawa was deeply affected by the demonstrations of the organized garment workers in New York which he witnessed in the summer of 1916. The sight of a mass of 60,000 workers of many nationalities marching through the streets made him feel the power of worker solidarity and strengthened his resolve to promote the union cause when he returned to Japan.[11] He vividly described the effect of the parade on his emotions:

> A procession was passing. It was a demonstration of the Needleworkers' Union, consisting of sixty thousand people. They were walking sixteen abreast and the procession took an hour and a half to pass. The masters of the four hundred and fifty tailors' shops in Manhattan had ordered a lock-out and sixty thousand poor workers on the East Side were affected. Under the August sun there were marching in the procession Italian workers, Jewish workers, Bohemian workers—workers from almost every country in the world.
>
> They carried banners with the words "We want bread" and also placards with "Down with Capitalism" on them. There were women from Syria who looked as if they had never worn European clothes before, and there were women who looked as if it was the first time they had worn high-heeled boots in the street, so painfully they walked. . . . All the colors of the unions waved and fluttered in the bright sunlight as the procession advanced. The appealing eyes of the thousands forming the procession made them look like a large flock of sheep being driven along the highway. . . .
>
> "Are these all the poor?" he thought. "Only these? And they are fighting only four hundred and fifty opponents. How useless to talk of relief! Labor unions! There is nothing for the worker to

do but to trust to his own strength. When I return to Japan I will preach the formation of labor unions."[12]

He went every day to a Japanese agency to find a place to work, and finally landed another job as a servant but was fired for not properly locking the house and tripping the burglar alarm. After this abortive experience, Kagawa returned to the resort area and was hired at another large house. But there again he left quickly because he had mistakenly put sugar instead of salt on the breakfast eggs of the family's teenage daughter. The embarassment of this mistake and a feeling of being ill at ease in the house caused him to leave voluntarily. From there he proceded to a butler's job on the Canadian border at Niagara, where by the end of the summer of 1916 he earned enough to make it to Chicago to continue his studies.

In Chicago, he visited Jane Addams' famous settlements and enrolled in the University of Chicago with intentions to pursue further his study of life sciences. He was running short of money, however, and a persistent cough increased his fear of a recurrence of tuberculosis. He had thrived in the fresh air at Princeton, but found the atmosphere in Chicago much less salutary. He abandoned further study, deciding to return to Japan as soon as he could earn enough for the trip.

He needed $150 to return, but had only $50. He heard from a fellow Japanese that an association of Japanese in Ogden, Utah was looking for a secretary. He journeyed west to Utah in the fall. In addition to the possibility of earning money for his return passage, he was also attracted by the romance of the west, so he "decided to go west to the Great Salt Lake Desert among the mountains. He wanted to pray in the desert and also to search for the fossils of mammals."[13]

The Japanese Association hired him as its secretary, paying him $50 a month for his services. He did office work, helped write letters and made the rounds in the Japanese community. He rode sleighs in the snowbound winter, visiting Japanese farmworkers in their crude houses and calling on the miners in this desert region. While making his rounds, he also found time to collect petrified wood, fossils, and some of the flora of the region.

Kagawa did not have to wait until returning to Japan to try out his new faith in unions. He suddenly found himself in the middle of a drive to organize Japanese tenants on sugar beet farms in the area.[14] The sugar beet industry was booming in northern Utah, having become the centerpiece of the local economy by the time Kagawa arrived. Harvest was about to begin, with processing plants paying $5.50 per ton for sugar beets. One Ogden plant was operating at an all time high and another had recently doubled its capacity. Two new sugar processing factories were being built, one of which was capitalized for $2 million.[15] One company alone in Ogden had the capacity to process 1000 to 1200 tons of beets per day. Some 9,000 acres yielding an estimated 125,000 tons were ready to be dug for Amalgamated Sugar.[16] Due to poor weather in the spring, the harvest began later than usual, but was well underway by the end of September.[17]

The farmers were far from satisfied with the price of beets, and the state's Farm Bureau began negotiating for better prices. The farmers gathered statistics showing that the sugar companies were making a net profit of $9.18 for each ton of beets they bought while the farmer made only 39.5 cents.[18] By the end of the year, the sugar companies had agreed to a large hike in prices, to $7 per ton.[19]

Since the tenant farmer received only a portion of this payment from the landlord, the Japanese tenants had good reason to demand increased payment. They asked Kagawa to help negotiate with their landlords, who were Mormons. Although the landlords seemed to be playing off the Mormon tenants against the Japanese tenants, Kagawa managed to persuade both to organize into one tenant union. They then demanded that the landlords pay more for the beets, and when the landlords turned them down, they refused to start the crucial spring planting. In March, the group won an increase from the landlords. The result was that the total income of the Japanese farmers increased by $50,000 a year.[20] The grateful Japanese farmers gave Kagawa a bonus of $100, which was sufficient to pay his fare to Japan.

Kagawa had come to the United States during some of the most turbulent times for the American labor movement. The demonstrations he saw in the East were part of a growing discontent which often met brutal resistance. Given his propensity to weeping, he undoubtedly shed some tears when he learned that on November 5, 1916, five members of the International Workers of the World (IWW) were murdered by a posse in Everett, Washington and 40 more were wounded. The IWW's balladeer Joe Hill, now a legendary figure in the left wing of the American labor movement, had been murdered in Salt Lake City the previous year.

The American Federation of Labor was lobbying at the national level for the eight-hour day and legislation against child labor. Coincidentally, not long after Kagawa arrived in Ogden, Bunji Suzuki, a leader of the Japanese labor movement and later an ally of Kagawa, was attending the California AFL convention in Eureka, California. Suzuki had learned much about labor organizing from the U.S. labor leaders.

Yet there were painful moments for both American labor and Japanese-American relations. The pressure of racism was so strong in the United States, that this AFL convention adopted a resolution advocating a boycott on Japanese labor and employment in the United States. This virulent prejudice against the Japanese was expressed more forcefully a few years later in the exclusionary immigration and anti-alien land laws, which stirred up strong anti-American feelings in Japan. The Japanese military regime used this issue to sell its own brand of imperialism to the Japanese people, packaging it as a legitimate form of self-defense. Having explored the slums, having worked as a house-boy, seeing first hand the discrimination against Asians in New York, and observing the treatment of blacks, Kagawa had learned much of what he later called "hell America." But he had also come to appreciate "heaven America"—the land of promise, freedom and hope.

Kagawa left Ogden, detouring through the Northwest, taking a boat down the Snake and Columbia Rivers, and finally departing from Seattle.[21] He had seized America, traveling like a Walt Whitman across her wide breadth, imbibing her in the green summer and pausing for contemplation on the high plains and desert of the West. A poet, he would give voice to this experience in future writings. Most importantly, it was in this sparsely populated territory that he first tested the new form of non-violent social action which would soon make him famous—the labor unions.

Passing the Aleutian islands and the glaciers of the northern Pacific on the way home, he dramatized his resolution to struggle non-violently for justice in Japan. He prayed on the ship's deck when the Aurora of the Arctic Ocean flamed in the sky at night. That resolve he described:

> He thought that when he got back to Japan he would become a shooter at the sun. For the sake of the poor and needy and for the sake of the oppressed workers he would go again to live in the slums. For the sake of the freedom of the country he would work for the freedom of workers' organizations. As a disciple of Christ he could take no violent part in the war between Capital and Labor, but rather than allow the people to be sacrificed he would sacrifice himself. . . . If the enemy came with a sword he would unsheath none. He would fight with the weapons of justice and humanity. He would continue the struggle till bedabbled in blood he fell from the Cross. There was no other way for the salvation of Japan save in the freedom of the worker.[22]

Chapter 5
Labor Struggles

*I*N MAY OF 1917, Kagawa returned home to a booming Kobe, with its shipping and industry basking in the cash flow from World War I. Just sixty years after the Western world had forced its way into feudal Japan, the island nation had been drawn into the Occident's "Great War," both as a major supplier and an ally of France, Britain and the United States. Under the expert tutelage and encouragement of these friends, Japan's military industrial complex had burgeoned.

Little of the war profits trickled down to the alleys and hovels in Shinkawa. If anything, conditions worsened due to a severe lack of housing caused by thousands of new workers crowding into the city and pushing up the population by another hundred thousand. Kagawa had to face the heartbreaking fact that some of his women converts had returned to prostitution or were sold into other services, while his men converts had gone into gambling, thievery, and assorted illegal enterprises.[1] Due to the postwar depression, unemployment was forcing more and more wage earners into marginal existence. But the core group led by Masaru Takeuchi remained a thriving, self-sustaining community, sharing income and giving the surplus to the poor, preaching and providing shelter, in the style of primitive Christianity.

Kagawa's thinking had matured considerably. His labors in the slums and his observations in the United States had shown him that personal acts of charity, however heroic, would never eradicate the desperate kind of poverty Shinkawa suffered. He saw that even better organized forms of charity, such as the settlement house, failed to reach the root causes of poverty, which he now believed were ingrained in the economic system itself. Until the entire political and industrial system was changed, the remedies to which he had dedicated himself with such passion were mere stopgap measures, in more modern terminology "band aids." He felt the need to turn to unions and political action in order to shake up the whole society. Through these channels Christians would seek to transform the system with an infusion of their religious ethics—ethics which he believed most Christians were failing to put into practice. He amplified this theme as follows:

> If we intend to eliminate the urban poor, we cannot do it by charity. The fact that charity tends to increase the number of the poor people can be proved by the fact that religious charity in ancient times produced beggars, or by the fact that the relief work of the poor in England failed. And if we seriously think of the relief of the poor, I believe, we will come to the point where we face the fundamental labor problems in the end. And for the solution of the problems, we can think of various doctrines such as socialism, the principle of social reform, and state socialism. But I believe that, as things stand now in Japan, nothing is more urgent for us to do than developing sound labor unions.[2]

This new political approach did not mean that he intended to abandon Shinkawa. Quite the contrary. A man with Kagawa's compassion had to continue easing the immediate pain around him, and the slums would remain a base of operations for both his religious community and his union activities. He found no antithesis between the urgent local tasks of feeding the poor and involvement in the larger issues of reform, particularly at this stage of Japan's development.

After rejoining Haru and taking a short vacation trip with her to Tokyo, the young couple returned to their headquarters. This trip included lectures, since he was already in demand because of the wide sales of *Hinmin shinri no kenkyu* (Study of the Psychology of the Poor). By 1922, this work had gone through nine printings and had helped draw the nation's attention to the plight of the poor. An attraction of this book and of Kagawa as a personality was authenticity. He was not a sociologist or journalist studying the poor for academic purposes; he had lived their squalor. The book was a compelling mixture of hard data, compassion, and novelistic attention to concrete details. He wrote with compelling simplicity at the beginning of *Study of the*

Psychology of the Poor, "I truly realize that poverty is impossible to bear since I myself am experiencing life in the slums from dawn to dusk. And when I think about and observe the effect of poverty on our spiritual lives, it is so miserable that it is beyond description."[3]

He wanted nothing short of a revolution in Japanese society, but as a pacifist, he could not side with those who advocated violent overthrow of the existing order. Kagawa's study of the French revolution, and news of the bloodshed in Russia had convinced him that revolution unleashed too much violence and in the end cost too many lives, especially if a peaceful alternative could be developed.

Therefore, he pinned his hopes on unions, because of their power to improve wages and working conditions and to be instrumental in creating social reforms far beyond the workplace. They could help secure desperately needed legislation by using their power to give voting rights to all 12 million male citizens over the age of 25 instead of the mere 3 million who were permitted to vote. (At this time, a Japanese male was ineligible to vote unless he paid at least 3 yen in taxes, thereby excluding the vast majority.)[4] In addition to unions, Kagawa believed that cooperatives would revolutionize the Japanese economy, and ultimately the world's, by giving workers and consumers ownership and control of key industries while redistributing profits to them rather than concentrating the wealth into the hands of the few.

Unions, cooperatives and universal suffrage were the three major causes to which he devoted his enormous energy and charismatic organizing skills over the next five years. Underlying his motivation for social action was his staunch religious faith. Within a year after his return from his Princeton studies in the United States, Kagawa was ordained a minister by the Japanese Presbyterian Conference in April 1918. Although this ordination was an important milestone in his career, it was given little publicity. All through his student years, Kagawa had been the unorthodox "loner" in terms of the denomination establishment. He was also torn between the more liberal Northern Presbyterians of the Meiji seminary and the "strict constructionist" Southern Presbyterians of the Kobe seminary.

The open theological and intellectual atmosphere of the former was more consonant with his outlook, but he never ceased to feel his deep loyalty to Drs. Myers and Logan, who had nurtured him in his earliest student days.

Along with improved conditions for the poor and working class, Kagawa, as an activist pastor, called for the transformation of the soul—a growth of the person. Without the spiritual dimension, Kagawa believed economic reform would be barren. He had witnessed enough of the spiritual emptiness of the middle and upper classes, both in Japan and the United States, to know that material comfort did not automatically create better or freer human beings, though it was a precondition for religious growth commanded by the gospel itself. An improved material condition was not an end in itself, but was the basis for the human personality to blossom and freely develop its full potential—in short, to encounter God.

Kagawa's view of evolution was that a higher level of awareness would evolve in the individual and the race itself, if given a chance. He did not accept the old religious dualism that separates soul from body, spirit from matter, and the things of this world from the next. He had no use for the teaching that bodily suffering in this life would be rewarded by a pleasant afterlife for the disembodied spirit. God was here and now, in the physical world. Spirit was neither higher nor better than matter. The two were intertwined. He summed this up:

> The purpose of our having a mystical experience is not that we may achieve our own personal satisfaction, but that we may succor the poor, help those who are in trouble, and educate the masses. If this were not Christ's teaching, we could not challenge the terrific power of this capitalistic civilization.[5]

Man did not fly to God to escape the world, but rather, God came to man to help build the world. This was Kagawa's whole doctrine of incarnation and his persistent argument for building the Kingdom of God on earth.

This movement of Kagawa's thought from individualistic charity toward a more political solution to social problems by no means diminished his charitable work in the slums. He kept various classes going. He opened his doors to day care and kindergartens for the children of the working poor. Aware that illness was the strongest barrier to improvement and education in the slums, he obtained help from businessman Sutekazu Fukui to open the Friends of Jesus Relief Clinic next to his headquarters. With support from this benefactor, Kagawa was able to hire some help, while a humanitarian physician Hiroshi Umashima donated part-time services. Haru, sister-in-law Utako Honda, and Hisa Umashima worked in the clinic and made visits to the sick.[6]

One of Haru's tasks was to clean and medicate the eyes of people suffering from trachoma, a disease caused by poor hygiene. An infection which initially attacks the inside of the eyelids, it can destroy the cornea and cause blindness. Both Kagawas contracted the disease after they returned to the slums in 1917, and it plagued them intermittently throughout their lives. At times Toyohiko became totally blind for several months at a time.

Kagawa set up another cooperative shortly after he returned from the United States. He and Takeuchi hauled equipment 50 miles from a toothbrush factory in Osaka and dragged it through the slums on handcarts. The idea was to turn the factory over to the workers eventually. Influenced by British guild socialism, Kagawa now believed in worker ownership of industry. It seemed clear to him that the workers who created the wealth were entitled to own and control the means of production. He believed that exploitation of labor in Japan would cease if the workers themselves shared the profits. Kagawa's vision was of a society based on worker or consumer ownership and control of industries. This factory project was to demonstrate that such a system would work.

Toothbrush manufacture was chosen because it had a steady, year-round market. To help Kagawa, Dr. Myers enlisted an Austrian merchant who donated 10,000 yen worth of raw materials and agreed to purchase the production of the factory. Although this project was more carefully planned than the pre-war restaurant fiasco, it nevertheless seems that Kagawa's idealism and enthusiasm for worker control prevented him from recognizing certain difficulties of such an enterprise. Brush manufacturing required a high level of skill and concentration, especially in inserting the delicate tufts. Many of the workers were unwilling or unable to perform such painstaking work. In addition, the factory was plagued by high absenteeism caused by drinking and illness. The staff constantly turned over, and pilferage of raw materials was a problem. By the end of 1917 the enterprise was losing about 1000 yen a month, and it was closed in March 1920.[7]

A revolutionary idea had failed, partly because Kagawa had pinned unrealistic hope on workers incapable of self-management and self-discipline. Assuming that they even made it to work in the morning, people shaking from hangovers were hardly suited for a meticulous operation. To lift the *lumpen-proletariat* up into the working classes was not an easy task. Kagawa's optimism appears to have gotten the better of his common sense, which should have warned him that the odds of redeeming slum dwellers and turning them into self-sufficient, productive individuals were very slim.

But this experience did not discourage him about co-ops. During this period Kagawa was having success with a cooperative employment agency he had also organized. Employment agencies were charging high fees to find jobs, so this co-op was able to compete successfully. Nor did he lose faith in the capacity for change and self-improvement which he had seen in many slum people, especially the younger ones who had come to his school and religious services. He also set up a day camp for the children of working mothers. These activities both helped the poor and furnished models of what could be accomplished in society. With political changes, the clinics, schools, employment agencies and consumer and worker-owned businesses would gradually become part of the system.

Kagawa saw that the time was ripe for social reforms. Discontent was increasing among Japanese workers, due to long hours, child labor and hazardous working conditions. It was not until 1912 that even such weak legislation as the Factory Law limited the workday to 12 hours for women and children under 15. Worker discontent was also fueled by the disparate effect of Japan's war prosperity on the lower economic stratum. Many workers made as little as 50 sen (25 cents) a day, while even the best paid, such as the mine workers, were earning less than 2 yen (about one dollar).[8] On the other hand the upper classes were enjoying war profits and indulging in conspicuous consumption. The workers' resentment rose as they watched their own standard of living deteriorate. The 50 strikes in 1914 involving just under 8000 workers increased dramatically to 417 in 1918 involving more than 66,000.[9]

Workers began demanding better conditions, despite the fact that oppressive laws made it difficult to organize labor unions. The Public Peace Police Law passed in 1900 required them to register with the police and obtain special permission to meet. Police were given sweeping powers to shut down meetings which they considered subversive.[10] In 1911, the clampdown was tightened in the wake of the trial and execution of anarchist leader Kotoku Shusui.

Japan's sudden leap from the feudal system to modern industrial society did not allow time to evolve the tolerance for dissent which had developed over several centuries in Western democracies. For that matter, the Western democracies themselves could not claim an exemplary record of peacefully resolving labor union clashes with the establishment, as can be seen by the numerous armed assaults on workers taking place in the West well into the 1930s. In addition to the kind of police surveillance which caused Kagawa to be interrogated by the police about his article on world peace, press censorship continued. In 1913 alone, newspapers editions were suppressed a total of 1,110 times.[11] In this repressive climate, the intimidated press performed a great deal of self-censorship.[12]

The threat of government intervention made union leaders quite cautious in their organizing efforts. Some maintained a low profile and did not even refer to their groups as unions. One labor group which had come into prominence was the Yuaikai, or "Friendly Society," founded in 1912 by the journalist Bunji Suzuki, a Christian Socialist who had himself penned a series of articles on the horrors of slum life. Starting from a small meeting in August in the Unitarian Church library in the Mita district of Tokyo, this organization grew to 30,000 members in just eight years. Suzuki would have preferred to organize a true labor union. This was, in fact, his long range goal, but he believed that the government would have abolished a union because of the law and its hostile attitude toward labor.[13]

Suzuki slowly began moulding the Yuaikai into more of an educational and mutual aid association. Through lectures, personal and legal counseling for workers, and a savings department, the Society helped members with their personal finances and encouraged them to deposit savings at the group's headquarters. A medical department arranged for free or discounted medical help through clinics friendly to labor and sponsored physical fitness classes.[14] Suzuki also established ties with liberal businessmen who advised and assisted the organization.[15] His strategy was to convince the workers and society in general of the value of labor unions as a method both to improve workers' lives and to foster orderly relations between capital and labor.

As discontent among laborers rose, the Yuaikai became increasingly militant. In Kobe, the local Yuaikai had 1200 members by the time Kagawa had returned to Japan in 1917 from his stay at Princeton. Takeuchi himself was active in the local branch and likely introduced Kagawa to the organization. Kagawa's first official contact was a lecture at the Kobe chapter meeting on September 9, 1917. Thereafter he was frequently invited to meetings and asked to speak. Strongly and urgently he spoke on worker's rights, salting his speeches with witty and sarcastic observations and illustrating abstract ideas about the dignity of man with cogent examples from daily life. This was no intellectual talking down to the crowd, but a man who had suffered with them and understood their plight.

He would tell the workers:

> Kobe, as you all know, is a harbor city where foreign trade business is prospering. Therefore, there are many warehouses. In them many cargoes are stored. And all the warehouses are stately looking buildings. Inside, the buildings are well cleaned and they are equipped with humidity-controllers. They are completely equipped with all other necessary things for storing goods. They are protected even by guards. The laborers who suffer from poverty are looking up at the cargoes piled up in the warehouses enviously and pitifully. Look! At the present time the cargoes are treated better than the laborers are. This is an age when material things are held in esteem excessively. The cargoes for profit are prized more than man, and man is held in contempt more than things. . . . We must reconstruct this wrong society in order to realize a society which is based on the principle of respecting human life.[16]

A month after he first spoke to the Yuaikai, he was elected to the council of the Kobe branch. Clearly, the society was comfortable with this dramatic orator. At the Sixth Annual Convention held in the Tennoji Public Hall in Osaka, April 1918, Kagawa along with others pushed for stronger demands. He called for a twofold policy of social reform, which included education and consciousness raising for workers and the establishment of a social security system. In May, he was named a trustee of the Kobe local and editorial advisor of its newly-formed newspaper, *Shin Kobe* (New Kobe). In print, as from the platform, he sounded the theme of reconstruction and a renewal of society: "Kobe City will become one of the leading commercial and industrial cities of the world in the future. . . . Greater Kobe has to be *shin* Kobe (*new* Kobe). And the new Kobe, to be sure, has to adopt a new industrial system which is based on labor."[17]

Kagawa's plea for justice for the workers came at a time of a rapidly deteriorating economic situation. Embittered by the obvious fact that they were not sharing in Japan's booming economy, the masses reached the breaking point in July and August of 1918. The cost of living had doubled since 1916, shooting up 50% between 1917 and 1918. A 30% increase in the cost of rice in July triggered rice riots that swept the nation and brought down the government of prime minister Terauchi. Government troops were despatched to quell the violence in the major cities. In Kobe, 20,000 rioters torched shops and newspaper offices, while they looted rice and sake shops. Kagawa had advised the officials to cordon off the sake shops, since he well knew that unlimited access to free liquor would incite the mob to greater violence, but his advice went unheeded as the riots continued. On the third day of the disturbance, troops and special policemen finally halted the riot.[18]

In this turbulent atmosphere Kagawa and others became more militant and began pushing Suzuki and the moderate Yuaikai leadership toward an outspoken position. Kagawa lashed out at the economic system with prophetic indignation, writing in *Shin Kobe* in a language that mixed revolutionary slogans with Christian ideals of brotherhood:

> Workers of the world unite! . . . Workers, awaken from your delusions. . . . Cross international boundary lines, and embrace thy brothers. . . . Dissolve in love the Diet system, suffrage, the

family system, capitalism . . . all systems and organs that oppress the workers on behalf of order. Laborers, in the name of love put aside the superstitious customs that bind you . . . for the day of love and freedom is on the way. . . .[19]

Insisting on human dignity, he demanded treatment of people "at least equal to that which capitalists give to their horses."[20] He railed against the long workdays, subsistence wages, and dreary and dangerous working conditions. He took a characteristic swipe at the organized church, charging it with catering to the bourgeois by piling up higher steeples and investing in stained glass rather than human beings.[21] In demanding social reform he scoffed at the popular Japanese slogan, *fukoku kyohei,* "rich country, strong army," pointing out that the workers were the last to benefit from this high-sounding doctrine used to promote militarism in Japan:

That we demand social reform does not mean to take large quantities of money from the laborer. Actually, we want to change from a civilization based on wealth to one based upon humanistic principles. . . . We are tired of a social structure that screams loudly about *fukoku kyohei.* . . . We demand social reform and a new civilization in which men will be treated like men, one which will not permit the existence of capitalists who only know how to waste money and play around. This civilization must be based upon the principles of labor. It must be spiritually and physically a civilization of laborers.[22]

Always a man of complex, powerful feelings, Kagawa at this time was full of prophetic anger. He was angry at the misery he saw, angry at an economic system which could grind people down while the wealthy profited from their misery. He was angry at the hypocrisy of the church which violated the brotherhood teachings of the Gospel he embraced, and angry at the government officials snuffing out the human spirit. The man who had grown up feeling the bitter sting of injustice in his family was now lashing out at the injustice of the larger family of Japan and the worldwide economic system.

This was a controlled rage, for he never joined the call for violent revolution that became more strident in Japan as the 1920s wore on. Kagawa abhorred violence as a solution to social problems, for moral and tactical reasons. Despite his use of Marxist terms to explain how the economic system drove people to desperation, he parted company with the doctrinaire Marxists on the issue of class struggle. He was critical as well of the totalitarian element in revolutionary groups, because he believed that it could pose as grave a threat to the freedom and dignity of a person and was as dehumanizing as capitalism.

> I want the destruction of capitalism. But, at the same time, I am opposed to the proletarian autocracy. I aspire after the materialization of industrial democracy. Capitalism is an industrial autocracy. So I am opposed to it. Supposing we overthrow the industrial autocracy, and establish the proletarian autocracy instead, we will find no difference so far as it is an autocracy. I do not want to live in a world of labor army systems where people are deprived of their freedom of exchange, freedom of occupation, and freedom of movement.[23]

Kagawa was convinced that in addition to pressures exerted by the labor movement, the other major instrument of peaceful progress and reconstruction would have to be universal suffrage, which would enable the legislation of changes. By fighting to extend the right to vote from a mere 3 million to 12 million adult males, the unions would be able to enact the reforms they were demanding. In urging that the Yuaikai become a strong advocate for suffrage, Kagawa and other activists differed with Suzuki and the more conservative element of the Yuaikai, who wanted to steer clear of political action for fear of government repression. Though he had blazed a trail for the workers, Suzuki remained too timid for Kagawa, let alone the firebrands in the revolutionary wing of the labor movement. They were growing impatient with Suzuki's leadership, questioning his ties with the business world and his emphasis on harmony between capital and labor.

When Suzuki left for the Paris Peace Conference in December 1918, Kagawa and the more militant leaders, Kozo Hisatome, and Gizo Takayama, steered the Yuaikai on a more aggressive course.[24] While Kagawa shared Suzuki's Christian beliefs and religious motivation for involvement in labor's struggle, they disagreed on the political issue, because Suzuki, as one writer describes it, was a "moderate reformer while Kagawa was a

moderate revolutionary."[25] Kagawa realized that the labor unions would not have the freedom to be genuine unions unless
they entered the political arena and put labor in a position
where it could legislate reforms.

The December 26, 1918, meeting of delegates from the various
branches of the Yuaikai in Kobe unanimously approved estab-
lishment of the Kansai Rodo Domeikai (The Kansai Labor
League) to coordinate activities of the labor union movement.
The name of the paper was also changed to *Rodosha Shimbun*
(Laborer's Newspaper) to give it a greater labor focus and
Kagawa was appointed the editor.[26] Kagawa poured his energies
into writing and lecturing on such topics as "Theory of the
Liberation of the Working Class," "Spiritual Motivation and
Social Reconstruction," "The Liberation of Wage Slaves," "The
Right to Live and the Right to Work," and "The Freedom of
Unions." The fact that the government soon suspended publica-
tion of the union's paper was proof positive of the weak position
of the labor movement under a repressive government.

Kagawa addressed a mass meeting of 3000 on January 16,
1919, together with Yoshiyuki Imai, a leading advocate of universal suffrage. Kagawa called for the legal recognition of unions and the mass meeting approved a resolution reading:

> We workers, considering the growth of Japanese industry and
> the development of culture, demand the public recognition of
> labor unions as necessary for our mutual relief, independence
> and self-defense.

Kagawa joined the leftist scholar Hajime Kawakami at another
mass meeting on February 2 to speak for the rights of workers to
have legal status for their unions. Along with Yukio Ozaki, the
grand old maverick of the Japanese Diet, Kagawa then set forth
on a whirlwind speaking tour to Kyoto, Osaka and Tokyo,
calling for universal suffrage. A welcoming group of 300 Yuaikai
members turned out to greet the two on February 15, and it
bloomed into a three-hour demonstration and march through
Kyoto singing Kagawa's hymn to labor:

> Awake, laborers of Japan
>   Break down old customs of the past
> Until the world's emancipation
>   Strive diligent with utter self-denial.

> Turning the soil, weaving the cloth, building the ships,
>   Groping the depths of earth to dig the ore
> Kneading bread, face bathed in perspiration
>   Laborers above all worth mankind's respect.[27]

When the group arrived at the lecture hall it was so jammed that those who couldn't get in smashed doors and windows to hear the speakers. The declaration, passed to the roar of applause, boldly demanded the vote and explained in unequivocal terms that suffrage was necessary to alleviate "the misery of the proletariat and their oppression by the propertied classes . . . by extirpating the injustices of the present socio-economic system."[28] A mass movement for universal suffrage was underway, with Kagawa in the forefront. Suffrage bills were introduced in the Diet in 1920. Though these initial efforts failed, the universal suffrage bill finally passed in 1925, abolishing tax requirements and increasing the number of eligible voters from 3 million to 12.5 million males over 25 years of age.

The Kansai Labor Federation was formally established in mid-April of 1919, with Kagawa elected chair at the inaugural meeting in the Osaka Central Public Hall. The group adopted a ringing manifesto written by Kagawa:

> We declare that labor is not a commodity. Capitalist culture made a commodity out of the laborer by the law of wage and by the pressure of machines, and demoted him to the bottom of the social ladder. Therefore, we claim freedom to organize; we demand the right to live and the right to work, the right to bargain collectively, and the right to strike for a just cause. And we demand abolition of Article 17 of the Peace Police Law of 1900, and revision of the existing Factory Law. We demand the eight hour day and legislation of a minimum wage.[29]

Improvement of conditions was not an end in itself, but a means toward the realization of human freedom. To Kagawa, this current system violated both the canons of Christianity and secular humanism, which is why he resolved his passion for justice into one compelling plea: "Our demand is not just wage increases. It is not just an eight-hour day. It is, foremost, to be men."[30]

The Seventh Annual Yuaikai Convention, which was held in Tokyo in August 1919, opened with Kagawa's labor song rather than the national anthem *Kimigayo*. It was a tense time, marked by increasing discontent with Suzuki's leadership and personality. The huge man, who dressed well and was noted for his prodigious appetite, hardly fit the lean and hungry image of a labor leader. Moreover, he and Kagawa had a falling out because Suzuki had interfered in a strike in Kobe that Kagawa was mediating, with the result that the strike was settled sooner than Kagawa and the workers had wished. Suzuki, however, in his address gave his blessings to the new direction of the union. Tension was still in the air when Kagawa asked for the floor, because the delegates expected a confrontation. Instead, Kagawa defused the situation by simply requesting permission for the delegates to take off their coats because of the summer's heat.[31] Having set aside their major disagreements, Kagawa and his allies worked with Suzuki to take the union in a new direction, and Suzuki was reelected president.

Restating many of the same points he had made at previous labor meetings, Kagawa wrote a platform of the reorganized union which was another declaration of the independence of the human spirit:

> Workers are people with personalities. They are not to be bought and sold with wages on the labor market. They must therefore have the right to form unions. . . . We are not machines. In order to ensure the development of individual character and a society of human beings, we demand an organization of society in which the producers can attain perfect culture, stability of livelihood, and the right to control our environment.[32]

Kagawa endorsed the declarations of the International Organization of Labor, adding:

> We workers declare to the world that the workers of Japan, with the League of Nations, will struggle like martyrs, in the spirit of the Labor Covenant of the International Labor Organization in order that peace, freedom and equality may rule the earth.[33]

The 20 demands written by Kagawa were similar to the ILO's platform and in line with labor's demands in many nations, including freedom for trade unions, abolition of child labor, minimum wage, eight-hour day and forty-eight-hour work week, public management of workers' housing; establishment of workmen's compensation system and insurance for workers.

A lifelong supporter of feminist causes who had fostered his wife's education and later encouraged his daughters in "male" careers of medicine and the ministry, Kagawa also called for equal pay for equal work of men and women and the appointment of female labor inspectors. The platform reiterated the demand for universal suffrage and an amendment to the Peace Police Law.[34] The platform also backed the principle of equal treatment for national and foreign workers in Japan.

Shortly after these heady times, Kagawa started to lose ground to rival factions in the union movement which pressed for "direct action," meaning violence. There were several reasons for this more militant stand. First, there was considerable disillusion because of the failure of the efforts to repeal the harsh terms of the Peace Police Law and to secure universal suffrage. Secondly, the economy took a plunge early in 1920, causing huge layoffs and worsening the already difficult conditions of the working people. This combination of frustration and economic trouble strengthened the appeal of the anarchists, who inclined toward violence as a means of change. Led by Sakae Osugi, who was brutally murdered a few years later by the police in Tokyo, the anarchists contended that it was futile to believe that workers could ever vote their way to a better life.

The tension built up through 1920, and when Kagawa went to the train station in Osaka to welcome delegates to the union's national convention in October, he was greeted scornfully by delegates from the Tokyo area waving black flags of anarchy and singing a song calling for violent destruction of the enemy. He defied them by leading the non-anarchists in his own labor songs, convinced that the Tokyo delegates' approach would only lead to chaos.

These strong differences boiled over into the convention that opened in the Tennoji Public Hall on October 3 and which reconvened at an Osaka church on October 4 and 5. Anarchist rage was expressed early in the convention, when one anarchist, Watsu Takata, drew loud applause by shouting, "We must absolutely decide between direct action and parliamentarianism." The hulking Suzuki had no sooner calmed the crowd when another anarchist cried "We reject the Diet."[35] Kagawa sought to reason against the anarchist position, saying "There are many faults in parliamentary politics, but it's rash to reject the Diet because unless we have universal suffrage the people will never develop experience in the Diet and will never play their historic role in Japanese politics."[36] Arguing that violent action was doomed as a tactic, Kagawa was shouted down with personal attacks "Down with the hermit monk. Down with the ruler of the slums." The anarchists lost out on some issues like the right to stage wildcat strikes without the sanction of the union's central governing body, but they had played the role of spoiler at a very crucial time.

A deepening struggle developed in the next few years not only within the labor movement, but between the totalitarianism of the right wing and the democracy which Kagawa had envisioned. Kagawa was realistic enough to see that the unions had to balance their activities delicately by being militant enough to make progress organizing and lobbying and yet avoid provocative action or rhetoric that could bring down the wrath of a government armed with broad powers of surveillance and censorship under the Peace Preservation Laws. It was a race to change the laws by diminishing police authority to the point where a genuine democracy could be free to develop. He repeatedly cautioned that threats of violence from the left would provoke a rightwing reaction that would crush the dreams of every ally of labor. The murder of Osugi and the crackdown on the Communist Party in 1923 would confirm his worst fears a few years later.

By this time Kagawa was a veteran strategist who knew how to test his opponents with a delicate sense of just how far to push them. He knew where to attack and where to feint, when to go on the offensive and when to appear beguilingly compliant. He had already been labeled as a "Red" and denounced as a "demon" even by the Japanese Christians, so he was keenly aware of the impression he created and of how the public reacted to the left. His friend and frequent traveling companion, Shiro Kuroda, described the risk involved for a respectable person visiting the troublemaker Kagawa: "I was disowned by my mother, a devout Christian, just because I went to see Kagawa often at his slum house in Shinkawa, and I was not allowed to return home for three whole years even though I was her only child."[37]

The anarchists found Kagawa's parliamentarianism and Christianity entirely too gentle. Yet while he was being criticized by the anarchists for being too conciliatory, Kagawa found himself in trouble with the police. Just a few days after the tumultuous convention in Fall of 1920, the prosecutor of the Kobe District Court, called him in for questioning about an article he had published in his paper.[38]

A few weeks prior to this on the evening of September 18, police had broken up a meeting of the Tokyo Union of Socialists in the public hall of Nakanoshima, where Kagawa was speaking on the seemingly innocuous topic of "The Health of the Workers." Uniformed police and the ubiquitous plain clothes spies were present before the speakers arrived and at the back of the speakers platform sat several of the local chiefs of police, undoubtedly in full uniform. There was a huge turnout, despite the fact that the entry fee was 30 sen (about 15 cents, a hefty amount for workers whose pay averaged a dollar a day). Those who couldn't fit in were massed outside in the night. Kagawa was on the platform with Kanson Arahata, later a leader of the Communist Party, and the anarchist Toshihiko Sakai. After Arahata opened the meeting, Kagawa started on his speech about the health of the working classes. The chief of police stepped up and yelled, "Stop your speech!" Kagawa withdrew from the podium while the crowd protested the order.

The next speaker discussing the living conditions of poor children was also ordered into silence, and succeeding speakers were interrupted in the same way, until the police simply called a halt to the meeting. This triggered more protest, and some 240 police who had been stationed in the basement stormed into the hall to keep the crowd under control. When asked to disclose his reasons for shutting down the meeting, the police chief declined to comment. Arahata responded by refusing to disband the meeting. Some of the audience were arrested simply for using bad language, and ten were sent to the police station for two hours of lectures. After most of the crowd was outside, Osugi summed up the situation eloquently by addressing the cheering multitude from a window:

> Children are under the false impression that there are fires because firebells are rung. Like these children, the authorities are laboring under the misapprehension that labor problems arise because of the speeches delivered by us. The idea is simply ridiculous. We make speeches because we are face to face with these problems.[39]

Two days later, the Union of Socialists encountered similar police interference at the Kobe YMCA hall, where an assemblage of 1200 met inside and a mass gathered outside because of limited space. The first speaker was silenced by a police sergeant moments after he began his speech with the phrase "Years ago, when the voice of freedom was raised in America . . ."

Kagawa next spoke on his ideas for reconstructing society, saying that equality for workers, freedom to organize and mutual assistance were the keys to this effort. When he reached the phrase "Come together, workmen," he was commanded to be silent, as were the subsequent speakers, except for Arahata who kept talking even after a police sergeant repeatedly grabbed his arm. Arahata continued his performance until the chief of the Aiobashi station stepped in and declared the meeting closed.[40]

The tragedy of attacking a man like Kagawa was the fact that he was not advocating violent action nor the overthrow of the government to further the proletarian cause. His program of union action, suffrage, and parliamentary reform was a peaceful and practical means to find justice for the workers. Yet the officials persisted stubbornly in hounding Kagawa, and to some observers he was becoming a sacrificial lamb. One observer points out the absurdity of persecuting a man like Kagawa, who "advises against strikes, urges the necessity of abiding by strict parliamentary proceedings, and on all occasions takes the most sober views."[41]

Kagawa's persecution was an ominous sign of the future in Japan and so was the fragmentation in the labor movement itself. In addition to the split between the anarchists and the parliamentarians, Kagawa faced opposition in other quarters. In

February 1921 he and Haru had had gone to speak at a local school to encourage the development of a cooperative buying club. They were interrupted by a rowdy group of self-styled socialists shouting, "You have capitalized our labor movement," expressing the fear that Kagawa's interest in cooperatives would siphon workers' energies from the class struggle. Some people in the audience objected to the interruptions and a fight broke out, causing a number of injuries and the arrival of the police to restore order.[42]

Despite the rapid ideological changes and the opposition, Kagawa remained active in the labor movement. He successfully organized an Osaka printers' union in June 1920, and wrote for its paper. In November, the union expanded into the Kansai Printer's Federation. He was also persuaded to become president of the Harima dockworker's union, while at the same time he was pursuing the formation of cooperatives among the dockworkers, the first of which was the Kobe Kobai Kumiai (Kobe Purchasing Union).

Drawing on the rich tradition of English cooperative organizers, social reformers, guild socialists and Fabians, he praised their vision of a society where factories were owned and managed by the workers themselves. While engaged in his union work he read a long list of authors, from the nineteenth century utopian Robert Dale Owen to Sidney and Beatrice Webb, George Bernard Shaw, Bertrand Russell and Ramsey MacDonald.[43] They led him to favor a system of ownership which would be an alternative both to capitalism and state socialism. Kagawa wrote:

> What I hope for from the Labor movement is, ultimately, that they will establish workers' control of industry, some form of Guild Socialism. I regard Socialism and the Labor movement as having essentially the same aim—that is, Labor control.[44]

The major dispute was whether "Labor control" should be attained through union action and parliamentary democracy or through direct takeovers of the factories. To the restive anarchists, the gradualist approach was an indication of Kagawa's compromise with the system. He drew more fire from them when he accepted an assignment from the government to investigate the conditions of 200 poor families as part of a study on labor insurance. The anarchists objected that agreeing to perform any such service was support for the oppressive regime. As with cooperatives, this was termed an ameliorating activity which would blunt revolutionary fervor and dampen the spirit of direct action.[45] Kagawa himself made a clear distinction between anarchists and Bolsheviks under Russian influence, and his objection to both groups. Discussing the meeting disrupted by anarchists, he said:

> In this particular case the opposition was anarchist. Not working men—there is little anarchism among the workers—but middle class elements, including students and salaried men. In Osaka and Tokyo, however, there are clear-cut Syndicalist and Bolshevik elements. In Tokyo one group calls itself the "Soviet of Tokyo!"[46]

Kagawa then rooted through some newspapers. He pulled one out and pointed to the name *Soviet* printed in the special Japanese script for foreign words, saying:

> This paper, *Rodosha*, represents rather Syndicalist tendencies. You will note, however, that it is published by the "Tokyo Soviet." This is in addition to the anarchist or anarcho-syndicalist paper put out by another group, *Rodo Undo* (Labor Movement), with which, I understand, Mr. Osugi is identified. There is at present a strong tendency towards Bolshevism among Japanese workers. I personally am working against it, because I consider it dangerous to the workers themselves. In a militarist country like Japan, at its present stage of development, such a movement will simply be crushed by armed force. It is difficult for me to imagine any other outcome.[47]

The one grim outcome the confident Kagawa failed to imagine was the government's attack on his own more moderate movement. Despite his keen perceptions of Japanese life and his immense knowledge of history, in one area he was painfully unrealistic, and that was in facing up to the totalitarian threat in Japan.

Ironically, the theatre for this pacifist's most stirring action at this time was at the heart of Japan's budding military/industrial complex. The region had prospered from building ships, manufacturing supplies and shipping for Europe's war. When World War I ended and the economy plunged, the port and manufacturing facilities in the region were hard hit. Thousands were laid off, and others had their hours cut back. This bred the anger that culminated in the summer 1921 strikes which captured the attention of the entire nation. Kagawa, as a union officer, nationally known author, popular lecturer and social worker, was in the forefront of the labor dispute. His chief antagonists were corporations which have since become household words in the West: Sumitomo, Kawasaki and Mitsubishi.

May of the long hot summer of 1921 began with a strike at the Fujinagata Shipbuilding Company in Osaka. The main issue was a demand that the company recognize the union and negotiate with it. Kagawa was called in to mediate. He spent several hours on June 5 talking with company officials, then met with the union leadership. The next day when the workers went to the plant, they were infiltrated by disguised police, who arrested about ten of them. Kagawa and the union resumed negotiations, finally hammering out a memorandum agreeing to union recognition, only to have management renege by insisting it was only an informal suggestion and in no way binding. The outraged union officials left the meeting and Kagawa withdrew from the mediation. Groups of frustrated workers vandalized the homes of management, and some laborers were injured brawling with police.

Union consciousness was now aroused as never before in the region. The workers viewed this dispute as symbolic of industry-wide troubles, awakening to the idea of solidarity. In a mass meeting at the Tennoji Auditorium, Kagawa as the keynote speaker cried out to the thousands there a demand for worker control:

> Come on, oppression! Come on, persecution. We defiantly stand here and cry out to industrial workers to arise. Bury the tyrants! We demand a constitutional society. Why should there be autocracy in industry alone? We demand constitutionalism in factories.
>
> Begone, polluted air. Rush forth, air of freedom. We shall fight on and on unceasingly until the workers gain their liberty.[48]

Demonstrations also took place in Kobe, with Kagawa addressing the crowds of aroused workers. Another strike broke out at Sumitomo's Amagasaki Copper plant, about 12 miles east of

Kobe. Kagawa was pushing himself hard, traveling from Kobe
to the union office to negotiate, sometimes sleeping with his
clothes on in the office to be ready for the next round. He
succeeded in winning the union demands for better conditions.

Kawasaki and Mitsubishi workers were receiving better pay
than many others in Japan, and Kawasaki had reduced the
workday to eight hours. As is often the case, the workers who
have made the greatest initial gains become the most militant,
having shaken free of paternalism and fear of authority. Much of
Japan's workforce was still too timid, entrenched in feudal
dependency, and worn out from 14-hour days, to organize
against their woeful conditions. The fact that workers still
depended on intellectuals like Kagawa and Suzuki for leadership shows how embryonic was union consciousness at the
time. These more sophisticated workers, however, were rapidly
coming to realize that neither the feudalistic landlord nor the
factory owner had inherent rights to the fruits of human labor.
Therefore, the Kawasaki and Mitsubishi workers, many of them
skilled laborers, were on the cutting edge of the young but
growing labor movement.

In June 1921, 350 employees at Mitsubishi Ironworks on Wada
Point, a peninsula that cradles the western end of the Kobe
harbor, demanded a reduction from a nine-hour to an eight-
hour day·and the right of their union to be recognized as the
bargaining agent. They also demanded that wages be increased
by 50 sen a day to bring them on a par with the nearby Kawasaki
workers. Further they sought guarantees of four months' sever-
ance pay, and failing to get a satisfactory response from management, they staged a slowdown.[49]

Though better paid than those at Mitsubishi, employees at the
Kawasaki shipbuilding yards were also angry. Some 900 in the
electrical department protested because the company had cut
bonuses to workers at the very time the company boosted
dividends and distributed new shares as a special 25th
Anniversary present to stockholders. A rash of labor disputes
had spread to other companies in the area. Already negotiating
with Sumitomo plus intervening in a labor dispute with the
Osaka division of multinational Lever Brothers, Kagawa was
asked to represent the Kawasaki workers. He addressed a big

rally on the evening of June 30, and worked with union leaders late into the night on a position paper to present to management. The company refused to negotiate on the pretext that the president was out of town. This further provoked the workers, who decided to expand their unionizing drive. Another mass meeting was held on July 4 to lay out the demand for worker control of the workplace and collective bargaining at all the large plants in the region. Kagawa was appointed to carry this demand to the plants. He was flatly rejected, and the companies fired the union leaders.

The Kawasaki disputes heated up on July 7 when thugs at the Kawasaki plant, wearing headbands and carrying clubs, beat up several workers at the gate and slashed another with a sword. The workers were convinced that the attackers had been hired by the company. Kagawa met with the managing director of the Kawasaki shipyard to protest this violence and to determine whether the gang was brought in by the management. Demonstrators massed early in the morning, an estimated 25,000 marching through the streets, many carrying black and red banners inscribed with such militant slogans like "Let us fight to the death."

Kagawa went to the police along with Kinoshita, head of the Osaka union, to discuss the tensions between the police and the crowds. He explained that if there was a lockout by management, the workers would have no choice but to take over the plants themselves. The police promised not to interfere in workers' activities, as long as the strikers maintained order. The authorities warned, however, that employees would not be allowed to enter the plants in the event of a lockout. Meanwhile, Kagawa and the other labor leaders planned a massive rally for July 10, coincidentally Kagawa's birthday.

That day started off with a shower as the workers assembled at 7 a.m. at Egeyama Park in the hills overlooking the harbor to participate in the largest labor demonstration in the history of Japan up to that point, but the weather soon turned to sweltering heat. The dissidents unfurled banners in a spectrum of colors emblazoned with slogans such as "Justice," and "Fight until We Die," along with Kagawa's calmer plea "We Are also Human Beings." At 8:30 a.m., they proceeded down from the hills, led by Kagawa and labor leader Kozo Hisatome. The crowd of an estimated 30,000 marched more than five miles singing labor songs. They arrived at the Kawasaki plant about 10 o'clock where police were on guard. After two hours of speeches and cries of solidarity there, the militant workers went on to Mitsubishi, also closely guarded. With Kagawa in the lead, this massive group proceeded from there to another branch of Kawasaki at Hyogo. The demonstration concluded in an open space, where a prison once stood, with singing and shouts of *banzai*, and praise to an Osaka contingent which had come in a gesture of solidarity.

Kagawa pulled all the stops at the close of the huge demonstration, emphasizing the peacefulness of the laborers, as proven by the fact that the demonstration was nonviolent. "In the United States," he cried, "the incidence of strikes has been reduced by 60% where they have allowed unions to organize."[50] He pleaded for the abolition of the regulations which prevented workers from officially organizing: "The present cry of the laborers is raised that they might make a living as men, and therefore they will not yield unless their companies recognize the rights of their labor associations to negotiate."[51]

The power of his oratory dazzled the audience. As biographer Mikio Sumiya pictured it: "Finally, Toyohiko Kagawa, with all his strength, showing tremendous emotion and courage, gave a white-hot address on the bright future of the labor movement, and amid thunderous hand clapping the rally came to a close."[52]

More instances of violence occurred when Mitsubishi announced a 10-day lockout. About 10,000 workers massed in front of the heavily guarded Mitsubishi plant and crashed through the back gates. At Kawasaki, they were admitted to the plant, where they took to their stations and sat idly in a slowdown. Troops were called in to reinforce the local police. Naval officers issued warnings against any attempt to damage the destroyers, ships and submarines under construction, and these crafts were patrolled by guards. Kawasaki followed with its own lockout. As the number of skirmishes increased and the situation became increasingly tense, more troops were rushed to the scene while the prefecture governor banned both demonstrations and the singing of labor songs.

In the midst of this chaos, Kagawa managed to negotiate a settlement at Lever Brothers, preventing proposed lay-offs, persuading the management to back down from its demand for a five percent pay cut, and obtaining acknowledgement of the union's right to be the bargaining agent. He also conducted a successful mediation at the Dunlop Rubber works, winning a number of benefits, including half-pay on holidays, a mutual relief association for workers to cover retirement and illness, and a two-week notification of layoffs with two weeks' pay if such notice were not given. The company recognized the right of workers to join the union and set up a worker committee system, and waived punitive measures against the strikers.

In the case of Kawasaki and Mitsubishi, however, the strikers were worn down by the companies and police by the second week of the strike. Kagawa spoke at theaters, public halls and temples exhorting the workers to hang on for the "final victory." The closest to a public demonstration the police allowed were baseball games and athletic contests, where Kagawa and other speakers appeared. When these crowds grew too large for the comfort of the law enforcement officers, they were unceremoniously dispersed.

Kawasaki fired the 125 employees on the union executive committees, refusing to budge from their paternalistic line that "outside agitators" were stirring up unnecessary discontent among the employees. In their view, the relation of employer to employee remained the feudalistic bond of master and servant, and the idea of worker control espoused by Kagawa was unthinkable. Kagawa angrily protested the dismissal of the workers, and vowed to continue the struggle, even if it included takeover of the factories. He insisted that companies which refused to recognize the legitimate rights of a peaceful labor movement were asking for a rude awakening.

Another measure of Kagawa's growing reputation as a social reformer and union leader was seen when Bertrand Russell steamed into Kobe on July 17, 1921, aboard the *Yeiko maru* during his tour of Asia. He was greeted at the harbor by a banner-carrying welcoming contingent from the dockyard organizations. Despite the fact that Russell had been ill, he attended a labor meeting at the Amidoji Temple in Kobe, with Kagawa at

his side interpreting his speech to the audience. Russell expressed his regrets that his health did not permit him to speak at
length, but his statement of support for the strikers was greeted
with rousing cheers. Encouragement from this famed British
socialist was obviously a boost to the morale of the strikers.

It became extremely difficult for the workers to hold out,
because of their meager personal savings and the lack of a
sufficiently large strike fund to support themselves. They had to
pawn their possessions to meet expenses, and some set up
vending stalls to earn temporary income to support them
through the strike. The police turned down requests for permits
to peddle door-to-door.

The companies had agreed to give the workers half-pay
during the lockout, but inside the first paycheck envelopes were
stern warnings that if they forced the lockout to continue there
would be no pay at all. Mitsubishi's letter was a cunning
combination of paternalism and toughness:

> Although the company is not called upon to pay you for the
> period of strike or sabotage, yet it is willing to stretch a point in
> your favor in this particular instance and give you full pay
> during that time lest your family should be reduced to distress.
> Should you go on strike or start sabotage in the future, you
> would not be entitled to such consideration.[53]

The entire nation was watching the strike because of its scope
and boldness, wondering how far the workers in Kobe would
go. The government was extremely wary. Although the workers
in Kobe were able to see a film of the demonstrations, the
newsreel was banned elsewhere. The unions had planned to
show it in Tokyo, charging admittance to raise funds for the
strike, but the metropolitian police flatly banned it.

When Kagawa released a statement elaborating on his idea of
worker control of the factories, immediate speculation arose that
this document violated the Peace Police Law. He defiantly
declared he was ready to accept the punishment if the document
broke the law. Even Kagawa was showing the fatigue of the long
rounds of strike activity. A reporter noted his impatience when
visiting the strike headquarters. Kagawa, sitting with his back to
a pillar reading a paper, curtly told the reporter he had time for

just a brief interview. Then, apparently repenting of this short-
ness of temper, he carried on a 2000-word interview about the
strike he was leading. The most significant thing, Kagawa
emphasized, was the sheer magnitude of the strike. With some
40,000 men on strike in Kobe, it was the nearest thing to a
general strike the district had known, and yet there had been
almost perfect order. He told the reporter:

> As for the issues involved, the most fundamental ones affect
> the organization of industry itself. We object to men being
> absolutely at the mercy of their employers, to be turned out to
> starve when it suits the interests or caprice of the latter. Such
> things are as a matter of fact impossible in most European
> countries—for example in England, where there are unemploy-
> ment pensions. . . . This matter of unemployment, however, is
> only one phase of the question. The problem is deeper than that
> of mere discharge benefits, or even of relative security in one's
> job. The problem, stated in political terms, is one of autocracy or
> constitutionalism in industry. What we are fighting for now,
> fundamentally, is an element of constitutionalism—the workers
> to have some voice, be it ever so slight, in the organization of the
> industries which they created and which they operate. . . . We
> will not stop until we have achieved industrial democracy, and
> the new serfdom has gone the way of the old.[54]

When told that the government was saying it interfered with
the strike for the benefit of the workers, the sting of Kagawa's
sardonic wit was felt:

> Well, you can tell your readers that the workers absolutely fail
> to appreciate the kind and altruistic motives of the officials. Such
> statements may be believed by little children at school, but we
> older people would like to have a little more evidence of official
> friendliness before placing any faith in it.[55]

Despite Kagawa's optimism about the solidarity of the strike,
it had begun to unravel by the middle of the third week of that
long hot summer. On July 26, 1921, over 4000 went back to their
jobs at Kawasaki, while 170 were arrested in scuffles with police.
By the next day, 5000 workers had gone back to Kawasaki, and
the total rose to 6000 on the day following. On July 29, Mitsubishi reopened, and the total number returning to Kawasaki

crept up to over 7000 by August 2, more than half the work force. Police continued to harass the strikers, even confiscating the record books of the union.

Because local officials had squelched public meetings, Kagawa proposed a new tactic that showed his flair for political theatre, dramatic irony and his continuing delight in catching authority figures in logical contradictions. The strike committee decided to do what would be the Western equivalent of meeting in church, offering prayers for the success of the labor movement and going to public Shinto shrines to pray en masse. This was calculated to embarass the police because the government encouraged visitation of state supported shrines. To break up religious assemblies would be a violation of official policy. The action also dramatized Kagawa's point that the strikers were acting legally and peacefully while putting the police in the embarassing position of potential lawbreakers.

Kagawa addressed crowds at these "religious" gatherings. On July 28, more than 10,000 visited several shrines. When a large part of the crowd broke away from the procession with the intent of storming the Kawasaki yard, he and the other leaders frantically talked them into remaining peaceful. The next day order collapsed when a large group of men broke from the procession and stormed the Kawasaki yard, starting a battle that ended with some 20 being stabbed by the police, mostly in the back, one critically wounded, and 200 arrests made. Kagawa blamed the police for precipitating the battle by approaching the workmen with drawn swords. That evening, the police raided the strike headquarters, arresting Kagawa and many other union leaders. One officer beat Kagawa with a sword and tore his clothing before they took him handcuffed and barefoot to the police station. Kagawa was charged with creating civil disturbance and sent to the Tachibana prison.

Never one to waste time, Kagawa busied himself writing poems with pieces of charcoal on scrap paper (he was denied writing paper) and planning out his next novel, *Kabe no koe kiku toki* (Listening to the Voice in the Wall). He wrote one of the most dramatic descriptions of the strike when he was in prison:

> In the evening of this hot day in July I find myself imprisoned, in fetters. It is told that the Apostle Paul, in prison, sang hymns

at midnight. But after some seventy speech meetings my own voice is so hoarse that I could not sing if I wanted to. But in my inmost ear there remain the sounds of tens of thousands of marching workers in giant demonstrations; and on the morning of my arrest, the victory cry of more than ten thousand, bringing all traffic to a halt in the streets of Kobe. I have never heard a hymn of such solemnity and grandeur. I was surely born in a wonderful day and age. I have heard the symphony of man's flesh and blood.

Not only that, but there still sparkles before my eyes a glorious scene—throngs of workers in overalls or in khaki-colored clothing running down the slopes from the woods of Ikuta. If a single person is something of dignity, the sight of ten thousands of producers charging onward toward the day of liberation—ah, how much grander by far! That was indeed a pure and noble morning, a day of bright hope and glory. It was Exodus over again, surely—from the place of slavery to the place of liberty; from the place of oppression to the place of emancipation; from the place of darkness to the place of light—truly a day of escape![56]

He also described the prison and his reaction to it in a long poem with a mixture of realism, irony, disgust, hope and religious ecstasy which said in part:

Midnight. The clock strikes one—two—. Wide awake I hound the
   prison vermin.
Oh, the noise of a prison! It surpasses all expectation. How lively
   is the neighboring cell. . .[57]

Haru managed to smuggle New Testaments to the imprisoned union leaders, an act of courage Kagawa would praise in later years in a poetic tribute to her.

The shrine visits were not the only creative flourish from the union. While Kagawa was in custody, an accident occurred that could be envisioned as a precursor to the American bombers pulverizing Japan two decades later. A fish dealer and strike sympathizer Ushimatsu Tokunaga was asked by union headquarters to make the flambouyant gesture of dropping strike literature from the air as he flew over Kobe in a plane piloted by an American. They were killed when the plane crashed at Naruo, slightly east of Kobe.

Another casualty was Shunichi Tsunemine, a Kawasaki worker who had died of stab wounds inflicted by the police on July 29. Thousands marched in the funeral procession from his house, led by the union members carrying their banners, some carrying the traditional branches offered to the dead from the *shikibi* tree. The streets were lined with sympathetic or curious spectators as the cortege wound its way to the Kasugano cemetery.

Journalists from other cities were especially harsh in their criticism of the imprisonment of Kagawa, because they felt that the jailing of an advocate of non-violent change would only aggravate the volatile relations between labor and capital throughout Japan. They cautioned that to make a martyr of Kagawa might trigger even greater militancy or full scale revolution. One commentator drew a parallel between jailing of Kagawa and the prisoners in the Bastille, whose liberation marked the beginning of the French Revolution.

> Mr. Kagawa, the well-known Christian Socialist, is now in prison, though he is a laborite of the pacifist school, who has always counselled against violence and against the use of militant methods. This arrest has done more than anything else to turn public sympathy against the authorities, as Mr. Kagawa is very popular, and very much respected generally on account of the high ethical tone of both his personal life—devoted to the poor, whom he (as a sincere Christian) believes are destined to inherit the earth—and his voluminous writings—devoted partly to telling educated people how the other half lives, and partly to educating the "other half" to higher ideals of life and labor.[58]

Although the brutal treatment of Kagawa may have aroused anger among the populace, there was no channel for the average person to express it. The military held the weapons and the upper classes held the vote. The arrest of the union leadership, combined with police brutality, several deaths, stabbings, impatience among the rank and file, and the hard fact that the strikers did not have enough money to survive, led them to capitulate on August 8 and return to work. Kagawa was released from prison two days later on the grounds of insufficient evidence, although he previously had to pay a fine for his provocative articles in the union newspaper. Greeted by his wife, Haru, and a banner-carrying group of 500 who came to the jail to meet him, he made a brief speech to a larger, cheering audience in the park of a nearby temple. Though admitting that the strike had failed, he reminded the workers that this was no occasion for despair. He and Haru were then driven home to Shinkawa.

While Kagawa joked about his restful time in jail, and spoke encouraging words to his constituents, the struggle seems to have taken something out of him. He was also hurt personally by the more militant workers, who blamed his non-violent approach for the ultimate failure of the strikes. He seems to have resigned himself to the fact that he no longer fit the violent mood that had arisen, and he expressed this with some self-pity, casting himself as the Christlike cornerstone which the builders rejected:

> When messianic movements flourish, the massses look for a messiah who will give them bread, but just as long ago they deserted Jesus, they are now undoubtedly tired of my doctrines of passive resistance, gradualism and human love.[59]

He began to reduce his involvement in the labor movement, but by no means severed his connections with it. It was not until May of 1922 that he turned over the editorship of the *Rodosha Shimbun* to Kunimatsu Ando. Toward the end of that year, he was busy organizing and seeking funds and faculty for a labor school in Osaka,[60] which numbered among its graduates men who were to play a large role in labor and socialist movements, such as Suehiro Nishio and Motojiro Sugiyama.[61]

At this point in his life, the astounding thing about Kagawa is that his commitment to service remained as strong as ever. His novel, *Crossing the Death Line* had become a best seller since its publication in October 1920, and was bringing in a phenomonal income. Even while he was in prison, the sequel was published and crowds lined up to buy copies. Yet all the income was turned back to his projects. Out of ¥100,000 ($50,000) which the novel earned in these years he spent ¥50,000 on the strike and the strike fund; ¥5,000 for the labor school, ¥10,000 for consumers cooperatives, ¥10,000 for other social projects and ¥5,000 for organizing the miners union. Another ¥20,000 went to help establish the Japan Farmers' Union, his next major endeavor.[62]

The man who had grown up on the land and knew first hand

the dilemma of rural life, was ready to turn his attention to the countryside. Though he substantially reduced his involvement in the urban labor movement, he certainly did not abandon hope in its future. He felt that the workers would eventually reject calls for violence and attempt change through legislation. His long range strategy was to develop a united front between urban workers and the farmers.

Chapter 6
Farmers and Outcastes

THE EARLY 1920S SAW increasing unrest in rural Japan, for many of the same reasons labor was becoming more militant in the urban areas. As those workers began to realize their power, the peasants also, especially the impoverished tenants, were beginning to rebel against centuries-old exploitation while questioning the paternalistic values used to justify it. This is not to say that tenant rebellions were new to Japan. They had been occurring for centuries, particularly in the last years of the Tokugawa shogunate.

During the 1870s and 1880s, the farmer's protests became more focused. The government's tax reform policies had put a heavier burden on rural areas. The peasants of the past had fewer examples of rebellion to follow. Their ideas about basic human rights were poorly-defined and most of them were illiterate. The rise of labor in the cities, military conscription which drew rural communities into a larger world, and widespread literacy resulting from compulsory education were shaking up the old order. The contrast with the standard of living in the cities was itself a powerful incentive.

Poverty in rural Japan often gave the countryside the appearance of an underdeveloped nation of today. Disease, famine, permanent debt and tenancy were the common lot of Japanese peasants. Because he was attuned to the social changes of Japan, it is not surprising that Kagawa had turned his attention to rural area problems as early as 1918. Publishing a thoroughly-researched article in January 1919, he noted that the people in the countryside had the lowest standard of living in Japan outside the harrowing slums where he lived. He cited infant mortality rates that were 16 to 29 deaths per thousand higher than in the cities. Among the *burakumin* (outcastes) in Okayama Prefecture the infant mortality rate was 224 per 1000. He decried the degradation of women in rural areas and the crime rate in

Hyogo Prefecture, which was five times the national average. The incidence of communicable diseases was treble that of the city.[1]

Kagawa had seen these agonies personally, having grown up on a country estate. As he said,

> I was reared in a farming village in Tokushima Prefecture. I saw the day by day breakdown of the farm villages, and grieved to witness it. I still feel the same sense of grief today. When, oh when, will come the salvation of Japan's rural people?[2]

There was starvation among the very people who produced the food. Debt, rent increases, and mortgage foreclosures brought about a cruel dilemma where peasants who produced rice actually had to buy it when they had none left after paying the landlord in kind. The Rice Riots of 1918 dramatized the absurdity of this situation.[3]

Farm families made about 70% as much as white collar workers, and about the same as urban laborers; but with bigger families to support, they had a lower per capita income. Over the past half-century, millions of small landowners had fallen into tenancy because they were forced to sell their land to pay their bills. A typical tenant family tilling only a small plot of 2.5 acres would turn over 50% to 60% of its rice harvest to the landlord for rent. After meeting operating expenses, there was a monthly income of about ￥20 ($10) from the main crop—a pathetic reward for long days of backbreaking labor in the fields.[4] The misery of the situation and the reasons for the farmers' anger were passionately stated by Hideo Yokota, one of the first tenant organizers:

> If we were to comment without reserve, it would be more appropriate to call the farmer's life today the life of an animal, not a man. At least if we take the middle class city dwellers' standard of living as average, the farmer's life is really half-human, half-animal. He lives in an unrepaired, ramshackle home, wears dirty, unmended clothing, sleeps on old, cold straw mats and eats food that city dwellers have turned their backs on. Who can really imagine what it is to live like a farmer, tyrannized by poverty and exhausted in mind and body? The starting point for discussing the farm villages is the phrase "among farmers there is no food to eat."[5]

Besides antagonism toward the cities, there was growing resentment toward absentee landlords who were bleeding tenant farmers and failing to live up to the few positive aspects of the ancient paternalistic values such as community responsibility. Although many landlords were themselves small farmers with holdings of less than 12 acres who worked side by side with the tenants, about 20% were not even engaged in farming.[6] It did not require much socialist theory to stir up resentment against these men who were living the good life, enjoying fine sake, women, clothes, and culture at the expense of the labor of their tenants.

These problems were aggravated by the fact that no firm legal guarantees existed for a tenant family to renew the lease on land they worked, and a number of disputes arose over evictions. This new unrest was expressed in an increase in the number of tenant unions. In 1917 there were 173 tenant unions[7] and 85 recorded disputes between tenants and landlords. By the time Kagawa was setting up the *Nihon Nomin Kumiai* (Japan Farmers' Union) in 1921, the numbers had multiplied to 681 tenant unions and 1680 disputes.[8]

Typically, Kagawa saw his role in this new organization as that of a financial supporter, propagandist and catalyst, rather than a permanent fixture. He realized that it was unsound for the farm movement to place primary dependence on intellectuals for leadership. He was anxious that the farmers carry on their own struggle without relying on outside help. Less than a year after he became involved in organizing the farm union, he expressed the hope that he would be able to withdraw from it.[9] He looked around for the right person to realize his dream of a national farm union and found Motojiro Sugiyama, a Christian minister with a degree in agriculture. His base for agrarian reform was a congregation in a farming village of Odaka.

Like Kagawa in the cities, Sugiyama was a Christian who employed a broad-brush approach to help the tenant farmers, trying everything from better farming techniques to tenant activism. (A versatile man, he also studied dentistry specifically to give care to the peasants.) He had converted unproductive rice paddies into orchards, drained swamps and applied his training in agriculture to other improvements. He led a highly publicized tenant dispute against a big landlord.[10] Elected to the Japanese House of Representatives seven times, Sugiyama eventually in 1955 became vice-speaker of the House.[11] He also served as a major leader in Kagawa's lay order, Friends of Jesus, and would become the first president of the Japan Farmers' Union.

In the meantime, Yoriyuki Murashima, a rural associate of Kagawa, published an article about plans for a union in the *Osaka Mainichi Shimbun* (Osaka Daily News). A strong favorable response to the article persuaded Kagawa to invite contacts from many parts of Japan to come to Kobe for a discussion. A group of sixty crowded into his mission hall in October 1921 and laid the groundwork for this new rural movement. The following February, the first issue of the union's newspaper, *Tochi to jiyu* (Land and Freedom), was published.

On April 9, 1922, Kagawa called a meeting of 100 delegates to the new Kobe YMCA building to proclaim the founding of the union, the first national farmers' organization in Japan. He wrote the manifesto for the Japan Farmers' Union, and it rang with the combination of compassion, a sense of justice and hope that inspired his speeches and writings for the urban labor movement. It proposed a practical program of education, and technical and moral improvement to revitalize the rural areas. Among the 21 specific goals Kagawa hammered into the platform were the following: "socialization" of farmland; guaranteed minimum wage for farmworkers; enactment of a farm tenancy law; enforcement of an arbitration law in agricultural disputes; stability of life for tenants; supplementary education; more schools; more support for agricultural cooperatives; banking facilities for tenant farmers; improvement of rural housing; improvement of hygiene; crop insurance; improvement of the status of women in rural areas; development of rural folk arts; development of science for farmers, and enjoyment of rural life. Convinced as he was that freedom to organize and the right to vote were crucial to securing tenants' rights, Kagawa again called for amendment of the repressive Peace Police Act and the establishment of universal suffrage.[12]

Motojiro Sugiyama was elected the president of the new

union, and Kagawa provided financial support of ¥20,000, crisscrossing Japan to make speeches for the organizational effort. The union had a relatively high number of Christians in the leadership. For that reason, Kagawa and other organizers had to be careful not to engage in overt religious discussion. Even so, there was still some suspicion among the farmers that the union was a front group for Christianity. Most farmers, however, were willing to judge by action rather than ideology. By February 1923, when the organization next met in Kobe, they had already established over 100 locals with some 10,000 members.

When Kagawa went out on his organizing forays, he found it encouraging that crowds of more than a thousand peasants walked as much as ten miles to hear him. They did this in spite of strong opposition from the ever-present police who frequently detained and jailed union leaders. Because of a bout with pleurisy in the fall of 1922, Kagawa was worn down and forced to take a break. In addition to his travels, he had continued to contribute articles to *Land and Freedom*, decrying the sufferings of the peasants and laying out proposals for alleviating their misery.

With all this organizing activity, Kagawa remained the pastor. Time and again, then and throughout his career, people expressed amazement that such a busy man rarely seemed impatient and always had time for them. This extended to doing the simplest, most mundane favors, as Kagawa continued to live the Gospel literally. One farmer from the Aizu district named Ken Kobayashi was influenced by Kagawa's best seller, *Crossing the Death Line* and by Kagawa's organizing activities to journey to Kobe for the initial Farmers' Union convention. Kagawa's kindness on that occasion was indelibly etched in Kobayashi's mind. In his own simple language he wrote:

> I visited Kagawa at his residence in the slums. He welcomed me and took me to a public bath-house in the evening. While washing myself on the floor, I felt someone rub me on the back with a towel. Looking back, I found it was Kagawa.[13]

The parallel with Christ washing the disciples' feet was not lost on the farmer:

After returning to my village, I realized that there was the Bible behind this humble attitude of Kagawa and began studying it. This was the motive for my becoming a Christian.[14]

Kagawa's organizing, preaching and writing continued on. Both their scope and the man's sheer stamina astonished observers. The official launching of the Japan Farmers' Union in April 1922 took place only a month after Kagawa's return from an evangelizing tour of Formosa. He had preached 50 sermons on that island which had become Japanese territory as a result of the war with China in 1895.

During this period he also worked on the founding of a labor school in Osaka, which opened in June, 1922. The school operated successfully, with Kagawa, Masamichi Shimmyo, Kanehito Matsuzawa, Yoshizo Takayama and Kisuke Murashima as lecturers and instructors. Kagawa also testified at the trial of 55 strikers who had been indicted for violations during the dockyard strike the previous summer.[15]

Kagawa himself was not charged in this case for inciting violent acts which erupted at the demonstrations, but he was grilled about his role in the mass visits to the Shinto shrines after demonstrations had been forbidden. He admitted that visiting the shrines was his idea, ticking off the reasons why such visits were acceptable. He argued that visits to shrines were not forbidden demonstrations, but rather spiritual and patriotic acts distinctly different from demonstrations.

He pointed out that the gatherings at the shrines had been non-violent. As a *coup de grace*, he postulated that if, in fact, the visits were illegal demonstrations, the police should have given an order to disperse them in the first place, which they did not.[16] Of the 55 strikers who were brought to trial, 26 received sentences ranging from eight months to two years. The remainder were given fines or sentences of six months or less.[17] Those with the longest sentence were freed on bail.[18]

Kagawa's strategy in the shrine visits was yet another example of the delicate cat-and-mouse game with established authorities, who in the years ahead would not only destroy his dream of democracy, but push Japan into wars in Manchuria and China during the 1930s and finally into World War II. In Formosa, he had been allowed to give sermons, but any talk on "social questions" was strictly forbidden.

Then—and today—Kagawa was accused of being a dreamer and a utopian. The fact is that his approach to the farm situation was extremely pragmatic and result-oriented. He selected capable people to assist him in the Japan Farmers's Union, and he was not afraid to delegate authority. The union rapidly gained membership, despite having to contend with feudalistic attitudes, fear of police, and opposition from landlords. Within a few months, it had recruited 30,000 members and set up 29 branches throughout the country.[19]

Sugiyama's involvement in a leading a major tenant dispute against the 5000-acre Fujita farms in the Okayama area drew considerable attention to the union. By 1926, membership had reached at least 68,000.[20] The union successfully negotiated rent reductions of as much as 30% in some areas and prevented other rent increases. Kagawa often went to the countryside for negotiations, as in one case where tenants on an Okayama estate were arrested for threshing the landlord's rice with his machinery and taking it for themselves. The tenants were driven to this action because they were close to starvation and the landlord had reneged on a pledge to reduce the rents. Kagawa's union gave farmers much more than ideology, though its emphasis was on the Christian ideas of social justice.

The peasants were attracted to a very concrete set of programs of lectures and peasant schools (including a research department which gathered facts on living and working conditions). In the 1980s, when education is taken for granted, and "information overload" is a favorite psychobabble term, it is difficult to conceive how important were the farm union's rural schools and publications. For peasants living in complete ignorance, the famine of information was almost as debilitating as the physical famine which swept some areas in Japan in the 1920s and 1930s.

Over the years, Kagawa established "Gospel Schools" and rural centers offering practical and religious training to thousands of farmers. He sponsored the work of rural leaders and instructors like Sotohiko Masuzaki, who established a thriving rural church settlement in Minabe, about 100 miles from Osaka. Masuzaki was an ideal disciple, because he combined religious fervor with practicality in introducing improved farming techniques into impoverished areas. The Farmers' Gospel School and conference center in Kawaragi, a village between

Kobe and Osaka, set up in 1923, was later remodeled and expanded largely from royalties from Kagawa's best-selling novel on rural reconstruction, *Hitotsubu no mugi* (A Grain of Wheat), published in 1931. Another important rural center contained both a school and pork processing facilities and was located in Gotemba, with a spectacular view of Mt. Fuji. Kagawa also called for cooperatives that would provide farmers low-cost purchasing of seed and equipment, free legal advice, guidance in new agricultural techniques to increase yields and develop new types of crops and livestock.[21] (See Chapter 8.)

Research and observation had convinced Kagawa that Japan was entirely too dependent on the rice crop. Furthermore he saw that it was being grown on terrain better suited to other types of crops, and that agriculture should be diversified. He recommended permaculture adaptable to the more mountainous areas, such as nut trees, fruits and the greater use of livestock fed from these crops. His writings on agricultural practices often sound like that of an enthusiastic U.S. Department of Agriculture county agent.

He also began calling attention to a number of problems in rural development such as environmental pollution and the lack of appropriate technology. As is evidenced from the following statement, his preaching of reverence for the land was not a neo-primitive rejection of technology, but a call for man to work in harmony with nature:

> Some people curse machine civilization and insist upon a return to the oxcart. . . . For my part, if it just wasn't for the capitalist's greed, I think there'd be nothing quite as beneficial for mankind as the machine. Thus, I do not in the least curse the machine. If the machine can be used as a blessing for all mankind and not as a tool to exploit labor power, I think it should be adapted to the farm village. But what worries me is that machine civilization is forgetting the soil. Man is lashing out at mother nature, the birds and the insects are perishing, and I fear the fish and creatures that live in the water are vanishing without a trace. Unfortunately without sufficient regard for the future, man will do something rash. Retribution will come without fail. And this may be one cause of the destruction of man himself. I want to preserve the land for mankind.[22]

His environmentalism stemmed from his observance of the

injustice of cash cropping. Peasants were growing silk and other crops for sale in urban markets while they themselves lacked a decent diet.[23] (Only recently, with the work of scholars such as Frances Moore Lappé and her Institute for Food and Development Policy, has wide attention been drawn to this problem.)

Kagawa's long range plan for the countryside was avowedly socialist. In the United States, where the terms "Christian" and "socialist" have been twisted into irreconcilable opposites, the idea of a Christian socialist still sounds strange to many people. Yet it was precisely his Christian ethics which prompted Kagawa to push for a political solution to the Japanese farmers' economic woes. He proposed a sequence of reforms, beginning with tenant legislation and rent reductions, followed by economic improvements that would give farmers credit, machinery, marketing and all the advantages of modern agricultural development. Farmer cooperatives would give rural areas the tools to accomplish this.

The ultimate goal was "socialization of the farm land," which was one of the demands Kagawa wrote into the organization's basic platform.[24] By "socialization," Kagawa meant the total ownership and control of the land by the people who worked it, in coordination with regional planning bodies and cooperatives which could bring some order into the agricultural economy. The end was revolutionary; it would result in massive land reform. He believed, however, that the means had to be gradual, given the political situation. He was deliberately evasive on the meaning of "socialization," even in the early stages of planning. When questioned about what he meant by "socialization" of farm land, Kagawa's answered:

> Socialization is a term frequently used among the industrial workers. Here socialization will mean the improvement and socialization of the life of the peasants. Therefore, you must be patient and wait for a few years.

The questioner was apparently satisfied with this answer.[25]

Considering the repression which Kagawa had experienced first hand, plus the legislation which was pending in the Japanese Diet, his cautious reply is understandable. The House of Peers had recently introduced a bill to tighten the clamp down on "dangerous thought."

The establishment's fear of disorder can be seen by the difficulties of another famous person whom Kagawa encountered during this period, the birth control crusader Margaret Sanger. Initially denied a visa to enter Japan. Sanger was invited to address Japan's pressing population problems by the liberal feminist Baroness Shizue Ishimoto and finally allowed to enter the country, on the condition that she refrain from speaking publically about birth control. She was met by enthusiastic groups from the progressive and labor circles. In the next month, scores of Japanese magazines carried articles about birth control.[26] (It should be remembered that Sanger and her supporters were jailed for her beliefs by authorities in the U.S.)

Sanger arrived in Kobe April 2, 1922 and attended a tea at the Oriental Hotel. Among the 26 in attendance was Kagawa, who must have been amused at Sanger's own sly bending of official policy. She defined this event as a "private" gathering, which allowed her to speak freely on birth control.[27] Before another year passed, the Japan Labor Federation was sponsoring public lectures on birth control by well-known intellectuals like Isoo Abe, and referring people to counseling. Kagawa was always a strong advocate of family planning and birth control.

Later that month, Kagawa had to appear in court on yet another charge of violating the Peace Preservation Law because of an article on universal suffrage published in his labor paper. The court levied a fine of ¥400 for this single article. He took another opportunity to oppose government policy by refusing to attend the International Labor Conference in Geneva. Kagawa agreed with the International Labor Organization's general policy and had borrowed many points from the ILO's labor demands when he drafted manifestos for the Japanese labor movement. The Japanese workers, however, were outraged by the method used to select delegates to the 1919 International Labor Conference. According to the international peace treaty of World War I, the chosen delegates were supposed to be "most representative" of working people in a given country. The Japanese government insisted on hand-picking the labor delegates, and completely ignored the Japan Labor Federation, passing up Bunji Suzuki. Instead Uhei Matsumoto, a chief engineer at the Kawasaki Dockyards, was selected to avoid the implication that the government officially recognized the union. The workers were so enraged at this slap in the face that they organized large demonstrations, and Matsumoto had to board the ship under cover.[28] To complicate matters further, the more radical workers refused to participate at all, because they considered the ILO a front for capitalists.

Faced with this protest, the government devised an elective process which permitted all factories employing 300 or more to send representatives to a prefecture selection committee. Each factory was allowed one for the first 1000 workers and an additional one for each additional 1000 workers. Kagawa was elected runnerup to Shinsui Kawai who declined because of ill-health. Kagawa refused to attend the 1922 ILO Conference. He distanced himself from the whole affair, staying with Reverend Izumida at Yoshida-cho, Yamanashi prefecture, while lecturing near Kawaguchi Lake at the foot of Mount Fuji, far away from the troublesome situation. (The one luxury Kagawa allowed himself throughout his life was to get away on his vacations.)

When interviewed, he used the occasion to direct some sharp criticism at the government's labor policies, saying it was pointless to attend the international conference because the Japanese government had totally disregarded the labor rights declarations of previous conferences. If the government had made an effort to carry out the ILO's recommendations for the recognition of unions and improvement of working conditions, then there would be some reason to attend. As it was, these worker demands were completely ignored. Secondly, Kagawa declared, he did not want to attend because he would have to be severely critical of the Japanese government for its refusal to recognize labor unions.

The third reason he gave is interesting because it indicates his continuing concern that the unions were relying too heavily on top-down guidance from intellectuals like himself. He was not interested in "labor politics"; he wished to be a "servant" of the labor unions. He also pointed out that the Japanese labor unions were developing slowly because there were "too many chiefs."[29] This was a criticism of the obvious career ambitions of certain labor leaders and of the factionalism which various leaders provoked. Kagawa was suspicious of Communists and others whom he condemned for using the labor movement as a vehicle for their own political agenda.

Kagawa might have received at least a respite from police harassment and a chance to rest aboard ship if he had opted to go to Geneva. As it was, he returned to Kobe, and suffered continued wranglings. The Labor Federation held a meeting at the Kobe YMCA on August 29 to discuss labor issues publicly. The large audience attracted the usual contingent of police to maintain order. (Surviving photographs of this type of labor gathering are often more dramatic than written reports, as they show uniformed police wandering through the audience.)

One report tells of the chilling example of the power of the police to squelch Kagawa's criticism of their activities:

> Towards the end of the function, Mr. Kagawa Toyohiko, the labor leader in the Kansai district, was addressing the meeting, which hung on his words with the profound and earnest attention they always receive. His speech had not proceeded far when he was also stopped, at a passage where he said that even in the principal cities of the country there is still suppression of speech, and a stern suppression of laborers.
>
> Mr. Kagawa would not leave the rostrum for some minutes after his speech was stopped, but stood in silence and meditation before the vociferous audience. Meanwhile a police inspector requested Mr. Kagawa to go over to the Aioibashi station, together with several other speakers who were also stopped. Mr. Kagawa and the others obeyed. Some inquiries seem to have been made at the police station into the behavior of the speakers and the greater part of them were allowed to go home. Two or three speakers who were considered to have disobeyed the police were detained.[30]

These episodes never stopped Kagawa from speaking his mind. In addition to his lecture tours, organizing and negotiating efforts for the farm union, Kagawa began to assist the burakumin, a group often called Japan's "hidden minority." His commitment to securing buraku rights, however, was quite limited, a fact which has drawn criticism from buraku civil right groups in recent years. The treatment of this class of "outcastes" is one of the greatest scandals in Japan and a blatant example of civil rights abuse. A large number of the slum residents to whom he ministered were burakumin (literally, "special village people") so Kagawa was already well aware of their plight at the very bottom of Japanese society. He did not discriminate against the burakumin in dispensing aid in the slums, but like most Japanese at the time, he likely harbored some discriminatory attitudes toward them.

Historically, discrimination against the burakumin has been as strong as discrimination against blacks in the United States. The treatment of the former has many parallels with the experience of the American blacks, right down to the details of daily life, such as segregated lavatories in schools.[31] The burakumin were officially "emancipated" about the same time (1871), yet like blacks they have had to battle continuously for basic civil rights in a campaign that continues to this day. They were not allowed to marry outside their group. They were subjected to degrading customs, such as a requirement to remove headgear and footwear when entering a courtyard, not being allowed to cross the threshold of a common citizen, nor to eat, smoke or even sit in the presence of others. Indeed, two of the more common names for them were *eta* (full of filth) and *hinin* (nonhuman), words which are avoided in polite Japanese talk. Official government documents described them as "the lowliest of all the people, almost resembling animals."

The rural villages in which they were concentrated were excluded from maps of 19th century Japan. One of thousands of recorded illustrations of the extreme hatred directed at the buraku is an infamous court decision in 1859. A young man was brought to trial for murdering a burakumin. In rendering his decision, the judge made this astounding statement to the buraku leader who brought the case to the court, "An eta is 1/7 of an ordinary person. If you would have me punish the guilty party, let him kill six more of your fellows." Although Japan has officially abolished the caste system which froze the burakumin into their degraded situation, the prejudice remains to this day, causing the group to endure segregation, limited job opportunities, inferior education, harassment, physical attacks, and the widespread belief that they are inherently corrupt and subhuman.[32]

What is so peculiar about this prejudice is that the victims are of the same ethnic stock as the Japanese and indistinguishable in physical appearance. The discrimination has its roots from a thousand years ago in the occupational caste system similar to that of India, with its untouchables. The burakumin were butchers and leather workers who apparently lost status when Buddhism, with its prohibition on slaughtering animals, became firmly established in Japan. This group was also relegated to other distasteful or "impure" tasks, such as undertakers, executioners, and night-soil carriers. They became beggars, dog trainers and traveling amusement people. They developed trades in certain other areas, such as basket weaving, straw sandal and mat making, weaving and textile dyeing. By Kagawa's time, about half of the burakumin still lived separate and unequal lives in segregated country villages.

The official census in 1920 put their number at 830,000, or 1.2% of the population, although it was surely higher. In the 19th century, buraku people had just begun to form organizations to protect themselves and obtain civil rights. Just like workers and peasants, however, they became increasingly militant by 1920, and turned to Kagawa.

The strongest new organization was the *Suiheisha*, "Levelers Society," which became the leading civil rights advocate until it was dissolved during World War II. There were burakumin among the farm leaders who held their organizing meetings in Kagawa's hall in the slums in October 1921. Others affiliated with the union, and laid the groundwork for their own organization at this time.[33] On March 3, 1922, the buraku organization was officially launched amidst a rousing declaration of their rights. Their dramatic flag was unfurled with a red crown of thorns on a black background, a conscious use of the image of Christ's suffering. (The liberation movement was influenced by both Buddhism and Christianity, as well as Marxism). The crown of thorns insignia is still used by burakumin civil rights advocates in Japan.

In addition to advising and encouraging the burakumin leaders, Kagawa responded to their request for a lecture tour in January 1923 to help publicize their efforts. He later distanced himself from the movement because he was put off by their militancy. When a buraku person was subjected to discrimination, the Levelers would announce the incident and demand a public apology from the person guilty of discrimination in the newspapers or through printed statements distributed by the Levelers. Kagawa came to believe that this technique stirred up too much hostility and he criticized the Levelers for preaching a "gospel of hatred."[34] But he failed to prescribe an alternative.

Such painful confrontations did stir up latent anger on both sides. The attention of the entire nation was drawn to one violent clash in Nara Prefecture in mid-March of 1923. An old man had made the derogatory gesture of raising four fingers at a group of burakumin (meaning "four-legged," thus "animal"). The buraku people demanded an apology, triggering the involvement of an ultra-nationalist group of bullies called the *Kokusuikai* (National Essence Association). When the Levelers returned to see the man two days later, they were met by an armed contingent of these rightists. Rallying their members, the burakumin leaders recruited 2000 to stage a battle against the Kokusuikai and their allies. The police had to step in and stop the fighting. When the matter came to trial, the Levelers were outraged that almost three times as many of their own were convicted and that they were levied much harsher sentences than the Kokusuikai supporters.

His insensitivity to their method was not Kagawa's only problem in relation to the burakumin. In his earlier years, he was very much a product of his times in his acceptance of certain beliefs about race. He had accepted the premise, backed by "scientific" ideas of the period, that moral and intellectual characteristics were hereditary and that certain ethnic groups and races were genetically inferior. He applied this thinking to the burakumin, which led him to the Social Darwinist conclusion that their condition resulted from inborn traits as much as from economic and social problems. Though Kagawa's *A Study of the Psychology of the Poor* broke new ground in Japanese sociology and powerfully exposed the scandal of poverty when it appeared in 1915, it accepted these derogatory assumptions about heredity, and applied them to the burakumin. This concern with genetics reached a point of absurdity when Kagawa tried to show that the burakumin are not "true" Japanese, but are "tainted" with Chinese, Korean, Caucasian and Negro blood.

In language that can only be called bigoted, he wrote:

> Outcastes living in the Nagata district of Kobe speak with a Chinese accent. The special people of Harima still preserve in their language Korean nouns. In the speech of the villagers of Minami-no-ura among the buraku of Omi there is also the retention of Korean words. It is already clear from these facts, especially if one studies their skin, that . . . the eta are a special race apart. This is a surprising fact, but I cannot help but believe that they are descendants of the Caucasian race.

After cataloguing some of their "offensive traits" like meat-eating and lack of ventilation in their houses, he employed tortuous logic in attributing their lowly state to the fact that they willingly accepted it because of their hereditary inferiority:

> They have always been satisfied with lowly work of all kinds, that is to say, the work of slaves . . . No one can deny that the burakumin are a criminal race in the Japanese empire. Minami-no-mura has a population of only 2,600. However, 305 of them are ex-convicts. I have heard that the rate of crime among Shinheimin ["new commoners"—a term for burakumin who were given citizenship rights in 1871] in Wakayama Prefecture is three and a half times that of ordinary people. In short, they are a degenerate race, or a slave race, or an obsolete, outdated ancient race of Japan.[35]

In Kagawa's defense, it must be remembered that this was written when he was about 25 years old, and when theories on racial degeneration were widely regarded as scientific truth. These ideas about heredity and degenerate types were so much a part of the era that they were almost universally accepted. Kagawa even applied such concepts to himself, with the morbid fear that he had inherited his father's degeneracy. Even as daring a reformer as Margaret Sanger accepted such ideas, as did the Japanese socialist Isoo Abe, who used the same terminology of eugenics during this period.

Not everyone embraced this view of race—least of all the burakumin themselves, and Kagawa's statements were strongly criticized by some at the time the book was published. In 1929 he agreed to take the book out of print, but evidently he never made a public apology, nor fully admitted the hurt that such remarks caused the burakumin and how such statements reinforced old prejudices with the cloak of "scientific" validity. Consequently, for today's burakumin, there remains a "Kagawa problem," one which painfully underscores the depths of discrimination they have experienced.

Another reason Kagawa separated himself from the buraku movement was his fear that their organization had been too tainted by the Bolshevik brand of Marxism, which he had increasingly come to fear and to oppose. He was particularly critical of their advocacy of violent means to secure their aims using Soviet techniques. In one of his dealings with the buraku group, he complained of the difficulties in getting along with them:

> I asked the Water Level movement to join our peasant union and make it an economic movement, and they did join us. But the Communist element of them made trouble inside the union and that was one of the factors which caused the peasant union to divide about a year ago.[36]

The rift between Kagawa and the burakumin was essentially as much political as ethnic. This is borne out by his 1927 statement:

> In the cities the sentiment against the outcastes is not so strong. They now intermarry with others and as a class they are disappearing. But in the villages it is very difficult to secure this hopeful result. The only solution is to have more religion combined with their economic uplift. Then we may hope to absorb them into the group of ordinary Japanese.[37]

Though he understated the degree of prejudice, it is clear that he no longer thought in terms of ethnic purity. He expressed no fear that the buraku genes would somehow taint the Japanese. There was in his reasoning, however, an element of denial of the depth of Japanese prejudice, not unlike that of a number of Americans who fail to address squarely the race issue of this decade.

Kagawa continued to push for a gradual approach to reform, through parliamentary democracy, trade unions and cooperatives as the most practical and painless way to bring Japan from a nation convulsed with the worst miseries of capitalism to a socialist system with political and economic equality. He opposed the belligerent rhetoric and the emphasis on class struggle of the syndicalists and Communists as too abstract and unproductive. They, in turn, branded his very pragmatism to be utopian, because the system was uncompromising.

It is futile to determine which side was "correct," since the right wing government and the military ended up destroying the Communist party and either emasculating or coopting most of the social democrats. The real mistake perhaps was in the complete inability of the left wing to agree and present a united front capable of resisting the totalitarians. Kagawa's quarrels with the syndicalists and Communists were a mere preview of the later 1920s and 1930s, which witnessed constant bickering and splintering in labor, farm and political movements,[38] and eventually suffered the creation of more than 20 proletarian political parties.[39] Kagawa himself was caught up in this bewildering tangle of alliances and breakdowns, as we shall see. The adage "the left wing firing squad stands in a circle" was never more true than for interwar Japan.

Kagawa did not confine himself to political and peasant organizing during this period. The faith that drove him to secular activism also fanned out in other directions. He established his own religious order, the Friends of Jesus Group in October 1921. Starting with a handful of his close associates in Kobe, this group emerged as the center of his future religious and charitable work. Its pattern was an amalmagation of the methods of the Catholic religious orders and the approach of the Protestant reformist lay orders. The Friends of Jesus combined the Franciscan compassion for the poor, the Dominican preaching spirit, Jesuit discipline, the methodism of John Wesley's spiritual group, and the hands-on activism of the Salvation Army.

Kagawa had always been critical of the sectarian rivalries within Protestantism, insisting that religious orders should coexist within a broad faith community, as in Catholicism and Buddhism. He considered his "sect" as another religious order within Christianity. The Friends of Jesus groups would meet to pray regularly, pooling their income as in the early church, and using their spare time to advance social reform, settlement house activity, medical care and education. Within a year, his organization grew to almost 900 members as it carried on the work of Kagawa's expanding community. Kagawa started a magazine, *Kumo no hashira* (Pillar of Cloud), to promote the ideals of the group and serve as a forum for its philosophy and discussion of its activities.

In addition to all this, Kagawa suddenly found himself a family man. Haru had become pregnant on the trip to Formosa in March, and gave birth to the couple's son Sumimoto, on December 26, 1922. Kagawa's daughter Umeko conjectures that Haru was unable to become pregnant earlier because of the couple's Spartan diet in Japan, as contrasted with the more nutritious food available in tropical Formosa.

Whatever the case, the birth would soon dictate some radical changes for the Kagawa family. It meant that they would have to leave Shinkawa. Though less than a year before the baby was born, Kagawa had publicly stated he would never leave the slums, he knew that remaining there would be tantamount to infanticide. He could sacrifice himself, but he could not demand the same of their infant. He wrote,

> From the time that my wife became pregnant I suffered anxiety, for all the while disorderly drunken people were about us and rogues would come in to threaten us. Knowing as I did the high mortality of infants in the slums, I felt that it would be absolutely impossible for us to raise our child in the slums. I had investigated the mortality of infants in our neighborhood and was astonished to discover that of 62 born in one year, 45 had died.[40]

So, for the protection of the infant, the family moved to Haru's mother's house outside Shinkawa while the Friends of Jesus maintained the headquarters in Shinkawa. Now a father, the 35-year-old Kagawa had by this time accomplished what for many would already be a life's work. He had published more than 20 books in addition to his union, farm and co-op organizing, while maintaining his religious community, and he was about to embark on some new ventures.

Using his international connections in religious and academic circles, he planned an extended world tour beginning April 1923 to lecture in England, Germany, France and the United States and to investigate conditions in these nations. His lectures were mainly to be sponsored by the YMCA. This trip had to be cancelled, however, because both he and Haru contracted severe cases of trachoma as a result of their intimate contact with the diseased poor in the slums.

A more drastic change of plans occurred later that year, when Japan was hit by one of the worst natural disasters in recorded history. At two minutes before noon on September 1, 1923, Tokyo was shattered by an earthquake that left the city in flaming ruins, killing more than 100,000 and leaving hundreds of thousands more homeless. The next day, Kagawa was on board the *Yamashiro maru* sailing from Kobe on a relief mission to the stricken capital.

Chapter 7
Crusader at Home, Ambassador Abroad

THE KAGAWAS IMMEDIATELY WENT to work on earthquake relief. When he heard the news of the September 1, 1923, disaster, Toyohiko dropped his writing and concentrated all his efforts on aid. Haru, carrying baby Sumimoto on her back, spent the next days going door-to-door asking for donations, while pushing a handcart in which donated items were collected.

Kagawa met with Kobe Christian leaders, who designated him as their representative to express sympathy to the stricken city, assess the situation and offer relief. The ship he boarded to go to Tokyo, the *Yamashiro maru*, had been halted on a trip to Shanghai when news of the earthquake came by wireless. It had turned back, unloaded its cargo, and reloaded it with food for delivery to the port of Yokohama. Kagawa himself traveled third class.[1]

The disaster drew the Japanese people together as few other episodes in their history. One of the Kobe workers' favorite targets, the Kawasaki Company executive Matsukata, made the arrangements for this particular shipment, while organized labor leaders like Kagawa and Suzuki were enlisted by the Tokyo government to assist in the relief effort.

Kagawa's ship traveled 300 miles and was passing the Izu peninsula, about 50 miles from the mouth of Tokyo Bay when the wireless operator received messages confirming the worst reports: massive damage in Tokyo and almost total destruction of Yokohama, its main port 18 miles to the south.[2] Upon arrival on the evening of September 3, fires caused by the quake still dotted the area. Kagawa saw the whole port town reduced to rubble, with smoke from three days of conflagration still hanging in the air. Other than a few fire-gutted buildings, the only structures left standing were the giant cranes of the port, their girders outlined against the smouldering background of the city. His ship pushed through a sea of debris and floating corpses.

The ruin encountered by Kagawa in Yokohama and Tokyo was grimmer than the hell of Shinkawa. More than 40 square miles in central Tokyo had been burned to the ground. The quake could not have occurred at a worse time, because the cooking fires for the midday meal were lit when the buildings came crashing down. Within a half-hour of the tremor, fire had broken out at 140 different locations. The rupturing of the water mains made it impossible for Tokyo's modern fire department to bring the conflagration under control. High winds, often shifting in direction, compounded the horror by fanning the flames.

The stench of decay was already in the air when Kagawa arrived. Tens of thousands of blistered and charred human bodies and animal carcasses lay in the rubble. Human bodies were floating in the city's many canals and bay. Thousands had drowned after leaping into the water to escape the walls of flames that surrounded them on all sides. Many were cooked to death in the canals when the intense heat had brought the water to the boiling point. Hundreds had been washed out to sea on the wide Sumida River, swiftly flowing through the east side of the city.

One of the hardest hit was the poor Honjo District on the east side of Tokyo. This is where Kagawa set up his first relief efforts in a low-lying area, crisscrossed by canals and bordered on the west by the Sumida River. Honjo had been made up mostly of factories and the crowded wood houses and shacks of the workers. The fire had quickly spread here and a huge throng had crowded near the river into a wide open space of several acres known as the Army Clothing Bureau. The flames burned across the bridges, igniting buildings next to the river, completely surrounding them with flames. Having nowhere to turn, 32,000 were incinerated into an immense pile of charred flesh and bones. The only way that the few survivors could escape was by climbing over burned bodies.[3]

Kagawa took on the relief work with the same relentless energy he had poured into the slums. After surveying the damage in the ruined city and touching base with friends there, he returned to Kobe. He lectured and even sold part of his extensive library to raise more money for relief work. As a result he was able to bring 40 big crates of bedding, clothes and futons back with him to Tokyo, accompanied by Haru and baby Sumimoto. Kagawa knew that this relief work would require the help of his wife, who was the manager of his extended household and a key figure in administering his charitable operations.

A crowd of homeless people had fled to the Buddhist Temple grounds at Asakusa, which was spared because it was surrounded by park land rather than flammable buildings. Kagawa first suggested to the temple priest that he put up a tent to shelter these people. When the priest failed to act, Kagawa went to city officials and was granted permission to do so in the city property around the temple. Kagawa pitched a large tent, donated by religious organizations, for temporary storage and shelter, supervised the distribution of food and clothing, and provided treatment for illness and injury to victims of the earthquake. The sight of a flag with a cross insignia flying above the tent shocked the Buddhist priests. Kagawa simply cited Buddhist texts which demanded compassion, saying "Even your temple is dedicated to the goddess of Mercy—yet all you are doing there is to worship idols." This argument convinced the priests to join in the relief effort, and the head priest not only continued doing social work but became well-known in the area for his efforts.[4]

This incident was typical of Kagawa's attitude toward non-Christian religions, which he studied intently and admired. He did not consider Christianity an "opponent" of Buddhism or any other religion, but rather its fulfillment, much in the same way that some early Christians saw the advent of Christ as the perfection of the religious and ethical systems of the ancient world. His ultimate goal was to Christianize Japan, but at the least, he would exhort his countrymen to live up to the precepts of their native religion.

Kagawa was quickly turning an overwhelming disaster into an opportunity to expand his social work, to build the Friends of Jesus religious community, and to use his spellbinding speaking skills in spreading Christianity among the people. He preached in every church that was left standing in Tokyo, addressing thousands and obtaining 5700 conversions.[5]

Within a few months, he helped to start the Industrial Young Men's Christian Association in a crudely built barrack-style building which served also as his headquarters in the Honjo area, not far from the red-light district. Under Kagawa's and Haru's guidance, the YMCA immediately started a variety of programs to educate and improve the lives of the people in the area, among them a special course on machine knitting, an employment agency and a private school for the poor. Kagawa also established another labor school, this one in the Asakusa district of Tokyo. He tapped many sources for aid, following the Biblical command "ask and ye shall receive." One was Count Rainei Arima who donated a site for the labor school.

In early 1924, Dr. Yutaka Majima and his two sisters came from Kagawa's clinic in Kobe to help. Their work in Kobe was continued by Haru's sister Yaeko Shiba, who was then graduating from Tokyo Women's Medical College.[6] Many people lived in hastily built barracks, while others less fortunate were in makeshift shacks of metal sheeting or whatever material they could find. Mothers had to leave babies unattended all day while they went to their jobs. Majima rescued a number of infants near death from hypothermia. A high rate of miscarriage occurred from a combination of malnutrition and overwork. To help solve these problems, Kagawa negotiated with city officials to procure more milk for the babies, better food in the schools, and cribs which would offer protection to babies who had to be left alone.

Collaborating with the Woman's Christian Temperance Union, he also set up a nursery and kindergarten in his headquarters. Kagawa was keenly concerned with the widespread problems of children's health. A reporter, describing the joy of children who participated at a traditional Japanese doll festival at the school, noted that 25 of the 55 children attending had sore eyes.[7] At Kagawa's insistence a milk distribution depot, pharmacy and dental clinic were also set up. Getting rid of pests was an urgent need so a delousing campaign was initiated. The pharmacy and medical office were outfitted with modern medical equipment, drugs and medical texts.

Life in these barracks was hardly comfortable. Families were crowded into compartments 10 feet by 12 feet that were full of cracks. The sole source of water consisted of a few hydrants surrounded by a plank platform in the middle of each cluster of buildings. No sewage system existed, only latrines at the edge of the barracks. Contemporary reports indicate, however, that remarkably clean conditions and high spirits prevailed in the barracks where Kagawa had an influence. No detail was too trivial to attract his attention.

His response to the earthquake and reconstruction was captured most vividly in his poetry expressing compassion for the victims, thanks to God, and anger at the bourgeoisie:

> Last fall,
> In burnt-out tin barracks
> Distributing clothing and bedding to thousands,
> I worried, fearing the coming winter.
> Compared with those days the reconstruction now
> Shines brightly on their faces.
> With tears of gratitude—
> Grateful that God so quickly allowed
> Our nation to rise up again—
> I could not stop crying.

Kagawa placed the responsibility for the continuing troubles on the rich rather than on God:

> Tens of thousands are still suffering
> With nothing to cover themselves,
> Under the tin roofs of Fukagawa.
> Have you forgotten this fact,
> O you frivolous men and women,
> Now well-clad in stylish suits?
> You must need another September First.[8]

During this time Kagawa also staked a claim at Matsuzawa village, just west of the city, where he found a rustic site near the woods with space to pitch tents loaned by the Red Cross. Ever the nature lover, he continued his efforts to bring children out of the city to the rural environment. By the summer of 1924, 60 children a week were flocking to this retreat. He rounded up 50 volunteers to work in shifts of ten to care for the children. Haru and her mother helped to run the camp, which served as well as a vacation spot for the relief workers. Later that year Kagawa also assisted in starting a women's refuge in the

Kameido district of Tokyo, a haven for prostitutes and battered women.

At the Matsuzawa retreat the Kagawas began to build the rambling structure he called the "caterpillar house," because of the rooms they kept adding to accommodate their many guests, co-workers, people seeking shelter and what the family termed "freeloaders." Kagawa's core group, the Friends of Jesus, set no limit to the projects they would undertake. He did not find it necessary to supervise every activity personally because he had gathered around him dedicated and capable people to whom he could entrust the growing work of his organization. Here was a movement based in his religious faith and intent on living a gospel of service to humanity.

It was this example, combined with the group's actual achievements, which kept attracting new people to his enterprises. Behind it all was his exemplary personal sacrifice. Everyone knew that at any time he chose, Kagawa Sensei could abandon his difficult routine and enjoy a comfortable life with substantial income from his writings. Yet he adhered to a doctrine of simplicity and a legendary work ethic.

The more Kagawa's reputation grew, the more he used his influence as a successful social reformer to elicit financial support from both liberal Japanese and the government itself. A Kagawa group led by foreign missionaries in Japan like Helen Topping set up relations in 1928 with a Kagawa Committee in the United States. *The Friends of Jesus* publication began to chronicle Kagawa's thoughts and actions for this expanding group of English-speaking supporters. By 1929 he had ten full-time, paid staff members doing everything from social work to translations of literary, theological and scientific texts.

An American woman and her father interviewing Kagawa in 1931 referred to Topping as Kagawa's "Boswell," and expressed their awe: "They feel that they are in the presence of one of the great characters of the age, and certainly his most extemporaneous utterances are worth recording."[9] Kagawa was proudest of his role as catalyst, an idea man who could spur others to action. His powerful capacity to rejoice at human growth, and his ability to make people grow were given ample exercise at this stage in his career.

While busily establishing his new relief and social work facilities in Tokyo, Kagawa continued writing and maintained his contacts with the farmers' union. He and his associates in the farmers' union organized "peasant gospel schools" where farmers came to study the Bible and learn about new agricultural techniques. Kagawa appeared at the schools to lecture on a variety of topics, speaking about "Biblical agriculture" in the simplest of language for less educated audiences:

> In Genesis we find that God gave permission to Adam and Eve to eat the fruits in the Garden. If we want real cultivation of the soil today so as to eat the fruits of toil, it is necessary to use the mountain sides everywhere and plant trees on the mountain slopes. . . . We learn much about farming in the Bible. In Proverbs there are many stories about farming—with honey bees, weaving, etc. In Isaiah there is restoration of desert land, and in the New Testament Jesus tells us many things about how to plant seeds, how to sell land, about growth, about seed-selection, etc.[10]

To those who objected to mixing spirituality with something as mundane as food policy, Kagawa explained that even a glimpse of the life of Christ showed a man profoundly concerned with food and other physical needs. Indeed, the central ritual of Jesus' religion was based on a meal. Kagawa, the non-dualist, insisted on a Christianity of the physical body like few preachers in the history of that faith.

At the same time, Kagawa's own body was taking a beating. He described the hectic year after the earthquake:

> On September 2nd of last year, I departed from Kobe, after which the nights in my home were hardly enough to count. To the east, to the west, racing about, giving little rest to my taut muscles, I went on and on for a full year, until finally reaching the restful shade of my Matsuzawa residence. As for any restful days during those travels, from the two or three nights spent in a tent pitched on the scorched ground of Honjo until these recent days under the trees of Matsuzawa, there have been absolutely none.[11]

Hoping to relax from such a schedule, he took the traditional Japanese hot bath every day, often remarking that without it he could not survive.[12]

His relationship with government officials improved but was still fraught with danger and contradiction. It was likely that the local and national government had involved the union in earthquake relief work in order to blunt their hostility, but the beneficial effects to the union were undeniable. The Japan Labor Federation was given a grant of ¥60,000 to build new housing for workers in Tokyo. Kagawa and Suzuki, the two purveyors of "dangerous thought" were appointed members of the newly-formed Imperial Economic Council, a body of 110 advisors chaired by the premier himself.

Kagawa was now in a vastly better position to lobby for social reforms, which he did with increasing effectiveness. Because of his knowledge of problems and his organizing ability, he was invited to serve on Tokyo's housing commission. The government commissioned him to do studies and statistical surveys on social problems in the areas of housing and medical care. He also served on the Central Employment Commission, particularly because of his background in setting up employment agencies. He was guardedly optimistic about this new level of official respectability which he had earned. He told one reporter that almost every member of the Economic Commission was "bourgeois," but then added, "They seem very much in earnest in their efforts to solve the social, industrial and financial problems of the country."[13]

This was a period when both government and business adopted a "carrot and stick" policy, making concessions to workers by improving labor conditions and welfare programs, and at the same time tightening its control of speech and press. The bright side was that some of the reforms advocated by Kagawa and his allies in the labor movement were being enacted, and brightest of all was the 1925 Universal Manhood Suffrage Act. On the dark side, the government was making an increasingly strong effort to stifle dissent. The men in power feared universal suffrage at the very time they granted it. They took calculated measures, therefore, to coopt the less militant dissenters on one hand and destroy the more militant on the other.

Among the reforms which Kagawa promoted and applauded was the passage of the 1922 Health Insurance Law which provided health, accident and maternity coverage to workers governed by the old 1911 Factory Act. (This law applied to all factories with 15 or more workers.) It was amended to include factories with ten or more workers, to raise the minimum legal age for child labor from 12 to 15 years, and to reduce the maximum legal workday from 12 to 11 hours. Other new labor legislation included minimum wages for seamen, provisions for labor dispute mediation, and improved safety in match factories notorious for causing lung damage by fumes (Kagawa has written a powerful chapter on a match factory strike in *Crossing the Death Line*). The government in 1924 also allowed the labor movement complete autonomy in selecting its delegates to the International Labor Organization.

This was the "carrot." In exchange the government demanded the right to wield the stick. Over the enraged objections of the labor movement, the Diet amended a Peace Police Law in 1925, making it far more repressive than before. The first article stated:

> Anyone who organizes a group for the purpose of changing the national polity or denying the private property system, or anyone who knowingly participates in said group shall be sentenced to penal servitude or imprisonment not exceeding ten years. An offense not actually carried out shall also be subject to punishment.[14]

If Kagawa tasted the carrot when men in power turned to him for advice, he also felt the blow of their stick. In something so benign as his earthquake relief work he had to deal with meddling authorities. When the YMCA was distributing 1000 futons among the homeless poor in the Honjo district, an official detective demanded a list of recipients. It was later learned that the police had gone to the homes of the poor and forced them to undo the seams of the futons to check for hidden subversive literature.[15]

When Kagawa appeared at a mass meeting of the Farmers Union in Osaka in February 1924, he was met by a heavy police guard. About 1500 people had gathered to discuss the formation of a new political party which would join the progressive forces of farmers and workers. Suzuki and other leaders of the urban unions were present. So fearful was the government of this kind of solidarity that the group was forbidden to sing as they marched, and the signs and banners they carried were confiscated as they entered the meeting.

Kagawa also felt the censor's big stick. The sequel to his two previous autobiographical novels, entitled *Kabe no koe kiku toki* (Listening to the Voices in the Wall), was allowed to be published in December 1924, but not until the censors had gouged parts of the text from the stereotype plates of the book. This novel portrayed the rice riots in Kobe and Kagawa's role in the strikes, with a scathing satire of the bourgeois lifestyle in Japan. The text was sometimes excised in places where characters had launched into dialogues or speeches critical of the authorities. In some instances, the censorship was so extensive that the thread of the narrative was lost.

The fact that Kagawa found time to write at all is remarkable, considering the pace of his activity and the ailments which bothered him during this period. His intermittent blindness from trachoma hit hardest in the spring of 1923. He had suffered a severe attack of nephritis earlier that year. Yet in 1924 alone, he managed to publish five books—three theological works and two novels totaling more than 1850 pages. The important *Ai no kagaku* (literally "The Science of Love," translated as Love the Law of Life) was composed mostly through dictation while he was hospitalized for six weeks due to temporarily blindness from trachoma. His prose style suffered because he had no time to revise the texts. His work became more hurried because of constant speaking trips, the pressing urge to communicate his ideas, and his bouts with blindness.

The situation was entirely different from the first draft of his big novel written in the solitude of the fisherman's cabin by the sea at Gamagori. An even more compelling reason for the great pressure to produce was that his publications continued to be the major source of income for funding his projects. Although Kagawa was an advocate of the simple life, and ascetic in his personal habits, neither he nor the Friends of Jesus had any monastic intention of spurning the world. The intent of their Christian socialism was not to retreat into solitary communication with God but to build the Kingdom of God on earth.

A project of such ambition required capital, begged, borrowed or earned, and Kagawa used all three methods to the hilt during this period of expansion. He earned an average of ¥50,000 a year until the outbreak of World War II, when his books were banned and he was not permitted to publish anything but a few volumes of jingoistic poetry. Almost every yen went to support settlement houses, churches, cooperatives, hospitals, agricultural research and other projects dear to him.

Kagawa's attention was also turned outward in the spring of 1924 from the devastation of Tokyo, the heart of Japan, to the United States. With all Japan, he anxiously watched the progress of the new immigration bill in the United States Congress proposing to ban all Japanese from entering that nation. Japanese immigration had already been severely restricted as a result of the "Gentlemen's Agreement" entered into by President Theodore Roosevelt and the Japanese government in 1907. When President Calvin Coolidge signed the immigration bill, it provoked keen outrage in Japan. The Japanese were quite aware of widespread and pernicious racial discrimination in the United States from news reports and the experience of relatives who had emigrated. To institutionalize such bigotry by making it the law of the land, however, was a stinging affront.

The Japanese papers were full of protest, and a number of large anti-American demonstrations took place. Demands were voiced for a boycott of goods from the United States. The Japanese were angry at the hypocrisy of the United States in claiming to be a bastion of human freedom and yet acting violently racist and driven by territorial ambitions. The Exclusion Act climaxed a series of troubling developments: oppressive treatment of the Philippines and other colonial territories; invoking of the Monroe Doctrine to protect the Americas while pursuing an "open door" policy in Asia; refusal of the United States to join the League of Nations; and naval treaties limiting Japan's fleet to a quota of ships below those of the U.S. and Great Britain.

As one professor commented:

> There are, indeed, very few peoples in the world whose actual deeds so completely belie their fine avowals. America entered the late great war to punish Germany, who was Imperialism incarnate, for the sake of world peace, but what she has been

doing of late years in Cuba, Santo Domingo, Haiti and Nicaragua has been even more Imperialistic than Germany's conduct before the war. . . . International peace and international friendship are things which carry no weight with the majority of American people, whose sole concern is to establish white Americanism.[16]

Stressing the racial aspects of the action, another commentator called for a conference of colored races:

If the Japanese can be subjected to such treatment, it is obvious that the Chinese, Negroes, Indians and other colored peoples would be reduced to a still more miserable position. In this way, the colored races, boasting three-fourths of the total population of the world, are to be stigmatised as peoples inferior to whites, and to be excluded from world civilization permanently.[17]

The United States had played into the hands of Japan's ultranationalists, providing yet another excuse for a military buildup in what finally became a holy cause for Japan to defend itself and Asia from the West's racism and imperialism. Japan, the nationalists argued, was a small island nation with limited resources, whose teeming population needed more territory to survive. If the United States, with its vast open spaces and immense natural resources, refused to tolerate peaceful immigration of Japanese, then Japan would have to find territory elsewhere. Kagawa, a man whose pacifism dated back 20 years, was appalled by the dangers latent in the tense relations between Japan and the United States. Few knew more than he the hazard of unleashing the military spirit in Japan. He was cognizant also of the racism and imperialism in America. In his writing and speeches on economics and labor he had analyzed and lamented the causes of poverty in international terms, and found the capitalist system wanting. This analysis was influenced by his theology stressing the need to return to the Gospel command of service to the poor. Japan's militarism and the United States' racism and imperialism were the antithesis of everything he stood for.

However, Kagawa's initial reaction to the immigration act was more balanced than that of many others. Some Christians, led by famous theologian Kanzo Uchimura, went so far as to demand the expulsion of foreign missionaries. Kagawa, with his characteristic combination of sarcasm and statistics, criticized both the foreign missionaries and the native Japanese. He pointed out that there were 1200 foreign and 4000 native missionaries operating on a total budget of ¥2.9 million a year. He noted that only 300 of the 1300 Japanese churches were totally self-reliant, although if the Japanese clergy were true followers of Christ it shouldn't be difficult to get along without foreign assistance. He likewise criticized the foreign missionaries for living more comfortably than was necessary.[18]

In reaction to these events Kagawa began to see himself as ambassador of reconciliation. As a man who with a growing international reputation as a Christian pacifist, he could play an important role in bringing harmony between Japan and the West. An internationalist both because of his wide reading and his long stay in the United States, it was time for his first major foray in a lifelong quest for world peace.

With his work well-established in Japan, he was ready to go abroad again. Articles about his projects had appeared in major publications in Europe and the United States, personal contacts had spread word about him, and his novel had been translated. The Kagawa legend was building up in the West. He was not about to attack the United States and Europe nor to jump on the patriotic bandwagon in Japan. Many benefactors in the States had contributed to his religious and social work. His conversion to Christianity, the central event in his life, occurred because of the dedication of two American missionaries, Logan and Myers.

Though strongly critical of colonialism, he did not condemn the entire white race as some of his more bigoted countrymen did. He had applauded the generosity of Western nations during his earthquake relief activity, noting that by the end of January 1924, Japan had received ¥14,750,000 in cash donations and goods worth ¥18,600,000. "Even the disorganized countries of central Europe" he wrote, "sent magnificent expressions of sympathy."[19] The entire white world obviously could not be written off as insensitive exploiters.

There was also the very practical matter of raising more funds for his growing enterprises. Kagawa intended to create good will for Japan by explaining his country and people to other nations. He hoped, too, they might demonstrate their good will by contributing to his cause. He accepted an invitation for a lecture tour by the Pan-Pacific Student Convention and the World Student Christian Federation in which he would appeal for friendship between Japan and the United States and urge a more reasonable approach to the immigration problem. After this, he would go to Europe for further lecturing, to meet with European leaders, and see what new developments in the European co-ops and educational system might be worth introducing to Japan. He had already been invited to meet with Labor Party leader Ramsey MacDonald and other officials of the British government, and he particularly wanted to meet with Gandhi as he circled back around the world.[20]

Kagawa prepared for his departure in the fall, journeying to Kobe to say good-bye to the Friends of Jesus group. Throughout his residence and relief work in Tokyo he had continued to coordinate the work there, shuttling between the two cities. He had been in Kobe and Osaka for events like the farmers' union meeting and for the purpose of voting. At the end of November 1924, he sailed for Hawaii on the *Shinyo maru*.

Ever the activist, within a few weeks he was encouraging striking Filipino and Japanese plantation workers in Hawaii. In California, Kagawa touched base with the state's Japanese communities, preaching in their churches and establishing a West Coast network of The Friends of Jesus, a group which offered him generous support over the years. As in Japan, no area was too remote or insignificant for his preaching efforts. He journeyed all the way to Livingston, a small town in California's Central Valley 120 miles southeast of San Francisco.

Hideo Hashimoto, a young man in Livingston who later became a minister and professor of theology, paints a vivid picture of Kagawa evangelizing in the Japanese American community, a portrayal of the tireless preacher already battling illness and fatigue to preach the Gospel:

> It was late at night of Christmas, 1924. A young evangelist was preaching to a small cluster of people, gathered around the potbellied stove, in a rural Japanese church near Livingston in central California.
>
> The preacher had become ill during the day following the Student Conference in Asilomar, where he was a featured speak-

er. The listeners had waited for a couple hours. The speaker appeared still suffering from fever, which did not diminish the zeal of his preaching. He illustrated his message with the familiar story of Sogoro Sakura, a leader of a peasant uprising in medieval Japan, who was captured and crucified. As he was dying a most excruciating death, he shouted at the lord who ordered his execution, "I will come back and haunt you till the end of time." True to his threat, he returned to haunt the family of the oppressor for generations.

Toyohiko Kagawa, the speaker, then told the story of Jesus: how he was crucified, and how he cried out "Father, forgive them, for they know not what they do."

I was one of the people who heard him that night. I was one of half a dozen, including my brother, who stepped forward to decide for Christ. This was a conclusion of a very dramatic six months and the beginning of a new life for me.

I had heard of Kagawa-Sensei, as he was usually called, or even more familiarly, Kagawa-san. My teacher at Hirose School in Hiroshima, Mr. Tsukano, had talked about a young novelist and a worker in the slums, who wrote the bestseller, *Shisen o Koete* (Crossing the Death-Line).[21]

Hashimoto, 13 years old then, goes on to tell how the religious, social messages were impressed upon him at the same time: "Having been converted to the Christian faith under the influence of Kagawa, I became a Christian, Socialist and Pacifist almost at once."[22]

Kagawa proceeded with lectures in a number of cities, visiting Lincoln's birthplace and attending the Foreign Missions Convention of the United States and Canada in Washington, D.C. He crossed the Atlantic to England, then over to the continent. He met with MacDonald, the Labor Party's prime minister, and other British leaders, and visited Denmark, where he was deeply impressed by the success of the rural educational system and the cooperative movement. He also visited the Holy Land.

A measure of his growing fame in the West was the publication of his Foreign Missions address in English and translation into German. The introduction proclaimed Kagawa as "without a doubt one of the most important spritual leaders in Japan."[23] The address was typical of the moving autobiographical accounts Kagawa gave in speaking to Western audiences. There is nothing of abstract theology, only his account of applied Christianity in the slums and his organizing activity for the labor and farmers movements. If Kagawa had a message to give to the West at this time, it was the message of himself as a person, applying the teachings of Christ to healing some of the miseries of the modern world.

Kagawa preached world peace, patiently explaining how the Japanese viewed racial discrimination as a direct contradiction of the Gospel. He presented an image of Japan that he hoped would blunt anti-Japanese bigotry. At times, his message was so frank that it shocked his audiences, as he gave expression to the hurt felt by the Japanese:

> By the recent Exclusion Act of the United States the Japanese as a whole have found that the United States is no longer a Christian Nation. In the classrooms of Japanese Grammar Schools the pictures of George Washington and Abraham Lincoln are hung, and the Japanese think these great Presidents belong not only to the United States but to the world and to Japan because they were the emancipators from the old bondage of tyranny. In the Spring of last year they were alarmed that the United States was acting to exclude Japanese from her territory, and they were sorry to find out that the spirit of George Washington and Abraham Lincoln does not abide in the hearts of the United States citizens.
>
> America today is only a land of liberty for the White race. It is no more a land of liberty for the Yellow race. America has closed her doors absolutely to the Oriental nations.[24]

He prophesied grimly to his Western audiences:

> In the future we Japanese must discriminate between two kinds of people in America, namely, those who are Christians and those who uphold the principles of senators. While we uphold the principles of senators we can never have a World's Republic. Warfare will continue between races. Hatred will be powerful rather than goodwill. We must arm and must be prepared to fight each other. We shall need more and more armaments against enemies. We shall not be able to believe in our neighbors. We shall repeat again the tragedy of the great wars, and civilization and culture will be destroyed over and over again.[25]

Blasting the exploitive policies of the West, he concluded:

> Look at the whole continent of Asia. Japan is the only nation
> which has independence and the whole of Asia is under the
> White man's control. Though the white races believe in Christ-
> ianity, they are not believing in true Christianity. Their Christ-
> ianity is only in words. The Sermon on the Mount has never
> been practised by the European nations. As individuals, quite a
> number of people follow in the steps of Jesus Christ, and today
> within a nation we have a Christian culture, but as nations we
> are brutal as wild beasts. The principles of Jesus Christ were not
> those of individualism. The idea of the Kingdom of Heaven and
> its realization is as much a social gospel as communism or
> socialism.[26]

At the same time, however, he was often less candid about
the problems within his own nation. He downplayed some of
Japan's serious problems and presented an overly benign picture of its attitudes. Chastizing United States senators, he
charged:

> They are still guided by nationalistic ideas and they consider
> that even Japan is agressive today against the United States. But
> Japan is very idealistic today. She has found that the world can
> never find peace while it is armed. . . . Leaders of Japan are
> following the Christian principles to abolish the wars among the
> nations and to uphold the Christian principles of loving-
> kindness between races. While the Japanese leaders and the
> nation have awakened to idealistic principles, the old idealistic
> nation of America has deserted her principles of the Christian
> faith and gone back to nationalistic and trivial instincts, and has
> discriminated between the White and Yellow.[27]

He assured audiences that the militarists were gradually
losing their hold on Japan, pointing to recent reductions in
military expenditures in Japan as proof.[28] His faith in human
intelligence was such that he believed that if people learned
about the Japanese and their struggles, the racism and paranoia
would be reduced. This would in turn relax the tensions which
already had people in both nations talking about the
possibility of war between Japan and the United States. In
effect, Kagawa was performing public relations for Japan with
peace as the ultimate goal. If he could prove that his country

was rationally addressing its problems and was not a threat to peace and commerce, then the Western powers would have no excuse for their belligerence.

The problem with this approach was that in presenting a positive image of Japan, Kagawa had to gloss over many repressive Japanese measures. This was not merely a public relations effort for peace; it came out of his basic optimism. He chose to view improvements in Japan as a sign of evolution toward the democratic society for which he had dedicated his life, and overlooked chauvinism, violence and increasing police control. In that same spirit, he painted an idealized picture of his earthquake relief work for the Western audience:

> In the midst of the great calamity the refugees, with the exception of a comparative few who became frenzied, were self-possessed, and manifested everywhere a beautiful spirit of mutual helpfulness.[29]

That was a serious omission of one of the most shameful episodes in Japan's history, when Tokyo residents went on a rampage, murdering 7000 Koreans living in the city. It was the underside of Japan's own racism that Kagawa ignored while stressing the nobility of the the quake survivers. It may have a connection to the prejudice against the buraku people previously mentioned.

There were other reasons for this gentle treatment of his native land. The spies and censors in Japan itself made him less bold. The very reforms he was promoting would have been jeopardized if he were seen as disloyal to Japan. This was a legitimate fear, as we shall see. Years later, he was jailed because of an article published in a magazine in the United States. Another reason was that Kagawa was still under patriotic influences and not inclined to launder the nation's dirty linen in public. Overall, his presentation of Japan was tinged with his basic optimism and faith. He was losing some of the hard realism he had learned in the slums, where he had frankly admitted that certain types of men were beyond redemption.

Following his return to Japan in July 1925 after the long tour, he was introduced to a new member of the family, daughter Chiyoko who was born on April 23. The Kagawa children would see little of their father in the hectic months ahead. His barnstorming within Japan and his travels abroad over the next 15 years left relatively little time to spend with his own children. Some years he spent but a month of an entire year with the family. He may have preferred being on the road engaged in his great mission to being at home with the family, despite his complaints about being away.

While he loved children in general and expressed this abstract affection through establishment of kindergartens, day care centers and writing children's stories, he tended to be emotionally aloof from his own family. He was reticent in expressing affection to the children. "He made an excuse saying he did not hug his children because he was afraid of transmitting his tuberculosis and trachoma," his daughter Umeko Momii, now a Presbyterian minister in Salinas, California, has confided, "but I felt this was just an excuse."

Yet he carefully cultivated the image of a family man, for he believed strongly in the ordered Christian family life. The famous Axling biography features several photos of the Kagawa family, as do other translations. Axling must have known that this was stretching the point, because he himself had been on the evangelistic circuit with Kagawa, traveling all over Japan at the time the pictures were taken. On another occasion, a film was made showing Kagawa helping his children with their homework. At a 1985 film showing when his daughter Umeko provided the commentaries, she jokingly remarked "A put-up job."

The real family story was that of a workaholic father dedicating most of his time and energy to his career to which he felt called by God. Kagawa was a master publicist who realized it was necessary to project an image to get the kind of attention needed to carry out one's mission, and he artfully developed what we now call charisma. He relished being photographed. One of the finest specimens of this period is the frontispiece in the German translation of *Crossing the Death Line*, (Auflehnung und Opfer), published in 1929. Kagawa is shown sitting at a desk frozen in a pensive pose, his left elbow on the desk and his left hand reflectively holding his chin, every inch the artist.

He continued the humble lifestyle, never once going to a barber in Japan. Haru cut his hair as she had ever since their wedding day. During this period he devised the "Kagawa suit," a low-priced, simple uniform made of black corduroy for the winter and gray cotton for the summer. It became popular with blue-collar youth. It was not until after the war that he began wearing his usual black gabardine suit. He then departed somewhat from the ascetic eating habits of his youth, eating meat and having Japanese breakfasts of rice, miso soup and sometimes eggs, or a continental breakfast of toast, butter and honey. A favorite food of his was white fish served with ground horseradish.

Once back in Japan, Kagawa plunged into his activities with the same intensity as before. During this time he established the large Shikanjima settlement house in Osaka, which had grown out of a small church. Under the direction of Genjiro Yoshida, this settlement expanded to the point where it contained a day care center, pediatrics clinic, prenatal care clinic and visiting nurse service available to over 300 families. Yoshida had converted to Christianity as a teenager, and was attracted to social work after reading Kagawa's *Study of the Psychology of the Poor* and his life of Christ. With Kagawa's assistance, he was able to attend the Auburn Seminary and Columbia University in the United States before starting his ministry and social work in Osaka.

Shikanjima also contained a library, kindergarten, and dental clinic, as well as a Sunday school. The Kindergarten was named Los Angeles Hall in appreciation of its construction being financed by contributions from the California Friends of Jesus group. Kagawa continued to donate his personal funds to these enterprises, and he might have had nothing left for his own household if he hadn't relied on Haru's cautious management. As his daughter observed,

> My father was very good at making money, but he did not know how to save it. My mother was the one who kept the money and tried to distribute it very carefully. When people came from various organizations to visit him, he always asked, "Oh brother, do you have enough money today?"

His public life also resumed after the return to Japan. He displeased the authorities when he signed an international "Anti-Conscription Manifesto." The declaration was considered an affront to Japan's militarists, because universal conscription was at the heart of their strategy. Among the other famous signers of this document were Martin Buber, Miguel de Unamuno, Albert Einstein, Gandhi, Bertrand Russell, Rabindranath Tagore and H. G. Wells.

Kagawa continued the attempt to forge a new political party which would bring together all the elements of the working class in Japan, including the Communists, although he was becoming increasingly critical of them. Still opposed to the Communist advocacy of using violent means to change society, he was also fearful of the highly centralized, dictatorial situation developing in the Soviet Union. Most important, he thought that Marxism ignored the necessity to develop the inner life of people, because its primary concern was understanding man as an economic creature. The Communist hostility to religion presented a limitation in Marxist thought. On the other hand, he fully expected Christians to offer a superior and more humane alternative to Marxism by living up to the demands of the Gospel.

He often remarked that Japanese workers could not be condemned for embracing Marxism when neither the state nor the church promised a better solution to their immediate problems:

> Our love of men, then, must be a love which embraces their life itself. Our appreciation of the positive contribution (omitting the negative side) of Marx and Proudhon, too, must be for the sake of life. In order to discover new life in humanity, we must revolutionize the universe and create it afresh.[30]

The whole point of social movements was that they set the stage for the transformation of the individual, where the creativity in every person could be unleashed. He continued to emphasize his view that the Gospel was a call to life—and life abundant:

> The transformation of the environment, or social revolution, is really no more than the first premise to the creation of the human soul; but Marx, by emphasizing the premise unduly, forgets the souls of men. O Marxists, cease placing emphasis on the premise, and attack the heart of the matter! Then, at the center of your environment, you will discover your recreated souls.[31]

Though he dedicated himself to the creation of a more just economic system, he argued that this was only the beginning of the redemption of the world. A few years before this 1924 publication he had written, "Even if a socialist world comes into being in our society, Utopia will not be realized. A mere guaranty of bread cannot allow us to consider that the work has been perfected."[32]

Disastrous developments in the labor movement began to threaten his dream of a unified front. The Japan Labor Federation in 1925 split into two factions, one remaining Social Democratic and the other Communist. The leadership of the Federation announced on May 16 the expulsion of all Communist individuals and organizations, accusing them of of subversion and collaboration with the Soviet Comintern. Within a few weeks, the expelled members formed their own new union, the Hyogikai.

Despite his deep disagreements with Communist strategy and his critique of Marxism's lack of a religious center, Kagawa deplored this fragmentation. It needlessly divided the working classes against themselves at the very time when they required a political party of their own to take full advantage of the newly-won right to vote. After the fateful split, he and the National Farmers Union invited both warring union factions to a conference to establish a united socialist party. Included in this organizing effort also were the *Suiheisha* (the Levellers Society for the Buraku) and the *Seiji Kenkyukai*, (Society for the Study of Politics), a group of leftist intellectuals for whom Kagawa had made the opening speech at their June 1924 inauguration.[33] He and Motojiro Sugiyama were convinced that a prerequisite for a strong party was unity both between the unionized urban and rural workers and within labor organizations themselves. Without such unity the political power of the struggling workers and peasants would be hopelessly dissipated.

The Japan Labor Federation (JLF) immediately protested, taking a hard line against the presence of the Communist Hyogikai and the Kenkyukai. The Hyogikai reacted with the countercharge that the the JLF was undermining the whole purpose of the meeting to form a united front. The two unions were never reconciled, and withdrew from the efforts to organize a political party. Kagawa and the farmers' union forged on anyway, and created the *Nomin Rodoto*, the Farmer Labor Party, on December 1, 1925, in the spirit of the original intent to unify the urban and rural Japanese. The government, which had already denied it permission to name delegates to the ILO conference, acted quickly. Within a few hours of its official formation, the Home Ministry banned Kagawa's proud new party on the grounds that it was too radical.[34]

The undaunted Kagawa and union leaders decided to try again, without the Communist, burakumin or intellectual groups. A new party was formed on March 5, 1926, with the names switched around to *Rodo Nominto* (Labor Farmer Party). Sugiyama was elected chair, Juso Miwa general secretary, and Kagawa, Isoo Abe, Iwasaburo Takano, Bunji Suzuki and other more moderate leaders were named to the central committee. Possibly because of the more moderate makeup of the group, the government this time took no repressive action.[35]

Kagawa and Sugiyama wanted the new party to have the broadest base possible by admitting all proletarian organizations, regardless of their affiliation. They attempted a backdoor maneuver, proposing to reinvite the Communists, burakumin and others to participate, with the stipulation that its members could join as individuals and not as official representatives of their organizations. The internal bickering continued through most of 1926, with the Japan Labor Federation persisting in its opposition to their inclusion.

Kagawa continued to argue for accepting the petitions of the radicals for admittance. The angered JLF leaders accused Sugiyama and Kagawa of having fallen under Communist influence. The Federation withdrew its support from the Labor Farmer Party in October and formed its own new party, the *Shakai Minshuto* (Social Democrat Party).[36] This party was soon beset by a factionalism that spun off more than 20 proletarian parties in the 15 years before World War II. The left was never able to form a cohesive force to combat the militaristic and nationalistic elements in the government and the ruling parties.[37]

The farmers' union was also bitterly divided between Communist and anti-Communist factions. Kagawa became increasingly opposed to what he perceived as a hostile takeover by advocates of violence. In turn, the Communists accused Kagawa and his faction of impotence and reactionary tendencies, much as they had earlier in the urban labor movement. These developments were heartbreaking for Kagawa the reconciler, who realized that the workers' movements had far too much in common to continue bickering and dissipate their strength.

Little wonder, then, that evangelism with a strong Socialist touch now seemed to offer more promise than his union or political activity. Kagawa expressed this in December, 1926:

> Japan's labor movement has been fragmented by political movements. I am truly disturbed by this. I am going to dedicate myself to the Kingdom of God movement with the time I have after leaving the proletarian movement. I will organize an association of consumers cooperatives for rural villages. I plan to combat capitalism with all my power. The consumers cooperative movement has gradually formed. Therefore, I have decided to publish a monthly journal on cooperatives. I want to put my best into this work.[38]

True to his word, Kagawa, now in the late 1920s, devoted more and more attention to evangelistic efforts and cooperatives. Despite universal suffrage, he was discouraged about a political solution to Japan's problems, and he was reaching the conclusion that his best contribution to Japan's progress lay in changing people's hearts and imbuing them with religious values. He would convert them, not to the Christianity of the established churches which he tended to criticize harshly, but a Christianity based on love and expressing itself in service to others. It would be the type of Christianity already practiced by the Friends of Jesus group.

He had expressed this desire for such a "pure" Christianity in 1922 by writing:

> I am going my own way, which is different from the church of today. The church is strict about insignificant sins and disregards the enormous sins committed by capitalism. When I look at the church in this light, I do not want to take its easy path. I do not want to walk the path of straight-line gospel people. . . . Mission work risking one's own life against capitalism is my path.[39]

A tragic accident pushed him further along this religious path.

Kagawa had acquired a motorcycle with a sidecar in order to save time on his constant travels around Tokyo. On September 9, 1925, his young assistant who was driving the car veered suddenly into a ditch to avoid an oncoming train. Kagawa was thrown from the vehicle. A blow to the base of the spine left him totally paralyzed, and the doctors predicted he would not walk again. During this period of terrifying immobility, Kagawa prayed and resolved that if he recovered he would dedicate himself to the conversion of Japan. It was a serious covenant with God, similar to the vow he made to serve the poor in the slums when he lay near death from pneumonia 15 years earlier. Once again, a miraculous healing occurred which defied the doctors' bleak diagnosis. He recovered just two weeks after the accident.

Immediately he initiated a two-month tour, preaching for 27 consecutive days in January 1926 without a break.[40] He continued at this furious pace until March, when his eye problems became so severe that he had to be hospitalized. He lost all vision in his left eye but resumed his exhausting round against the advice of both his doctors and friends.

He began to tone down his criticism of the organized churches, knowing that he would have to enlist their aid in such a massive campaign. It would be his most strenuous evangelistic effort. Based on study of the Huguenots in France, Kagawa had concluded that if one million Japanese became Christians, it would transform the Japanese society.

He began his crusade with the help of the Friends of Jesus and his traveling companion and his seeing eye, Shiro Kuroda. He would preach in the most obscure towns and villages, spreading his message of the social gospel of Christianity. Those interested in Christianity would sign declaration cards, as in traditional evangelism. At the National Christian Conference in Karuizawa in June 1927, Kagawa proposed that the organized churches join in a massive evangelistic effort. With his typical verve and humor, he urged Rev. Kimura: "Let's reach one million for Christ."

"One million?" the astounded man asked.

"Yes," replied Kagawa. "Twenty-seven million frequent the licensed quarters. Let's reach just one-twenty-seventh of them!

We cannot do it by ourselves alone, but let's all work together to do it!"[41]

Kagawa launched his campaign in 1928 as the Kingdom of God Movement. During the next three years, he estimated that he had preached to more than a million people, of whom 65,000 had signed decision cards. The churches grew by 19,000 a year, and Kagawa felt that with more follow up work, the harvest of souls would have been much greater.[42] Between June 1928 and June 1929, he spoke at a grand total of 635 meetings attended by more than 270,000, among whom he garnered 13,000 converts.[43]

Kagawa's evangelism was not the commercialized spectacle usually seen in contemporary America, but a program to effect the spiritual and social transformation of Japan. He had obeyed the Biblical injunction to go forth and teach, and he saw preaching not as a drain on spiritual resources, but as integral to his faith life. Though he admired Buddha and his contemplative ways, he paid his most affectionate and perhaps suprising tribute to the master's dedication as an evangelist: "It is evident that Buddha was a wonderful priest. He would respond to any invitation to preach."[44]

In order to have a "break" from this exhausting program, Kagawa made evangelistic travels abroad. He was off to China in 1927, 1930 and 1931. He visited the United States, Canada and Siberia in 1931. In February and March of 1934 he was in the Philippines and China. From mid-February to the end of July 1935 he was on the preaching and lecture circuit in Australia and New Zealand.

Kagawa was abroad when the infamous Manchurian Incident took place. This sad triumph of militarism cast a long shadow over Japan's future. Japanese army officers had plotted to provoke war in that territory by exploding a bomb on the Japanese railroad north of Mukden on September 18, 1931, and blaming it on the Chinese. The Japanese army quickly advanced, outside the control of the civil government, until it had taken the whole of Manchuria and set up a puppet government by March 1932. The army then attacked other points on the mainland.

These grim proceedings marked the beginning of the war with China, a conflict that was to merge into World War II, hundreds of thousands of deaths later. Elements in the Japanese military had come to consider themselves above the law, claiming that their judgment was superior to civil authorities and that they had a right to act on that judgment. The government lacked the will and the power to reign them in. To complicate matters, the headlong rush to war took place during the worldwide depression, when military agression provided an outlet for economic frustration. Japan was correctly wary of Western imperialism, but now had embarked on its own course in China that was in every respect as unjust and brutal.

Although Kagawa deplored this Japanese expansion on numerous occasions, he failed to mobilize against it. In 1933, he was called in for questioning at least three times merely because of the anti-militarist poems he had published. The exuberant preacher of the 1920s suffered a depressed sense of fatalism as the military seemed beyond control. To American guests visiting him in August 1933, he promised an apology to China, but he showed such weary resignation that one visitor, Presbyterian minister Clyde H. Roddy concluded, "It is very evident from his heavy heartedness that Japan must suffer for her blindness."[45]

Looking "tired and downcast" while sitting on the floor in his blue suit, Kagawa leaned against the doorframe, yellow matter filming over his left eye, and wearily explained to his guests his limited options: "If I say too much, my helpers will be without me in all this work. If I fly too high," he added, stretching out his arms, "I will have my wings clipped!"

Kagawa sadly but accurately prophesied:

Japan muddling. Losing money. Spending twenty billions in Manchuria and in twenty years China will suck it up—absorb all Japan is now doing. Japan will lose it. In fifteen years Manchuria will be under the Shantung coolies.

Korea is a loss to Japan. The cheap labor of the Koreans has put the Japanese farmer out of commission. Japan's mills are closing. Japan is suffering because Korea has been annexed. The militarists are too stupid to see this. They know nothing about politics or economics. . . . Araki, Minister of War, is trying to play Mussolini. He is representing the military in Japan. . . .[46]

In the end, he forecast: "Europe will build a wall around Japan. In six years, Europe will wage an economic blockade against Japan."[47]

Perhaps his most poignant statement was given in a Sunday sermon on March 11, 1934, when he made good on the pledge to apologize to China. On his way back from the Philippines, he stopped in Shanghai which had suffered fierce Japanese bombing two years earlier. Japanese forces now occupied the city and soldiers were present everywhere, drilling in the municipal park, riding in convoys of armed motorcycles and tanks in the streets, and living in new block-long military barracks. In a room still riddled with bullet holes, Kagawa dined on Saturday night with K. S. Lee and a group of local Chinese Christians, and he met with people whose homes had been destroyed and whose children had been murdered by soldiers of Kagawa's own nation.[48]

Kagawa was asked to address a service the next morning in Rev. Z. K. Zia's Fitch Memorial Church, a fairly new, thousand-seat facility at the hub of Shanghai's Christian activity. Rain was pouring down, but the church was filled despite the fact that the visit had not been widely publicized for fear of disruption. A church elder introduced Kagawa by paraphrasing St. Paul: "We are not men and women, old or young, Japanese or Chinese. We are all one in Christ Jesus."

Kagawa stepped to the pulpit and said:

> Dear brothers and sisters, I have prayed the Lord to let me stand here. If we did not have Christianity, I could not stand here. I personally regret the things we have done as a nation. Because you are Christian and forgive, you let me stand in this pulpit. . . .
>
> Militarists throughout the world do not understand the Holy Spirit. They have the spirit of military aggression, of colonization. When we are invading the territory which belongs to another nation, we are really trespassing against the kingdom of God. We must stand firmly in the Spirit of God. Let us pray that He may be heard in the world, when there will be no war, no militarists, no revolutions.
>
> Because you have already manifested the most ethical, gracious result of His Spirit on this occasion, let us pray the Lord that real Christianity may be established permanently in the Orient. . . .[49]

Privately, Kagawa was paralyzed with pessimism and emotional confusion about how Japan might be freed from the military stranglehold. Publicly, he still spread the Gospel, speaking with more authority in foreign countries than he was permitted in Japan, as the 1930s wore on. His pacifism was complicated by his patriotism. In his popular novel of 1931, *Hitotsubu no mugi* (A Grain of Wheat), the hero dutifully serves in the Japanese army. The novel, which was later made into a film, also expresses a hostile attitude toward the Communists which could only excuse official persecution of them. His drift toward the political center led one observer, John Gunther, to remark, "For a time, authorities regarded him a dangerous radical, but his work organizing relief after the 1923 earthquake made him respectable."[50]

Nevertheless, people in the United States saw Kagawa as a radical because of his emphasis on the social gospel and his support of the cooperative movement. Despite ambiguities about his behavior at home, he would preach an uncompromising message of activist Christianity and cooperation to millions across the ocean.

Chapter 8
The Cooperator's Message to America

O F ALL THE PROJECTS INTO WHICH Kagawa poured both income and energy, the one which has made the most visible impact on Japan is the cooperative movement, both consumer and farmer. The Japanese Consumers Cooperative Union (JCCU), which he founded in 1951, coordinates the activities of 660 different cooperatives in food, consumer goods, insurance, medical care, housing, international trade and other enterprises. These cooperatives have 10 million members, employ about 70,000 and generate a total patronage of $11 billion. The most successful of these has been the Nada-Kobe Co-op, which began as two small retail cooperatives, one of which Kagawa was instrumental in founding in 1921. With annual sales of $1.6 billion, Nada-Kobe is presently considered the preeminent retail cooperative in the democratic world.

The growth of consumer cooperatives in Japan has been explosive. Since 1972 the number of members increased from 3.6 million to over 10 million. Sales increased by a factor of 35 in the past 20 years—an impressive record, even taking inflation into account. Cooperative wholesaling operations distribute more than 2000 products and their plants produce tofu and various other soy products, noodles, baked goods and other consumer edibles.[1] This rapid growth has taken place despite a hobbling Japanese law that restricts cooperatives within the borders of the prefecture where they are headquartered, except for those whose membership consists of nationwide occupational groups like teachers.

Statistics, however, merely begin to tell the story. Cooperatives are a force in both the Japanese consumer and peace movements in Japan. They have lobbied for stricter health regulations, opposed price increases on important consumer staples, and campaigned vigorously against environmental pollution. They have objected to reductions in welfare spending and fought tax increases onerous to low income consumers. The larger cooperatives operate their own testing laboratories in which they have pioneered the development of food items with fewer additives and other products that are environmentally sound, such as non-polluting detergents.

Significantly, too, the cooperative movement has been concerned with issues that extend beyond its basic role to deliver goods and services efficiently. One reason for this broader involvement in social responsiblity was the powerful influence of Kagawa, or what the long time JCCU President Sadao Nakabayashi termed the "Kagawa spirit." It is exemplified in the slogan of the JCCU, *Heiwa to yori yoi seikatsu no tameni* (For Peace and a Better Life). From the grassroots to the national level, the cooperatives have contributed to the peace movement through education, promotion of peace activities, and participation at the World Conference against Atomic and Hydrogen Bombs.

In 1982, Nakabayashi headed the 1400 Japanese delegates to the 2nd United Nations Special Session on Disarmaments held in New York, where they presented a petition for nuclear disarmament signed by 30 million Japanese. Within this delegation the cooperative members numbered 200, and the co-ops obtained 3.8 million of the signatures. Nakabayashi declared, "Kagawa's greatest contribution to our cooperative movement was his leadership in the peace movement. He insisted that the maintenance of peace was the highest ideal of the co-op movement."[2]

To those who see cooperatives as purely economic and business institutions, such activity might not appear relevant, perhaps even distracting from their main business functions, but Kagawa's vision of cooperatives was all-encompassing. He believed, and fervently preached, that cooperative development was not only a major element in economic reforms but the key to world peace. Because they give democratic control to members and return their "profits" ("savings" in co-op terminology) to members rather than concentrating them in the hands of a few business owners, cooperatives become an instrument of economic reform. In short, Kagawa regarded co-ops as instrumental in battling poverty in Japan and humanizing the economy. In the longer term, he hoped the world economy could be converted to a cooperative basis.

From his earliest years, he was convinced that war was caused by economic imbalances and by intense economic competition among nations for markets, raw materials and, above all, profits. What was needed, Kagawa tirelessly argued, was a system which replaced the profit motive with the service motive. Because consumer cooperatives are mutual aid businesses whose principal aim is providing goods and services to all their members, rather than piling up profits at their expense for a few entrepreneurs or investors, he saw co-ops as the ideal vehicle for this change in motive.

Kagawa wanted the movement to be imbued with the religious values of unselfish behavior and concern for others, if it were to effect the transformation of society. Nakabayashi once wrote:

> As a Christian with high principles, Kagawa always taught us a personalistic way of life in connection with the co-op movement. When he attended meetings of the Japan Cooperative Federation he refused the offer of a taxi and always took the street car home. He stubbornly practiced this even after his physical condition deteriorated.[3]

Many Japanese probably are unaware that Kagawa also had a profound impact on the consumers cooperative movement in the United States, where he inspired thousands to develop, support and make careers in cooperatives. Wallace Campbell, the United Nations representative of the International Cooperative Alliance and former president of CARE (Cooperative for American Remittances Everywhere), while on The Cooperative League of the USA staff, became acquainted with Kagawa. Campbell expressed the feeling of hundreds of American co-op leaders from the 30s:

> I was greatly impressed with Kagawa and feel that a great deal of the leadership that grew up in the cooperative movement in 1936 and in the years that followed came from his tour, because he stimulated the interest and provided the motivation and objectives that led many of these people to pursue leadership roles in the cooperative movement.[4]

Kagawa's relation with cooperatives in the United States

helped create a healthy international cross-fertilization, through his extended lecture tours in this country and his writings. While many American cooperators were inspired by Kagawa, the Japanese cooperative movement in turn has benefited from the visits of more than 2000 of their staff people to American co-ops and business enterprises since the 50s to observe and study the latter's facilities, merchandising techniques and distribution system.

Ties between the two cooperative movements were further strengthened by the actions of organizations like the Consumers Cooperative of Berkeley (CCB), whose supermarket operations peaked at an annual volume of $83 million and membership of 100,000 families in 1980, and its regional wholesaler Associated Cooperatives (AC). That historical background began at the outset of World War II in 1942 when the United States government engineered the massive evacuation of 120,000 citizens and aliens of Japanese ancestry on the Pacific Coast, sequestering them inland in tar-papered barracks of what were euphemistically called "relocation centers" but which were, nonetheless, concentration camps.

This internment has been exposed recently in Congressional hearings and the federal courts, from government documents obtained under the Freedom of Infomation Act, as the calculated result of the same kind of racial prejudices that Kagawa condemned. Although government and military officials knew that no act of espionage or sabotage had been committed by any of these residents, their removal was justified on the pretext that they constituted a threat to national security. These internees lived behind barbed wires for the duration of the war, except for those who were able to find employment in the Midwest and East (some with co-ops), enter colleges, or serve in the armed forces. The heroic all-Nisei 442nd Regiment merged with the Hawaiian all-Nisei 100th Infantry and became the most decorated American unit of the war, while many of their families still languished in the camps.

The War Relocation Authority, which had been established to administer the camps, sought to ameliorate some of the harsh conditions. One of its acts was to permit the internees to set up cooperative "canteens" to provide dry goods, personal items, and many services for the internees. Larry Collins, the first buyer-manager for the University of California Students Cooperative Association and later president of AC, was employed to direct this program. Associated Cooperatives itself assisted by servicing some of these canteens. When the war ended, the evacuees returned in many instances to the same kind of racial prejudices that had caused their evacuation. Both CCB and AC were foremost in the San Francisco Bay Area in countering such discrimination by hiring Japanese Americans along with others of ethnic minority background.

Members of this Berkeley cooperative in particular had been directly influenced by Kagawa's writings and his lectures to church and academic groups in the 1930s. These actions created the ties between cooperatives in the two nations and led to a sister co-op relationship between the Consumers Cooperative of Berkeley and Kagawa's own Nada-Kobe Consumer Cooperative Society in 1965. Prior to that a personal letter from Kagawa in 1959 culminated in two young JCCU employees Shigeru Fukuda and Masao Ohya, now two of their top executives, spending six months in California on the staffs of the Berkeley and Palo Alto co-ops. Years later in 1982, in one of those gestures of international harmony that would have delighted Kagawa, the Japanese co-ops' peace delegation, on their return home from delivering their plea for nuclear disarmament to the United Nations, stopped overnight at the Berkeley and Palo Alto co-ops, broke bread with them, and jointly pledged to work for world peace.

Kagawa's own knowledge of cooperatives dated back at least to 1905, as mentioned earlier, when he read *The Story of Co-ops* by Sanshiro Ishikawa. Over the next decade, this knowledge broadened considerably. He familiariarized himself with the work of the British social reformers who advocated cooperatives throughout the economic system, especially the guild socialists. He was impressed by the humble beginnings of the cooperative movement in England, where in 1844 a small group of striking weavers and social and religious reformers opened their tiny retail store on Rochdale's Toad Lane, near Manchester. By 1920, the British cooperatives had attracted 4.8 million members whose patronage exceeded £250 million.

To a man who had passionately argued for the dignity of each individual, the democratic structure of the cooperatives was compelling. The policy of one member, one vote, meant that individuals in the co-op were equal in their power to determine policy, regardless of their wealth or the number of shares owned. The poorest member had an equal voice with the richest. Among the other innovations of the Rochdale pioneers was the idea that earnings be returned to members, based on a percentage of the amount they had purchased. No individual could amass "profits" from the co-op, because it distributed them among the people who owned it and used it. Profits were transformed into savings.

This type of business corresponded to Kagawa's dreams for a reform of Japanese society that would empower the individual and distribute the wealth of society among the masses. He considered open membership and democratic control of business as the extension of the rights of universal suffrage for which he had crusaded. The democratic control of the factories had been a major demand in the long, hard strike in Kobe. Worker cooperatives provided democratic control, instruments to "humanize labor." Nobody was the boss and nobody could corner the profits. Cooperatives were businesses of, by and for the working people. They were the have-nots whom Kagawa hoped would become major factors in commerce and industry and thereby effect a non-violent evolution to a democratic cooperative society. This is why he repeatedly emphasized cooperatives as the "middle way" between unfettered capitalism and violent revolution.

The advocacy of cooperatives as the middle way was deadly serious business for Kagawa. Although he criticized capitalism for the suffering it imposed on humanity and for the wars it created, he also publicly attacked Marxists who argued for violent revolution and emphasized class struggle. Regardless of his acceptance of parts of the Marxist diagnosis of the economy, he could not approve what he felt was a dehumanized approach viewing the individual as merely an economic entity and mechanical cog in the machinery of the state. Regardless of his recognition that capitalism had been a liberating force from feudal society, he likewise could not condone its ruthless exploitation of human beings and the spiritual emptiness of a system shot through with greed and cut throat competition. Sometimes he put the choices in almost apocalyptic terms. At a gathering of the Kagawa Fellowship members in their annual retreat at Karuizawa in November 1934, he said,

> The world today is weighing in judgment two economic systems, capitalism and communism. There are many good features of capitalism which should be recognized as having made contributions to modern life, among them the principle of free trade, the historic destruction of serfdom, and emphasis upon individual freedom. Capitalism has, however, produced evils which now threaten to overbalance all the advantages derived therefrom, and seeking to supplant it there appears the doctrine of communism based chiefly on the principles of revolution, materialism and the rationing of goods.
>
> Communism, too, has many good features, chief among which is a more equitable, presumably classless distribution of material goods among all workers contributing to production. The evils of communism are principally those involved in the abandonment of the practices of free exchange, and in the loss of freedom in religion and ethics, especially the repudiation of non-violent morality. For communism, it develops in practice, is fully as dependent upon force for achieving its goals as is capitalism in preserving its privileges.[5]

In the same speech, so typical of his statements on cooperatives, he continued:

> We need a state or social order in which no exploitation is possible, no accumulation of capital or privilege, no class strife. If no exploitation, then no proletariat; if no accumulation of capital, then no unfair distribution of wealth and privilege, and therefore no class war or other conflict. Now how can we get this kind of state? Only by the cooperative movement, which is Christianity in action socially and economically.

If cooperatives appealed to Kagawa the guild socialist, they also corresponded to his religious beliefs, not that there was a strict difference between the two, since he considered guild socialism as Christianity in action. As a man who risked his life to put Christian theory into practice, cooperatives were similarly for him the Gospel in action. They provided a concrete system to carry out the Gospel's demand to feed the poor, shelter the homeless and cure the sick. Their ethic of mutual aid was a literal expression of the Gospel command to "love one another." Among the Japanese Christians and their missionary friends there was incessant talk and theorizing about the "Kingdom of God," but Kagawa constantly pointed out that all too little was being done to build the Kingdom. Heaven, whatever it was, certainly did not include in its domain the slums, rural poverty, ultranationalism and wars of modern Japan.

Over and over, in his writings and in his incessant tours through Japan, and in his actual efforts to organize co-op businesses, Kagawa emphasized that the cooperative movement was the way to bring these ideas into social reality. At the height of his popularity in the West he exhausted himself in preaching the Gospel of cooperation to hundreds of audiences as he toured the United States, Asia and some of the European nations. He brought the discussion down to the concrete level of daily life where Christian values were put into practice. Talk about love meant nothing to him unless it translated into life. Cooperatives were the unique fit of ideals and action, because mutual aid, economic democracy and social equality were structured into the business.

From 1927 until 1940, in addition to those marathon lecture tours which awed his followers and exhausted his co-workers, he published a dozen books and numerous articles on cooperatives, ranging from discussions of the philosophy of cooperation to analyses of the particular models of cooperatives he organized or inspired, including consumers, medical care, health insurance and fishery co-ops.

Yet we should be careful not to exaggerate Kagawa's role in the cooperative movement in Japan nor to regard him as the Messianic leader of cooperation. Cooperative-style enterprises had their origin in the 14th century. In fact, when Kagawa promoted co-ops in Japan, he freely acknowledged that he was drawing on cultural traditions which already stressed a high degree of cooperation and mutual aid. He saw this as a perfect argument for their further development. Japan had been a nation of thousands of small agricultural villages where cooperation in its generic sense was essential for survival. The cultivation of rice, with its communal irrigation systems, demanded a high degree of collaboration in order to function. Repeated earthquakes and other natural disaster in Japan also had a way of bringing villages together in cooperation to dig their way out.

The earliest form of cooperative enterprise, dating all the way back to the 14th century, was a type of credit organization known as *koh*. The koh consisted of a group who would simply pool their savings and make loans available from the pool. Loans were repaid by a series of deposits back into the fund. "Interest" was the basis of a bidding system, where the loan was assigned to the person who offered to repay the highest amount of additional money beyond the original loan. Not permanent financial organizations in the modern sense, the koh more often addressed a specific set of credit problems, and was usually dissolved when all the money had been repaid. It would also collapse completely in the event of defaults, because there were no other types of financial activity on which to fall back.[6]

A more modern form of credit union, *Hōtoku sha*, was developed by the agrarian reformer Sontoku Ninomiya in 1843, about the time the Rochdale pioneers were organizing their cooperative retail shop. To obtain loan capital, members were required to save a specified sum of money in proportion to their income. Those successful in the enterprises created from the money they borrowed reinvested part of their new profits in the organization, as an expression of "thanks for the favor." That is what the word hōtoku means. This approach taught the values of mutual aid and interdependence which are at the heart of the cooperative philosophy. By the end of the 19th century, these societies existed in more than 900 villages in Japan.[7]

In addition, tea and silk marketing cooperatives were formed in the 1870s, along with cooperatives for fertilizer purchase and credit. The need for cooperative action was especially important because of the small size of the Japanese farms. Individual farmers on two or three acres benefited when they could band together to sell their products.

Contact with the West introduced the Japanese to a wide variety of other cooperative enterprises which were developing in Europe. The Japanese quickly adopted the techniques of the

Schultze-Delitzch credit cooperatives and the Raiffeisen agricultural cooperatives. Although cooperatives have faced opposition from government in many nations, those in Japan had the blessing of officials like Home Minister Yajiro Shinagawa and Count Tosuke Hirata. As early as 1891 these men proposed legislation to establish credit cooperatives. When this legislation was defeated, they still continued to write and lecture on cooperatives, so that by 1898 there were 346 co-ops with a membership of more than 63,000 and capital of ¥968,000.

A law providing a framework for cooperatives was finally passed in 1900. The passage of this law and the establishment of the Central Union of Cooperative Societies in 1905 accelerated the growth of credit cooperatives. Conspicuously absent was a legalized form of producers' cooperatives. This would have been a concession to the labor movement, which the government feared and repressed.

By 1930, there were over 14,000 cooperatives in Japan, with a membership of 4.8 million and a total investment of ¥307 million. The vast majority of these were credit cooperatives. Only 151 consumers cooperatives with a membership of 212,100 had been formed. The government proposed a "Five Year Plan" for cooperatives to encourage rapid new growth in the rural areas. Kagawa often pointed out, with some satisfaction, that the government itself had recognized that the most efficient way to alleviate rural poverty was to build cooperatives. This he had been urging all along.

In a way the government was using cooperative development as a means of quelling rural discontent and blunting the militancy of the impoverished peasants. That created some painful ambivalence in Kagawa's attitude toward cooperatives. He was deeply concerned that they not be preoccupied with economic or material matters, and he could be sharply critical of those which were. He was convinced that a cooperative dedicated solely to business would lose the larger vision concerned with peace, justice, and general moral and religious principles. He argued that if the cooperatives remained parochial in their outlook and looked only to satisfy material needs, they could not achieve social reconstruction. Since Kagawa was never comfortable with the Japanese government, he was dissatisfied with a cooperative movement which existed primarily as an arm of governmental economic policy.

A cooperative without spirit was not the powerful alternative he sought to either capitalism or Marxism. In the end, its members might become as acquisitive and self-centered as anyone else. This quest for a religious and philosophical impulse and his impatience with people's lack of conviction provoked him on occasions into occasional harsh assessments of the Japanese cooperatives. He told a reporter early in 1930, "The cooperative movement in Japan is useless because its leaders are absolutely useless. The Danish people are teaching us a great deal. Spirit is at the center of the cooperatives when they are really successful."[8]

Ultimately, Kagawa taught, the local cooperative should set an example for global cooperation with an entirely different approach to international relations. Since economic conflicts were at the root of war, endless discussions solely about armaments control could not bring a lasting resolution to international conflicts. After outlining an ideal cooperative system within a nation, he proposed at a 1934 Kagawa Fellowship meeting:

> This same principle of cooperation should be applied to international trade. We must have international cooperatives! . . . If representatives of the nations can spend endless time and money discussing questions of armaments, why can they not meet to solve international questions of production, marketing and consumption?[9]

He envisioned cooperatives as "an international network of mutually dependent yet locally independent and socially conditioned economic cells, without exploitation, without competition, without panic, without unemployment, without poverty, and without either class strife or international conflict."

These were the major elements in Kagawa's cooperative theory. Yet as with his Biblical readings, he could not refrain from putting them into practice. Kagawa had started his first practical experiments with co-ops very early in his career by organizing the cooperative restaurant and the toothbrush factory. The consumers cooperative store he founded in Osaka in 1920 failed in a few years after having lost ¥23,000. This failure did not discourage him. He looked at it as a learning experience, one which made him more attentive to the practical side of cooperative management. The cooperative ideals were splendid, but the business had to be managed as well as any private enterprise if it hoped to survive. To this end he set up a school for cooperative managers to help insure competent administration.

Kagawa didn't found co-ops singlehandedly, for the simple reason that a cooperative is never the result of one individual's work. What he did was provide inspiration, help to find capital, and recruit people to do the organizing. Besides generously pouring his own funds into the co-ops, he was never afraid to ask those who could afford it to do the same. This boldness sometimes combined with good luck to raise substantial capital, as in the instance when the wealthy businessman Sumiyoshi visited Kagawa after reading *Crossing the Death Line*. Inspired by the hero of the novel, Sumiyoshi wanted to do some kind of social work after he retired. Kagawa suggested to him that the best social work he could do was to help to start a cooperative. That resulted in the organizing of the Kobe Co-op in April 1921.

Through his work with Sugiyama and others in the Japan Farmers' Union, Kagawa was directly involved in the creation of rural marketing and supply co-ops. Working with Daikichiro Tagawa in 1928, he formed the Nakanogo Credit Union in the poor district of Honjo in Tokyo, where he had previously done earthquake relief. It soon grew to a membership of 2500 and deposits of ¥238,000. Another cooperative project he started at the time was a pawnshop charging low rates. A pawn shop may sound like a strange cooperative enterprise, but for those who lived in poverty, getting cash from the pawn shop was sometimes the only way to feed a family. Five other pawn shops were set up after the initial one.[10]

The delivery of decent health care to the Japanese people was a deep concern to Kagawa. He had provided medical help to the poor in the Shinkawa slums; now he set up clinics in Kobe and Tokyo. He had experienced enormous pain from ill health himself, contracting various diseases, and more than once he had wept publicly at the sight of someone suffering from severe illness. A poignant part of the Kagawa mystique was his willingness to sacrifice his own health to care for others. His damaged, sometimes bandaged eyes were the direct result of his physical contact with people suffering from trachoma. This was not a man who merely talked about charity, but one who bore the scars and paid a heavy price for his love.

Medicine was such an important topic in the Kagawa household that he convinced his son Sumimoto and daugher Chiyoko to study medicine. Dr. Chiyoko (Kagawa) Tomizawa today manages a cooperative hospital in Japan. Kagawa's research into health problems scored the urgency he felt to improve health care. He believed that cooperatives could help provide some of this badly needed care, both in the cities and in the rural areas, where the shortage of doctors was even more severe.

Kagawa collaborated with Dr. Inazo Nitobe and Dr. Fusajiro Kato, as well as Michio Kozaki, a member of the Tokyo city council, and others, in applying for permission to establish the Tokyo Medical Utility Cooperative. The group was strongly opposed by the national medical association. The physicians' group felt threatened by medical cooperatives, fearing stiff competition from enterprises which placed service ahead of profit. A national controversy raged on the subject, and the co-op's permission to open was delayed for an entire year. The hospital was finally set up in a converted hotel in the Shinjuku district. The rapid growth in membership under the management of S. Yamanouchi led two years later to the construction of a new building in the Nakano district. Kagawa could proudly report by 1935 that his Tokyo cooperative had 5600 members who had purchased 7000 shares at ¥10 each. The hospital had 51 beds, and about 170 patients were treated daily by a staff of 9 doctors and 16 nurses.[11] A new wing was added in 1936 as the membership rose to 8600.[12]

Around the same time, another medical cooperative was begun in Akita City in January, 1932, soon attracting 6000 members. By 1935 it had doubled to 12,000, one-fourth of the population of the city, and succeeded in rebuilding its facilities.[13] With characteristic enthusiasm, Kagawa traced these and previous developments in his book about medical co-ops, writing with fire imagery, mentioning the "beacon fire" of one earlier medical cooperative. He proclaimed,

The medical cooperative movement, stimulated by these good results spread simultaneously to every part of Akita Prefecture. The sparks which had been smouldering here and there were changed, in a twinkle, into a wild fire by this blast of north wind which arose in Akita, and today they are spreading over the whole country.[14]

The prospectus for the Tokyo Medical Cooperative is a classic Kagawa plea for justice, alternately condemning the profit health care system and looking forward to his dream of cooperative health care permeating the society:

In present day society, when everything, even the medical art, is carried on under the profit system, the result has been that those who could not bear the expense of medical treatment have been placed in a condition of finding it difficult to find medical security.

Of course, in the face of such a social defect, charity hospitals as a form of social work for the very poor, were brought into existence. Also, for factory laborers and miners there was enacted the health insurance law. But still the greater part of the population, which is not included in these plans, is troubled by the necessity of meeting high medical expenses. The Union Cooperative Hospital which is here planned will provide a new economic organization in the original spirit of medicine as a benevolent art, instead of the present medical system. . . .[15]

Opposition from the medical association actually strengthened the resolve of the medical co-op group, hastening the development of new medical co-ops to the point where 150 of them were formed by 1935. In discussing these cooperative hospital ventures, Kagawa offered practical advice based on what had been learned in the movement, such as the minimum size necessary to insure success, the type of medical services and technology required, and the territory which had to be covered. He gathered the necessary data through the labors of his own research staff.

Food was another of the basic needs cooperatives could fulfill, and Kagawa's later attempts to set up low cost public eating places were considerably more successful than the first disastrous effort in Kobe. In the 1930s his Nutritious Foods Distributing Co-op in Tokyo's Honjo district was serving 6000 meals per day at the low price of 28 sen (14 cents) two months after opening. In 1937 a second kitchen with a capacity of 10,000 meals a day was opened, using modern equipment and taking advantage of the services of a dietician from the municipal government. Kagawa also helped to establish a cooperative store nearby, which soon signed up 1800 members and paid patronage refunds of 2%. It joined with the Nutritious Foods group to build a summer seaside retreat with accommodations for 50 members.

A down-to-earth aspect of these cooperative efforts added a charming touch to Kagawa's serious work. Near his home in Matsuzawa he and an agricultural specialist Fujisaki started a chicken-raising cooperative to help local farmers. The farmers were unbelievably outdated in their methods, according to Fujisaki, who said:

> The church was in a bad quarrel so we could not make an approach to the community through the church as an institution, that is, through the regular evangelistic channels. So we started with a poultry cooperative society. We started with four eggs. People were laughing at us. Now it is our turn to laugh for it has been a great success. Out of 70 families in the neighborhood, 57 are members of the cooperative. It has an annual budget of over ¥1000.[16]

Fujisaki also conducted a night school for the local residents in which he taught regular subjects and the Bible, while a sewing co-op was organized under his wife's guidance. Other enterprises like a credit co-op later developed from these efforts.

Talking on a rainy afternoon in his little office, Kagawa announced his discovery of an unique new way to feed his chickens with the nuts of the *kunugi*, the silk-worm oak. He had gotten the idea from reading a book on the topic of nut trees, and starting a study to find out how to make use of them as part of his program of "vertical agriculture," which he preached as an effective way for the Japanese to increase their food supply by taking better advantage of tree crops on mountain slopes. He launched into an enthusiastic recitation of the possibilities of a reformed agriculture:

> If we can discover the means of enriching the villages in the mountains which occupy 85% of the land of Japan, the country can easily support another 100,000,000 of population. . . .

But it will do no good for the villages simply to be rich. Some spiritual content must be infused into the village life. This will be the work of the cooperative unions. It cannot be done by the individualistic way of thinking of the past. Neither is the family principle sufficient. The family consciousness, which thinks only of improving one's own family, must be awakened into a village consciousness. Then this village consciousness must be broadened into a national consciousness. In this way, if one desired to develop a cooperative, he would be doing it for the whole village. That is to say, unless an all-inclusive movement of rural folks arises, in which each will sacrifice himself for the village by putting forth his very best in the way of knowledge and power for the whole village, it will be impossible to revive the villages of Japan.[17]

It was this creative combination of the concrete and the visionary, the attention to everyday details and the global picture, and a mind darting about on every conceivable topic that would dazzle those who met Kagawa. His gentleness, humor and self-irony added to the already intriguing picture of the man who had carried a cross of self-sacrifice and heroically faced the horror of life in the slums. His resolute living of the simple life, when he could have enjoyed many luxuries, was a continuing testament to his religious values. He enhanced his reputation by downplaying his sacrifice through humble behavior, a saintly virtue. He gave the impression of being infinitely more excited about his projects or about social problems than about himself.

An aura of sanctity surrounded him with the perception that in addition to being engaged in his multitudinous works, he was a contemplative in touch with the divine through his prayer and meditation. The sheer success of his cooperatives, schools, social work, clinics and settlement houses was itself proof of his power. The time had seemingly arrived for him to extend beyond his native land the preaching of the Gospel of cooperation and the financing of his endeavors to put the Gospel in action. He was ready to visit the United States; in fact, he took it by storm.

His fame in the West had reached new heights, elevated by the popular and worshipful biography by the missionary William Axling and articles in the religious and secular press. Beginning in 1924, when *Crossing the Death Line* was published, his reputation was further boosted by the generally favorable, sometimes cloyingly reverent reviews of his newly-translated books. Supported by the Kagawa Fellowship and the Friends of Jesus in the United States, he planned his third and most celebrated world tour in 1936. Helen Topping, who as missionary, translator and "Boswell" made the advance arrangements, had so many requests for speaking engagements that she could have booked Kagawa for five years.[18]

The preparations were carefully planned. Regional directors set up hundreds of speaking engagements and secured media coverage. Religious magazines, especially the liberal *Christian Century*, had the presses rolling ahead of time to announce the intinerary and cover the lectures. Kagawa's admirers in churches, universities and cooperatives did commendable work preparing the way. The Revs. J. Henry Carpenter and James Myers of the Federal Council of Churches and E. R. Bowen, general secretary of The Cooperative League of the USA and long-time member of the American Friends Service committee, coordinated the tour, jointly sponsored by the Federal Council and The Co-op League.

The list of co-op leaders involved in the arrangements or attending the lectures included many who now are in the Hall of Fame of American cooperatives. Besides the earlier mentioned Wallace Campbell, there were: Murray Lincoln, then the head of the Ohio Farm Bureau (predecessor of Landmark, Inc., and Nationwide Insurance Company) and later president of the Co-op League; E. G. Cort, general manager of Midland Cooperatives in Minneapolis; Harvey Hull, general manager of the Indiana Farm Bureau Cooperative; Howard Cowden, general manager of Consumers Cooperative Association (now known as Farmland Industries), Kansas City, one of the largest farm co-ops in the United States; and Robert Neptune, who became general manager of Associated Cooperatives, the nation's largest consumers co-op grocery wholesaler. Also inspired by Kagawa were co-op writers, educators and administrators, among them Art Danforth, Jack McLanahan, Walker Sandbach and Emil Sekerak, to mention a few.

If these young activists were inspired by Kagawa, there were others who had the opposite reaction. Conservatives warned of his arrival and expressed dire doubts about the cooperative movement he was promoting. Even before Kagawa landed in San Francisco on December 19, 1935, he was greeted with both extravagant praise and blame.

On the one hand, an advertisement for his most recently translated book, *Meditations on the Cross*, slightly ahead of time proclaimed:

> Rousing America and Canada like some new Peter the Hermit preaching a crusade for the capture of the City of God, Kagawa will be the most discussed Christian leader in the world during the next six months. Everywhere men will be asking, "What is the secret of this man's power? What has driven him to his apostleship in Japan's slums? What has made him the champion of a Gospel for the Lowly? What has he to preach that makes his coming an event everywhere in East and West?"[19]

The famed poet Edwin Markham composed the following Messianic sonnet:

> I hail you, Kagawa, son of the One on high,
>   Great social dreamer, rebel against wrong.
>   Whenever I see your name I rise to song:
> You are the leader sent from the watching sky,
> Greater than Gandhi, greater than Hu Shih.
>   Proclaim the Brother-World, for in your voice
>   Is strength to endure and strength to make the choice.
> In your strong cry we hear the Father-cry.
> You build the hope of nations, and we sing:
>   You see the Hero of the Cross supreme
>   Above this chaos as the world's one dream.
> Hold firm, great comrade, cry one crowing thing:
>   "God and the People!" For these words we wait:
>   This is our blazon, our apostolate.[20]

On the other side, the advertising magazine *Tide* saw him in an entirely different, less favorable light. Especially concerned about the growing "menace" of cooperatives and the upstart consumer movement, *Tide* worried that Kagawa's efforts might spell the end of advertising as they knew and loved it (advertising for his books apparently being the exception). In its October 1935 issue, the magazine noted that the trade of consumer cooperatives had enjoyed a 40% increase between 1929 and

1934, and attested to its genuine threat because the Roosevelt administration, the unions and the churches all appeared to encourage the cooperative method of business:

> What Dr. Kagawa and his cohorts mean to advertising in the long view is more serious by a good deal than anything Dr. Schlink of Consumers' Research and his cohorts mean. For one thing, more people, by far, will be reached and excited by Dr. Kagawa. And for a second, a cooperative movement working full hilt doesn't just snipe at commercial advertising—it dispenses with it.[21]

Kagawa and the cooperatives he advocated did not need their own public relations people to obtain national attention.

His very arrival in the United States had occasioned another twist of fate that turned adversity into an opportunity. The *Chichibu maru*, on which he came, was delayed a day by bad weather, preventing him from attending a gala reception in Oakland on December 18, 1935. The disappointment and anxiety were heightened when the ship arrived and he was not permitted to debark. Instead he was shunted to the Angel (sic) Island detention center in San Francisco Bay by the Federal Health Service because officials discovered that he had trachoma, which the service termed a "serious malady of the eyes prevalent in the Orient."[22]

Two of his followers, Dr. Stanley Hunter of the Graduate Theological Union in Berkeley and Dr. C. C. Cunningham, in charge of tour arrangements, telegrammed the U.S. Secretary of Labor, Frances Perkins: EARNESTLY EMPLORE YOU TELEPHONE ANGEL ISLAND EXPEDITING KAGAWA'S EYE EXAMINATION. The Kagawa network swung into action with similar telegrams to the government requesting prompt attention to the matter, as did the Federal Council of Churches, co-sponsor of the lecture series.[23]

President Roosevelt himself took a personal interest in the matter at an afternoon cabinet meeting, asking cabinet members Cordell Hull, Hans Morgenthau and Perkins to take necessary steps to make it possible for Kagawa to enter the country. Less than two hours later, at four in the afternoon, Perkins announced that the Board of Review of the Immigration Service, a branch of her department working with the Public Health

Service, had granted Kagawa's appeal for a seven-month visit. They ordered that he be accompanied by a doctor or nurse and take other steps against contagion.[24]

The President's direct intervention and the mobilization of Kagawa's disciples turned the entire episode into valuable publicity for both Kagawa and the cooperative movement. It further dramatized his selfless service to others. It was hard to miss the irony of this gentle man cast out as a pariah, forbidden to preach the Gospel because of the disease he had contracted "doing" the Gospel. It touched a deep nerve to see the "Saint Francis of Japan" treated like the Son of Man without a stone on which to rest his head.

Time magazine in an article on the "Quarantined Christian," included a photograph and a history of the illness, commenting:

> He contracted this highly infectious eye disease during the 14 years he voluntarily spent in the filthiest slums of Kobe, laying a solid foundation for his views as a Christian radical. After 13 operations, Dr. Kagawa has lost the sight of one eye, must use a powerful magnifying glass to read with the other.[25]

Time also summarized the itinerary and billed him as an expert on cooperatives who had been summoned partly because of his knowledge of the topic. The fact that Roosevelt supported cooperatives, having recently signed enabling legislation for both the rural electric co-ops and the credit unions, added to the American interest in Kagawa.

Kagawa treated the entire episode with the humor and detachment which most people found so charming. He observed: There is an American heaven and an American hell, and I want to see them both. . . . I hope I shall be permitted to enter.[26]

Throughout the six and one-half months Kagawa toured the country, he scrupulously followed the prescribed health rules, making sure that utensils and linen handled by him were sterilized, and accompanied by a nurse, Marguerite Duthrie. Handshakes were forbidden, so he developed the habit of shaking hands with himself when he was introduced to people on the tour.

The prescribed hygiene hardly placated the bigots, right-wing fundamentalists, superpatriots and paranoid nativists, who pestered Kagawa and assailed his sponsors throughout the tour.

John B. Trevor, president of the right wing American Coalition, an association of patriotic societies, sent his own telegram to Roosevelt protesting Kagawa's admission, calling it a "flagrant violation of the spirit and, I venture to believe, the letter of Section 3 of the Immigration Act of 1927." He told a reporter that Kagawa was an "alien propagandist seeking to tour the country for an organization closely associated with groups carrying on a campaign to undermine all our agencies of national defense." Trevor asserted that no attendant or practical precaution could relieve the "peril of contagion."[27]

After touching base with the Japanese-speaking Friends of Jesus group in California, Kagawa flew to Texas to begin the tour. Ultimately, it included hundreds of appearances before more than 750,000 people in 150 different cities in the United States and Canada, ending with a June 30, 1936, broadcast on the NBC network. During one 12-week stretch he spoke at 200 meetings in 84 cities and towns. As in his Japanese tours, Kagawa astounded his sponsors with his stamina, sometimes speaking 11 hours a day and driving himself to such exhaustion that he was forced to cancel part of the tour in February. His sturdy voice at times was reduced to a such a thin squeak that crowds had difficulty understanding him. His accent compounded that difficulty, despite all the time he had spent practicing English pronunciation with his friend Axling.

Those not convinced of his sainthood were certainly impressed by the endurance of the "mighty little man from the Far East" as one reporter referred to him. A typical day was like the one spent in Cleveland on March 4, 1936. He began with an 8 a.m. breakfast speech before a circle of ministers, co-op leaders and members of a social gospel group at the Euclid Avenue Baptist Church, went to the Old Stone Church to officiate at a noon lenten service, returned to the Baptist church for a 4 p.m. youth service, and later addresssed an 8 p.m. mass meeting.

Wherever he went the audiences were taken by his combination of an aura of gentle sanctity, biting wit and prodigious memory. At a Washington, D. C.'s gala affair in the Mayflower Hotel he told his listeners humbly, "I deserve no reception in this mansion—I belong in the slums, really."[28] In Detroit he needled his Protestant audience, "You have too many sects. The last time I was here I looked it up, and there were 266. Too many. Are you going to live in compartments in heaven?"[29] In Cleveland, where he addressed 10,000 that day, he chided the men, "Eighty percent of our birds are monogamous. Are American men like that?"[30]

In a more serious vein he advanced his message of Christ and co-ops:

> The cooperative movement would put jail wagons out of employment. . . . If any of you want to make the American people a good nation, don't be ambitious to be a leader. Be a servant. . . . Can you keep God separate from your life and commerce? Are you ambitious for the kingdom of God on earth? Then you must adopt it in your economy. . . . Virginia, with 2.5 million population, has 7,000 in its prisons. England, with 45 million, has the same. . . . I am a radical if the cooperative movement and the New Testament are radical. . . . When we believe God is our real Father, mountains, clouds, stars, trees, rain, even motor cars, belong to us. . . . Jesus was not an engineer, a scientist or an inventor, but just a carpenter. He is remembered because of His consciousness of God.[31]

A brief summary of an early portion of his travel will give some idea of his frenzied pace. He was in Indianapolis December 30 and 31, 1935 at the Student Volunteer Convention, speaking to co-op and church groups. Immediately thereafter he began his swing through the South, visiting Birmingham, Atlanta, New Orleans, Nashville, Louisville, Lexington, Memphis, Nashville, Norris Dam, Asheville, Durham, Richmond, and numerous other points in between before landing in Washington D.C. on January 18, 1936. After this he swept along the eastern seaboard until the end of that month.

He next went to Missouri, visiting Columbus and St. Louis before moving on to Kansas City to meet with the Consumers Cooperative Association from February 3 to 5. Then the tour scheduled February 6–9 for speaking engagements before the Illinois Council of Churches, winding up in Chicago for the International Council of Religious Education. He spent two weeks traveling in Nebraska and the Dakotas, with a stop at the Midland Cooperative Oil Company in Minneapolis, a large farm supply co-op whose dealerships and gas stations have been a familiar sight in the Great Lakes region. From Lake

Superior at Duluth, he swung down through Iowa, and then headed back east, motoring to halls and churches in Ohio, Indiana and Michigan.[32]

Undertakers as well got into the action, volunteering in some towns to haul his three steamer trunks full of books. Kagawa rode a mule into the Grand Canyon, a big Packard from town to town in Southern California for 10 days, visited his alma mater, Princeton Theological Seminary, paid a call on the inmates at the Elmira Reformatory in New York, and met with the famed atomic physicist Robert Millikan. His down-to-earth humor and warmth won friends, and his insatiable curiosity about everything amazed them. In a few short hours, his research stretched from the formula for Coca Cola to the outer reaches of the galaxy.

Wallace Campbell was charmed by Kagawa's range of interests. Driving Kagawa back to his hotel from a lecture which drew an overflow crowd, Campbell asked what he did for leisure. Kagawa's reply was,

> After talking about the social and political conditions of the economy, it is helpful to turn to a book of geology and read about earth formations hundreds of thousands of years ago. It gives me a perspective and an assurance that I do not have with the more ephemeral things of our economy.[33]

Kagawa made it to New York state in late March, where he spoke in a different city almost every day until mid-April. He then arrived in Rochester at a climactic point of his tour to deliver the Rauschenbusch lectures. They were published in book form as *Brotherhood Economics*, his most popular and inspiring publication on cooperatives. In May he crisscrossed back West, to Chicago, Denver and all the way to Seattle for a two-day seminar, which was originally planned for 150 people but expanded into a group of 420 from three states and Canada.

Except for that precious time of prayer and meditation in the pre-dawn hours, Kagawa's typical day on this tour, according to *The Christian Century*, sounds like that of a lionized celebrity:

> Kagawa will arise at 4 a.m., spend an hour in meditation, read and write for two hours, go out to some home for breakfast, hold two meetings during the morning, lunch as a guest at a luncheon club, hold a conference or two, make an afternoon lecture and

answer questions from one and a half to two hours, accept an invitation to dinner, address a throng at night, meet a group in conference after the lecture, greet the endless number who crowd around him at all times, autograph books until someone drags him away, answer all queries politely, though crisply, and get to his room late for the five or six hours that suffice for his night's rest. He literally wears his entourage out though they rest while he talks.[34]

True to his ecumenical spirit, Kagawa spoke before Southern Baptists, Methodists, Presbyterians and dozens of other denominations, from Bible Belt fundamentalists to ardent liberals of the social gospel persuasion. One of his favorite jokes on the lecture circuit was a gentle barb at himself and at the Protestant disunity he often criticized in Japan: "I am surprised that you have as many as 260 denominations. I am told that I pronounce this word to sound like 'damnations' and I am not sorry that I do. You have the opposite of Christian unity." He mined his own life for anecdotes, like the time he concluded the story of the Shinkawa thug knocking out his front teeth by saying, "I now have an alibi for not pronouncing the English language correctly."[35]

He appealed to the more fundamentalist Christians by using their cherished religious belief in the redeeming power of the blood of Christ, while liberals were attracted by his social gospel and advocacy of cooperatives as Christianity in action. He could combine a rather fundamentalist interpretation of the Bible with his Darwinistic idea that Christ was the culmination of evolution, saying, "I believe in the virgin birth, resurrection, ascension, and divinity of Christ. But I believe in much more."[36] The "much more" was the entire plan of Christian economics, centered in co-ops and a democratic social order.

As if the size of the overflow crowds was not enough, he was showered with adulation and generous contributions. Contributions far exceeded the $100 a day budget for the tour. In Nashville, simply passing the hat at one meeting raised $540. In Philadelphia the amount was almost $2000, in Detroit $1000, and groups were organized to do follow-up work to keep the funds flowing in for his projects.

Kagawa never ceased to preach the Gospel of cooperation,

challenging the audience to live its religion. Because of his failing voice and pronunciation problems, he was more successful with smaller audiences and in face to face dialogue, but everywhere, even when people did not fully understand him, they were moved by a sense of calm that he projected in the midst of the bustle and stress of a busy schedule. They were also impressed by his emphasis on the delicate balance between a religious experience and social action. As one writer put it:

> He came as a flaming prophet of a balanced Christian gospel with both evangelistic and social accents. The light and calm of a mystic shone upon his radiant face. The confidence of a scholar illumined his messages. For the competition of the old order, he would substitute the cooperation of the new order.[37]

No less than his Japanese audiences, Westerners were impressed with the range of his discussions. Kagawa could intellectualize to the point where he confused his listeners and then move on to speak to another group in the most colloquial manner. He would scramble ideas from Kant, Marx and Darwin in one lecture and then say with utter simplicity, "It is a miracle that I was born, that I live, body and soul, an object of God's care in a ruined world."[38] (These diverging styles also characterized his writings.) At some meetings he surprised people by reading to himself the 900-page tome *Soil Microbiology* in between speeches.

A candor in his English added weight to his words about cooperatives. On the platform with E. R. Bowen of the Cooperative League in Indianapolis, he offered the message of nonviolent revolution through cooperative economics:

> As you understand, the cross of Jesus stands at the center of life. When we apply the principles of the cross in economic life, we must observe four things: first, the principle of non-exploitation, which is the spirit of sacrifice; second, the principle of brotherhood; third, the principle of sharing and fourth, the principle of social solidarity.
>
> Now the principle of non-exploitation stands in contrast to the profiteering motive of the capitalistic system. The principle of accumulation of the capitalistic system is contrary to brotherhood. The concentration of capital by a few rich people is contrary to the principle of sharing. And the class struggle which

eventually results from the capitalistic system is contrary to a true sense of social solidarity. . . . Christianity is well preached throughout the world but in economics we forget to put the principles of the cross into practice so we have competition. Well, competition is good as long as it is for psychological effect on the individual, but if it is applied to the getting of daily needs, we have a chaotic situation. It leads us to gambling and speculation and war. We must, therefore, change this idea of competition into the spirit of cooperation. . . .

When I speak of brotherhood I mean we must have a good system with the spirit of sacrifice and cooperation. The cooperative system has the spirit of sacrifice and the spirit of brotherhood.

But sometimes, we have too much system. When we have something like the Soviet Bureaucracy or Fascist control by the state or Nazistic control we have a big system with great power. But we lose our individuality.[39]

Kagawa insisted that economics were the roots of war. In another talk he declared:

The world is suffering from economic chaos. Italy invaded Ethiopia to capture some territory. Japan invaded Manchuria to capture natural resources. In Europe today we have terrible chaos. In Asia we have the dark clouds of war hanging over the nations.

Now throughout the world Christians are eager to find some path to international peace. We have many conscientious objectors against war. I think they are the finest people in the world, but there are many who do not understand that kind of philosophy of life. For instance, in Japan we have militaristic tendencies, and there are secret orders which are very much against conscientious objectors. There are about 100,000,000 people in Europe who do not understand Christianity. . . .

There are other people who are philosophically inclined to peace. We are convinced that the man who wrote the essay "Eternal Peace" was a great philosopher. We need reasoning to stop war. But in times like these, philosophy alone will not stop war. We need a way to eliminate the causes of wars before we talk the philosophy of peace. . . . But politics can never solve the problem. When the League of Nations was established in the year 1919, there was much zeal and enthusiasm for peace in Europe, but it has failed. Unless we can solve the question of economics it is utterly impossible to solve the question of peace.[40]

He proceeded to criticize religious individuals for their lack of involvement in solving these secular problems:

> Today, spiritually-minded people are trying to seclude themselves from economic entanglements. In Japan some monks and priests seclude themselves from worldy things; they go to the mountains, to the forests, and to monasteries, and meditate and entirely ignore economic questions. They let other people capture the economic system and greedily accumulate capital.
>
> Some Christian leaders, when we talk about economics, think it is not spiritual. But as you know, Jesus came in flesh. In his flesh he had wonderful manifestations of the presence of God. When our flesh shall be controlled by the consciousness of God, the laws of God will be manifested in the material things and economics shall be controlled by the law of God. The teachings of Christ will be applied in economic matters.[41]

Kagawa brought up specific examples of how international trade could be accomplished through cooperatives:

> Now we should adopt International Cooperative trade like between Denmark and England. . . . Denmark sells her farm products to England through the Cooperative Associations and Great Britain buys Danish farm products through the British Wholesale Consumers Cooperatives. They have an agreement that they will not exploit each other and they will turn the profits back to the people who have produced the profits. They don't talk about free trade and protective tariff. There is no need to think about such things where there is no competitive trade.[42]

He concluded by arguing for international cooperative banks built on a uniform monetary system to bring stability to world trade:

> Because we have terrible disasters from time to time, we depreciate our currency. So cheap goods are exported to America, and you are suffering from Japanese cheap goods. If we could have only one monetary system throughout the world, having International Cooperative banking, then Japanese cheap goods would not flow to this country.[43]

By the time Kagawa arrived in Rochester for the Rauschenbusch lectures, the trenchant opposition from the right wingers had built considerably. The Rev. Dr. Harold Strathearn, executive secretary of the Interstate Evangelistic Association, Inc., started agitating against Kagawa and cooperatives by raising the spectre of socialism: "Kagawa preaches a sinister plan to advocate consumers' cooperatives and socialism under the cloak of the Christian Church."[44]

Forming a "Committee of Fifty" to combat the twin demons of Kagawa and cooperation, Strathearn persuaded the Masons to withdraw permission for Kagawa to use their hall in Rochester, but the Masons relented after protests from the Council of Churches in Rochester and Monroe County. Then Strathearn decided to bring in a fundamentalist hit man, Rev. Dr. J. Frank Norris, a Baptist from Fort Worth.

Called "Two Gun Norris," the flamboyant preacher had been acquitted of a murder by a plea of self-defense. He red-baited the Federal Council of Churches as "Communistic," launching a caustic tirade that impelled Rev. Dr. Samuel McCrea Cavert, the FCC general secretary, to demand a retraction. Norris retorted, "Out here in the west where every man puts his breeches on one leg at a time, you will find out that we are still Americans that believe in God, home and native land, and have no fear of all the red flag crowd."[45]

On the evening of the showdown in mid-April, Kagawa drew a crowd of 3000, while Norris attracted 2500 at nearby Convention Hall in Rochester. The charges of communism were somewhat blunted when Kagawa was introduced by Mrs. Harper Sibley, the wife of the president of the U.S. Chamber of Commerce who was also on the platform. Kagawa spoke gently on one of his favorite topics, the medieval guilds, which he looked upon as an ideal of harmonious labor and Christianity in action. He dismissed Norris and Company saying "Because I want the love of God to be applied in industry, in economics, in daily life, I am criticized as a Communist. What a joke!"[46]

Meanwhile, Norris was fulminating to a cheering crowd: "Co-ops are more dangerous than outright Russian communism." He asked rhetorically, "Do we need to import the Japanese to tell us how to run our business, our homes, our churches?" To this his instant disciples responded, "Amen, Amen." Norris then moved on to Chicago on a three-month campaign against the Federal Council of Churches. He also begged the Baptists to oust the Rev. Dr. Albert W. Beaven from the presidency of their Colgate-Rochester Divinity School because of his radical activities and sponsorship of Kagawa's lectureship.[47] There were attacks by other clergy like Dr. W. B. Riley of Minneapolis, who labeled Kagawa an "anti-Christ."

Further attacks emanated from secular quarters, such as the publication of the coal industry, *Black Diamond,* which printed a speech given by E. W. Dobson criticizing the churches for their involvement in cooperatives. The executive vice president of the bituminous coal merchants association Kline Roberts also cautioned, "The more successful these zealots are the greater will be the number of existing enterprises put out of business." The paper urged the coal dealers to battle the cooperatives:

> Now is the time to use your influence in damming this movement by insisting that your church have no part in furthering it. Get the cooperation of other retailers in other fields to register opposition; let the church know that it has a job still undone in its chosen field, and that, at least until that job is well done, its efforts in fields it does not know will be resisted.[48]

An insurance agents' publication in Ohio hurled racial slurs into the fray, calling Kagawa "the Jap" whose meetings have been "ballyhooed from the pulpits." It warned that "the growth of the cooperative movement will strike directly at your agency. It will strike at all private business. Those who are propagandizing the cooperative movement dream of a cooperative state in which all business is cooperative. They would put you out of business." The bulletin urged the insurance agents to "Do your part in blocking its spread!"[49]

As in Japan, such attacks tended to be counterproductive, stimulating more sympathy for the cooperative movement that had been battling constantly against charges of socialism or communism. The rural electric cooperatives and the credit unions were beneficiaries of federal legislation, but the consumers and workers cooperatives did not win the same kind of support, partly because of greater hostility to those types of enterprises and partly because certain segments of the consumers cooperative movement were themselves reluctant to accept government aid and involvement.

Kagawa had faced far more severe opposition in Japan, so he was not shaken by these assaults, and was able to give the

Rauschenbusch lectures on schedule. The lectureship was an endowment named for Walter Rauschenbusch, a leading theoretician of the social Christianity movement. He had been a professor at the theological seminary at Rochester Theological Seminary, later named Colgate-Rochester Divinity School. Kagawa's first draft of the Rauschenbusch lecture was written in Japanese aboard ship when he was en route to the United States. It was sent back to Japan for translation into English, and after review by Helen Topping and others, it was published in 1936 by Harper and Brothers under the title *Brotherhood Economics*.

The result is anything but a dry treatise on economics. The opening is a poetic lament for the lost potential of the modern world:

> Aeroplanes wing their way across the airways of the world; radio's shrill voice echoes through the ether waves; television conquers great distances, making us conscious of the limitless power of man's invention and intelligence. But it is a bewildered world, trembling with unrest and tortured with poverty. The world is in chaos.

> The poverty of today is not the poverty of want but the poverty of plenty. It is the agony of over-production of goods, machines, labor and intelligentsia. We suffer not from scarcity but from surplus. Wealth is accumulated in the hands of the few and the mass of society is crushed down into a world of unemployment, unrest, dependency and non-credit. They lift their voices in a cry of eternal helplessness. The policy of *laissez faire* has led us into hell, and millions of unemployed are starving in the shadows of overflowing warehouses.[50]

After this opening, Kagawa criticized both capitalism and Marxist economics as having a common major flaw—materialism. This was a theme he often sounded. He also criticized "creedal Christianity" as being impotent. He praised those institutions which he had long admired as precursors of the modern cooperative movement. They included the communalism of early Christianity, the reforms of the monastic orders, the medieval guilds, the Anabaptist movement and liberal Protestantism, all of which he had attempted to incorporate into the structure of his Friends of Jesus Society.

Kagawa argued that traditional history, whether capitalist or

Marxist, overemphasized war, competition and class struggle. He asserted that the long history of collaborative self-help efforts was never given its proper due, though this communitarianism had actually contributed far more to human progress. Giving it proper cultural emphasis and studying its method and spirit would speed the evolution toward a truly cooperative society, where "brotherhood economics" was the order of the day.

Much of Kagawa's efforts sought the spread of cooperative culture, where peacemaking and mutual aid replaced hostility, war and violence as the typical reaction of individuals and nations. Cooperation, he repeated over and over to his American audience, meant far more than the physical plant and the balance sheet of cooperative businesses. It involved the universal development of a whole new philosophy of life, one which had existed in isolated cases, but was now waiting to be born the world over.

In the Rauschenbusch lectures Kagawa expanded on the points he had been making throughout the tour, calling for cooperatives in seven areas of society, so that an entire system of cooperative enterprise would embrace the economy. The seven were: Insurance, Producers, Marketing, Credit, Mutual Aid, Utilities and Consumer. The advantage of this system over standard socialism was its decentralized and democratic character. Borrowing the ideas of the British guild socialists, the lectures even outlined a form of government where economics and politics were conjoined in two legislative houses, the "social congress" and the "industrial congress." Members of each would be elected by the cooperative federation and the labor union federation, but they would each deal with different sets of issues. Instead of elections at large, representatives would be selected to represent the various cooperatives and labor groups.

Kagawa observed:

> Some members of legislative bodies now act as if they were the business managers of capitalists. If members of the legislative bodies were elected from the various coordinated organizations, their duty would be clarified for them. They would represent the body of the people rather than a few capitalists. Furthermore, there would be little need of campaign funds, because the

bounds of each electoral precinct would be well defined from the beginning. The vexatious election rules of today would be avoided. There would be no temptation to members to resort to underhanded acts to promote their own interests.[51]

This construct was more a response to the corruption in Japanese politics than a blueprint for democratic governments, and caused the lectures to stray from the cooperative topic. It is perhaps an example of Kagawa at his weakest, drifting off into utopian ideas because he had become somewhat disillusioned with the parliamentary procedures which he himself had worked so hard to promote in Japan.[52] Whatever the flaws in some of his speeches, no individual in the history of the cooperative movement in the United States had ever put forth such an effort to crusade for the development of cooperatives as Kagawa.

In the wake of his speaking tour, meetings of cooperatives were thronged with new participants. The Cooperative League of the U.S.A. had an all-time high in its publications sales. One man he profoundly impressed was Jerry Voorhis, who subsequently become a U.S. Congressman from California and after that executive secretary and president of The Co-op League. A liberal New Deal legislator who had been named in his initial term as the outstanding freshman Congressman, Voorhis was unseated in 1946 by Richard Nixon in a savage red-baiting campaign.

Voorhis vividly recalled Kagawa's visit in 1936 to the boys school in Claremont, California, which he operated. Kagawa, standing outdoors in the sunset next to a wooden cross that the young boys had erected, led a service. In Voorhis' words, "He poured forth the purity of his Christian message of love and faith, identifying with all his fellow humans regardless of their station in life." Voorhis was particularly inspired by Kagawa's cooperative ethos, as it was outlined in *Brotherhood Economics*, affirming that cooperative enterprises were putting into practice the Second Commandment, "Thou shalt love thy neighbor as thyself."[53]

Kagawa's tour and writings were a strong moral force in encouraging cooperative development in the United States. His mere presence inspired many. Kagawa's combination of practical social reform and mysticism was so appealing that the translation which expresses it most vividly, *Meditations on the Cross*, sold tens of thousands of copies by the spring of 1937. His philosophy of cooperation and his interpretation of the social gospel offered an alternative to the violence of class conflict that troubled liberal Christians. It gave them a path to reform which coincided with their religious needs.

His final message before departing for Europe, broadcast over NBC, was full of hope: Urging international cooperation in trade and praising the U.S. willingness to grant independence to the Philippines as "one of the greatest achievements in American history that has happened in the Orient."[54] He closed with,

> I have learned to love the American people. . . . You have a wonderful future. . . . I ask your prayers for the maintenance of peace between this country and Japan. I bid farewell to you and I pray God's blessing upon you.[55]

Chapter 9
Toward War

*H*IS TRIUMPHANT WORLD TOUR would soon stand out in stark contrast to the grim years ahead for Kagawa and Japan, as the police state tightened its grip and the nation marched into total war. He sailed from the United States for Bremen at midnight July 1, 1936, with the applause of his admirers ringing in his ears, ready to meet the European throngs. Less than five years later, one of those admirers returning from Japan would call him "a man with a broken heart."[1] In bringing these sad tidings, Dr. Luman Shafer also cited the contrast between Kagawa's religion and the world situation, describing Kagawa as "a man with a deep Christian philosophy looking over the ages and yet living in the melee of today."[2]

Kagawa agonized between feelings of loyalty to Japan and contempt for its growing militarism; admiration of the West and scorn for its racism and colonialism; belief in non-violence and the reality of a world rushing toward war; faith in democracy and disillusion with the parliamentary system in Japan. In the midst of these contradictions, he was torn apart.

These problems can be glimpsed in his approach to U.S.-Japan relations during his 1936 tour. As a peacemaker, he tended to paint a rosy picture, as in his luncheon declaration at the Hotel St. George in Brooklyn:

> Both houses of the Japanese Diet have passed laws prohibiting expression of bitterness toward the United States by Japanese writers. I wish your country would pass that sort of law. . . . Ninety-nine percent of the intellectuals in Japan are against war, and labor groups there, through demonstrations, express dissatisfaction with the war spirit.[3]

Shortly thereafter in Des Moines, Kagawa received the shocking news of the assassination of Finance Minister Korekiyo
Takahashi and three other high officials in an attempted coup
engineered by 1400 ultranationalist soldiers. Prime Minister
Keisuke Okada barely escaped in this abortive February 26,
1936, takeover. Kagawa's comments to the first vague reports of
the attack on Takahashi was: "He was held in high honor. If he
was killed, he'll be a saint. The nation will never excuse his
slayers."[4]

The nation did prosecute the insurgents and executed 17 of
them, but in court martials held in absolute secrecy. The episode
roused the Social Masses Party and the labor movement into a
vigorous election campaign that later succeeded in capturing 8%
of the Diet seats, making them the third political force behind
the major Minseito and Seiyukai parties. Kagawa and other
prominent cooperators marked that election as a turning point
for the social democrats. Others considered it an aberration that
would be wiped out by the overpowering forces of militarism,
nationalism and government control of the media.

A subsequent "incident" the following year on July 7, 1937,
caused the entire nation to lurch to the right and gear up for
war, erasing whatever gains Kagawa and his allies had made. A
skirmish between Chinese and Japanese troops broke out at the
Marco Polo bridge near Peking and soon erupted into a full scale
war, which really marked the beginning of World War II in the
East. Nationalist China stubbornly stood her ground led by
Chiang Kai-shek. The Japanese prime minister, Prince Fumi-
maro Konoye, proved to be a hawk, calling for a "war of
annihilation" against Nationalist China. Japan mobilized for
war; the Diet passed the National Mobilization Law in March
1938, giving the government emergency powers to run the
economy, control the flow of labor and material, and direct the
major industries. The military budget leaped to 70% of the total
national spending of ¥4 billion.

It was only a matter of time before the labor and farmers'
unions Kagawa had helped to establish, and many of the
Christian churches where he had preached the gospel of peace,
all fell in line and declared their solidarity with the military
effort. They did so from motives of self-preservation, as it

became clear that opposition to the war would not be tolerated by the authorities. They also acted out of that pathological state of sheer patriotism and war hysteria—an experience of people in all tribes and nations at one time or another. At its October 1937 convention, the Japan Labor Federation passed a "Resolution of Appreciation to the Officers and Men of the Imperial Army," stating: "We give our most sincere thanks to the officers and men of the Imperial Army who with the Imperial Navy have done so much to add to the nation's glory throughout China since the incident began."[5]

Kagawa's colleague Sugiyama began to appear on the speaking platform with military officials. The National Christian Council set up a special Committee of 30 whose numbers included anti-militarists, but their manifesto was a disturbing expression of faith in the war policy:

> In this emergency: (1) We recognize our great responsibility as Christians for bringing about a spiritual awakening in our nation, and we shall redouble our efforts to this end. (2) In order to express our appreciation of the toil of our Imperial troops, we will undertake projects to comfort them. (3) We earnestly desire that this difficult crisis may be solved as speedily as possible and with a minimum of sacrifice. (4) It is our hope that this incident may result in the establishment of relations of good will definitely and for all time. To this end we ask our fellow Christians throughout the empire to pray most earnestly.[6]

The full impact of these events was yet to hit Kagawa. He had returned to his rambling Matsuzawa house in the fall of 1936— that is, when he wasn't out on the lecture or evangelistic circuit, or inspecting the agricultural experiments at his farm. Haru was firmly in charge of the local church and household affairs. Sumimoto was going on 14, Chiyoko was 11 and little Umeko's seventh birthday was celebrated on June 20. Though he was away much of the time on his endless speaking engagements and evangelistic tours, he still enforced rigid standards of simple living on the children. This meant that they often did not get the new clothing or toys they wanted. They came to regard him as somewhat of a tyrant because of his insistence on the doctrine of simple living in conformity to gospel values.

His little farm experiments, undertaken in the joyfully adventurous yet serious spirit of "vertical agriculture," often made it to the Kagawa family table. "Won't you have another helping of ham?" was the question posed by Haru serving a meal to a visitor in March 1937. With the infectious enthusiasm that captivated those who met him, Kagawa expounded his agronomical thesis:

> This ham ought to make you strong, because our pigs are fed on acorns. I got the idea from reading a book by Professor Russell Smith of Columbia University. There is an unlimited supply of acorns, but they have never been used. We buy them at about a cent for a bucketful. My novels have popularized two other new things, the raising of honey and mushrooms of a new kind. Then for five years I have been promoting the planting of nut trees, especially walnuts, on the mountains, to increase the farmers' income and enrich their food supply. Recently we have stimulated rabbit-raising by digging holes for them in the hillsides. One pair increases to forty in a few months.[7]

Agricultural research was not the only investigatory work at the rural establishment. Two rooms were occupied by three researchers constantly collecting information which Kagawa used in arguing for improved social services. One product of their efforts was a book entitled *Moral Statistics of Japan*, filled with data and commentary on crime, juvenile delinquency, liquor, marriage, suicide, prostitution, labor, religion, social work, recreation and other topics. Such data backed up Kagawa's plea to the cabinet for funding the National Health Insurance Act, which later passed and authorized cooperatives to provide sorely needed medical insurance in rural areas.

This research operation was only one part of Kagawa's humanitarian empire, which now had encompassed 35 different organizations with a paid staff of over 200 in the cooperatives, settlement houses, schools, hospitals, founded and/or supported by Kagawa. The Kagawa Fellowship in Japan and the United States was mobilizing to raise ¥500,000 by Christmas of 1938, to commemorate the 30th anniversary of God's gambler's lonely foray into the slums of Shinkawa.[8]

The unrelenting self-discipline that had driven Kagawa for the 30 years since his entry into Shinkawa continued, resulting in a dozen more books in 1936 and 1937, from children's fiction to

theology to a textbook for cooperatives. He continued his studies, sermons, and lecturing. As always, much of his preaching
was a combination of personal experience, vivid recollection and
historical events. It sounded many of the same themes he had
preached for years, such as his admiration for Asian religions
combined with his own conviction that Christianity perfected
the work of the great masters, Confucius and Buddha. It also
preached a doctrine that was becoming less and less acceptable
to the officials in Japan—the ideal of brotherly love and internationalism that extended beyond the borders of one's own race
and nation.

He recalled how he had visited Confucius' grave in the
Chinese countryside at Santo Sho in January 1931, and how this
experience strengthened his Christian faith. Preaching to a
crowd in his own church on November 1936, he said:

> From boyhood I had been taught of Confucius and had re-
> vered and admired him. . . . In the midst of a thickly wooded
> forest of about 100 acres there is a cone-shaped mound. This is
> the grave of Confucius. After seeing it I went back to Kyokufu
> and visited the halls of the old castle there. Inside of it there are
> over one hundred stone tablets, upon which is written the
> biography of Confucius. This quite fascinated me and I eagerly
> began reading, but suddenly my idea of Confucius underwent a
> change. I felt my esteem and admiration beginning to wane. But
> I also felt the sorrow of disillusionment when I found that
> the Confucius of whom I had studied since I was five years old
> and whom I had considered a Saint was nothing but an ordinary
> man. When I read the teachings of Confucius, after knowing
> Christ, I could plainly see that Confucius was naught but an
> ordinary politician. I was completely disillusioned. Compared to
> the great love of Christ, it was evident that Confucius' mercy
> was only for his native country. When he came face to face with
> another country he no longer exhibited mercy. . . . he taught
> that you may kill your enemy if by so doing you protect your
> country. This teaching is very different from that of Jesus who
> said, "Love your enemies."[9]

Kagawa went on to praise Buddha's selflessness and willingness to forgive, referring to his death:

> It proves he had been truly cultivating himself. If on top of our
> heritage of Oriental Culture we have the love of Christ we will

have everything—mercy, compassion and love. For this reason, I maintain that we should be proud of our Japanese background.[10]

It was a thin line that Kagawa was soon forced to tread between reverence for his tradition and the patriotic hysteria which gripped Japan after the China war had begun. Insisting on ever greater emphasis on Shinto, the indigenous religion of Japan, the government was pouring money into building and refurbishing Shinto shrines and demanding shrine worship as a means of stirring up patriotic fervor. Those killed in war were deified in ceremonies at the Shinto shrines. The strong revival of Shinto was permeated with nationalism and racism, designed to bolster the patriotic spirit for the war effort. Religious awe was thus used to evoke reverence for the state and its all-embracing militarism.

The confusion of the sacred and the secular was expressed thousands of times over in words like these:

> The shrines of Shinto bring unity to the faith of our nation. They strengthen the corporate fusion of the race. They furnish the supreme and central power for refining the feelings, manners and customs of the people. . . . Reverence for the shrines is rich with the significance of a solemn oath of loyalty to the great duty of improving and consolidating the state. The relationship of the shrines and the state is so intimate that they cannot be separated.[11]

By placing more emphasis on the compatibility of Christianity with the native religion, Kagawa hoped to deflect the patriotic criticism of Christianity as a "foreign" religion. Other Christians went much farther, desperately attempting a synthesis between Shinto and Christianity, and declaring their loyalty to the state.

As a Christian, Kagawa never believed in the deity of the emperor, but he would not openly declare that the concept was a complete fabrication nor even that it was misused to support a fascistic regime. Like other sceptics, the most he could dare were some rather delicate theological distinctions between reverence for the national heroes and worship of the state. In *Christ and Japan*, a book written explicitly for a Western audience, Kagawa stated:

> The Department of Education attempts to differentiate between state Shinto and religious Shinto. This may be wise, but

its success is doubtful. According to the department's interpretation the state Shinto shrines are like national monuments which commemorate heroes who have rendered meritorious service in the building of the Empire. Therefore, the department insists that these shrines are not of a religious character. Nevertheless, through the existence of these monument-shrines the forms of ancient Asiatic Shamanism are preserved. Yet it is true that the shrines of state Shinto are the monuments and tombs of men who have rendered conspicuous service for the state. In this respect they differ not at all from the Lincoln Memorial in Washington and the Cenotaph in London. Therefore, when visiting them I remove my hat and bow in reverence, just as I do when I visit my parents' graves.[12]

He further elaborated:

Let me define my own position. Whenever I visit the Great Shrine of Ise I do not worship Ama-Terasu-O-Mikami as a goddess. I do, however, remove my hat and bow reverently. The guard on duty finds no fault with this. The educational authorities ask nothing more. Some missionaries, however, look upon this as idol worship and clashes occur. These missionaries may find satisfaction in ignoring Japan's whole past history, and in destroying the memorials of the nation's builders.[13]

He concludes:

This question of Shinto shrines will probably be made an issue again and again. Personally, I find myself in agreement with the attitude of the educational authorities, that the shrines of state Shinto should be treated as monuments to the builders of the nation and not be looked upon as religious institutions.[14]

The identification of God and country in a sentimental blend of religion and nationalism was not unique to Japan. In the United States, there has been insistence that American flags be displayed in churches. What is frightening is when state and religion become profoundly entangled and religion is made a fetish of the state, as it was in the fascistic countries. The fascist madmen of Europe were already slaughtering the first of millions at this time. The question here was how profoundly Japanese authorities were imposing the state religion upon their people, and whether Kagawa misled himself in failing to recognize the gravity of the impending totalitarianism that would soon engulf Japan.

Kagawa had gone out of his way to demonstrate that Christians could be good patriots, saying:

> The people of Japan, however, always keen on preserving things of value, will discover that Japanese Christians take second place to none in their eagerness to conserve the nation's historical traditions. For instance, it was Christians who promoted the movement to preserve the traditional relics of Ninigi-no-Mikoto, the grandson of Ama-Terasu-O-Mikami. If Christians give evidence that they also have a high appreciation of Japan's past and its culture, it will help non-Christians to understand the true spirit of the Christian faith.[15]

Kagawa the rebel was accommodating to the system, partly because the system was allowing him less and less freedom.

At the same time he was attempting an international balancing act by downplaying Japan's problems in the hope that he might tone down the anti-Japanese feelings in the West. At home, however, he continued to chastize the military spirit. Earlier in 1928, he organized the All-Japan Anti-war League, which had little impact since it was soon suppressed by the government. An opponent of militarization, he had long been concerned about Japan's belligerent attitude toward China. In the preface to the Chinese edition of *Love the Law of Life* he wrote a poignant apology and a confession of failure. That document later landed him in jail.

The apology was not simply an attack on Japanese militarism. It was a passionate plea for peace, international and racial tolerance actuated by love:

> I have been asked to write a preface for the Chinese edition of *Love the Law of Life*. It has made me very sad, for my nation is constantly breaking the law of love toward the Middle Kingdom. I myself love China as I love Japan. And for a long time I have been praying for the speedy coming of peace in China.
>
> It causes me intolerable shame to reflect upon the violence that Japanese militarism has done and is doing in China, in spite of all my prayers. And I am surprised at the leniency of my Chinese brother who has translated my book in spite of Japan's immoral acts. Though a million times I should ask pardon it would not be enough to cover the sins of Japan. I am ashamed, because I am too impotent to influence the militarism of Japan. Chinese leaders may well accuse me of impotence. I deserve the charge.
>
> If only Japan will repent, and establish and keep permanent

friendship with China. There is no other way than by the law of love. Nay, not only in the relations between China and Japan—if we hope for a progressive uniting of all the cultures of the nations and races of the whole world, there is no other way than through the principle of redemptive love. The law of redemptive love is the fundamental law of the universe. Kropotkin's instinctive love is not enough. Instinctive love does not transcend race. It is the redemptive love that Christ lived and practiced that alone transcends race. This type of redemptive love must grow in us, and acquire universal consciousness, and labor to save the most unhappy peoples of the world. Since the Japanese nation was unable to taste that great redemptive love, I suffer the sorrows of the prophet Jeremiah. Forgive us! You sons of Confucius and Bok Su, forgive us in the name of your great peace-loving sages! Someday the Japanese will cast away the sword and gun and awaken to the love of the Cross. Just now I can think of nothing but to beseech your pardon. And there are an uncounted number of young souls in Japan who like myself are asking for pardon.[16]

Kagawa's confession of failure prophesized a dismal future for Japan. If people as influential as himself were impotent in curbing the military, then there was scant hope of any effective opposition. This preface to *Love the Law of Life* echoed earlier statements of Kagawa to the Chinese people. In his open letter to China in 1931 following the Manchurian Incident, and in his sermon in Shanghai, he indicted the Christian community in Japan for the failure to curb the military: "Pardon us, pardon me especially, because our Christian forces were not strong enough to get the victory over the militarists."[17] In *Tears* he expresses poetically the grief he felt living like a ghost, desperately searching for a way out of the war that he simply could not bear.

In his own country Kagawa now began to acknowledge that war fever and patriotism were becoming a depressing obstruction to a major part his life's work, the spread of Christianity. He noted the decline in the number of people signing inquiry cards at evangelistic meetings, and a marked reduction in church attendance. He cited three reasons for what he called this "lamentable regression": extreme nationalism which promoted the theory of the Japanese as the chosen race, the opposition to pacifism, and the revival of Shintoism.

According to the Japan Christian Yearbook for 1938, Kagawa

faulted the Japanese churches for falling in line with this nationalism to save themselves, and he deplored attempts to "nationalize" Christianity:

> These people would unreasonably try to fit the world-wide religion of Jesus of the Cross into the restricted confines of a particular mould. Hence they have forsaken the absoluteness of the religion of redemptive love for a narrow standard of criticism of those who differ from them. Furthermore, the religion of Christ, which as a religion of love should be warm and attractive, has become cold and repelling. Consequently they have lost the vitality and freshness of Christ.
>
> Moreover a number of people in their zeal to oppose internationalism have thought it necessary to oppose Christianity. Some nationalistic organizations in the provincial districts, welcoming such attitudes have begun to persecute the educational organs of Christianity. Fearing this persecution, many Christian institutions have become extremely nationalistic even exceeding such compromises as were permitted in the Old Testament.[18]

His hardest hitting denunciation of the war effort was in his description in 1938 of how the nation eagerly mobilized and how dissent was crushed:

> With the outbreak of the Sino-Japanese incident, national mobilization of persons and their thoughts, was efficiently carried out. Symbolic of their readiness to help at all times, certain women's organizations adopted kitchen aprons as their badge of patriotism. Clad in these all-enveloping white garments, they could be seen marching on the streets and filling the stations as they cheered the departing soldiers on their way. The movement for peace was ridiculed and all utterances against the actions or pronouncements of the military were prohibited by law. To even mention the word peace is not now permitted in newspapers or magazines.
>
> Though the emperor gave to the Diet his Imperial Rescript expressing his hope for world peace, many organs of nationalism seem to have forgotten it and are busily engaged in trying to crush out the intelligentsia who advocate peace movements.[19]

This was the naked truth about Japan, stripped of the apologetics of the good will ambassador, and Kagawa took a heavy risk in publishing it. His chilling appraisal ended on a note of rather desperate optimism:

The foregoing would seem to present a gloomy picture of our Christian movement in Japan. But I am not discouraged nor disappointed. Love and the Cross cannot fail. They promise victory. Our past experience teaches us that thought waves in Japan move in ten-year cycles. I am confident that ten years from now this period of perplexity and darkness will have given way to an era of light and hope.[20]

His prediction was accurate. Had Kagawa foreseen the full extent of the "coming period of perplexity and darkness," however, even these last traces of optimism might have disappeared from his prophecies. Life went on for the Kagawas, but as in the rest of Japan, with increasing fear. The situation was ameliorated by Kagawa's contacts in high places, like Minister of Agriculture Count Arima, who had backed his agricultural projects and was a former officer of the cooperative movement. Other officials may have considered Kagawa useful to the Japanese government in maintaining good relations with the United States.[21] A considerable amount of material essential to Japan's war came from American corporations. (So much, in fact, that prominent liberal Christians in the United States like E. Stanley Jones called for a boycott of Japan, saying, "Apply Gandhi's method to Japan.")[22]

As a man with a pacifist reputation dating back to adolescence, Kagawa was an obvious candidate for surveillance. He also was the kind of independent-minded troublemaker who might "confuse the thought of the people," in the terminology of General Hideki Tojo seeking tighter control of information in Japan. Kagawa had been sharply critical both of Nazism and Russian Communism, and that was exactly the wrong kind of attitude at a time Japan was considering the advantages of improved relations with both these countries.

Through this treacherous situation, Kagawa's social work was thriving. His allies in the Friends of Jesus, Kagawa Fellowship and other organizations continued to run the kitchens, settlement houses, cooperatives and other enterprises. The Fellowship staged a celebration of the Kagawa's 25th wedding anniversary, inviting 200 guests on May 27, 1938. Kagawa paid this tribute to Haru:

I am the workman and she is the superintendent, and on that

principle only have we been able to maintain our family. In the first place, I, the so-called head of the family am practically never living at home. Often during an entire year I cannot return home to sleep more than thirty days in all . . . .

Without hesitation I also call her my "Minister of Finance." The maintenance of that large family is entirely in her hands. From the point of view of the family, I am certainly an absurd husband. Many times I have asked her to spend every penny we had for some social project, with the result that she had no idea where money for the next day's food was coming from. Without a word of complaint, even at a time like that, she has somehow or other always provided. As the problems have come up day by day, she has thought the way out. Nor has she made me feel the least bit uneasy or insecure.[23]

Kagawa was still permitted to preach and travel. On a 1938 lecture tour in Manchuria, he first became attracted to Yosuke Matsuoka, a political figure whose ideals were considerably different from his own. Eventually indicted as a war criminal, Matsuoka was the pro-war official who led the Japanese delegation's walkout from the League of Nations in 1933. He was dumped as Foreign Minister in 1941 because his hawkish stance was too aggressive even for the other militarists. Kagawa's attitude toward Matsuoka, an advocate of Japan's sacred role in protecting and developing the Asian continent, was surprisingly favorable.

Kagawa wrote:

I was also invited to dinner by Mr. Yosuke Matsuoka, the head of the South Manchurian Railway. We had a very intimate talk. He explained his continental policy, which has its religious overtones. His sincerity almost brought me to tears . . . . Mr. Matsuoka is determined to love the Chinese people to the end. In him I had a glimpse of the most purified Japanese spirit.[24]

That Kagawa could be sold on the imperialist Matsuoka's "love" and paternalistic rationalization for invading the mainland under the guise of protecting Asia was somewhat alarming, to say the least.

Kagawa's most spectacular journey during the late 1930s was to Tamburam, Madras, India, for an international Christian conference of Protestant denominations, December 12–29, 1938. The grim transactions in the secular world were like a negative image of the spirit of international cooperation permeating the conference. At the very time when so many nations were involved in or moving rapidly toward war, the International Council of Missions staged this historic conference, the first since 1928. Almost 500 delegates from 64 different nations attended, with strong representation of non-white clergy from the world over. The conference was a celebration of brotherhood and equality predicated on the dignity of indigenous cultures, a striking renunciation of the old colonialist and imperialist element of Christianity. Gandhi himself saw it as "this world in miniature," alluding to the representation of all colors from the various continents.[25]

It was a colorful festival of the Third World, held in a place where even the weather was outside the Euro-American Christian tradition, with blazing sunshine, flowers, birds and outdoor tea parties during the yuletide. The daily religious services were a veritable Pentecost of tongues, with delegates singing hymns in the style of their native music. Apropos of the tropical latitude, one white observer remarked,

> The forty Bishops among the delegates were Bishops brown, black, yellow and some very red-faced so-called white men— their vestments as varied as their skins and as their methods of directing our thoughts.[26]

The Indians and Africans were at ease in their nation's costumes, since coats, ties and clerical collars were not required. The most conspicuous evidence of the waning colonial Christianity was the pith helmets worn by some of those red-faced white brethren seeking relief from the burning sun.

As Japan's most famous Christian, Kagawa was one of the 23 delegates sent to Madras by the Japanese community.[27] With him were his biographer Axling and three Christian women's leaders, Michi Kawai, Ochimi Kubushiro and Fumiko Kobayashi—women's rights being a major concern of Japanese Christians, especially Kagawa.

Kagawa's influence on the declarations of the conference is readily seen throughout the seven volumes of proceedings. The six main points in the declaration of the social significance of Christianity were:

1. We would look on every man as a man apart from race, birth, color, class or culture.

2. We would make the unit of co-operation the human race.

3. We would demand equality of opportunity for every man for his complete development.

4. We regard the present economic opportunities open to various nations as most unchristian, giving to certain of them a privileged position in access to the world's raw materials, financial assistance, and open areas which is denied to others.

5. Since war is a violation of human personality and repugnant to the Christian conscience, we repudiate it as a means of settling international disputes. We reaffirm our faith in the Christian weapons of overcoming evil with good, hate by love and the world by a cross.

6. To a torn and distracted and sinful world, we offer God's offer—the Kingdom of God.[28]

Only the representatives from Germany, obviously under Nazi constraints, dissented from this statement.

Kagawa participated in leadership discussions, drafting of resolutions, and the spontaneous conversations that sprang up as the delegates wandered about the ample grounds or conferred in the white, tile-roofed buildings of Madras Christian College. With his characteristic mixture of secular and religious concerns, he addressed the assembly on the wide scope of his work: social justice, health insurance, rural poverty and the efforts of cooperatives to bring relief to rural areas.

He peppered his speech with a mixture of bluntness, statistics and eagerness to show how Japan had looked to international models for cooperative techniques:

> Our first cooperative association for farmers was introduced from Germany a few years ago. Until then the farmers borrowed money from the loan sharks, with interest sometimes 25% and sometimes 30% per year. The government had a regulation that interest was to be only 20%, on a debt, but the loan sharks were able to squeeze the peasants for more. Today more that 14,000 cooperatives have been organized for the farmers. . . .
>
> Through the cooperative plan that we got from Denmark, we have four different forms of insurance for the people in rural areas. We have a harvest insurance for the rice crop and the silkworm crop; a livestock insurance; a health insurance cooperative; and a national health insurance cooperative. . . .[29]

Despite enthusiasm for these improvements, he was realistic in assessing the suffering of the peasantry and the utterly unfair system of absentee land ownership in Japan, a system which his farmers' union had battled but one which would not be over-turned until the massive land reforms decreed by the Allied Occupation after World War II:

> In 1931 the farmers of Japan suffered from a depression and a panic. As one result many lost the ownership of their lands and today about 40% of the 5,700,000 farmers are landless. Thirty percent of them have a little land; 70% are tenant farmers; 28% own small lands; only 2% of the farmers are well off. Sixty-five percent of the owners of farms live in the towns and cities. . . . Each year there are about 3000 cases of land disputes—labor disputes are almost stopped, but not land disputes—because of what the Japanese farmers suffer from the city owners of their farms.[30]

Turning from economics to Kagawa's theology, we see his distress at the sin of humanity, expressed at a morning service:

> On Calvary I see the blood of Jesus dropping down from His body on the cross. I hear the sound of the agony of the Lamb of God for the sins of mankind. It was for me and for my nation and for my race and for the whole world. I have committed sins and Jesus died for my sake. My race has committed sins and He died for my race. And the whole of mankind had fallen into sin, so He died for us all.
>
> Forgive us, Lord, for His sake and for the sake of the blood of Jesus Christ, our Redeemer and Savior.
>
> In the nineteenth century, some theologians could not under-stand the wonderful revelation of redemption because they were overshadowed by the amazing development of science and industry. But now, in the twentieth century, because we sit in darkness and depression after the breakdown accompanying the great European war and the following economic difficulties, we have come to understand more of the meaning of redemption.
>
> The inner consciousness of Jesus Christ was rather too deep for His disciples. Therefore they could not understand it. And even today, many people cannot understand this mystery. . . .
>
> Redemption means the remaking of mankind.[31]

As always, redeeming love was the heart of Kagawa's theolo-gy. Because Christ had suffered and died to redeem the world,

Christians must continue the work of redemption by giving up themselves to transform the world. Kagawa repeatedly used the "grain of wheat" image to illustrate how transformation took place through death. As the grain of wheat was sacrificed in order to produce a new plant bearing many grains, so the genuine Christian had to sacrifice self to create a new world, both at the personal and social level. This act of dying would produce both a fuller self and a fuller world.

Kagawa's words continued to carry weight because they were not mere talk about the traditional dogma of redemption. In his theology, Christ's death did not mean that mankind could claim salvation forever through one redemptive transaction. He insisted that the sacrifice of Christ must be reenacted in the life of every person who claimed to be a follower of Christ. What continued to give credence to Kagawa's theology of redemption was that his own life mirrored that of his teacher, Jesus, and was a public exhibition of sacrifice. He had emerged with what many perceived as an aura of sanctity that signified personal resurrection.

The ultimate sacrifice, however, eluded him. That sacrifice would have been the crowning redemptive act in a life dedicated to redemption—to save his nation and the world from war. The fact that Kagawa had contemplated such a sacrifice can be seen from accounts of his visit to Gandhi, two weeks after the conference on January 14, 1939. Kagawa's willingness to be a sacrificial victim was the central question of a tense conversation between the two international heroes. Kagawa traveled to Bardoli where Gandhi had arrived about ten days earlier.[32]

"Your reputation has preceded you, Dr. Kagawa," Gandhi said, standing up to greet Kagawa. Kagawa knelt to return the greeting, then opened their conversation with questions about the drought in South India and how the cooperative movement was doing.

"I cannot say that it is flourishing," Gandhi replied. "It is going on somehow. It was initiated by the British Government. It did not come from within, but was superimposed upon the people. It is managed after a certain stereotyped pattern and therefore has no room for growth according to the exigencies of time. Whereas I know you have a big cooperative movement."

"Yes, it is growing every day," Kagawa answered. "There are 3500 producers' cooperatives organized by themselves. There are national health insurance cooperatives, harvest insurance cooperatives and storage cooperatives."

Gandhi then bored in on the question of war with China. "What is the feeling of people in Japan about the war?"

"I am rather a heretic in Japan," Kagawa quietly announced. Then, "Rather than express my views, I would like to learn from you what you would do if you were in my position."

"It would be presumptuous for me to express my views," Gandhi replied.

"No. I would like very much to know what you would do," Kagawa said.

"I would declare my heresies and be shot," Gandhi pointedly replied. "I would put the cooperatives and all your work in one scale, and put the honor of your nation in the other, and if you found that the honor was being sold, I should ask you to declare your views against Japan and in so doing make Japan live through your death. But for this, inner conviction is necesssary. I do not know that I should be able to do all that I have said if I were in your position, but I must give you my opinion since you have asked for it."

"The conviction is there. But friends have been asking me to desist."

"Well, don't listen to friends when the Friend inside you says, 'Do this.' And friends, however good, can sometimes well deceive us. They cannot argue otherwise. They would ask you to live and do your work. The same appeal was made to me when I took the decision to go to jail. But I did not listen to friends with the result that I found the glow of freedom when I was confined within the four solid walls of prison. I was inside a dark cell, but I felt that I could see everything from within those walls, and nothing from outside."

Kagawa, who had been behind prison walls himself, must have felt the sting of these remarks, for he changed the subject. "Have you some irrigation cooperatives in India?" he asked.

"I do not think so. Of course you have all these things. You have done marvelous things, and we have so many things to learn from you. But how can we understand this swallowing alive of China, drugging her with poison and so many other horrid things that I read about in a book called *What War Means* which Pandit Jawaharlal has given me? How could you have committed all these atrocities? And then your great poet called it a war of humanity and a blessing to China."

Kagawa then turned the conversation to religion, asking Gandhi how he reconciled his teaching on non-violence with the *Bhagavad Gita*. After a bit of rather tense theological fencing about the meaning of violence of the *Gita*, Kagawa shifted to agricultural conditions in India. "You get famine once in every *ten* years?"

"We get it every year. Famine is our constant friend."

"Then you should have more tree culture, more trees for fuel and for cattle fodder. Rice and barley are not enough, you need more protein trees."

"No. We need a change in the method of government," Gandhi replied.

Gandhi then asked about Kagawa's itinerary, exhorting him to visit India's great poet Rabindranath Tagore at Santiniketan.

"How can you leave India without seeing Santiniketan?"

"But I have read the Poet's poems, and I love them," Kagawa answered.

"But you have to love the poet."

"If I can repeat the *Gitanjali* every day, I can see the Poet every day and do I not love him? Maybe he is greater than his poems," Kagawa said.

Gandhi countered, "Sometimes the reverse is the truth, but in the case of the poet he is infinitely greater than his great poems. Now, another question. Have you included Pondicherry in your programme? If you want to study modern India, you must see both Santiniketan and Aurobindo Ghose's ashram. I wonder who your tour advisers are. I wish you had appointed me your adviser in this matter."

"No. You are a good guide for life," Kagawa replied. This was certainly more than a polite compliment, for Gandhi's lucid remarks must have cast a darker shadow of the cross than Kagawa had ever seen before. Gandhi had put the dangers of civil disobedience as starkly as possible. Kagawa the pacifist was also the Kagawa who had grown increasingly nationalistic. The pilgrim to Gandhi had also looked to the hawkish Matsuoka for salvation. It was a contradiction he never fully resolved.

In the summer of 1939, relations between Japan and the United States were greatly strained when the United States gave notice of intent to terminate its commercial treaty with Japan. Kagawa sent this cablegram to friends in the United States and to *The Christian Century* in August:

REGRET PRESENT AMERICAN JAPANESE CRISIS. PLEASE EXERT YOUR CHRISTIAN INFLUENCE FOR RESTORATION OF OUR COMMERCIAL TREATY FOR THE PEACE OF THE PACIFIC AND TO AVERT WORLD CATASTROPHE.   TOYOHIKO KAGAWA[33]

The magazine paid Kagawa a tribute but still reiterated its criticism of Japan's military expansion and the fact that imports from the United States which flowed into Japan under the terms of the commercial treaty were being used in the war against China:

Such a message as this makes a strong appeal both to the heart and to the head. Every well informed Christian in America thinks of Kagawa as a brother in Christ, an alien only by legal definition but a fellow citizen in the kingdom that is above and beyond all nationalism. The memory of his radiant face and burning words and the impress of his nobly sacrificial spirit, known so well to many thousands of us through personal contacts and through the records of his work, have made it easier for our sympathies and our sense of fellowship to span an ocean and to transcend differences of race. There are doubtless unnumbered Japanese Christians whose mind is as his mind, but his has been the peculiar gift and function of serving as the link between them and us. In so far as his influence has reached, he has immunized Americans against the poison of any propaganda which would infect them with an indiscriminate hatred of the Japanese people. He has, in short, done all that one man could do, and more than any other has done, to enable us to consider dispassionately the import of such a message as that which he has just sent.[34]

The editorial added:

We want to be friendly with Japan and, come what may, we shall not hate. But we cannot be hand in glove with a government which acts as the Japanese government is now acting. . . .

We cannot use our influence, such as it is, for the continuance of a commercial treaty under which Japanese-American commerce has for its end result the dropping of bombs made of American metal, from planes powered by American motors and fueled with American oil, upon the congested areas of Chinese cities. We shall gladly join with Mr. Kagawa—himself a lover of peace whose sincerity none can question—in working for such changes in national policy, whether in his country or in ours, that mutual confidence between our nations may be restored, and that a treaty of amity and commerce may truly serve the cause of peace in the Pacific and in Asia may help avert world catastrophe.[35]

The moral and political confusion Kagawa faced was heightened by the non-agression pact between Hitler and Stalin. Japan had cast its lot with the Nazis partly to neutralize Russia, and now in the deranged chess game of international politics Hitler had betrayed the Japanese, but nevertheless remained an ally.

In spite of, or perhaps because of his access to officials in the Japanese cabinet, Kagawa was being watched more carefully by the secret police, who were suspicious of his past criticism of the Chinese war. On a 1940 visit to a Manchurian cooperative group founded by the Friends of Jesus, he was almost deported for criticizing the behavior of Japanese troops stationed there. During 1939 and 1940, however, his opposition to the Chinese war became increasingly cautious and he made few unfavorable remarks about government policies and actions.

Kagawa's best hope for the China war solution was the idea that once it was brought to conclusion Japan would "serve China." This was dangerously close to the rationalization of the Japanese leaders in justifying their concept of the Greater East Asian Co-Prosperity Sphere, wherein Japan would bear the burden constructing a new and just order in Asia. It was based on a widespread feeling in Japan that the Japanese were a chosen race charged with the sacred mission to protect and defend other Asian nations from Western imperialism and Russian Communism. Unfortunately, the Western powers provided just enough reason to give the militarists' argument plausibility.

Kagawa himself began to drift further toward the patriots, echoing some of their pious rhetoric about the power of the

Emperor, the unity of the Japanese race and the need for harmony. He asserted that Christianization in Japan did not necessarily imply Americanization or Westernization:

America's Lincoln, great as he is, cannot be the inspirer of Japan. We have our heroes too, like Nakae Tojiu of the early 17th century, who have seen that our great need is for that which binds us together and prevents disastrous cleavage and social disorder. That uniting factor is our conception of the Throne. The Throne is something which we Japanese accept without discussion. When I do not touch on problems of the Throne, I have freedom to talk of anything else I wish, even about the existing government or the army or the navy. I must be a Christian patriot. If I were suspected of disloyalty, next day I could not preach. But woe is me if I preach not the gospel; so I preach Christ the savior of the world and of Japan.[36]

Small wonder that in less than a year what little remained of the tolerant and progressive world Kagawa had built with love and exhausting effort came crashing down. The churches were placed under control of a national religious body and Christians were exhorted from the pulpit to practice self-denial in the interest of national policy. Those Methodists, whose quiet style of dissent Kagawa had praised, were ordered to rewrite their constitution to conform to national policy. The missionary community which had nurtured the young Kagawa and called the world's attention to him began its exodus from Japan.

Daikichiro Tagawa, head of the Christian Literature Society in Japan, was summoned before the Osaka gendarme to answer charges that he had violated the criminal code by speaking of a settlement of the China war. The Social Masses Party for which Kagawa had campaigned tirelessly was disbanded July 6, 1940, when the premier Prince Konoye formed a single national unity party. The Japan Federation of Labor convened in Tokyo for the last time on July 21 to disband and merge with the official government-sponsored union. At a signal from Kagawa's old ally, Bunji Suzuki, the embattled union officially dissolved amid patriotic cries of *banzai* for the Emperor.

"Kagawa the spellbinder," as one scholar called him, found his own enormous popularity as a speaker waning. He was now greeted by heckling, anti-Christian placards and other signs of the discrimination against Christians which was increasing as Japan became ultranationalist. It was only a matter of time before Kagawa himself faced formal official opposition whose existence he had denied to the outside world. After delivering a Sunday morning sermon on non-violence at his church August 25, 1940, he was arrested by military police on suspicion of violating the military code. They took him to the Shibuya Military Police Headquarters along with his associate pastor Kiyozumi Ogawa. The congregation was stunned by the arrest, and one of them, Tetsuya Kikuchi, shaved his head and fasted in protest. Prayer meetings were held for Kagawa's release. Haru visited officials and was unsuccessful in persuading them to release her husband.

The police interrogated him for the next 18 days, investigating his actions, speeches and publications, including those appearing in English. His monthly magazine, *Kumo no hashira* (Pillar of Cloud) and another of his periodicals were shut down on the pretext of a paper shortage. He was transferred to Sugamo Prison September 11, to be grilled further by military police. Only after Haru personally persuaded Foreign Minister Yosuke Matsuoka to intercede was he was finally released.

The *Kagawa Calendar* in particular drew special attention of authorities. Published seven years for distribution abroad, this little booklet contained photos of Kagawa, quotations from his writings, and news about his work. The 1940 version led off with excerpts from the Kagawa apology to the Chinese: "Though a million times I should ask pardon it would not be enough to cover the sins of Japan, which cause me intolerable shame. . . ." Other material must also have annoyed the militarists. There was a photo of Kagawa with the Chinese Christian Dr. Cheng and a message from Cheng mentioning the spiritual unity of the Chinese and Japanese Christians.

A prophetic quote from his *Meditations on the Cross* read: "The nation, or the society that indulges in sin is on its way to death. A nation that kills other people, and thus sows hatred and enmity, will come to destruction, reaping what it has sown." Even more damning was an excerpt of a conversation Kagawa had held with Chinese students, criticizing the military and openly discussing his own choice:

I cannot foresee success for Japan. I thought that because Japan joined the League of Nations our militarists would not act independently any more. But I miscalculated. We lacked a solid education of the common people in Japan for peace. And now I ask you, which should I do? Go to prison or work to educate? It's very easy to go to prison, very easy to be killed, but I have chosen the task of educating the people for peace.[37]

Kagawa was released without charges, but it was quite evident that there would be no more peace education on his agenda. He announced his retirement to Toyoshima Island in the Inland Sea, where he would dedicate the rest of his life to tuberculosis patients in a sanitarium he had founded there. After a six-week recuperation, however, he resumed preaching, making another tour of Manchuria with Kenichi Yarita and after that going on the evangelistic circuit again.

The police were surely more baffled than annoyed with Kagawa's attitude toward prison. Like other noted mystics throughout history, Kagawa could turn jail into an opportunity for meditation and communion with his God. He did have a powerful mystical experience during this imprisonment that seemed to have helped sustain him through the agony of the war years. After sitting erect on the prison floor for two consecutive days, the military police said "Kagawa, you had better lie down on the floor. You will become sick." Kagawa could not lie down because of emotional distress.

He later described the event, saying:

I prayed and wept because I knew that Japan and China were twins in the Far East. If Japan should destroy China, the next day Japan would be destroyed; and if Japan should be destroyed, China, too, would be ruined. So I put my head between my knees, weeping and weeping. Then through the grace of God a verse recalled itself to me, "By faith may Christ dwell in you." Suddenly there was a glow of light in the prison and in my heart. I felt an ecstasy, obsessed with the idea that Christ lived within me. I had a kind of an illumination that enabled me to see through the shadow of the present and visualize the New Japan of the future. A great joy dried up my tears and I became very courageous and bold. Christ isn't a mystical person only: He lives in my soul and body . . . . I came out of prison realizing that I might be killed, but I was not afraid.[38]

The Christian Century, one of the magazines which had published some of the articles examined by the police, interpreted the arrest as a way of frightening the Christians of Japan into total submission. It warned: "But let those who have imprisoned this Christian servant beware. Kagawa in prison may be stronger than Kagawa free could ever be.[39] Reports about Kagawa's arrest, such as one in the *New York Times* which called him "Japan's Gandhi," could undermine Japan's military interests far more than any action in Japan by Kagawa himself at this dismal point in history.

Regardless of Japanese strategy and international power plays, Kagawa still hoped to salvage peace between Japan and the United States. Peace was his ultimate goal, and he would make a last minute attempt to help avert war. In early 1941, the National Christian Council in Japan was in communication with the Federal Council of Churches in the U.S. and the New York-based International Missionary Council which had sponsored the Madras Conference. Arrangements were made for a delegation to meet with a group of American church leaders to exchange ideas and discuss a formula for peace between the two countries.[40]

Five members of the Japanese delegation sailed on March 27, followed by Kagawa, Ogawa and Bishop Yoshimune Abe nine days later.[41] Beginning on April 20, the group met for five days at the Mission Inn, Riverside, California, praying together and discussing the differences between the two nations. The Americans expressed concerns about the Japanese government's support of the Shinto religion and the forced unification of all the Christian churches. The Japanese devoted considerable energy to distinguishing secular Shintoism, as a means of honoring the dead and national heroes, from religious Shintoism. As Protestants, they also found themselves in the uncomfortable position of trying to defend the almost Papist centralization. There appears to have been no effective dialogue on the central issue of dispute between Japan and the United States, the war in China.

While it offered spiritual solace to the participants, the conference accomplished little in the political realm other than a rather general declaration of fellowship between the Christians of the two nations. Religion became for them "the heart of a heartless world." The fundamental differences underlying the declaration of Christian solidarity were so great that there was, in fact, little else to do but pray.

Some members of the group met again from May 9–11 at Atlantic City, and a final conference in Chicago from May 29–31. Kagawa gave lectures and attended meetings with various Protestant groups in St. Louis, Wichita and New York, as well as a convocation at Princeton. Some observers commented on the depression which recent events had created in the man who had always been known for his humor and spiritual aura. They also noted some evasiveness in his discussion of serious issues in Japan. An interviewer put it:

> Today a profound sadness enfolds Kagawa. The threat of a war between his own nation and ours pervades his life with deepest tragedy. His love for Japan, with its mystical family tie between all its citizens and between the living and the dead, finds itself in tension with his affection for America, which gave him a part of his education and has generously provided both spiritual and financial support in recent years.[42]

Relations between the two nations became increasingly strained. U.S. Secretary of State Cordell Hull protested that any peace agreement with Japan would be virtually impossible as long as key officials in the Japanese government continued to support Nazi Germany. Japan signed a Mutual Security Pact with the Nazi-imposed French Vichy government June 21, opening the way for Japan's occupation of French Indochina. The United States retaliated by freezing Japanese assets in the United States July 25, effectively ending trade with Japan. On August 1, petroleum exports to Japan were embargoed, while Japanese leaders were worrying about improved relations between the United States and Russia. The power plays of global warriors had leaped forward infinitely beyond the control of any group of well-meaning clergymen.

Still, Kagawa pleaded for peace as he traveled through the United States, speaking over 300 times. He exhorted large religious audiences to practice redemptive love, urging in New York: "If you want Japan to be a Christian nation, you must give her Christ. We could not stop the second European war because we did not know the real meaning of redemptive love."[43]

To co-op members and leaders he extolled the idea of co-ops

empowering the common people and called for a universal spirit opposite to the nationalistic mood in his own nation:

> There are three types of consciousness—national conscious-ness, class consciousness and universal consciousness ignoring racial, color or any discrimination. We must have universal minds. We must have not group but universal education. Group consciousness brings bombardment by airplane. Universal con-sciousness will develop material and power for mutual aid and brotherhood.[44]

His trip ended abruptly as the war clouds drew closer. Kaga-wa departed in August 1941 on the *Tatsuta maru*, not to return for another 10 years. Back in Japan in the last days of August, he was part of the group of 50 Christian leaders who met at Kutsukake, near Karuizawa, to discuss the new united church in Japan. The activist Christianity which had stimulated many of Japan's social reformers for so long had become an active if reluctant partner of the war government.[45] A patriotic declara-tion sought to interpret the unification of the churches as an example of divine providence.

Kagawa made one last-ditch desperate attempt to avert war. On September 5, apparently after a meeting with the Japanese premier Prince Konoye, he sent another cablegram to his Amer-ican friends and allies:

> SITUATION TAKEN EXTREMELY SERIOUS TURN STOP IMPERATIVE TO FIND SOME NEW WAY AVERT PENDING BREAK BETWEEN TWO NATIONS STOP FUTURE OF HUMANITY AT STAKE STOP URGE YOU TO EXERT YOURSELF TO UTTERMOST TO PRESERVE PEACE IN THE PACIFIC STOP DOING MY VERY BEST HERE WITH UNFAILING FAITH.   TOYOHIKO KAGAWA[46]

Kagawa and his Japanese associates began an international prayer vigil with E. Stanley Jones, his friend from theology school days at Princeton. This popular evangelist, missionary to Asia, and liberal advocate of the social gospel, had spent time with Kagawa at a summer conference in Lake Geneva, Wiscon-sin, when the two went out to the lake together at dawn to pray for peace.

"You go to see Admiral Nomura, the Japanese ambassador at Washington. He wants peace," Kagawa assured Jones. Kagawa's thought was that the militarists in Japan would be deflated if the United States made some dramatic gesture for Japan, a gesture that had to do with *Lebensraum*—more territory for the Japanese people. "Japan needs a place for her surplus population, warm enough to take off our coats," Kagawa had said, suggesting that Dutch New Guinea be ceded to Japan for her overpopulation outlet.

Jones was impressed with the proposal, since New Guinea had a population of only a million and a quarter. In his view, turning it over to Japan could sabotage the militarist claim that the nation had to fight for more territory and resources for its overpopulated islands. It would also serve as a psychological ploy to provide a graceful way for the image-conscious Japanese leaders to withdraw from China. Jones believed that they wanted out, but that they were far too proud to disgrace themselves by backing down after five years of battle. If, however, the government could present its people with new territory, the leadership would be exonerated. Finally, Jones felt that this territorial concession would also allow Japan to drop out of the Axis alliance.[47]

To the missionary Jones, who had spent much of his career in Asia, shared Gandhi's contempt for Western imperialism, and opposed racism, there was a dismal logic in the proposal. As he explained it "the Western nations grabbed these islands in the Pacific when grabbing was good, before Japan woke up. New Guinea belonged to Australia and Holland, neither of whom needed it."[48] Jones was in no sense naive nor an apologist for the Japanese; in fact, he had sternly condemned Japan for going to war in China.

Jones spent a good part of the next three months discussing this move with the Japanese and lobbying American officials. Finally, at the behest of Japanese diplomats in Washington, he paid a personal call on President Roosevelt on December 3, sneaking through a secret White House entrance to avoid the press. He discussed with Roosevelt a proposal made by the Japanese officials in Washington to send a cable directly to Emperor Hirohito asking him to intervene to stop war in the Pacific. The cable was sent on December 5 and reached the emperor on December 6. At the same time, Kagawa himself also sent cables to Jones and Roosevelt, informing them that the Japanese Prime Minister wanted to arrange a negotiation meeting with the President.

During this last week before the Japanese attack on Pearl Harbor, Jones set up an around-the-clock international prayer vigil, cabling friends in Japan, Australia and China and asking them pray with him. Kagawa cabled a message: JAPANESE CHURCH LEADERS HOLDING VIGIL FOR WEEK. WE ARE DOING WHAT WE CAN AT THIS END.[49]

This was the last message his friends in the United States were to receive from Kagawa until the end of the war. It was also the last that many Japanese were to hear from him. The prolific writer's books were banned, and he was allowed to publish almost nothing. With the police watching him closely, he could preach the gospel of peace and social justice only in vague and abstract terms. That was the cruelest kind of censorship for a man who for over 30 years insisted that the gospel be put into action and who practiced what he preached.

Jones had written that prayer was "the naked intent stretched toward God. It is giving vent to our deepest selves in the silence before him." Kagawa had spoken of the "pain of God," of God's agony in beholding the insanity of man destroying man. Kagawa returned exhausted from the prayer vigil, only to hear on the radio the wrenching news of the attack on Pearl Harbor. The president's cable had not arrived in time to affect the decision for war. Kagawa was now left with the naked intent of prayer and a searing sense of the pain of God.

Chapter 10
The Pacifist at War

Although Kagawa ceased opposition to the Japanese war effort and at times expressed sympathy for it, he remained under suspicion throughout World War II because of his pacifist background. In the autumn before the attack on Pearl Harbor, however, he was allowed to address Japanese Diet representatives in both houses, opposing Japan's entry into war and stating that the American people wanted peace. Nevertheless, Kagawa fell under the thought control dictates of the totalitarian regime, and the Kempeitai (military police) brought him under tighter surveillance, interrogation and on several occasions, arrest.

The dreaded Kempeitai stated its case against him:

> When preaching at the church, Mr. Kagawa referred to the war (Sino-Japanese conflict) saying this war is not a war of justice. This war will only result in making the Chinese people suffer and will bring no benefit to Japan, and therefore should be terminated at once. If, however, it is dragged along as it is, Japan will meet with the indignation of God and fall into trying circumstances. In his speeches and behavior, Mr. Kagawa indicates an anti-war opinion which is opposed to the policy direction of the government authorities.[1]

After Pearl Harbor, Kagawa's work was severely censored. This prolific writer who used to churn out half a dozen or more books annually was allowed to publish only a few volumes of poetry and fiction, *Tenku to kurotsuchi o nui awase te* (Stitching together the Sky and the Black Earth), *Ginzame no shinro* (The Course of the Silver Shark), and a translation of *Wissenchaft und Gott* (Science and God), by a German theologian, B. Babing. Even his politically neutral essays on agronomy and agricultural innovations ceased to appear.

The spying of the military police and their sympathizers also restricted his sermons and lectures. Kagawa could not oppose the military government publicly without risk of imprisonment. If not censorship, the shortage of paper would have greatly curtailed his publications in any case. Despite his precautions, he was arrested twice during the war for "anti-war thoughts"; once in May 1943, and again in November of that year, when he was interrogated for nine days in Tokyo. Much of the time Kagawa was essentially under house arrest.

War against the Allies was a difficult period for the Kagawa family, as for most Japanese families. Kagawa's son Sumimoto, married Michiko Tomai and attended medical school at Chiba University, where the couple had an apartment. Eldest daughter Chiyoko enrolled at Toho Women's Medical School and later moved to Nagano prefecture. Haru's mother was evacuated to Toyoshima during the war and did not return until it was over. The remaining family members stayed at Kamikitazawa, and Kagawa's niece Shige lived with them and went to Keisen Girls School with Umeko. The girls wore Sumimoto's hand-me-downs until the end of the war when donated secondhand clothing came in from the U.S.[2]

Kagawa buried himself in study at home because his evangelistic barnstorming was limited both by wartime transportation shortage and government repression. Most of his traveling was between his Toyoshima settlement and Tokyo. After his first arrest in August 1940, fear of the authorities gripped Kagawa's own congregation and reduced attendance at his church, but most of them and core groups like the Friends of Jesus remained loyal.

The family faced the typical food and supplies shortages and the scarcity of clothing as the war dragged on. Kagawa was enough of an agriculturalist to raise crops like potatoes and sweet potatoes in the back yard. He trained the children to gather edible weeds, which were dried and ground into powder to make dumplings. When the supply of rationed goods like sugar dried up, Kagawa resolutely refused to purchase anything on the black market.

The family also experienced numerous episodes of police harassment. Daughter Umeko recalled a typical incident, "One day when I came home from school, I found our books were scattered all over because police had gone through them in order to find out my father's thoughts and words."[3]

The military police either jailed opponents of the war or intimidated them into silence, and Kagawa was no exception. Already in the October 1940 issue of his magazine, *Kumo no hashira* (Pillar of Cloud), he was impelled to offer an apology to the government:

> I feel very sorry to have bothered the authorities in this way when the State has more than enough to deal with. It is quite natural that the authorities interrogated me. While Japan was still a member of the League of Nations, I consistently placed the primary emphasis on the importance of co-operating with the League. It is natural that the authorities should have suspected me of similar ideas after the outbreak of the China War.
>
> But I cannot help loving my country when it is facing a national emergency. Ideals are ideals, but even the Bible forbids that we break the law of the country for our ideals. That is why, ever since the outbreak of the China War, I have been emphasizing that we should defend our country even to the last person.[4]

This kind of public repentance was often extracted from dissenters, including the Communists, who were perhaps the fiercest opponents of the regime. Kagawa was, in effect, retracting his previous opposition to the war in China, a stance which had drawn admiration in the United States.

In the same issue of the magazine, he paid tribute to the emperor, celebrating the 2600th year of the Imperial Reign and endorsing Japan's goals in Asia with no mention of his nation's profound malaise:

> The Almighty has directed a miraculous providence toward Japan and has provided a ruler unparalleled in the world who, with the full benevolence of an uninterrupted Imperial line, showers love on the Japanese people. . . .
>
> The path of military rule will fall; power which is not based on justice cannot last. However, our country does not have the barbarous custom of slavery nor the fetters of the caste system. The spirit of moderation and conciliation spontaneously wells up from the people themselves. They love nature and are content with being honest. These millions of people see the trials of their nation and risk their lives for it. It must be believed that these

good customs, so unusual throughout the world, are completely and inevitably the result of the benevolence of the Imperial line and the illustrious virtue of His Majesty the Emperor. . . .

We are not merely made to shoulder the struggle of creation at this time in history; we are given the burden of the great call to repair the world. When love and justice has disappeared from the West, we should extend the hand of salvation from the Japanese nation and preach the gospel of the rebuilding of human society.[5]

These interpretations of the Bible and history were far different from those preached by the defiant young Christian who had led the 1921 dock strikes. Kagawa was now dutifully glorifying the Japanese tradition and supporting the regime that was controlling the people's thought. As he had softened his opposition to the government through the 1930s, his pacifism had been compromised as well. In the end, he could not abandon his patriotic allegiance to Japan, in spite of his internationalism and his opposition to violence.

Once the war began, the situation was further complicated by the fact that he could not obtain accurate reports about the conflict in the Pacific. The censored news he was receiving made it appear that Japan was engaged in a fight for its very survival against the Western powers. Under such circumstances, the existence of his nation superseded all other values. Little wonder, then, that he became a man with a broken heart. He did not believe in war, and yet found himself supporting Japan's war effort. He loathed violence, but was advocating it as a last measure of self-defense. He ached for the non-violent reconstruction of Asia, yet was acceding to Japan's violent agenda of reform. He wavered between a sort of fiery jingoism and half-hearted incantations of loyalty. He could not stand up as a consistent and wholly ardent backer of Japan's aggression, but neither could he repudiate it fully. It might be said that his heart was not so much broken as torn apart by the contradictions.

Kagawa's naive sense of patriotism showed itself even before the outbreak of World War II. Kan Majima, a social worker in Nagoya, reported his conversation with Kagawa:

Shortly before the war, I mentioned to him that the militarists were driving toward a war with America. Much to my surprise he said "If the war starts I will support it." When I wanted to discuss this with him he called me a coward. . . . About a year after the war started, Kagawa told me that Japan is very strong and on the road to victory and that we must do everything we can to help her win.[6]

Kagawa was deluded by the propaganda machine and by the Japanese cabinet's own sloppy appraisals of the nation's logistical strength.[7]

His followers in the United States knew little or nothing of these profound changes in his attitude. What later alarmed and disillusioned some of them were reports that Kagawa had engaged in propaganda broadcasts for the Japanese government. These broadcasts in English were strongly worded condemnations of American war atrocities and of American racism and imperialism.

With reference to reports of U.S. soldiers sending home bones of the Japanese dead as souvenirs, Kagawa had castigated those acts as:

> . . . a kind of savagery comparable to the lowest cannibalism. . . . Today I see America as a white grave. I cannot believe that the Almighty God for all the earth will permit the success of their inordinate ambitions for world domination which forged the spirit of racial superiority, but at the same time talks of freedom and liberty, using these words while waging this unjust war on the Oriental race. Ah, woe to America for so degrading the name of Christ by this butchery.[8]

The purpose of this and and all Japanese propaganda broadcasts, including those of the widely publicized "Tokyo Rose," was to demoralize American troops and convince them that Japan had a will to win. The Japanese media reported examples of American war crimes, but omitted mention of similar deeds by its own soldiers. Because of these reports of propaganda activity, Kagawa was investigated after the war by U.S. military officials and considered for purge from holding any responsible position, in accord with the policies of the Supreme Commander for the Allied Powers (SCAP). That investigation revealed an apparent attempt to frame Kagawa. FBI investigators received a letter purportedly written by a Japanese minister in Shanghai, indicating that Kagawa had functioned as an espionage agent during his last tour of the United States before the war.[9]

It would be simplistic to regard his broadcasting as pure

complicity with the military government, as some of Kagawa's detractors did. There were also impassioned protests against real atrocities which had taken place. Kagawa had learned of a picture in *Life* magazine which showed an American girl admiring a Japanese soldier's skull sent to her by a boyfriend. There were other pictures of souvenirs made from Japanese bones, including the letter-opener carved from a Japanese soldier's leg bone and actually sent to Roosevelt. After the President had displayed the macabre gift, he repudiated it when a protest from the Catholic bishop in Tokyo was transmitted through the Vatican.

Kagawa's derogatory statements about America were repeated in other articles, interviews and speeches during the war, and likewise his affirmations of loyalty to Japan. On October 24, 1942, when he was planning for a trip to the Philippines, he declared:

> I will go anywhere if it is for the good of our country. . . . When I was in the islands (before) I was surprised to learn that the tenant farmers of the islands were living a miserable life. This state of affairs can be explained by the fact that the American capitalists made it a point to exploit the farming population of the islands. . . . The Filipinos, especially the farmers, have to be educated properly before they can be brought to make a contribution toward the reconstruction of the islands as a component of the Co-Prosperity Sphere.[10]

At Christmas 1943, Kagawa broadcast to American prisoners of war renouncing the bombing of the Japanese civilians by the United States. In August 1944, he thundered this powerful statement by radio:

> Woe to you, America. . . . You talk about equality, yet you oppress the minorities, manipulate freedom and try to maintain the superiority which the Almighty God would never permit you to do. Repent America. The name of Jesus is smeared by the heavy bombing. . . . Alas, Japan would never experience Christianization due to America. As the crusaders isolated the Asia Minor from Jesus, this Pacific war removed the Far East from Christ forever. America is like the white washed tombs. Their children play with the scalps of the Japanese soldiers and the President of the USA received a paper knife as a souvenir, which was made out of the bones of a Japanese soldier. How can it be

possible to exist without the judgment of the Almighty, if the conscience of America is paralyzed this far?[11]

Kagawa came close to portraying Japan as the hero in a war of liberation for Asia, and the Co-Prosperity Sphere as a means of securing Asia from imperialism. Yet even at this point he was not in favor with his government. The proposed trip to the Philippines never took place because the army refused to grant him a passport.[12] He remained suspect because of his past record of denouncing Japan's own militarism and imperialism. It is also possible that authorities worried that if he had gone to the Philippines and seen first hand the atrocities committed by Japanese troops, Kagawa might have renounced the grand design of the Co-Prosperity Sphere.

The only trip abroad that he was permitted to make during the war was a two-month speaking tour in the spring of 1944 to Shanghai, Peking, Nanking and Hangchow. There were post-war accusations that Kagawa used this trip to rally support among the Chinese for the Great East Asia declaration. In the SCAP investigation, Dr. Chung Ke An, a missionary for the Presbyterian Church and a YMCA officer, filed an affidavit that Kagawa had told a Tokyo YMCA meeting that he had taken the Great East Asia Declaration to persuade the Asiatic puppet governments to support Japan's war effort. Kagawa denied these charges, saying that he had gone at the invitation of Chinese Christians solely for religious purposes. Kagawa's assistant pastor, Kiyozumi Ogawa, confirmed this, telling the investigators that while Kagawa may have told the Chinese that the principles of "good neighborliness and international coop-eration" set forth in that declaration were worthy of endorse-ment, it was incidental to the religious program. Unfortunately, in the context of war, even "religious purposes" can serve the propaganda aim to encourage collaboration or subvert resist-ance.

Other Kagawa statements expressed familiar anti-imperialist themes. On the occasion of Gandhi's birthday on October 2, 1943, Kagawa criticized the spread of the war into India:

Americans have sent armed forces into India. Thereby they've aggravated the famine which threatens the existence of millions in India. This will be considered by historians the blackest page in American history. All peoples in Asia are now striving to gain their freedom.[13]

Earlier that year, in the preface to *Stitching together the Sky and the Black Earth*, he gave vent to his angriest expression of anti-Western sentiments:

> The strange logic that only Roosevelt's people should be free and that the people of Asia should be slaves makes even the sun laugh. . . . Churchill and Roosevelt, who regarded Asia as their protectorate, at last dyed the Pacific Ocean eternally red with blood.
>
> A tornado of blood rose. A tornado of blood of righteous indignation, of blood of the heroes of Pearl Harbor and of the loyal brave soldiers of the Solomon Archipelago, rose boiling to heaven. We would like to die near our sovereign lord. We would not regret such a death. The sincere spirit of the soldiers who, oblivious of self and transcending life and death, strove only to serve Imperial Japan, enabled the Morning Star to see that the dawn was not far away. . . .
>
> Ah, Asia has wakened. India has cried for liberation. The Republic of China has cursed America and Britain. . . .[14]

On the other hand, Kagawa's patriotic rhetoric did not afford him immunity. After he was arrested and interrogated by the Kempeitai again in 1943, he resigned from two pacifist organizations, the War Resisters' International and the Fellowship of Reconciliation. To the former he wrote:

> I have come to be ashamed of my membership in the War Resisters' International whose headquarters is in an enemy state, so please delete my name from the membership list.
>
> The United States first strengthened discrimination against Japanese; it forbade Japanese immigration completely, deprived Japanese children of primary schools. Further, the United States repealed the treaty of amity and commerce with Japan, and finally it threatened Japan by the ABCD encirclement and dared to attempt the murder of the Japanese economy by freezing Japanese assets in the United States. At that moment I had to throw into the Pacific Ocean the pacifism which I had been embracing for many years.
>
> Beginning with the invasion of India by the Portuguese in the 1490s, European powers—Spain, Holland, England, and so on—

have been competing with each other to invade the Orient. This tendency was intensified in the nineteenth century, until even the United States occupied the Philippines in 1898, and Japan became isolated in the Orient. Even today Japan is the only independent country in the Orient in the true sense of the word. The most ardent pacifist cannot retain his conviction when he sees that Churchill and Roosevelt are planning to destroy even this last independent country of the Orient.

I have made a firm resolution that even if other Japanese are all annihilated and I alone survive, I will continue to defend Japan so that independence and freedom shall not vanish from the Orient.[15]

Kagawa's abandonment of internationalism is further revealed by intelligence reports indicating that he publicly criticized the UN Conference on International Organization as an example of U.S. designs for world domination.[16]

The most compelling evidence of how the war had transformed Kagawa's attitudes may lie in his poetic use of Christian rhetoric in the struggle. In 1943, the United Church of Japan published a hymnal, *Koa sanbika*, with 36 hymns. Kagawa's contribution, entitled "Song for the Great East Asia Co-Prosperity Sphere" (Dai toa kyoeiken no uta), links the war of liberation with the Christian cause:

> Though the darkness of the world is thick,
> Dawn is breaking.
> Call for the light of East Asia.
>
> Though in the midst of trial
> High-spirited by carrying the cross,
> Rain of grace is all around us.
>
> The Okhotsk Sea is packed with ice,
> Let's melt it with blood of love,
> Let's realize the Fathers will.
>
> Let's awake the sleeping India,
> Let's free its chains of suffering,
> Let's build the Kingdom of God.
>
> Ah dawn, ah dawn!
> History is awakening by grace,
> Asia has at last seen the light.

His rage against America turned to lament in an October 1944 article that the American bombardment of Japan had made the Christianization of Asia impossible forever:

> Think again, America! How terribly the name of Christ is sullied by your artillery shells! The people of Asia lose their footing because of America. As Central Asia was cut off from Christ by the Crusaders, the Far East is eternally isolated from Christ because of this Pacific War. . . .
>
> America! Don't take pride in your superior resources. What hope can you have when you sell your conscience and buy slaves; when you use your machines to make all of humanity materialistic but you yourselves lose your human nature.
>
> Woe on America! Rid yourselves of the false belief that world civilization consists of a single, Anglo-Saxon culture. Just as the human body is made up of millions of cells, true civilization must be a unified cooperative culture.
>
> Lippmann says that America began war with Japan because the Philippines had been surrounded. But is the Monroe Doctrine going to teach that Asia is included in the American Continent?[17]

It appears that Kagawa's radio propagandizing was limited. He denied that he himself did any broadcasts other than a few at Christmas. One broadcast, he asserted, was in response to American propaganda that he would be installed prime minister after the war. Such a rumor would not only have made him an assassination target of the right wing, but it could have been used against the Japanese churches as well because of his prominence as a Christian.

Because Kagawa was unable to read or hear about the war atrocities committed by the Japanese, the American bombardments appeared to be even more diabolical, one-sided and undeserved. Kagawa's horror of the war reached its height in the Tokyo bombing raid of March 10, 1945, in which 100,000 civilians were killed in a few hours. His June 1945 article in the magazine of the Friends of Jesus Society, *Hi no hashira* (Pillar of Fire) again blasted the hypocrisy of the Americans:

> In America too they read the same Bible. But they do not have the religion of Christ. They are pharasaic; they are heretic. A way of thinking which discriminates against the Asiatics and is satisfied if only its own country is well off, no matter what

becomes of the Asiatics, or how much they suffer. It is absolutely opposed to the spirit of Christ. . . .

Now almost all the countries of the world have declared war on Japan. Neutral Sweden alone understands Japan, says that Japan's war aims are right and that Japan is not bad.[18]

This and other statements make it clear that Kagawa felt a powerful anger interwoven with patriotic sentiments. Up to the very eve of surrender, he expressed this mixture of feelings. The savagery of the American bombing drove him to reiterate his support of Japan's holy mission to save Asia from the greed and racism of the West. His *Nippon Times* article on August 8, 1945, pleaded Japan's case and recoiled at the spectacle of Tokyo in flames:

Mr. Essen of Sweden, a newspaper critic, says that if America is going to practice real idealistic international policy, she must pursue a policy similar to Japan's international purpose as expressed in the Declaration of the Greater East Asiatic Nations. So if America is coveting the oil of Borneo, the tungsten of China and so forth, this war is utter folly.[19]

Appealing to the spirit of his "heaven America," he continued:

George Washington fought for the liberation of America, and if America believes in the freedom of a nation, she is the very one who can best understand how Japan is fighting for the independence and freedom of its race and state. . . . Abraham Lincoln fought for the liberation of Negro slaves. Should there still be in the conscience of the people of America the least particle of the spirit of Abraham Lincoln? They are the very ones who can really understand and sympathize with Japan's struggle for the liberation of the Asiatic races. . . .

When this war ends and when the time comes for a world historian to pass a fair and cool judgment upon the methods America used against Japan, America and the world will realize that there was no more horrible cruelty than is recorded even by Genghis Khan in India and Afghanistan. The present form of indiscriminate bombing by the American air forces upon the cities of Japan is unlike Japan's careful and thoughtful air raids on Shanghai and Nanking. Take the case of the air raids of Honjo and Fukagawa-ku of Tokyo on March 10th, 1945. The bombs came down suddenly from the clouds in a rainy day, and massacred innocent women and children, and the old and the sick, and even in that one day alone about one hundred thousand non-military civilians were burned to death. Against such American methods of cruelty, world history can never be silent. . . .

This war began and was born in racial prejudice. It was aggravated by the ambition for the expansion of the American financial interests in the Orient, and by American capitalistic ambition for the domination and control of Oriental markets. The methods go beyond that of Emperor Nero. America might be excused for this if she were a country that had no New Testament. But for a country that produced George Washington and Abraham Lincoln such a moral degeneration is beyond imagination. . . . If America's policy, as well as that of Japan, goes back to the spirit of Washington and Lincoln, there is sufficient ground for America and Japan to be reconciled—to give freedom to China, to liberate the Philippines, to cut the iron chain of India and to give independence to Indonesia. Oh America! Stop and think! Stop and think![20]

Kagawa's outbursts were more complex than mere wartime propaganda, and deserve to be assessed in broader terms. They arose from his agony over the death and destruction being visited on his nation. They were the cry of a fundamentally non-violent man appalled by the horror of 20th century war, yet aware that he had complicity in it, and they expressed his outrage at Western imperialism. That such an outburst was based partly on a "shallow" view of the United States, as Kagawa himself later admitted, does not mean that his grievances and passion were not deeply felt at the time.

The Kagawa who had always firmly opposed violent class struggle now found himself reciting the Marxian rhetoric of violence and portraying war in the Pacific as a class struggle between the have-nots of Asia and the racist conquistadores of Western capitalism. This was Asia's war of liberation from the yoke of the West. Japan had no choice but to fight on because its very survival was at stake.

This line of thinking was an intensification of his long standing condemnation of racism and imperialism. He had been consistent in denouncing Western racism and colonial ambitions since his first 1924 tour of the United States when he sounded a prophetic warning about the consequences of the Exclusion Act. A decade later, he had stated these views explicitly for the English-speaking world:

> Japan is jealous for the cause of justice and national honor. Above all things, her people hate to lose face . . . it was not so much the literal fact that the United States refused to put Japan on a quota basis that aroused the Japanese. It was the feeling that this action was an insult to the yellow race that maddened our people and made them want to fight. To this degree Japan is jealous that justice shall prevail and her honor be maintained. . . . In a case where she feels that justice and honor are at stake Japan will never yield, even though it should mean utter annihilation. To this extent does the feudal spirit of *bushido* control the soul of the Japanese.
>
> Don't laugh at Don Quixote! Was not Japan isolated out here in the Farthest East for three hundred years? Gladly will she go through another three hundred years of isolation, if thereby justice as she sees it, and national honor as she feels it, will be maintained.
>
> Don't laugh! Have not the leading nations of the West taught her this kind of internationalism? America's advocacy of the Monroe Doctrine teaches her the American brand of international isolation. Is not Great Britain, now that after age-long aggression, she has taken possession of one-fifth of the earth's surface, crying Peace! Peace! with no intention of disgorging her ill-gotten gains?
>
> Well, when will Japan awaken from her childish, feudal dream? When England awakens. When the United States awakens. Then and only then. Japan is to blame. Yet who can say that the Western nations are blameless?[21]

While his admirers in the West may have been shocked by his apparent abandonment of pacifism, the truth is that Kagawa never claimed to be an absolute pacifist, that is, a person who categorically refused to bear arms, even in self-defense. He always connected his ideas of pacifism to economics, insisting that unless nations eliminated the economic causes of war, abstract discussion of peace would be fruitless.

He had thought this out as early as 1931, drawing distinctions between four types of pacifists: the sentimental, moral, rational, and economic or cooperative pacifists. He expressed his sympathy for the first three but pointed out that they wielded insufficent power to bring peace to the world. He criticized the sentimental and moral pacifists for being too individualistic to have any lasting influence. Of the sentimentalists he said:

> They are emotional. They don't like to fight. Their ideas are very good. . . . They have good feelings and ideals, but they are very individualistic, and with their good feeling and their good emotion, they don't see through the social turmoil. Therefore when some bad situation comes around they have no influence, and that kind of movement disappears after a short period.[22]

The absolute pacifist Kagawa was more a projection of sentimental or moral pacifist thinking in the United States. The real Kagawa was skeptical of arms agreements and peace negotiations which were not backed up by economic changes to root out the causes of war.

As has been mentioned, an important part of Kagawa's teachings was his warning that Western imperialism and racism could provoke a reaction that would lead to disaster. This concept was never fully understood by the bulk of his disciples in United States and Europe. While they imbibed his religious, pacifist, and cooperative message, they failed to internalize his plea for justice from the white world.

Kagawa's tide of rage against war and imperialism crested as Japan suffered the continued onslaught of massive bombing by the U.S. Air Force, while Japan's allies, the German Nazis and the Italian Fascists, were capitulating in Europe. His message of September 1945 reiterated the lament that the devastation wrought by the bombings would make Christianization of his nation impossible:

> The Americans burned down 2,100,000 houses, so the common people don't like Christianity. Thousands of people— 250,000—living in dugouts in Tokyo alone. More people cannot come back till we have food and houses, but winter coming, no food, no clothes, no storage. . . . March 10th, within three hours, 100,000 people killed in eastern Tokyo. Only kindness can revive Christianity, not mere words or creeds.[23]

He was unquestionably deeply shaken by the wartime behavior of the United States, and it was this that he was protesting.

Kagawa frankly admitted his anti-U.S. propaganda efforts. When quizzed by a reporter from *Time* magazine, he said:

I did. I did intentionally. The Americans said that when America won I would become Premier of Japan. That made me and all Japanese Christians traitors. Therefore, intentionally, I said America must return to the spirit of Abraham Lincoln. I was sorry I had to come down from international Christianity to national Christianity. I had no choice.[24]

On more than one occasion he explained his motive in making the broadcasts:

Everyone in Japan knew that. Therefore I was in danger and the life of a Christian was in danger. That was why I went on the radio, speaking for Japanese policy, not to protect the militarists of Japan but to protect the Christian church. I do not like America to conquer Japan because this is my country.[25]

Let it be added that his failure to level the same fierce criticism at Japan's own wartime barbarism is a measure of Kagawa's failure as a prophet. He may have been kept ignorant of Japan's atrocities by a regime with long experience in suppressing the truth, and was led to portray Japan as the innocent victim of American savagery because this image was needed to maintain the nation's fighting spirit. Yet he had to have known of Japan's saturation bombing of China and the unspeakable atrocities in Nanking, because the American press were full of such reports during Kagawa's U.S. travels in 1941. To have written, as he did, of Japan's "careful" bombing raids was an exercise in self-delusion.

What is surprising is that there is no evidence of anyone in his American audiences questioning the brutal Japanese attack on China, even though it was one of the major areas of dispute between Japan and the United States. Certainly his listeners included liberal Christians who were highly critical of Japan's actions and had proposed a boycott to cripple the invasion.[26] Had Kagawa acquired such a nimbus of sanctity and celebrity that people were reluctant to raise painful questions?

It is more realistic to accept Kagawa at face value, as a man outraged by war but who still subscribed to some of the tenets of the Greater East Asian Co-Prosperity Sphere—Japan's excuse for invading the mainland. He acquiesced to Japan's sacred mission to lead Asia out of bondage. The fact that after the war he offered no apology for his personal behavior confirms this. Americans tend to forget that there were two sides to this war.

With this mind-set that the attack on Pearl Harbor was an atrocity committed on an innocent nation by a belligerent aggressor, they fail to understand the complexity of Japanese thinking—how anger and fear could be manipulated and turned back upon the United States. When the Japanese looked to the continent and the sea, they saw Russia to the north, the rape of Asia to the west, and the colonization of the Philippines, Indochina and Indonesia to the south. They were wary of Anglo-American intentions. They could proudly observe that they alone were one of the rare major nations unconquered by Western powers.

From this perspective, one can understand how Japan could construe its imperialism in Asia as a Holy War. Its sense of empire was not much different from the United States' postwar position of saving the world from Communism and/or Socialism, yet not as ambitious, confining themselves to Asian territory and not trying to police the entire globe. That does not absolve the Japanese nor Kagawa. The use of the defense of Asia as a pretext for Japan's bloody invasions and the hypocrisy of signing a treaty with the racist Nazis, while claiming to defend the nonwhite world, laid bare the ruthless ambitions of the militarists.

Once the bombing of Japan began, Kagawa saw his life's work being obliterated. In the Kobe area, all the facilities of the original Friends of Jesus group were completely burned down. In Osaka, churches, day care centers and the Shikanjima settlement were destroyed. The bombing of Tokyo wiped out the credit union and other co-ops he had founded, killing some of the employees. A bomb exploded near the family compound but the Kagawas and their guests escaped injury.

In the end, Kagawa became a refugee in his own land. During the last weeks of the war he ran for his life, convinced he was being hunted down by right-wing fanatics bent on assassinating those they believed responsible for Japan's defeat. He was warned to leave Tokyo by an official who had heard about the assassination plans. Kagawa believed that the motive for killing him arose from American propaganda that he would be installed as prime minister after the war and would collaborate with the Allied occupation of Japan. The mere fact of being considered would have made him a target for these ultranationalist fanatics. He fled to the forests 40 miles northeast of the city where he went into hiding near Mamada, Tochigi prefecture. The food shortage was severe, and he had to forage on mulberry leaves in order to survive.[27] He managed to find refuge in the factory of an associate, Yasutaro Goto, who had been active in Kagawa's church.

The war's end in the Pacific is a familiar story, and yet of such unfathomable horror that it is almost impossible to find authentic language to describe it. Mere words fail to explain a madness beyond rational comprehension. The massive obliteration of Hiroshima and Nagasaki on August 6 and 9, 1945, was at the same time a symbol of modern war and a threat to life on this planet. Two sudden explosions culminated mankind's entire history of war weaponry. On the country whose native name *Nihon* literally means "sun root," we unleashed powers like those which before existed only in the distant explosions of the sun.

Even after Hiroshima and Nagasaki, some chieftains of the Japanese military establishment were determined to continue fighting. It was the emperor who took it upon himself to decree the decision to surrender at the Imperial Conference on August 14. After the surrender, a new government was hastily formed to lead a confused and devastated nation. To help them, one of those they summoned out of hiding was a rather unlikely looking figure—a sloppily-dressed, fragile little man, almost blind, wasted thin by illness and hunger, and near despair. That man was Toyohiko Kagawa.

Chapter 11
Reconstruction and Repentance

K AGAWA PARTICIPATED WHOLEHEARTEDLY in the reconstruction of postwar Japan, a most remarkable episode in history. That the Japanese accomplished it with the blessings and assistance of the enemy makes it even more remarkable. Thoroughly defeated, their nation in rubble, many Japanese had feared a retribution from the United States as brutal as the war itself. Instead, the former enemy extended desperately needed aid, encouraged and often demanded sweeping reforms.

Democracy replaced totalitarianism, freedom of speech and press were granted for the first time in Japanese history, women received the right to vote, the rights of workers to organize was guaranteed, and massive land reforms lifted million of peasants out of the feudal system. Viewed even from the cynical perspective that Occupation policy was prompted by American economic motives and defense strategies, this remains one of the finest hours in United States history.

The Occupation had its low points, such as the squelching of strikes, the ruthless purge of thousands of Communists, and the failure to fully wrest power from the monopolies. Such shortcomings, however, do not cancel out the immensity of the reforms nor the value of the forgiveness and justice fostered by Occupation policy. That policy stands as an example of what can be achieved when human freedom, human rights and human needs take precedence over the violence, vengeance, greed, and racism that have sometimes marred U.S. foreign policy in other regions.

Despite the bleak history of United States-Japan relations, their former enemy surprised the Japanese with benevolence. The American Occupation confirmed Kagawa's oft-repeated Manichean view of the "hell America" and the "heaven America." The hell America—that had dropped the atomic bomb on Japan and interned Japanese Americans residents on the Pacific Coast—had given way to the heaven America. That was the America Kagawa had always loved and praised. Little wonder that he welcomed the heaven America with an enthusiasm so strong that it seemed suspect to some.

Kagawa's attitude was typical of millions of Japanese. They had exhausted the possibilities of militarism, had been soundly defeated, and now resolved to embark on a new course. Drained and disgusted by war, they would rebuild in peace. Mingled with their feelings of despair and disgrace was a determination to move the nation in a different direction. The utter defeat and the physical destruction also created an opportunity for complete reform, lifting the terrible burden of militarism that enlightened Japanese had despised from the time of the 1905 war against Russia, when the young Kagawa had thrown down his gun on the school grounds. Kagawa compared the aftermath of the war to the 1923 earthquake, which had devastated Tokyo but also provided a chance for reconstruction— slum clearance on a grand scale.

Physically spent from his flight into the countryside at war's end, Kagawa underwent an emotional ordeal that was a mixture of patriotism and pacifism, of desire for the liberation of Asia and distrust of militarism, of desperation and enthusiasm, of repentance and defiance, and of love and anger. Less than a month after the surrender, when asked by an American whether he was grateful to the United States for conquering Japan and creating the possibility for him to assume a position of influence in the government, his blunt and sorrowful reply was, "I would rather be dead."[1]

Kagawa sat in the large conference room of the premier's palace, a pitiful emblem of Japan's defeat, emaciated and wearing a donated blue suit that was several sizes too large. It had been pinned up to fit him, his shriveled neck not even touching the shirt collar. "We are sitting now in the house of blood," he grimly observed, "Two of the emperor's ministers were killed here."

He groped for a comprehension of the causes of the war, the defeat of Japan and his own role in events. Asked how militarism in Japan could have been abolished without the American victory, he could only reply: "It would not have been necessary to borrow foreign weapons to eliminate militarism here. We had a proletarian movement."

"You mean that you still had a labor movement in Japan from 1941 to the present?" the reporter pressed him.

"No," admitted Kagawa, "It was intentionally disorganized because since the war with America, America was so big and Japan so small, America would eliminate us." His attempt to shift blame to the United States for the downfall of Japan's labor movement was amiss, since the unions had capitulated long before war with the United States.

In answering what the United States should have done after Pearl Harbor, he projected his own guilt onto the enemy: "If President Roosevelt had been a Christian, why did he also want to wage war against Japan?" With respect to Japan's policy in the Far East, he expressed his own unresolved conflict: "I am against militarism, but I am also against domination by the white races in Asia." This same conflict between the goal of Asian liberation and Japan's own imperialist designs showed in his reaction to Pearl Harbor: "Though I did not like it, I thought it would lead to independence for Asia. . . . My ideal, and that of the militarists, are two things—it is a dilemma." He resorted to uncomfortable sophistry when asked point blank how he interpreted the gospel's injunction to love thy neighbor: "You must love your neighbor but with conditions. Jesus put conditions on it. Anyone who would blaspheme the Holy Spirit is not forgiven."

Kagawa admitted that he had not protested against the war after Pearl Harbor because the government had cautioned him to keep quiet. He defended his lack of action by offering a fundamentalist interpretation of the Bible which rationalized the emperor system as the divine right of kings. The following sequence of questions and answers is illustrative of his waffling:

> *Question:* In view of your faith as a Christian, as absolute above Japan, would you be willing to say that the Emperor could be wrong?
> *Answer:* No. I can't say that.
> *Question:* Does that mean that the Emperor is always right?

Answer: I refer you to the 13th chapter of Romans, which says, in effect, "Obey the authority who is endowed with power from above," and the Emperor is.[2]

Vestiges of his Meiji upbringing remained, and Kagawa would not acknowledge the flaws of the emperor system itself. Like many others, he held the emperor blameless, but allowed that the emperor had been misled by bad advisers, from the 1931 Manchurian Incident through World War II. It was as if the person of the emperor was the last repository of Japan's self-respect, a jewel still shining in the ashes of war. The guilty ones were the advisors, the military, and the entire population who followed their orders. As the weeks went by, however, he toned down this absolute view of the emperor and started to encourage a change toward European-style constitutional monarchy.

In stating the case for Japan, Kagawa admitted her war guilt and the need for repentance. "We were too proud, lacked self-examination, love and intelligence and were too much misled by the militarists and shallow judges of America," he said. "Everyone must repent, including me."[3] When asked if he thought freedom and democracy had arrived in Japan, Kagawa enthusiastically responded: "Oh, sure. The Army is gone. The Potsdam Declaration promised to revive democracy in Japan— revive, not create. We are very glad. But Americans must not expect democracy here with American zip. What Americans do in one hour takes Japanese a day."[4] His mood was almost joyful relief when he talked about the dismantling of the Japanese military machine that he had opposed so long.

Looking back, he characterized Japan's infatuation with the military as an aberration in its history:

But the Army and Navy cannot form a party. They have disappeared. Japan had a good whipping. The emperor signed away the Army and Navy—permanently. Not just for now, but permanently. . . . Japan is like Sweden, which was once a very warlike nation. Gustavus Adolphus fought many battles, sometimes winning, sometimes losing, but in the end Sweden found that war was no use. All that is past now. Prisons have been made into art galleries. Under the shogunate Japan had 250 years of peace, developed the tea ceremony, color prints, and love of nature. This terrible war experience shows us that we have made a serious mistake. The atomic bomb was rather a terrible thing, but it also shows how much Japan fell behind by neglecting culture and science.[5]

Kagawa meant what he said, and his words "were not calculated, but spontaneous, ringing with conviction. Plainly he believed and rejoiced."[6] The point he made about "reviving" democracy is extremely important, because it was another way of affirming the dignity of Japan. Many Americans, while congratulating themselves for bringing democracy to Japan, were often skeptical of men like Kagawa who quickly proclaimed acceptance of democracy after failing to resist totalitarianism. There was suspicion that the Japanese had a hidden agenda and were simply going through the motions of accepting democracy to placate the Allies, after which they would revert to their feudal, militaristic past. What those Americans overlooked was that Japan for decades had been moving toward democracy, and Kagawa was one of its propelling forces.

Weeks later, Kagawa went so far as to say that Japan's defeat was a "great blessing" because it actually set Japan free from its "military bondage."[7] He publicly welcomed proposals for reforms such as female suffrage. He paid tribute to the American Occupation at this early date, repeating the heaven/hell theme: "There are two kinds of Americans—those who follow Abraham Lincoln and those who follow Al Capone. I believe in General MacArthur and his spiritual life. In some respects he is winning us by being generous."[8]

Yet Kagawa did not back off his contempt for imperialism or his anger at the violence inflicted on Japan, nor did he apologize for his retreat from the high ground of pacifism. He explained: "When 10,000,000 people lose their homes, you can't be a pacifist. We had to defend ourselves."[9] He was consistently supportive of MacArthur's Occupation policies, which he strongly endorsed and to a significant extent influenced. Kagawa expressed his personal trust in MacArthur: "He knows and understands us."[10] Of MacArthur critics who condemned the Occupation strategy as "kid glove treatment" and advocated punishing Japan he remarked: "Those who say that do not know the Orient. Supreme Commander MacArthur's three points—generosity, liberty and justice—are wise. It would be tragic if he were to change."[11]

What made his lavish praise of MacArthur's policies ring true was that it was the counterpoint of his continued criticism of American and Western imperialism and racism as causes of the war. Though he could have been silent about this in order to curry favor with the Allies, he continued to air Asia's long history of grievances. One statement appeared in a Japanese newspaper on October 9, 1945: "Most of the American correspondents ask me what was the true cause of the war. I reply that it is the 400-year history of your aggression in the East."[12] That was considered dangerous enough to warrant placing it in the investigation file of the Supreme Command of the Allies in the Pacific (SCAP) as evidence for purging Kagawa as a war criminal.

Because he had also considered economic problems as major causes of war, Kagawa was anxious for revival of the Japanese economy. He predicted that the nation would start down the road to prosperity because it no longer had to bear the enormous burden of arms expenditures: "Being unarmed, Japan can carry on a prosperous trade with all other countries. . . ."[13] He talked about specific needs, such as for oil, which he wanted Japan to buy "on credit" and repay by revenues from sales of manufactured products. He continued to make his case for cooperative economics, "Christian cooperatives must be the foundation not only of Japan, but of the entire world."

The Japanese government initially sought Kagawa's help when the first postwar Prime Minister Naruhiko Higashikuni asked him to serve as a cabinet advisor. Higashikuni specifically wanted Kagawa to use his Christian perspective to help reform the nation.[14] To the gaunt little man who was squinting through yellow-tinted glasses, Higashikuni said,

> Mr. Kagawa, Japan has been destroyed not because we had not a sufficient army, but rather because we had suffered the loss of a good standard of morality and engaged in war. If Japan should now seek to revenge itself against the Allied Forces, there would be wars going on permanently in the Pacific Zone. So we need a new standard of ethics, like that of Jesus Christ. Bud-

dhism can never teach us to forgive our enemies; nor can Shintoism. Only Jesus Christ was able to love his enemies. Therefore, Mr. Kagawa, if Japan is to be revived we need Jesus Christ as the basis of our national life. Kindly assist me to put the love of Jesus Christ into the hearts of our people.[15]

Kagawa was moved by this request, and responded with a quick evangelizing attempt: "Your Highness, Christianity is not a mere creed or doctrine, nor is it just a system of ethics. It is a conviction about God and Christ. It is better for you, yourself, to become a Christian first, and set an example for the nation."[16] Even in such a situation, Kagawa would lecture on Christianity, because it was for him more than the dogma of traditional Western faith or an ethical system. Higashikuni, however, considered Christianity as a useful moral tonic for Japan, not a soul-shaking encounter as it had been for the convert and mystic Kagawa.

Higashikuni had appointed Kagawa as an advisor at the behest of Lt. General Kanji Ishihara, whom General Tojo had forced to retire in 1944. Ishihara had advised, "Get a person like Toyohiko Kagawa as a cabinet consultant."[17] Aside from the practical advice available from a man so experienced in welfare and relief work, Kagawa's international image was certainly a key consideration. The appointment of a Japanese Christian with a wide following in the West was a powerful signal of Japan's willingness to cooperate with the United States.

To Kagawa the West's role in provoking the war was not an exoneration of Japan. He exhorted his people to repent of its own military madness. A campaign for total national repentance (kokumin sozange) was proposed by Kagawa, together with Mitsuru Tomita, Koji Suzuki, Shiro Murata, Takeo Katsube and Satoshi Kimata at the August 29, 1945, meeting in the United Church of Christ. Kagawa enthusiastically took it to Higashikuni.

His main goal was to proceed with the vigorous kind of evangelizing tours which he led during the Kingdom of God Movement 15 years earlier. This, he believed, was still the most effective way to spread Christianity in Japan. While he welcomed Higashikuni's enthusiasm for Christianity, he cautioned the premier to avoid any hint of state sponsorship.

The pleas of Higashikuni to the United States asking for reform of Japan, rejection of militarism, and forgiveness of the Japanese were quite similar to Kagawa's and undoubtedly influenced by him. The premier asked:

People of America, won't you forget Pearl Harbor? We Japanese people will forget the picture of devastation wrought by the atomic bomb and will start entirely anew as a peace-loving nation. America has won and Japan has lost. The war is ended. Let us now bury hate. This has been my policy since the organization of the present cabinet.[18]

He commended, too, the attitude of the United States Occupation forces, expressing relief that Japan was free of its military leadership:

We intend to build a completely new and peaceful Japan; we intend to build a country of high moral principles and culture. I think it will require years for us to complete the task. All our internal inconsistencies will be brought to light as a result of Japan's defeat. The conflict between the old and the new may take the form of a struggle among political parties or of strikes, but I do not think such conflicts should be avoided. It is my firm belief that a new Japan, progressive and just, will be born as the result of these conflicts.

The premier added that steps would be taken to ensure freedom of speech, which he admitted had been long suppressed in Japan. Referring to economic issues, he declared,

We are looking forward to a continuous flow of American capital and technique. Real friendship cannot be created unless the people of the United States and Japan can come together and be friends. Diplomacy should not be left entirely to the diplomats. There must be direct intercourse between the peoples concerned.

He announced dependence on the power of religion to help Japan, and went on:

Democracy in its true sense will be realized in all phases of political, economic and social life under America's sagacious guidance. . . . I hope the people of the Allied Powers will extend a helping hand to the Japanese people, who are now completely exhausted.

His criticism of Japan paralleled Kagawa's:

> Morality had lost its hold in Japan. We can say that one reason for our tragedy was that no great statesman appeared in Japan. We can also count as one reason lack of courage on the part of the Japanese people to defend justice, so they were unable to correct the mistaken guidance of militarists and bureaucrats.

The initial response to this statement was regretably cool—indeed, so cold that it marked the beginning of the period in which the United States first envisioned itself as policeman to the world. Acting Secretary of State Dean Acheson's negative response was:

> Nothing could show more clearly than this statement the failure of the Japanese to understand the nature of their own conduct or the mind of the American people. Pearl Harbor is not a symbol of hate for Japan but a symbol of Japanese perfidy. We are determined that there shall be no opportunity for such perfidy again.[19]

Acheson was wrong. The statement showed considerable understanding of both the Japanese and the Americans. On the Japanese side, it clearly recognized their capacity to make a drastic change in attitude. Those who think of Japan as a tradition-bound nation, forget the startling examples of revolutionary change, beginning with the introduction of Buddhism, the first wave of Christianity, the establishment of the Tokugawa shogunate, then its overthrow and the restoration of the emperor, and the quick adoption of Western political structures, technology and philosophy in a xenophobic country almost totally cut off from the rest of the world for 250 years. Higashikuni and Kagawa had also accurately gauged the constructive and forgiving side of the United States, one that combined pragmatism with generosity, goodwill and knowhow.

From the Occupation's very outset, Kagawa used his influence to obtain merciful treatment for Japan, stressing that his nation would completely convert from war to peaceful membership of the larger world community. He published a long "Open Letter to General MacArthur" in the August 30 issue of *Yomiuri Hochi*, calling on the Supreme Commander to treat Japan sympathetically and to retain the emperor system. The translation in the *Nippon Times* a few days later created a stir because it exhibited reverence for the emperor and the emperor system, which most Americans then regarded as the the cause of Japan's war mania.

Kagawa's words were:

> Your Excellency: On August 15, Japan was labeled as a defeated country. That is a grim fact and everybody had to admit it. Till one minute before the proclamation of the Imperial Rescript terminating the war, the Imperial Forces including the Army, Navy and Air Forces were burning with an unflinching fighting spirit. However, with the issuance of the Imperial Rescript, Japan immediately stopped all her military action and began to tread on a new road.
>
> Your Excellency: You must have already received news as to the peaceful landing of the vanguards of the Allied occupation forces amid a friendly atmosphere due to the thorough preparations made by the Japanese side. You must have by now met many Japanese people and noticed that their mouths were set firmly. All the Japanese were determined to fight to the last. Everybody was aware of the power of atomic bomb attacks. None of them doubted that the war would have to be continued even if he or she might be blasted to bits or burned to ashes, while His Majesty the emperor willed so. Following the proclamation of the Imperial Rescript, however, Japan made a quick turn from war to peace. The determination and efforts of all the Japanese to start out on a new path are shown in their tightly-set mouths. Can you find any other people like the Japanese?[20]

Citing examples from Japan's past to show how resolute their turnaround would be, Kagawa continued:

> Your Excellency: The Japanese people are always ready to conduct themselves in compliance with the Imperial wishes. By proclaiming the Imperial Rescript, His Imperial Majesty took over the sufferings and privations which were brought about by the war, on his own shoulders. Every one of his subjects wept upon receiving the Imperial Rescript and expressed his sincere regret for not having done as much as he ought to have. You know that many military men and patriots killed themselves to apologize with their lives for their inability to perform their duties. Others who also regretted that they were not able to serve His Imperial Majesty as expected, have become resolved to

exert their utmost to contribute toward the development of the world civilization and realization of world peace, in compliance with the Imperial wishes.[21]

Having demonstrated the people's allegiance to the emperor, Kagawa proposed a world economic order based on an international system of cooperative economics. He submitted that despite the good intentions of the San Francisco Conference for establishing a world government, it would fail and world peace would be impossible if the fundamental problems of poverty and unemployment were not first solved.

Kagawa proceeded:

The 31 resolutions adopted at the San Francisco Conference, and the setting up of the security guarantee system and the international court and police will not prevent many countries from suffering acute unemployment. The defeated countries must travel over a thorny road. How could the defeated people, whose arms are seized and who are obliged to pay enormous reparations, stand up again on their own feet unless they are sure of friendly help and assistance? From degeneration, they will eventually come to complete collapse. They cannot participate in the activities of the world organization advocated by Your Excellency's country and others.

Your Excellency: Japan has no intention of isolating herself from the world organization. You will be able to understand easily that it is much wiser to extend a helping hand than to torment a defeated country and welcome its early participation in the march toward a new world civilization. By a helping hand I mean the establishment of an international cooperative system. . . .

Your Excellency: Victor countries must be broadminded and sympathetic. Japan, in observance of the Imperial Rescript, is ready to start on a new road as a member of the world nations. If you attempt to confine the Japanese to a small space, the result will be contrary to your expectations. Should the loyalty of the Japanese and their true strength be further fostered, Japan will be able to contribute toward the establishment of a new world much sooner than expected. . . . The wisest policy is to rule with kindness and consideration. This is an immortal truth.

Your Excellency: Please do not crack your whip, but help the Japanese to give full play to their characteristics so that they may forge straight ahead to participate in the development of a new culture and a new world. I believe that is the wisest and most important policy in putting the decision reached at the San Francisco Conference into practice.[22]

Kagawa's plea thus reinforced the general policy for the reform and reconstruction of Japan which had been formulated by the Allies and the United States as the postwar strategy. He risked considerable criticism from Americans by his reverential attitude toward the emperor.

An article in the Army paper *Stars and Stripes* attacked him, charging that he "was on the platform at the inaugural meeting of the Social Democratic Party where he distinguished himself by giving three loud banzais for the emperor."[23] This reaction may have reflected the bias of the reporter more than anything else. Japanese liberals who never believed in the divinity of the emperor still recognized the value of retaining him as a symbol of national unity. The Social Democratic Party itself was in fact strongly divided on the question of retention of the emperor, and Kagawa was among those in the party who favored a type of constitutional monarchy.

Kagawa entered a busy routine of relief work, as well as political, peace, evangelical, publishing and cooperative activities that he had known before the war. Shortly after his appointment by Higashikuni, he went to Occupation headquarters to meet with MacArthur's staff and request both food and timber to reconstruct housing destroyed by the air raids before the winter set in. He had taken the initiative because the Cabinet ministers were hesitant to do so. Negotiating with Brigadier Generals Bonner Fellers and T. F. Farrell, and others, he obtained a large supply of wood, rice and medical supplies.

Widespread press coverage was given Kagawa, informing the public that timber originally designated for military use would be supplied for 300,0000 homes, and he was negotiating for 2 million *koku* of rice and ¥500,000 worth of medicine. It was helpful in his work both to "sell" the Occupation to the Japanese and let the public know of his good relations with the Occupation authorities. Kagawa announced:

> It happens that the General [Farrell] is a friend of mine who 25 years ago wrote a biography of me. He is a person of strict morals who listens willingly to my earnest requests. . . . I have

seen the General in the capacity of chairman of the Christian Commission for the Relief of Air Raid Victims.[24]

Kagawa, putting himself at center stage, caused some to accuse him of being a publicity seeker and others to see him as a great leader and man of action. It also showed a mind alert to all the possibilities of a situation. At one and the same time he was reassuring the Japanese, reminding them to treat the Allies with respect, cementing relations with MacArthur's headquarters, and signaling that his own enterprises needed help. He was telling the world that he was back at work on Japan's welfare, promoting moral repentance with the image of swords beaten into ploughshares—or in this case, military timber hewn into homes for the homeless.

His private interviews with U.S. intelligence officials were consistent with his public statements. He was especially careful to emphasize that Japan's willingness to make peace with the Americans was genuine. He told an investigator on October 10, 1945, that a strong feeling existed that losing the war was ultimately best for the Japanese character. That the feeling extended even to the Army people he had found "amazing."[25]

Like thousands of Japanese activists who had been stifled, censored, spied on and jailed during the war, Kagawa was buoyed by the restoration of the political and intellectual freedom decreed by SCAP. He was in the public eye as a spokesman for reform and reconstruction, and the foreign press frequently interviewed him because of his prestige abroad. He became involved in a variety of groups which took advantage of his reputation, his experience in relief work and his organizing ability.

He was appointed director of the People's Nutrition Council in September, and he organized the International Peace Association in the same month, using seed money from Higashikuni. He was on the Research Commission on Diet Reorganization in October. He was elected President of the Japan League of Cooperative Unions in November. He helped to organize the Japan Educators' Union (Nippon Kyoikusha Kumiai) and presided over its inaugural meeting on December 2 as its head. He teamed with Isoo Abe, Iwasaburo Takano and others to form the new Socialist Party of Japan (Nihon Shakaito), which scheduled its first official postwar conference for September 22, 1945. He was named to a variety of other relief and research groups such as the Commission on Food Supply and the Social Insurance Inquiry Commission.

His war-crushed exuberance returned. He made speeches, advised politicians, preached the gospel of cooperation, exhorted the nation to repent and represented Japan to the world community. Less than six weeks after the end of the war, he was devoting major efforts to a complete transformation of Japanese attitudes. Yes, Western imperialism had given the militarists an excuse to attack, but Kagawa insisted that Japan's own militaristic disease was also responsible for the war and that it must be purged forever by a complete spiritual renewal. He said:

> Re-education of the people is an absolute necessity. We must repent because our fellow countrymen were responsible for the black deeds which were brought to the light very recently, and realize our responsibility to all humanity. Once when I met Mahatma Gandhi, he pointed out the cruelties perpetrated by Japanese soldiers and said that if they entered India, they would repeat the same atrocities, adding that the Indian masses would never welcome Japanese troops. The misconduct of Japanese troops has been thus pointed out by the whole world. . . . A new-born Japan must be protected by laborers who are awakened to the real values of love and laborer's cooperatives, so that Japan will be purged of militarism which is rooted deep into the minds of all Japanese. I am confident that after a year, Japan will become ruled with justice and high principles.[26]

Whatever the sins of the rest of the world, Japan now had to squarely face its own. Whatever the evils of Western imperialism, whatever the horror of the American bombings, the Japanese had to acknowledge their own territorial ambitions and their own war crimes.

The whirl of activitity continued into 1946, when Kagawa was appointed National Food Commissioner in February. He raised sufficient capital (¥300,000) to found a new Christian publishing company and newspaper *The Christian News* (Kirisuto Shimbun) with his friend and future biographer Tomio Muto as editor. He joined the Board of Directors of the National Relief Commission and became President of its Tokyo Branch in May. Between

December 1945 and June 1946, he published no less than five books and pamphlets on the themes of a new Japan: *Democracy, Food, Clothing and Homes for New Japan, Guide to New Life, Theory and Practice of Cooperatives,* and *Reconstruction.*

One significant assignment was an invitation from Emperor Hirohito to lecture at the Imperial Palace in February. Kagawa came in his baggy suit, talked for an hour and a half, and ended up preaching to the emperor. He pulled out a dog-eared Bible and flipped the pages to Christ's exhortation that serving others was the key to salvation: "Whosoever shall be great among you . . . shall be servant of all," and added, "A ruler's sovereignty, Your Majesty, is in the hearts of the people. Only by service to others can a man, or a nation, be godlike."[27]

Despite all these efforts, Kagawa was investigated for purge from public life. His appointment by the emperor to the Japanese House of Peers in March automatically triggered an investigation for purge, because SCAP headquarters was required to clear appointees for such positions. Kagawa was temporarily suspended from taking the seat in the upper house, and by the time he was cleared, the House of Peers itself had been eliminated by the new Japanese Constitution, promulgated on November 3, 1946, and placed into effect the following May.

The investigation attracted wide attention both in Japan and the United States. His friends deplored the attack on a man with such a fine record of peace advocacy and social service, for that would deprive Japan of exactly the type of person needed to help the nation recover. A Church of Christ group of 300 ministers and laymen met in Tokyo on May 21, 1946, to pass this declaration:

> Recently there have been certain malicious attacks made against Christians, especially against Dr. Toyohiko Kagawa. Through radio broadcasts and newspapers, he has been attacked by charges based on either unfounded or twisted facts, and thus the public has been greatly misled and he misunderstood. This is clearly a case of evil propaganda against him. We hereby certify, on the basis of his consistent faith, thought and deeds, that he has been incessantly working for the uplift of international justice and for absolute peace even at the risk of his own life during the war.[28]

In July, Kobe Mayor Kazuo Nakai sent a letter of support to General MacArthur, saying:

> The fact of Dr. Kagawa's position as a man of God, an ardent advocate of peace and democracy is without question. He is the most unique and qualified character to be the leader of New Japan after the war. If he is ever to be purged by the Directive, no Japanese will be safe. . . . Now is the time he can exert his great influence to realize his long cherished ideals and principles. And what a pity and a great loss to the people of Japan when this unique opportunity for him to execute his grave responsibility and carry out his important mission toward democracy has been blocked.[29]

Newsweek reported in spring 1945 that Kagawa had broadcasted propaganda for the Japanese during the war. This was followed by an inflammatory *Stars and Stripes* article by Barnard Rubin with the headline "Under Christian Guise, This Jap Fostered War." He accused Kagawa of being an agent for the Japanese government:

> A man who has propagandized for an aggressive war; a man who has called for the defeat of the United States on Nazi-like racial grounds, and who still has to a large extent, the reputation in the States of being a Christian pacifist and a social reformer, must be a very clever man indeed.
>
> The man is Dr. Toyohiko Kagawa, who used to be one of the favorites of American lecture booking agencies. The combination of Kagawa's "magnetic" personality, and the build up accorded him as a "Christian reformer" from the "mysterious" East proved an irresistable attraction to wide audiences. . . .
>
> Kagawa's camouflage was as skillfully worked out as that of a Nazi agent in a Hitchcock movie. And just as surely came the denoument.
>
> The story of his American reputation was being relayed to the Japanese people by the Nippon government controlled press. Thus Kagawa's war-mongering was supposed to be that much more effective in convincing the Japanese people that the war against the United States was a just war. For was it not supported by a man who knew America and who was known by both Americans and Japanese to be a Christian man of peace?[30]

The article then quoted one of the radio broadcasts.

The SCAP purge program was an attempt to keep militarists

out of power in postwar Japan. A wide range of people were
subjected to scrutiny, from war criminals who were later tried,
sentenced or executed to minor officials and journalists.[31] Seven
categories were candidates in the purge. The first six were the
true architects of the war, such as military officers, members of
ultranationalist groups and semi-private and public officials.
Kagawa was investigated under the following ill-defined catch-
all category:

> . . . any person who in the capacity as scholar, journalist,
> member of a newspaper editorial staff, reviewer or writer for
> magazines or other publications, or in any similar capacity,
> comes under one of the following categories because of his
> writing, lecture, speech, article, news report . . . or advocated
> aggression or militant nationalism or actively contributed to such
> propaganda, or who through his political or philosophic doctrine
> laid down an ideological basis of the policies for the Greater East
> Asia, or New Order in the East Asia or policies of similar nature,
> or the Manchurian Incident, China Incident, or the Pacific War.[32]

A closer look at some of the charges flying around about
Kagawa at the time reveals as much about the motives of people
making the accusations as about Kagawa himself. While the
facts reported are essentially accurate—and have been recapitu-
lated in this book—a careful examination of the articles by Rubin
demonstrates a vigorous twisting of those facts. Rubin stated
that:

> Kagawa only lately was stumping side by side with Yoshio
> Kodama, former leader of the Patriotic Mass Party. During the
> war Kodama made a fortune confiscating properties and com-
> modities in China and then selling them at fantastic prices to the
> Japanese Navy. Until recently, Kodama was using some of the
> profits to subsidize many of the now one-man unltranationalist
> "parties" that have sprung up with the avowed intention of
> protecting the emperor system. . . . Kodama was arrested the
> other day as a war criminal suspect. But Kagawa is still playing
> the game—as a Christian pacifist and social reformer.[33]

The ex-Communist Rubin was using the same guilt-by-
association tactics with which the American government perse-
cuted Communists and their associates in the early 1950s, in
what is called the McCarthy Era. In the chaos of the immediate

postwar period and the prodigious reconstruction work at hand, neither Kagawa nor anyone else had the luxury of choosing with whom to work or stump. Kodama was one of the half-dozen or so special advisors Higashikuni had appointed along with Kagawa, and the latter had no dossiers on them. In fact, Kodama had become something of a hero by risking his life in a futile attempt to prevent a group of nationalist fanatics from killing themselves immediately after the war.

Rubin paid a price for his efforts, as MacArthur ordered an investigation. He was removed from his post at *Stars and Stripes* when Counter-Intelligence chief Brigadier General Elliot Thorpe concluded that his reporting was a "disguised shield for propaganda."[34]

An article by Hugh Deane published in April 1946 in *The Christian Register* rehashed many of the same charges made by Rubin, again without interviewing Kagawa or making the slightest attempt to put Kagawa's actions into the context of the times. His conclusion was even harsher than Rubin's:

> Kagawa's thinking is obviously wedded to the ideology of feudalism and ultranationalism, to the concepts the Allies are trying to root out of the Japanese mind. Clearly Kagawa does not belong in the ranks of those leading the fight for democracy in Japan.[35]

This assessment was particularly unfair since Kagawa had often applauded the collapse of feudalism and ultranationalism, and enthusiastically supported democracy. His support for the emperor was not a clinging to feudalism. He made it clear that he favored a constitutional monarchy because he believed the emperor to be a symbol of national unity that would ease the transition to democracy.

Some of the American reaction to Deane's article was fierce. One reader regarded Kagawa as:

> . . . a skillful propagandist who makes use of the credulity of some American missionaries who are either vain or simple enough to be taken in by his words. His actions have always contradicted his words. No man with a deep belief and a solid backbone can ever be "forced to stoop as low as he stooped."[36]

But one of those missionaries referred to above, Thoburn T.

Brumbaugh, saw it otherwise. He answered back that the charge was:

> . . . such a tissue of half truths and skillful perversion as to make appraisal difficult. For the fair-minded, however, a warning should be raised lest we permit ourselves to be victimized by forces purporting to be democratic and Christian, but falling seriously short of the spirit and ethic of Jesus, in an effort to smear Kagawa in the same manner as Martin Niemöller's fair name was besmirched following Germany's capitulation. . . .[37]

The "Kagawa question" became such a hot topic in America, especially in Protestant circles, that one author in 1947 referred to "the debates which today rage around the person of Toyohiko Kagawa,"[38] while as late as 1951 another said in reference to the Rubin article, "Widely quoted in America, the broadside shook churchmen's faith in Kagawa. Its echoes are still being heard."[39]

After accumulating hundreds of pages of information and discussion, the Supreme Command on March 18, 1947, finally cleared Kagawa of the purge and approved his appointment to the House of Peers. Even so, SCAP's final assessment of him was mixed with hostility and a lack of understanding:

> Despite the technical non-purgeability of the subject, Kagawa's thinking is obviously confirmed in the ideology of feudalism and ultranationalism; the very concepts that SCAP is committed to eradicate from the Japanese mind. Occupation policies cannot hope to be realized if the leadership of Japan is bestowed on pseudo-liberals like Kagawa who exploit the trappings of democracy for political purposes. Kagawa is considered the type of person who would tend to obstruct rather than promote the development of individual initiative on the part of the people and retard the establishment of social and political democracy in Japan.[40]

The document went on to recommend "reluctantly" that Kagawa's suspension be terminated.

This crucial paragraph in the official ruling, passing harsh judgment on Kagawa, bears striking similarity to Hugh Deane's article of a year earlier. Much of the surviving rough draft of this paragraph is a verbatim copy of that article. Certain words and phrases are crossed out and replaced by others, as if to mask the plagiarism of Deane's damning assessment.[41] The likelihood of a conspiracy is further apparent from the fact that thousands of others with deep involvement in the militarization of Japan were permitted to hold office. The selective use of information by both the journalists and the investigators was inexcusable, since ample evidence had been published, in English as well as in Japanese, of Kagawa's support for democratic reforms.

A recommendation against holding office would have meant little to Kagawa anyway, because he repeatedly had refused to run for office since the early twenties. He always maintained that his mission in life was that of a catalyst, adviser, organization builder, preacher, and moral and religious teacher. The life of a politician, with its often routine work, compromises, and in-fighting, was too confining for his prophetic temperament.

There was too much of the artist and the autocrat in Kagawa for him to have been happy as a politician. His departure from the labor and peasant political movements in the 1920s and 1930s indicated his dislike with playing a secondary role or with tedious in-fighting. He was a visionary who loved spinning out new ideas for projects, leaving the administrative details to others. This may be why a great deal of his later career was dedicated to preaching and lecturing, for it was from the lectern that he wielded the most power and, in his own judgment, had the broadest effect. He was constantly starting and supporting organizations, but he could not be long content in a bureaucratic role. He put it best when he said, "I am a free-lance, a tramp—a vagabond for Christ. . . . I must go on until Christ's work is done. . . . I go like the wind."[42]

Kagawa began his postwar speaking tours with the endorsement of the All-Japan Christian Convention, which he chaired on Pentecost Sunday, June 9, 1946. A huge overflow crowd of 10,000 had come to the auditorium of Aoyama Gakuin in Tokyo. The services were conducted by Takeo Katsube, Soji Saito, Rinzo Onomura, Shiro Murata, Tsunenori Takase, Michio Kozaki, Akiji Kurumada, and C. Kawamata. Other prominent Christians like Soichi Saito, Michi Kawai, the Minister of Education Kotaro Tanaka and Col. Ivan Bennett, the chaplain from MacArthur's headquarters, were speakers.

The convention launched an evangelistic campaign, issuing a declaration stamped with Kagawa's desire for both repentance and renewal. This campaign, which was to run for three years, was in some respects a repeat of the Kingdom of God campaign of 20 years earlier with Shiro Kuroda assisting him. This time it was more ambitious with the goal of "3,000,000 souls for Christ" and "repentance for a hundred million."

This task of preaching Japan's moral and physical reconstruction was intimately connected with Kagawa's growing concern for world peace. The International Peace Association which he founded with the help of Kiyozumi Ogawa and Kanji Koshio in the fall, was the original focus of this peace work. The association had as its major purpose a sort of "deprogramming" of the Japanese from a military spirit by guiding them to a peace-loving attitude. Peace education and preparation for entry into the United Nations were its specific objectives. The appeal for donations and membership contained both a condemnation of Japanese militarism and manifesto of cooperative economics.

Still believing that issues of bread, peace and cooperative economics were inseparable, Kagawa stated:

> To meet with the critical condition of our food shortage and the lack of various necessities, the importation of these goods from abroad seems to be the only hope left for us at present. For this purpose we must get rid of the old capitalistic profit-making ideas and accept the principles of democracy. We most follow the model set by the countries in the Scandinavian Peninsula of western Europe and the way of permanent world peace which is to be worked out by the League of International Cooperatives.

In the area of education, Kagawa took a personal hand in revising the textbooks used to inculcate militarism. He anticipated and helped prepare the way for acceptance of the new Japanese constitution prohibiting Japan from using war as an instrument of policy and granting women the vote. Women's rights advocate Tsuneko Gauntlett became head of the league's women's section, which was charged with expanding women's ideas and initiating them into roles in the sphere of politics, economics and foreign relations.

With his typical can-do attitude, Kagawa launched a magazine for promoting peace. He purchased the publication, *Kokka to shukyo* (Religion and the State) in 1947 and changed the name to *Sekai kokka* (The World State). He wrote monthly articles on pacificism and his idea of a world federation. He renewed old contacts with the world peace movement, becoming one of the charter members of Union of World Federalists in August 1948. With the help of Yukio Ozaki, an ally from the days of the suffrage campaign, he established a Committee for World Federation in the Japanese Diet. He translated *Draft of a World Constitution*, the global plan for government written by former World Federation president Robert Hutchins.

Kagawa's Japanese pride found a powerful channel after the new Japanese constitution was approved in November 1946 with Article 9 categorically rejecting war as an instrument of policy. Kagawa was unabashedly proud of his country's revolutionary renunciation of war, something unprecedented in human history and an example for all nations. It mattered little to Kagawa when opponents of the new constitution complained that it was forced upon the Japanese by the Supreme Command. The point was that the new law of the land absolutely prohibited war, and it was a cause for rejoicing. Consistently defending this renunciation of war against attacks by military-minded Japanese conservatives, he also proclaimed it as a model for the entire world. He rejoiced not only because it freed his country from the agony of war itself, but because it threw off the social and economic burden of militarism.

Kagawa declared:

> A typical modern state, encumbered with its heavy armament but well-nigh bereft of other values, reminds one of nothing so much as a naked savage, lugging around his javelin and poisoned arrows. States today seem nearer to the stage of barbarism than do many individuals.
>
> By the abandonment of war, we in Japan have emerged from the era of barbarism. Thus we have been afforded a chance to make ourselves the most progressive and civilized of all nations.
>
> If only we had done this willingly ten years ago, history would have taken another course. But it is not too late for us.
>
> Our new constitution will become a milestone in the realization of world peace. For the first time in human history, by our abandonment of war, the warning of Christ has been accepted by a national government: "All they that take the word shall perish by the sword."[43]

While Kagawa was buoyant about this and the other sweeping reforms brought about by the new constitution, he was not content. Periodically he bemoaned Japan's moral degeneration in the postwar period and the fact that true spiritual reconstruction was not taking place. The black market, prostitution, materialism, Communist agitation, armed robbery, pornography, dance halls, liquor and moral decadence in general all were targets in his preaching and writing. Although he welcomed the United Nations enthusiastically, he became gradually disillusioned with it because the Security Council was controlled by the major powers. At first sympathetic to the UN's "police action" in Korea as a legitimate attempt of world government to keep the peace, he later came to regard it merely as another war between the dominant nations.

Reborn as an author, preacher, pacifist, political adviser, social worker and activist in Japan, Kagawa was ready to take his message abroad. Unfortunately, he was unable to attend the World Federation Conference in 1949, when he was denied a visa by Occupation headquarters, despite his promotion of the reforms mandated by Allied policy in Japan. He was able in December 1949 to begin a world tour that was to last an entire year, visiting England, Germany, Denmark, Sweden and Norway before flying to the United States on July 14, 1950. The European tour was immensely successful, with crowds as large as the 35,000 massed outside in Oslo to hear him speak. He was well received by both the House of Lords and the House of Commons in England, and the German churches were filled with overflow throngs coming to hear the sage from Japan.

The controversy about Kagawa's wartime stance had soured some Americans, but he remained a celebrity. At Idlewild Airport news photographers and a welcoming party, headed by Kagawa Committee secretary J. Henry Carpenter, greeted the aging but vigorous and stocky man in the rumpled black suit with its pockets bulging with papers. He waved his hat to the crowd, and began to shake hands with his admirers. "Thank you, thank you so much for coming," he greeted them. "It is good to be back. Good to be back in this country where I have so many friends."

On his car ride to city, he was already giving an interview to a *New York Times* reporter, spilling out comments on world affairs in his charmingly offhand manner. Of the Korean war that had just begun, he said, "I have no use for atom bombs against Korea or any other nation."[44] He argued that a better plan would be to extend the police action until a world government evolved. He remained critical of the doctrine of class struggle, proclaiming "Russia must repent of its doctrines of violence before it can join a world government."[45]

He managed to squeeze in a few words about his mystical view of science, reminiscing about a visit he had made to Bell Telephone Laboratories in 1936 to observe electron diffraction experiments by Clinton J. Davison: "We must understand atomic science from the religious standpoint. I am interested in the wonderful construction of the atom. We must use it for the benefit of mankind."[46] As they proceeded down FDR drive, he critically commented on the brute architecture of the UN building. That was merely a warmup for an interview on NBC radio at the Rockefeller Center less than an hour after he landed. Then followed a meeting with 200 religious leaders who had already finished their luncheon at the McBurney Young YMCA by the time Kagawa arrived.

Clearly, the zeal of his still loyal American admirers was as strong as ever. They were overjoyed to see that he had recovered his old energy, sense of humor, and could entertain them with a mind that darted among diverse topics that reflected his omnivorous reading. They were still awed by the sense of tranquility he projected. They came prepared to venerate, starved for a figure to revere, and revere him they did.

Kagawa was introduced in glowing terms by longtime supporter, Dr. J. Henry Carpenter, executive secretary of the Kagawa National Committee, which was sponsoring his tour. The following description by Emerson O. Bradshaw, Kagawa's tour guide on this journey, expressed the thrill felt by the faithful:

> The introduction by Dr. Carpenter was short. "We all know why we are here," he said. "We are here to honor and to welcome to our country the greatest living Christian leader in the world today, Dr. Toyohiko Kagawa." He turned his head slightly and smiled affectionately at the man beside him. Applause burst forth. It welled louder and louder, and then everyone in the room was standing in ovation to the distinguished guest garbed

in black, and tears were in my eyes and in the eyes of others. It had been nine long years—devastating, war-torn years—since he had been among us. It had been nine long years that we had been praying for him, for his well-being and for his return. And now he had come, and there was gladness in our hearts and we felt somehow that truly the spirit of Christ was in the room.[47]

"Thank you, thank you all so very much," Kagawa acknowledged,

I wish to say to everyone in the United States "thank you" and I will go around the United States saying "thank you, thank you, thank you." After the defeat of the war you sent over to Japan many missionaries and also many packages of very great necessities which we lacked in Japan. So will you please permit me to express our heartfelt appreciation for these wonderful gifts. Thank you.[48]

His gratitude and his plea for further missionary assistance to Japan were added to the themes of social justice, cooperative economics, the power of redemptive love, and the need to apply Christianity. He stressed the revolutionary nature of Japan's pacifist constitution and the need for a new world order along the World Federationist lines. These ideas were closely interwoven with his highly personal account of his own life experience.

As before, he spoke of his perennial concerns with the relationship between the inner life and the social world, continuing to insist on the dialectical relation of the individual to society. Inner spiritual transformation must express itself in Christian social action, and participating in social action would, in turn, lead to a deeper spiritual life. This was precisely how he interpreted the Protestant Reformation itself, saying to a throng of 6000 at St. John the Divine in New York:

The Reformation was the restoration of man's inner soul through the grace of God. It means the remaking of mankind. The Japanese have received five gifts from God through reading the Bible. These are a true spirit of personal piety; purity of soul, of home life and of social life; respect for labor and laborers; service of neighbors; and a spirit of peace.[49]

This is not to say he was content with the Reformation, because he continued to criticize pietistic individualism and doctrinal divisions, saying fervently: "The religion of Jesus is not mere creeds and doctrines, it is a life. The salvation of Jesus is not only of the individual, it is also for home, life, society and mankind."[50]

He retained his knack for turning an aggressive inquiry into a puzzle that forced the questioner to think about the very grounds of his question. When asked if he was opposed to Communism, he would reply that he was opposed to violence. Such an answer was a criticism of the violent aspects of Communism, but it also reprimanded those advocating violence against Communists to search their own hearts.

Only rarely did anyone in the audience confront him with questions about the storm of controversy which had surrounded him a few years before. When they did probe the war issue, his reply was essentially the same as those of five years earlier:

> Of course I became indignant when American bombs took the lives of two million citizens, drove ten million people from the cities to the rural areas and destroyed five hundred Christian churches. But I never doubted the loyalty of American Christians. I recalled that when nations engage in war they become brutal.[51]

Or, he would deflect the question by saying, "Americans should forgive and forget as all Japan is doing."[52] Kagawa felt that little could be accomplished dwelling on the war. He deplored the horror of Japanese militarism, but he believed that the focus of discussion with Americans should be on solving Japan's immediate postwar problems rather than on assigning blame for the war. Because Japan was still suffering from poverty, unemployment, inflation, and food and medical shortages, Kagawa discussed the immense task of rebuilding the nation, and trying to make sure that such a war never occurred again. These were the critical issues that he took to his friends in the United States. His talks emphasized his Christian notion of forgiveness and rebirth, of putting the past behind to enable his nation and the world to build the Kingdom of God, a physically and morally reconstructed world.

Kagawa likely had tactical reasons for not dwelling on the war. He had an image to maintain in America. If he had been totally candid about discussing the tragic degree to which his pacifism had been compromised, he might have seriously damaged that image. On the other hand, his American followers did not want to damage the image either. They still needed a Kagawa to believe in, a hope, a model, a greatest living Christian, and proof that their missionary efforts were not in vain. It is as if there were a tacit agreement not to delve into the past, because it might have been an uncomfortable act of demythologizing, both for the hero and for his devotees.

The news media did not give Kagawa the huge volume of coverage which he had received during his triumphant 1936 tour, but he still received substantial attention, most of it quite positive. Photo coverage appeared in papers ranging from the *New York Times* to the *Sacramento Bee*, in addition to radio appearances. Although he now took a rest day each week, he continued to amaze everyone with his stamina, traveling over 50,000 miles speaking to over 300,000 people at 137 different locations in the United States, Canada and Hawaii. During the first two weeks alone, he went from New York, to various locations in Ohio, Iowa, Oklahoma and California. His appeal was still so strong that on this tour he managed to collect more than $100,000 in donations for his work in Japan.

Nor was his popularity limited to the Christian community. When Rabbi Israel Goldstein, president of the American Jewish Congress, gave his suggestion that twelve Jews and Christians get together to work out a plan for world peace, he listed Kagawa along with Einstein, Schweitzer, Russell, Jacques Maritain, Martin Buber, Eleanor Roosevelt, Arnold Toynbee and Reinhold Niebuhr. He described Kagawa as the "Japanese Christian Leader whose religion is contagious."[53] In the final analysis, faith in Kagawa, then, was bigger than Kagawa himself. It was faith in the future of a humanity that could pull itself out of the hell of war and poverty.

World peace became Kagawa's major concern during his last decade until his passing on April 23, 1960, at age 72. As age and illness began to slow him down, he summoned his energies to campaign for a world order of peace built on an economic system of international cooperation and inspired by the love at the core of his faith.

Chapter 12
The Peacemaker

IN HIS LAST DECADE as long as his health permitted, Kagawa remained both the pastor of his home congregation at Matsu-zawa and the roving evangelist. At home he preached, conducted services, baptized new converts, and talked to the faithful.

On the road, he still preached himself into exhaustion, to the increasing dismay of friends concerned with his health. He exhorted his audiences on the value of love as exemplified in the life of Christ. He spoke of the the need to follow Christ's command for action to alleviate the physical suffering of the poor and to heal everyone's soul. To the less educated rural audiences, he talked in simple terms of "biblical agriculture," drawing examples from daily life. He was legendary for continuing to preach the Gospel and social reform in towns far off the typical lecture circuit.

In the years after the war, he was credited with assistance in the founding of more than 250 churches, mostly in the rural areas. When, at Kagawa's urging, his old mentor Charles Logan came out of retirement for an evangelistic tour of Japan in 1951, he was amazed at the extent of Kagawa's influence. In August and the first two weeks of September, Logan spoke at 23 locations in the northern island of Hokkaido and 21 more in Tohoku. He reported that "Everywhere that I have been I find that Dr. Kagawa has been there before me putting his gospel of love into practice."[1] As was often the case with those who watched Kagawa, he was inspired by Kagawa's way of backing up his spiritual exhortations with attention to seemingly trivial details of life:

In one place they told me that he had the young men gather acorns from the mountains, grind them into flour and mix with caramel to give them a good taste and feed them to the 3000 lost children whom he was saving. In Hokkaido I found that the Governor had given him 5000 *cho* of land for the establishment of a Christian village for some repatriates from Manchuria.[2]

Though Kagawa could claim many titles because of the diversity of his interests, he enjoyed being called *evangelist* or *pastor*, for this vocation of ministerial service remained the heart of his activity. Even the preface to a German translation of one of his novels was signed, "Dr. Toyohiko Kagawa, *Pfarrer*"—that is, "Pastor." There was something touchingly humble about a man of his stature simply calling himself a pastor. It was related to his self-effacing humor which captivated the audiences of "the saint who laughs," as he was sometimes called.

His own introduction to this translation is one of the most moving little expressions of his compassion and of his belief in sowing the seeds of genuine Christianity:

> The needs of rural people are not confined to Japan. In China and India, and even in the United States and Europe, farmers are suffering in similar ways. To relieve this suffering, is a command of love of God and neighbor.
>
> It is one of my greatest joys that the message of God's love has spread over the entire nation. When this mission is fulfilled, and Japan has recognized the Light, then the entire Asian world will turn to the light. But until this day dawns, we must sow and let die yet many more grains of wheat.
>
> The world cries from care. As long as the cross is kept down, the power of darkness rules. We must understand and contemplate the Gospel more deeply. These kinds of grains of wheat are the most essential.[3]

In this spirit, he continued to advise and assist numerous religious leaders, social workers and socialist politicians in the postwar era. Christian social workers like Reiji Takahashi, well known for his assistance to the homeless in Tokyo, were typical beneficiaries.[4]

Kagawa's once-feverish writing went on at a reduced pace, especially in the late 1950s. Poor health, bad eyesight, and his immersion in countless projects, all detracted from his writing.

He was, moreover, no longer the popular author of the early years, when his byline alone could attract thousands of new subscribers to a magazine. The best sellers no longer poured out as they did in the tiny cabin along the sea or the slum or jail or on board ship. Since his writing was rarely an end in itself, but a means of earning money to support his projects, there was less of the urgent need to churn out a half-dozen marketable new books each year.

He devoted considerable effort to what he thought of as his philosophical testament, a difficult work called *Uchu no mokuteki* (The Purpose of the Universe), which finally appeared in 1959. In this book, he used scientific thought to explain the basis of his mystical intuition of the universe as a purposeful evolution toward ever greater beauty and complexity with God at the center. It was also an attempt to grapple with the problem of evil.

This *magnum opus* was deeply influenced by the vast amount of his scientific reading and by writers such as Pierre Lecomte Du Nouy, who attempted to demonstrate statistically that evolution could not have taken place through chance alone. When someone visiting Japan in the late forties mentioned that he had read Du Nouy's *Human Destiny*, Kagawa surprised him by saying, "cynical young materialists ought to be reading that splendid book. I want very much to translate it."[5] With typical zest, he then asked the man to help him obtain permission from the publisher. The translation into Japanese appeared in 1950.

There were also other publishing projects, such as Kagawa's personal funding of a fresh translation of the New Testament into colloquial Japanese. Tomio Muto undertook the work, while Kagawa pored over the Greek lexicons, scrutinizing the translation chapter by chapter, advising Muto and sometimes offering alternative readings. On Christmas of 1953 this version was published.

In connection with this Bible publishing venture Muto describes an experience which shows that Kagawa had lost neither his emotional intensity nor his concern for worldly matters. Kagawa, who always had a strong practical side (his novels are full of little economic details), inquired how the sales were going a few months later. Muto replied that they had sold 20,000

copies and were already printing the third edition. When Kagawa asked if payments for the books were coming in regularly,
Muto replied they were doing very well, except for a missionary
in the Osaka area who had paid only 20 percent of his bill, and
had not paid up despite repeated requests. To add insult to
injury, the man refused to say exactly when he would pay,
arguing that this would amount to taking an oath, which was
forbidden by scripture. At this point in the narrative, Muto
became angry, and said he would take the man to court:

> Sensei, I had two years' experience at the Tokyo Local Court
> when I was young. I'll sue this missionary and put a bailiff in his
> house to seize the contents of his wardrobe. The Osaka papers
> will be interested in this incident and report about it. Then he
> can no longer stay in Japan. I can't bear having such a missionary
> in Japan.[6]

Suddenly, Kagawa went to the floor, kneeling, with his hands
folded and with a look of sorrow said "Pardon him for me,
Muto-san, pardon him for me." Muto, of course, took no action.
Two months later the payment was received. On one of his
evangelistic junkets to Awaji Island with the missionary, Kagawa had spent the night with him at an inn, giving him a "hint"
to pay what he owed.

The aging Kagawa was not always so saintly. Eager for action
and impatient with disciples who failed to live up to his standards, he could still be stern and vocal in his later years. Before
coming in the house for a visit or to make a request, his
associates would often ask, "How's the old man's temper
today?"[7]

The peace movement continued to absorb Kagawa's attention
in these later years. During the course of his 1950 tour, he had
become increasingly worried about the Cold War mood in the
United States. Another of Muto's reminiscences gives a hint of
this concern. When Kagawa landed at Haneda Airport on
December 27, 1950, he was greeted by a large crowd of reporters, photographers, Socialist Party leaders, members of his
organizations, and other Japanese admirers. Describing this
scene, Muto said that Kagawa went through the crowd shaking
hands. Then he pushed through the people to Muto. First, he
had a bit of good business tidings: "For the fund of the *Christian*

News," Kagawa said, "I raised $3000 from the Japanese in California." Then he whispered: "Muto-san, America is going to wage war. She intends to make Japan her fortress to defend herself aginst the Soviet! Be cautious!"[8]

Kagawa's approach to world peace was to urge an international order along the lines of the world federationist movement. He worked in both the Japanese and international cooperative movements, touting cooperatives as instruments for a peaceful and rationally planned commerce. Through his writings, especially in his magazine, he continue to further these causes. He was building on the ideas summarized in *Brotherhood Economics:* the cause of war was rooted in greed and economic exploitation by the major powers. Peace and a more equitable distribution of the world's wealth could be secured only by an orderly world economy and a global federation.

As in *Brotherhood Economics,* he criticized the injustice of economic colonialism, which kept underdeveloped nations in poverty. Although he placed great hope in the United Nations, even to the point of endorsing the UN forces in Korea as a peacekeeping police action, at the same time he favored a revision of the UN charter to give the organization genuine legal authority. While on his tour in 1950, he had carefully explained his position to an American audience, analyzing the Korean situation by comparing it to the League of Nations response to the Manchurian incident in 1931:

> When Japan occupied Manchuria in 1931, the League of Nations procrastinated for a year and a half before finally adopting the Commission of Inquiry's report censuring the Japanese action. When this report was accepted, Japan simply resigned from the League and continued her acts of aggression against China. The League, by not acting in this crucial instance, failed to fulfill its basic purpose of maintaining peace through a collective system, and from that time on was powerless.
>
> When the North Koreans invaded South Korea, the United Nations organization was confronted with a situation that was in every way parallel to that which faced the League of Nations nineteen years ago. By acting almost instantly to block this unprovoked aggression, the United Nations took a major step toward the ultimate achievement of world peace and has strengthened, rather than diminished its influence among the nations.[9]

Kagawa emphasized the need for a police system to protect the smaller nations of the world, both in the East and West. He told the Americans that this system would be especially important for his own country, because it had renounced war:

> We Japanese especially welcome this initial step toward the formulation of a police sytem, for by having adopted a pacifist position which outlaws armament of any kind, we are completely dependent upon the United Nations for protection against outside aggression.[10]

The key word was initial step. Because he had some faith that this police action would evolve into the global peacekeeping force, he even praised the United States for its role in the intervention:

> The manner in which the United States moved promptly and unflinchingly to the defense of South Korea has increased our respect for this country and has removed all doubt of the sincerity and good intentions of its government and citizens.[11]

In praising the United States, Kagawa was attempting to persuade the Americans to support the much more comprehensive vision of a world government which he shared with the world federationists. He emphasized that the situation in Korea demonstrated the practicality of a global order, but reminded Americans that no individual nation had the right to appoint itself as permanent global policeman. The action in Korea was perhaps the crude beginning of a global order. A legitimate global system, however, would require considerable evolution from this isolated effort.

Kagawa elaborated further:

> The necessity of having a world police system has now been demonstrated, but to actually establish a real world police system we must have parliaments of the various geographical sections of the world which can then unite to form a true federal world government. The parliament of Europe, which even includes Western Germany, is now functioning well. A similar parliament is badly needed in the Far East. The federal world government, which might be called the "United States of the World," would have a world court and an effective police system which could enforce the government's laws and the court's decisions.[12]

Neither the UN nor the U.S. policy makers were ready for this concept, despite the international support it had from many prestigious individuals, including Albert Einstein, William O. Douglas, Norman Cousins, future California senator Alan Cranston, and even the President of Standard Oil, W. T. Holiday. Kagawa viewed with increasing alarm the United States' role of global vigilante in the the Cold War. Instead of the hopeful beginning of global government, the Korean crisis became a symptom of global hostilities that continue to the present day.

Kagawa's first involvement in this movement for a world government dated back to 1947, when he translated the *Draft of a World Constitution*, written by world federation activist Robert M. Hutchins, president of the University of Chicago. Kagawa had come to the belief that the veto powers of the UN Security Council thwarted democratic processes, and, in fact, made the UN more a tool of the superpowers rather than a just and effective means of world goverment.

He also called for quicker admission of the many nations which still were not seated in the general assembly. Finally, he proposed a bicameral method of assembly delegates, with an upper house analogous to the United States Senate, with one vote per nation, and a lower house, with proportional representation based on a formula of one vote per five million in population. The International Court at The Hague would be the forum for resolving disputes among nations, and the international police force would be charged with enforcing the decisions of the court. Knowing that such a world government would not materialize overnight, he often pointed out that his model, the United States Constitution, was thirty years in the making.

Kagawa was a key participant in the first Asian Congress of the World Federation held in Hiroshima for four days from November 3, 1952. He was elected president of this conference, which included 350 delegates from India, Indonesia, Malaya, Cambodia, Vietnam, the Philippines, China, Taiwan, Korea, Okinawa, Germany, the United Kingdom and the United States. There he met the great British agriculturalist, Lord Boyd-Orr, 1949 Nobel Peace prize winner and head of the United Nations Food and Agricultural Organization.

After the conference, Kagawa shared his agricultural interests with Boyd-Orr, taking him on a tour of Japanese farms. Boyd-Orr was amazed at the efficiency of the farming, and took note of Kagawa's pet projects in vertical agriculture.[13] The Kagawa influence was clear in the declarations of the conference: (1) to ban the production and use of any atomic weapons, (2) to reduce armaments as completely as possible, making complete abolition the ultimate goal, (3) to abolish racial discrimination and realize fundamental human rights, (4) to exclude religious bias, and bring about cooperative action between world religions, (5) release war prisoners as early as possible, and (6) to look·forward to the development and use of the world's resources as a solution to the problem of over-population.

Kagawa still drew upon his basic religious tenets in facing up to the hard realities of the political scene:

> Japanese Christians are challenged now to work for world government as no other group of Christians in history. . . . Almost the entire nation is of one mind on the subject of permanent world peace; and the majority, including the great political parties of the Social Democratic Movement, are ever more and more clear about the methods of attaining this aim. They are sure that world government is the only way to move forward. There is, moreover, a basic relationship between the growth of Christianity in this country and the Social Democratic Movement. Since it is the leadership of this Movement who are spearheading the work for world government, many Japanese Christians are contributing to this goal.[14]

Christians, he felt, must be prepared to "give our very lives to heal the world's crimes. Unless some nation is ready to take the risk, to pay the debt of sin and crime, crime will not be redeemed."[15] The willingness to sacrifice for peace was based on the parable of the grain of wheat, which in dying itself begets a new and greater abundance of life. The parable of the vine and the branches was, to Kagawa, yet another call for solidarity. It expressed for him the need to organize all society into a relationship of mutual aid. He wanted the love and mutual aid which existed in early Christianity to become worldwide and supplant constant conflict between nations.

Complementary to the world government would be the international cooperative economic system which was the concrete expression of the solidarity demanded by Christ. Kagawa said:

> Without the daily struggle to achieve desirable ends within the spheres of socio-economic, educational and religious activity, as preliminary to the necessary political changes, ideas of world federation may end in utopian dreams. At the present time, it is the international economic cooperative movements that are showing most clearly how the whole of mankind can effectively be bound together in one body. Related to every kitchen and every pocketbook, they indicate the most dependable way to social solidarity. They do away with the profit motive, the accumulation of capital, the concentration of money power; they are less concerned with material resources than with the great potential resources of moral character; they insist upon the actual practice of full democracy. Through voluntary control, the cooperatives establish a balance between production and consumption; they prevent unemployment; they raise the standards of living and bring about social security. Yet without international peace, their full benefits and the completion of true consumer-economics cannot be achieved.[16]

He continued his travels outside Japan to promote his ideas, making a religious lecture tour of Brazil for five months early in 1953. He didn't confine himself to purely "religious" topics, because he never accepted the old divisions between sacred and secular. For Kagawa, building the Kingdom of God continued to mean what it always had: healing the material world and treating all things and people as manifestations of the divine. Therefore, he freely gave agricultural advice to the Brazilians, dwelling on his ideas of permaculture and environmental protection. Kagawa's daughter Umeko was surprised, on a visit to Maringa, Brazil, in 1985, to find her father memorialized by a eucalyptus grove. The villagers said "Your father advised us to plant these trees in order to stop the soil from washing away after the original jungle had been cut down. And still now, the trees are really helping to save our fields."[17]

Though health problems slowed his activity, Kagawa kept hammering away for the international cause. In March 1954, at Boyd-Orr's request, he became vice president of the World Movement for World Federation. Boyd-Orr had spent £2000 of his Nobel Prize money to help the organization out of debt when he took over. In May, Kagawa presided over a conference of nonmember countries of the UN.

The thrust the World Movement for World Federation and like-minded groups, such as the United World Federalists, was to revise the United Nations charter along the lines suggested by Kagawa and others, to secure genuinely representational world government which had the force of law. Kagawa continued his plea for this cause, both to the churches and with secular organizations.

From July through October 1954 he made his final journey to the United States and Canada. This visit differed from the previous tours, with fewer public appearances and little of the advance publicity that had made him into a celebrity before. He attended the Second World Church Conference, which began on August 15, in Evanston, Illinois, on the campus of North-western University. Sponsored by the World Council of Churches, this conference was a major event for Protestant churches and one of the biggest news events of the year, with massive coverage from the media by hundreds of reporters. There were 1298 official participants representing 179 churches from 54 countries. Over 125,000 attended the spectacular nighttime opening ceremonies held at Soldier Field. President Eisenhower and UN Secretary General Dag Hammarskjold were among the dignitaries who addressed the throngs.

Unlike so many meetings and conferences of the past, however, Kagawa now played a minor role. He was an accredited visitor and not part of the official delegation from the Japanese Church of Christ, which included Michio Kozaki, Shiro Murata, Shigeharu Oishi, and Professor William Enkichi Kan representing the Anglicans of Japan. No longer sought after, interviewed and photographed, the aging Kagawa had a much quieter and less influential stay than before.

His body was less able to battle with his "catalogue of diseases," and he was losing the energy needed for the intense crusading which had been so much a part of his life. The onset of congestive heart disease and the cumulative effect of his many bouts with illness, were beginning to drain his seemingly inexhaustible energy.

On August 17 he spoke and conducted a discussion session along with British Methodist Victor Jones, on "Reaching Non-Christians in Our Own Lands," where he outlined the difficulties facing the church in Japan and reminded the audience of the importance of evangelizing the working classes:

> Unless we win the souls of the laborers for Christianity, the destiny of Japan and of the Orient will be black for centuries to come. While we Christians sit back contentedly and contemplate ideologies, the Communists act to help the laborers on strikes and sabotage, and spend much money for such movements.[18]

He deplored the fact that the Communists worked as an organized body while Christians were divided by denominationalism and lack of financial support for evangelization. These, of course, were old themes for Kagawa, as he had often exhorted the Christians of Japan to do more work among the common people rather than preaching to the converted, living in comfort and indulging in doctrinal debates. Yet while he often criticized the emphasis on violent class struggle and the lack of spiritual depth in Communism, he credited it with showing a dedication to the poor which he thought was sadly lacking in many Christians.

As he had maintained since the war, the conduct of the "so-called" Christian nations was itself a major obstacle to the spread of Christianity in Asia. In particular, he protested nuclear testing in the Pacific by the United States, because the radioactive fallout was causing health problems in Japan. "Not only Christians, but all Japanese, say if you want to experiment with H-bombs, do it in Alaska," he sarcastically remarked at the conference.[19] Kozaki presented the Council of Churches a petition signed by 33,000 Japanese youths opposing atmospheric testing. The petition said "every nation should prohibit the production, use and experimentation of atomic and hydrogen bombs" and called for exertion of all our efforts "to end war and at the same time endeavor to establish true peace."

While Kagawa was lecturing in air-conditioned Cahn Auditorium, the delegates were battling over major religious issues in the sweltering heat of an Illinois August. Dramatic as the conference was, it showed up many deep divisions in Christianity and the world which Kagawa had spent an entire career attempting to heal. Roman Catholics were forbidden to attend, some conservative Protestants boycotted, and the clergy visiting from Communist nations were attacked in the press and trailed by the FBI.

The conference deeply divided along doctrinal lines and wrangled over what position to take on communism. A major rift occurred between the theologians on the ancient debate of justification by work or by faith. One wing emphasized man's utter dependence on God, maintaining that the Kingdom of God would result from divine eruption into the secular world. The others stressed man's duty to take action to bring the Kingdom of God to earth. They were exactly the kinds of theological differences with which Kagawa had little patience, since faith and work had always been closely interwoven in his thought and pastoral practice.

Again in November of that year, the Second Asian Conference on World Federation was held in Tokyo, followed by a series of special meetings and the Second Asian Cooperative Conference, which Kagawa also chaired. He vigorously defended the anti-war article of the Japanese constitution against revisionists in Japan and continued to promote it as an example to the world.

In his last years, he sometimes had to make his plea for world peace through world government from a sickbed. He suffered a collapse from his weakened heart in Osaka in March, 1955, that was so serious he could not be moved for two weeks. He continued to frustrate family and associates by stubbornly writing, preaching, overseeing his projects and receiving the combination of guests and freeloaders who found their way to his rambling headquarters.

Though not as large as in the pre-war era, his charitable enterprises had recovered substantially from the ravages of war. The Kagawa National Committee proudly reported that he had 46 staffers employed in 39 projects: slum centers, day nurseries, farmers' schools, a widows' home, a halfway house for ex-convicts, a leprosarium, and an orphanage. His American friends continued to send $1000 a month to support this activity, until the American Kagawa committee disbanded in 1962.[20]

Again and again he sounded the message for peace, affirming, reaffirming and defending Article 9 of the Japanese constitution. Refusing to play into the hands of those who argued for arming Japan to stave off communist aggression, Kagawa contended that Japan's response to external threats lay in the establishment of a genuine world government whose police force could prevent acts of aggression. In his view, Japan's war tragedy had made the Japanese a chosen people in the sense that they were the first nation in history to categorically renounce war. He took this message to the world with a missionary zeal, as in addressing the Conference for the Renunciation of War, begun in Tokyo on November 26, 1956:

> The Japanese people declared a permanent renunciation of war, in article nine of the new constitution. This was a great event in world history. We must not only observe this Article at all costs, but also persuade the world's peoples to follow this principle.
>
> With a drastic reformation of the political economic and social structure of our country, we must stabilize the economic life of the Japanese people.
>
> At the same time, we must hold to our neutral position in international tensions, making an endeavor to mediate the conflicts between countries.[21]

He worked on other fronts as well, seeking to improve relations between Japan and Korea, meeting with Japan's Prime Minister Hatoyama in 1956 and with other Japanese and Korean officials. His concern found public expression in an open letter to Syngman Rhee.

In 1957 he spent January in Thailand on another speaking tour, and again in the fall presided over the Third All-Asian Congress for World Federation, held at Kyoto in the fall. In January of the following year, he was off to Malaya, for the South East Asia Conference of the International Cooperative Alliance.

In 1958, along with two other great peacemakers, Albert Schweitzer and Bertrand Russell, he signed an open letter to the world powers negotiating in Geneva for the suspension of nuclear weapons testing:

> What we offer you is the most precious thing human beings have to give. We offer you our hopes.
>
> We want you to feel you are representing not just a nation, powerful though it may be, but two billion human beings who represent the ultimate authority on earth. . . .
>
> We know there will be in the background many voices actually pushing you in the direction of failure—for it is hard for some men to comprehend the needs and dangers of our times.

But this is not the source of your mandate. Your mandate comes from one and only one source—the sovereign will of the human community. It is to this community you are primarily responsible. . . .

Naturally, the peace of the world depends on many things besides control of nuclear weapons. It depends on the control of the basic causes of war—injustice, hunger, oppression, aggression, ambition. To meet these dangers, we must look to the cause of a stronger United Nations into which has been built the required powers of world law. . . .[22]

One of his last major public appearances was in August 1958, when he participated in the World Conference on Christian Education in Tokyo. This event was a great honor for Japanese Christians—a symbol of Japan's eager return to the world community. Reportedly the largest international meeting ever held in Japan, it hosted 12,000 people at the opening ceremonies on the evening of August 6 in the Tokyo Municipal Gymnasium in Sendagaya. There were 1400 official delegates from 63 nations, 3000 from Japan plus another 8000 observers.

The opening ceremony had all the international drama of the Madras conference of 20 years earlier, with representatives wearing their native costumes and marching in procession to a raised platform, over which towered a giant white cross and a banner in Japanese and English proclaiming the theme of the conference: "Christ is the Way, the Truth and the Life." The Indian bishop, Shot Mondol, opened the ceremonies for the huge audience, and Michio Kozaki, president of the National Christian Council of Japan, delivered the opening address. Even the hymn for the conference was a Japanese product, written by Tokuo Yamaguchi, minister of the Toyohashi Church of Aichi Prefecture with music composed by Hidetoshi Ikemiya, music instructor from the Tokyo Women's College, a Christian school.

The proudest moment for Kagawa and his fellow Christians was the address of Japanese Prime Minister Nobusuke Kishi, who stood at the podium with a cross on its front and praised the influence which Christianity had on modern Japan:

Japan is not a Christian country, as those professing Christianity constitute a small minority of its vast population, but it is beyond dispute that Japanese Christians—humble followers as well as outstanding leaders of the faity—have made signal contributions to the social progress and spiritual uplift of the nation, and worked a powerful moral influence out of all proportion to their numbers through their exemplary conduct.

The same may be said, I believe, of not a few countries which are represented at this convention. In this sense it is of special significance that you are meeting in Tokyo.[23]

The non-Christian Kishi said in effect that Christianity had been St. Paul's "leaven" in Japan, as Kagawa had insisted it must be ever since he had launched his "million souls for God" campaign 30 years earlier. The impact of Christianity on Japan had always been far greater than the actual number of church members would signify. Knowing well the experience of Paul in a pagan empire, Kagawa did not dream of an immediate conversion of the entire land. He was more concerned with producing enough Christians to help transform secular society by infecting it with love in action. At the concluding sermon at this opening ceremony, he sounded one of his favorite biblical themes, Christ's command to love and trust as children do:

You teachers must love. Love the children God entrusts to you, and learn from them. Learn to be like them in their eagerness, their ready response of love to love. For unless you learn to be like them, you will never enter the Kingdom.[24]

The conference grounds were the campus of Aoyama Gakuin University, where Kagawa had spoken on many past occasions. As a Japanese representative along with Tetsu Katayama, former prime minister, fellow Christian and socialist, Kagawa met with 70 delegates who formed the International Christian Conference for World Peace. The group resolved to publicize the facts about the devastating effect of the bombing of Hiroshima and Nagasaki and to work for the prohibition of nuclear weapons. Kagawa was named chair of a committee to organize a similar conference every four years in various locations to promote these efforts.

The group was also involved in the Fourth World Conference Against Nuclear Weapons which opened in Tokyo on August 15. That conference opposed Japanese importation of nuclear weapons and demanded immediate suspension of atomic tests by the United States and Britain. It urged these nations and Russia to agree on an unconditional test ban. The Japanese delegation introduced a specific resolution to demand a halt to

Britain's plan for a new series of tests in the Christmas Island Area.

Kagawa tasted the joys of age as well as its pains. His two oldest children, Sumimoto and Chiyoko, had graduated from medical school, and his daughter Umeko was becoming a minister. His circle of church, schools, co-op stores and demonstration farm continued to be a buzz of activity, filled with students and workers.

The house was jammed with more books than ever reflecting a wide range of intellectual interests. The old man with the thinning black hair was at center stage, dispensing wisdom, limping along with his cane, greeting visitors, wearing baggy trousers held up by suspenders, squinting through his glasses, and boasting that his eyesight was inside. When he stepped outdoors, young people working on their projects would pause briefly and bow to the beloved Sensei.

His admiration of Haru continued as strongly as ever. It was best expressed in one of the poems he wrote to her in 1950, when he was on his tour:

> My wife I love, O my wife
> Who with me for thirty years
> The muddy road of life has trodden.
>
> My wife I love, O my wife
> Who knelt with me on that slum lane
> Or by the factory wall to pray.
>
> My wife I love, O my wife
> Who stood tearless at the backdoor
> Or by the window of a prison house.
>
> My wife I love, O my wife
> Who with millions of yen in hand
> Patched her sleeves to finance others.
>
> My wife I love, O my silent wife
> Who went to a store to sell the books
> To make money for my urgent use.
>
> My wife I love, my courageous wife
> Who used to run without umbrella
> In hailstones or thunderstorm.

My wife I love, O my wife in spirit
Whose beauty faded, whose hair turned grey;
Yet I love my spiritual wife.

My wife I love, O my wife.
Who takes the hand of her husband blind
And numbers the divine blessings.[25]

Neither the physical weariness of old age nor basking in the glow of his achievements dampened Kagawa's love and his righteous indignation. His fury at injustice burned as strongly as ever, though often transmuted into humor and irony. When one American visiting Tokyo for an education conference suggested that some people seem to get a new lease on life at 70, Kagawa replied sharply, "Not in our part of the world."[26]

He did not abate his criticism of the Japanese for their "growing materialism and the breakdown of sexual morality," diagnosing the cause as "the price we are paying for modernism and capitalism. The impulse of greed has begun to dominate our lives. Our economy still needs to learn Christian ethics in respect to property."[27] Nor was he any happier with other countries or with the organized church itself, as he once stated:

I have never joined any kind of religious synod, because I am opposed to religious politics. That is why I have never received a salary from any church. And unhappily I cannot feel a sense of identification with the A B C D nations: America, Britain, China and the Dutch. All are exploiting nations.[28]

Asked for an example of American exploitation he shot back "Okinawa—study its history, and you will discover that Okinawa was the birthplace of the Japanese nation. Yet the United States has seized it for its own purposes."[29] He was still critical of American racism, too. Referring to the civil rights struggle unfolding in Little Rock, Arkansas, he said "America's treatment of the Negro in the south is outrageous. I still remember, in 1936, refusing to speak at a southern church, when I found the congregation segregated."[30]

Kagawa was lavish in his praise of America's heavenly conduct during the Occupation, but just as quick to criticize the hell America. He rarely passed up an occasion to lecture on the dangers of nuclear testing. He would remind a visitor "There is radiation everywhere. The water in the tea which you and I just drank is polluted. Radiation is in the vegetables we are eating. America is committing suicide without war."[31] Depending on his mood, he would sometimes make this kind of statement with a sort of scientific detachment, while on other occasions he would raise his voice in anger.

Because of his life's work, some of Kagawa's friends and admirers began lobbying for the Nobel Peace Prize as early as 1954. Carola Barth, a German biographer of Kagawa who was editing a collection of writings to honor Albert Schweitzer, had asked Schweitzer for support in nominating Kagawa in 1954. According to her diary, she sent a letter to Schweitzer in June asking his support for nomination. She also discussed the matter with various individuals, among them Buskes Jom Heugenholt, Frau Pohlmann, and Herr Plank. Plank promised to lobby Schweitzer and advised her to write to a Nobel prize winner in Tubingen about the matter.

Others, such as Schweitzer's friend Frau Buvi, also wrote requesting his backing for the Kagawa nomination after Barth had brought up the matter. As early as January, Barth had corresponded with Helen Topping, who had inquired about the Kagawa nomination, and informed Topping that it took years to nurture a candidate along to the prize.[32]

At some point, Barth also met with Schweitzer to discuss Kagawa's nomination. A letter to her from Schweitzer dated 8 July 1954 includes the comment that he said he not forgotten their meeting and their discussion of Kagawa. Schweitzer added that he had not forgotten his promise to help Kagawa obtain the prize because he held him in very great regard. He then thanked her for the "Calendar which he found very interesting."[33] (This was probably a reference to the "Kagawa Calendar," published in English, as described in chapter 9.)

Kagawa never received the Nobel award despite this support, for reasons that remain unclear. No Peace Prize was awarded in 1955, although 37 candidates were nominated, including Kagawa.[34] One explanation was that the propaganda broadcasts still tainted his reputation, and he had never adequately accounted for the motives for the broadcasts.[35] Others, like

Kagawa's daughter, Umeko Momii, felt that Kagawa was denied the prize because of his sympathy with Bertrand Russell's anti-nuclear campaigns, long considered by many as too extreme. A third factor might simply have been the bias in the Nobel selection process itself. The year of Kagawa's death, 1960, was only the second time in its 60-year history that the Nobel Peace Prize was awarded to an individual outside of Western Europe or the United States.

Kagawa's insistence on continuing his evangelical work hastened his final illness. He called it "desperate evangelism," as Tomio Muto, the editor of *Christian News*, reports in his reminiscences. Kagawa was so weak by 1958 that he had begun to stagger merely climbing stairs. Muto warned him, "Sensei, don't go out anymore on evangelistic trips!"

"But the churches ask me to come. I can't but comply with their request," Kagawa answered.

"Refuse," Muto shot back. "Your existence itself is meaningful for the churches and for Japan. Stay at home and take care of yourself."

"Muto-san," Kagawa replied with mock solemnity, "Since the state of things is like this, desperate evangelism shall be my task."[36]

The old man's dedication was unswerving. He had nearly preached himself to death in the rain in the Shinkawa slums over a half century earlier, and he was quite willing to take the same risk again. Although suffering from a severe cold in January 1959, he insisted on going to his home island of Shikoku for an evangelical tour, saying "it is a glory for an evangelist to die on the way of his evangelism."[37]

Kagawa resisted the advice of friends and sailed for Shikoku after a Friends of Jesus meeting. By the time his ship arrived at Takamatsu, he was in such severe pain that he was unable to stand. He was taken to Saint Luke's Hospital in Takamatsu and remained in bed for almost three months before returning home in March. His worsening heart condition forced him to spend most of the time in bed. Even then, his passion for peace was undiminished. This was expressed movingly in Kagawa's unadorned English in a letter sent to Indonesia in December, 1959:

Dear Friends in Indonesia:

Christmas is drawing near at hand. This year, I am going to celebrate in bed the birth of Christ who brought peace on earth. My heart is now filled with sorrow to hear that many of the lives of the brethren in Indonesia have been lost day after day in the bloodshed of the civil war in your country. My heart aches as I long for the coming of true peace in the world. There is no greater tragedy for a nation than bitter struggle between brothers even if they are of different opinions.

As I lie in bed at this Christmas time, I fervently pray and wish that peace might again come all over Indonesia and that my Indonesian brothers would cease fighting and enter a stage of peaceful talks.[38]

He remained bedridden much of the time in the home in Matsuzawa, his strength steadily waning through the spring. Though he seemed to rally in mid-April, when the cherry trees were in bloom and his beloved nature pulsed with spring, he took a quick turn for the worse. When his physician, Nobuo Odagiri came to visit on the evening of April 23, Haru told him that Kagawa had been unconscious for three hours. The doctor went in to look at Kagawa, and realized that the end was near. Another hour passed. Then, Kagawa suddenly opened his eyes for the last time and smiled at those around him before he died at thirteen minutes after nine. "Please do your best for world peace and the church in Japan," were his last words.

He was laid in state and given a simple funeral service in his own church on April 26. The immensity of his loss was beginning to sink in. One witness described the scene: "The humble home of the Kagawas behind the Matsuzawa Church was thronged with mourning friends who passed beside the bier to look upon his wasted features, once so alive with outgoing human kindness."[39] Three days later a public ceremony was held at Aoyama Gakuin University. At this service, it was announced that the emperor had posthumously awarded him "The Order of the Rising Sun," one of Japan's highest awards.

He was laid to rest in Tama cemetery, under the shade of spreading oak and gingko trees in a small enclosure bordered by privet hedges and a bamboo fence. On the simple memorial pillar was the inscription beginning: "Toyohiko Kagawa . . . In my Father's house . . ."

Epilogue:
Kagawa Today

*B*ECAUSE THE SITUATION IN THE WORLD today stems directly from the economic exploitation and violence which Kagawa condemned in his time, his thought and example deserve to be retrieved and rethought by Christians and non-Christians, believers and agnostics, alike. There are even some terrifying lessons to be learned from his failures and weaknesses.

Many of the reforms Kagawa fought for have been incorporated into modern Japanese society. It now enjoys universal suffrage, freedom for unions and political organizations, adequate medical care, good education, decent housing, vastly improved land ownership rights and numerous other social services which he tirelessly promoted. The cooperative movement has flourished. The peace movement is one of the world's strongest. Article 9 of the Japanese constitution, forbidding war as an instrument of policy, survives despite attempts of nationalists to rekindle the military spirit. While Christianity has not spread as Kagawa had hoped, at least in numbers of conversions, it continues to have a significant impact on the nation's values.

Were he alive today, however, he would be far from satisfied with this progress. He would remain in the forefront of the peace movement, undoubtedly questioning the role of Japanese corporations in arms manufacture and environmental pollution. He would challenge corporate executives wherever he saw exploitation of workers, whether in Japan or in underdeveloped nations. He would continue to criticize the spiritual emptiness and malaise of selfishness which he detected in the developed nations. He would deplore the fact that capitalist culture and values still have a far stronger hold on our souls than cooperative or Christian ethics.

Clearly, Kagawa would not be comfortable in a world where more than ten million people starve to death each year while humanity squanders a trillion dollars annually on armaments, and where five million people were killed in more than 30 wars in 1986 alone, according to a United Nations report. These are the kind of numbers Kagawa tried to erase by an unswerving application of the Gospel to every area of life—personal and political, spiritual and economic.

Kagawa has always had his critics. From the beginning there were detractors who dismissed him as a publicity seeker. They were absolutely right that Kagawa had an enormous ego, basked in public attention and was an inexhaustible self-promoter with a driving need for recognition. Similar charges are often leveled at leaders of social and religious movements. Like most of them, Kagawa knew that one does not get far by hiding one's light under a bushel. Those serious about spreading their convictions have to be adept at self-promotion, or risk failure. The issue is not the size of the ego, but what one does with it, and the judgment must ultimately be of the man's works. Kagawa surely enjoyed public attention, but he used it primarily to gain support for humanitarian and religious projects, while living almost ascetically himself. He was thoroughly in possession of his personality, conscious enough of his egotism to cut himself down with self-irony throughout his career. His self-deprecating humor was one of his charms, and by playing the humble comic, he added to his popularity as a very human sort of a saint.

Since World War II, Kagawa's reputation has been reduced from the international stature of a Gandhi to relative obscurity. His reputation may have been harmed as much by his admirers as by his detractors. The desire to revere him was so strong that his followers in the West placed him on an altar that removed him from the tensions of a genuine dialogue, and when he tumbled from the altar, it aroused enough disaffection and scepticism that the "Kagawa cult" lost its massive appeal.

The comparisons with Gandhi were inappropriate from the beginning, although the two had in common an aura of saintliness, a belief in non-violence, a spirit of self-sacrifice, compassion for their people and a capacity for revitalizing religion.

However, the 'historical situations in which they found themselves were strikingly dissimilar. Gandhi's cause was to drive colonial power out of his nation through non-violence. Kagawa's Japan, on the other hand, was one of the few major nations not victimized by colonialism, and it turned to violence in a misbegotten war to drive Western imperialists out of Asia. Gandhi's antagonist was the imperialist intruder; Kagawa's was the militarist dictatorship within his own nation—a much more formidable opponent than the embattled British Empire, which had lost its will to maintain its holdings and was finally exhausted by war.

Thus, where Gandhi had an unambiguous goal, Kagawa was trapped between two conflicting sets of values, non-violence and the struggle against both foreign and domestic imperialism. Gandhi could harness the forces of nationalism to further his cause, while Kagawa could not because Japanese nationalism itself was the focal point in a cult of violence. Gandhi was able to use the potent force of his native Hinduism, whereas Kagawa's Japan had a mixture of religions and value systems, one of which, Shinto, was tightly bound to nationalism. Kagawa converted to Christianity, in contrast to Gandhi who converted Christianity to Hinduism by incorporating the New Testament and Tolstoyian pacifism into his thought and action. Gandhi saw his indigenous religion as a spiritual engine in the fight for social justice. Kagawa, on the other hand, thought his native creeds lacked the moral resources to redeem Japan.

Gandhi had the old romantic antagonism to modern technology, regarding it as rather unholy, whereas Kagawa wanted to pursue it. Kagawa had no quarrel with science and industry, nor did he see them as an evil in themselves. It was their misuse that drove him wild with indignation. One of the more pragmatic mystics the world has ever known, Kagawa reveled in putting science in the service of God, building the Kingdom. While Gandhi was turning his ancient spinning wheel and preaching vegetarianism, Kagawa was pushing for better farm machinery and urging peasants to raise pork and rabbits. He was advocating appropriate technology, environmentally sound agriculture and birth control—three of the most desperate needs of the underdeveloped nations 75 years ago.

Kagawa's disciples in the West exulted over "Kagawa's cooperative movement" and looked to him as "the leader of 40
million laboring people in Japan." In reality, neither the cooperative nor the labor movement was his or anyone else's,
especially after they had both been subverted by the militarists
as Japan geared up for the fast developing war in the Pacific
with the United States. Kagawa's admirers in the West had an
exaggerated notion of the extent of his popularity in his own
country. He was, in some respects, more influential abroad than
at home.

Instead of engaging in a tough, realistic dialogue with him,
Kagawa devotees too often subsumed the frightening pre-World
War II developments in Japan into a sort of ecstatic hymn of
praise to Kagawa. The following is an example:

> Within the last few years, the name of Toyohiko Kagawa has
> blazed like a comet across the world's horizon. Out of Japan
> from whence have issued so many disturbing rumbles has come
> the voice of a great religious leader. Throughout the Protestant
> churches of America a few years ago ran the question "Who is
> Kagawa?" With the forthcoming answer there arose a deeper
> and more profound question "what is the meaning of Kagawa?"
> The answer which America is receiving today is having a moving
> effect upon Christianity in America. For Kagawa's message is
> one of international brotherhood, of peace and Christian
> unity. . . .
>
> This is the voice from Japan that has been ringing in the ears of
> Western Christians these last few years. While others point
> tremulous fingers and utter disquieting forebodings as to the
> possibility of war with Japan, these men smile confidently and
> say, "You forget Kagawa."
>
> These men know whereof they speak. They knew that among
> the humble 95% of the Japanese, the real peace-loving people,
> Kagawa has assumed the aspect of a saint. They turn to him for
> guidance and counsel. . . .[1]

This kind of hero worship ascribed superhuman powers to
Kagawa—or if not superhuman, certainly powers far beyond
those he actually had in Japan.[2] No one individual, not Kagawa
nor those who had greater sway than he, could lead the masses
to some "promised land" Kagawa's American admirers were
projecting the Western "great man" theory of history on to a

different culture, one which deemphasizes individuality and operates on a collective and consensual basis.

Unfortunately, instead of trying to work out a strategy to curb totalitarianism in Japan, the disciples came to Kagawa believing that with the great man in charge, the will of the humble 95% was being fulfilled. To the contrary, the two major political parties, the military police, big business, landlords, bureaucrats and government censors held all the real power. Millions of Japanese were still so steeped in feudalistic values that they were often reluctant to follow any leader who challenged authority, let alone an individual like Kagawa who was suspect because he preached an alien religion. With the government's omnipresent propaganda and censorship, the supposedly peace-loving folks were molded into warriors. Kagawa himself, as we have seen, became a victim of this powerful disinformation apparatus.

Kagawa's popularity in the United States was a social and religious phenomenon. Charisma such as he possessed is a very difficult power to define. Because of the human need to venerate, to experience that *frisson* of awe, people came to Kagawa looking for an encounter with the divine. That magnified his already impressive character. As a man from Asia he had appeal beyond charisma. He helped to restore American faith in their own tradition in a number of ways. Those troubled by doubts that the whole missionary endeavor was worth its expense and effort could see in Kagawa a justification for it. Here was living testimony of the value of foreign missions. One Kagawa was a dramatic vindication of global evangelism.

Most important was the fact that he helped to resolve some of the deepest anxieties about a Christian faith shaken by the Darwinism, secularism and revolution of the 19th century. With Christendom further convulsed by World War I and the Great Depression, the religious mood for many intelligent people seemed better expressed in T. S. Eliot's *Wasteland* than in the hollow exhortations of the established churches. The horror of modern history had brought on such relativism that there were profound doubts as to whether the "good news" of Christianity could claim any moral superiority to other belief systems.

Kagawa arrived with living proof of the power of that faith, and he preached a social program which demanded that faith be incarnated in action. He had been reborn through Christianity and he talked about the tremendous influence for reform which this religion exerted in Japan, both individually and collectively. Kagawa the Asian could affirm what Western Christians themselves had come to doubt—that the Gospel remained the light of the world. Kagawa's experience convinced the skeptics that it was not time to abandon Christianity, but to begin practicing it again.

He was a man steeped in the tradition of his own land in a perfect position to exhort the West to return to its own tradition—for Christendom to come home to true Christianity. His Christianity was wholly his own, adopted to serve Japan. It was not the ethnocentric Christianity intent on giving the non-white world an inferiority complex, and of which the West was beginning to feel ashamed. Nor was it the tool of conquest which Christian nations had used in their hypocritical quest for world domination. Quite the opposite, Kagawa's Christianity was an instrument of liberation.

Through his actions, writings and an indefinable aura of holiness, he showed how to recover and "enjoy" a religious faith which had been frayed by doubt. His combination of practical social reform and mysticism was especially appealing to those struggling to make their faith relevant in a suffering world rather than merely a private exercise. In addition, his philosophy of cooperation and his interpretation of the social gospel demonstrated that social reform could be achieved through non-violent means.

Some of this aspect of the "Kagawa phenomenon" was astutely described by Yusuke Tsurumi, in 1935:

> If one had asked thirty years ago what Japanese was most widely known in the world, the answer would have been Admiral Togo. Fifteen years ago perhaps it would have been Sessue Hayakawa; and today it would be Toyohiko Kagawa. . . .
>
> The fact that Western civilization is not so superior as they had thought has gradually opened their eyes. They have found out, as though it were just new, that Asia possesses some things which they themselves do not have. One of these is a way of looking at things which Asia has. In a word this is what is called

"Culture." In addition to this "way of looking at things," which Asia possesses, does she not also possess more deeply and in a purer form, even that which Westerners thought they themselves had produced? What about Christianity? Even this religion which they thought they had been observing for 2,000 years—its pure spirit, however, having deteriorated in their own hearts—is it not rather finding a resurrection in the Orient from which it sprang?

Because of this, the great admiration of foreigners for Mr. Kagawa and Gandhi is the product of their own self-condemnation. It might be called the groan of the white race on awakening from its dream of superiority.[3]

Those who insisted on calling Kagawa a prophet didn't realize that, in some respects, he had abdicated the prophet's role as an uncompromising critic of society. Kagawa withdrew from this dangerous role by becoming a partisan for his nation and more of a good will ambassador for Japan in the 1930s. His strategy in discussing Japan with outsiders seemed to downplay its problems, to give the impression that matters were in hand and that the forces of good were quietly prevailing. Japan had its problems, but there was no cause to panic.

His reason for taking this line was a noble one, in that he hoped to help preserve peace by toning down hostility toward Japan. But merely smoothing over relations was not enough. Festering problems at times are best aired and subjected to painful discussion and confrontation so that a healing can take place. As great a Christian as he was, Kagawa was not equal to Christ's most troubling words and deeds, such as throwing the money changers out of the temple or warning the disciples that he had come to create division on earth.

Kagawa appeared to have been emotionally unable to face squarely the pathology of pre-war Japan and battle through such a recognition to its conclusion. His capacity to endure painful conflict with others was not without limits. Rather than continue battling for his beliefs in the labor, peasant and political movements in the 1920s, he gradually retreated. Instead of continuing to defy his government, he toned down his harsher criticisms and found himself drawn closer to the center of political power. The end result was that instead of dramatizing the real differences between people, he tended to deny the existence of such conflicts by appealing to abstract concepts of love and cooperation.

One can only speculate on what other courses of action he might have taken. Instead of spreading good will, he might have devoted his energies to a more scathing attack on Western racism and colonialism, which the Japanese militarists used to justify Japan's empire building. At the same time, he would have had to mount an international movement to curb oppression in Japan, perhaps through calling for stronger international sanctions and a boycott of his own nation. The boycott that finally was launched against Japan, when the United States froze assets and embargoed oil, came a decade too late and ended up provoking war rather than preventing it.

Mounting such a double-edged crusade might have brought exile or death to Kagawa. Aware of his many opponents, he once stated,

> It seemed that everyone was attacking me—the Soviet Communists, the anarchists, the capitalists, the foul-mouthed literary critics, the sensationalist newspaper men, the Buddhist who could not compete with Christ, and those many Christians who profess Christ but believe in a Christianity which is sterile.[4]

Kagawa consciously portrayed himself as the cornerstone that the builders rejected, as the Son of Man who had not a stone on which to rest his head:

> It seemed that enemies came at me from every direction; that everything I had worked for was being undermined and soon would crumble. I felt that I had been beaten until I bled, and many times the thought forced itself into my mind that somehow I must have failed. Then I remembered that Jesus was willing to fail in the attempt to establish a better social order. If a person goes against any sort of social evil he will be persecuted. So we need the courage of Jesus to carry through the fight for social justice. We need to be subjected to pain and suffering to make us want to fight for the cause of righteousness. There can be no progress without sacrifice. If you can't understand pain you can't understand God. If you do not understand how to fail, you do not know how to follow Christ. Jesus fought and he was crucified.[5]

It was precisely this lonely hike up Golgotha which Kagawa could not take, and so he fell short of his attempt to imitate Christ in an act of redemptive love which would have stripped him of life itself. He needed friendly American audiences, and he needed acceptance in Japan, whether from the officials with whom he associated, the millions on his evangelizing tours, or his devoted co-workers in the Friends of Jesus society and other organizations. He needed too much the friends of whom Gandhi had warned him, the friends who asked him to desist.

Yet when all is said and done, Kagawa ascended much farther up Golgotha than most of us can even hope to do. He served as a rich inspiration for faith and social action. For that reason, he deserves to be remembered, studied and emulated today.

Notes

Introduction.

1. Gerhard Rosenkranz, *Flammendes Herz in Gottes Hand, von der Christlichen Ritterschaft des Dr. Kagawa Toyohiko* (Stuttgart: Evangelische Missionsverlag, 1948.)

2. *New York Times*, 5 September 1940, p. 5.

3. Allan A. Hunter, *Three Trumpets Sound: Kagawa—Gandhi—Schweitzer* (New York: Association Press, 1939).

4. Kenneth Saunders, *Whither Asia?* (New York: The MacMillan Company, 1933).

5. *Modern Japanese Literature in Translation* (Tokyo: Kodansha International, Ltd., 1979), pp. 90–91.

6. Alfred Kazin, "Pilgrims of Japan," *New York Times Book Review*, 9 February 1936, p. 6.

7. Barnard Rubin, "Under Christian Guise, This Jap Fostered War," *Stars and Stripes*, Pacific edition, 20 December 1945, p. 2. This was the first of several articles in this publication which accused Kagawa of collaborating with the Japanese government and of "stumping" with Yoshio Kodama, a leader of the ultranationalist, pro-military Patriotic Mass Party, who was later convicted as a war criminal.

8. Shiro Kuroda, *Ningen Kagawa Toyohiko* (Toyohiko Kagawa the Man) (Tokyo: Kirisuto Shimbunsha, 1970), p. 9, trans. Yuzo Ota, "Kagawa Toyohiko: A Pacifist?" in Nobuya Bamba and John F. Howes, *Pacifism in Japan: The Christian and Socialist Tradition* (Vancouver: University of British Columbia Press, 1978), p. 169. For a discussion of Kagawa's reputation in Japan, see Yasuo Furuya, "Toyohiko Kagawa (1888–1960): Blessed are the Poor," in H. T. Ker, ed., *Sons of the Prophets* (Princeton, N.J.: Princeton University Press, 1963), pp. 192–204.

9. "Kagawa Arrives on Revival Tour," *New York Times*, 15 July 1950, p. 14.

10. Ibid.

11. These and numerous other details of Kagawa's personal and domestic life are drawn from a series of interviews in 1986–1987 with his daughter, Rev. Umeko Momii of Salinas, California.

Chapter 1.

1. The first major biography of Kagawa in English was William Axling's *Kagawa* (New York: Harper & Brothers, 1932). Two postwar biographies published in English are Charlie May Simon's *A Seed Shall Serve: the Story of*

Toyohiko Kagawa, Spiritual Leader of Modern Japan (New York: E. P. Dutton, 1958) and Cyril J. Davey's *Kagawa of Japan* (New York: Abingdon Press, 1960).

Four other excellent modern sources in English on Kagawa's life are available, the most intriguing being George B. Bikle, Jr., *The New Jerusalem: Aspects of Utopianism in the Thought of Kagawa Toyohiko* (Tucson, Arizona: The University of Arizona Press, 1976). Bikle's study of Kagawa's political thought is indispensible in understanding Kagawa's spiritual growth and his relation to Japan. In addition to Bikle's thorough and insightful work, the following unpublished doctoral dissertations are quite useful: Arthur C. Knudten, *Toyohiko Kagawa and Some Social, Economic and Religious Tendencies in Modern Japan* (University of Southern California, 1946); Willie Tsunetaka Nagai, *A Christian Labor Leader: Kagawa Toyohiko (1888–1960)* (University of Colorado, 1976); Ken Nishimura, *The Idea of Redemption in the Writings of Toyohiko Kagawa* (Emory University, 1966).

The standard biography in Japanese is Haruichi Yokoyama, *Kagawa Toyohiko den* (Biography of Toyohiko Kagawa) (Tokyo: Kirisuto Shimbunsha, 1951). Other valuable sources are Mikio Sumiya, *Kagawa Toyohiko: jin to shiso* (Toyohiko Kagawa: the Man and His Thought) (Tokyo: Nihon Kirisuto Kyodan Shuppanbu, 1966); *Hyakusan nin no Kagawa den* (Biography of Kagawa by One Hundred and Three People), Tomio Muto, ed. (Tokyo: Kirisuto Shimbunsha, 1960) and Tomio Muto, *Kagawa Toyohiko* (Toyohiko Kagawa) (Tokyo: Kirisuto Shimbunsha, 1981).

2. Toyohiko Kagawa, *The Challenge of Redemptive Love*, trans. Marion Draper (New York: Abingdon Press, 1940), p. 100 or *Christ and Japan*, trans. William Axling (New York: Friendship Press, 1934), passim, contain descriptions of this early religious development.

3. Emerson O. Bradshaw, *Unconquerable Kagawa* (St. Paul: MacCalester Park, 1952), p. 80.

4. Masuyoshi Kagawa, "Gokaini kurushimu," *Bulletin for Kagawa Toyohiko zenshu*, no. 23 (August 1964), pp. 2–3, cited in Nishimura, op. cit., p. 20.

5. Toyohiko Kagawa, op. cit., pp.61–62.

6. Nishimura, op. cit., p. 19.

7. H. W. Myers, "Toyohiko Kagawa—Japanese Apostle to the Poor," *The Missionary Review of the World*, vol. 54 (July 1931), pp. 501–502.

8. Toyohiko Kagawa, in "Kagawa's Boyhood Teacher and Friend Becomes His Coworker," *Kagawa Comes Home: Friends of Jesus*, vol. 9 (June 1937), p. 12.

9. Ibid., p. 13

10. Ibid., p. 12.

11. Ibid., p. 13.

12. Umeko Momii interview.

13. The Logans, who arrived in 1902, had an address at 82 Tokushima-machi, the same as Myers, who had arrived in 1897, when he was only 23 years old.

14. H. W. Myers, "Toyohiko Kagawa, Christian Labor Leader," *Missionary Review of the World*, vol. 46 (October 1923), pp. 807–811.

15. Myers, "Toyohiko Kagawa—Japanese Apostle to the Poor," p. 502.

16. Toyohiko Kagawa, "Revealing Christ in Japan," *The Missionary Review of the World*, vol. 54 (March 1931), p. 166.

17. Idem, *Kami to shokuzai ai no kangeki* (The Challenge of Redemptive Love), *Kagawa Toyohiko zenshu* (The Collected Works of Toyohiko Kagawa), 24 vols., ed. Tomio Muto (Tokyo: Kirisuto Shimbunsha, 1964), vol. 3, pp. 383–384.

18. Helen Topping, *Introducing Kagawa* (Chicago: Willett, Clark and Company, 1935), p. 4.

19. Helen Topping, *Kagawa in Australia* issue of *Friends of Jesus* (Tokyo: [Friends of Jesus], 1936), p. 54.

20. The date may have been February 21. There are conflicting accounts.

Chapter 2.

1. For a discussion of the peasants' reaction to militarization, see Mikiso Hane, *Peasants, Rebels and Outcastes* (New York: Pantheon Books, 1982), pp. 18–20.

2. Cyril J. Davey, *Kagawa of Japan* (New York: Abingdon Press, 1960), p. 20 and Kenichi Yarita, *Nihon no yoru wa akeru* (The Day Breaks in Japan), 2 vols. (Toyohashi City: Daiichi Shoten, 1948), vol. 1, pp. 135–138 have accounts of Kagawa's refusal to carry the gun.

3. Tomio Muto, ed., *Hyakusan nin no Kagawa den* (A Biography of Kagawa by One Hundred and Three People) (Tokyo: Kirisuto Shimbunsha, 1960), pp. 53–54.

4. Robert E. Speer, "Kagawa, the Man," in Toyhiko Kagawa, *The Religion of Jesus*, trans. Helen Topping (Philadelphia: John C. Winston, Co., 1931), p. 3.

5. William Axling, *Kagawa* (New York: Harper & Bros., 1932), pp. 20–21, and Haruichi Yokoyama, *Kagawa Toyohiko den* (Biography of Toyohiko Kagawa) (Tokyo: Kirisuto Shimbunsha, 1951), pp. 25–29, describe Kagawa's compulsive reading habits.

6. Yokoyama, ibid., pp. 28–29.

7. Ibid., p. 27.

8. Kiyoko Takeda Cho, "An Essay on Kagawa Toyohiko—the Place of Man in His Social Theory," *Asian Cultural Study* (Tokyo: International Christian University, n.d., [1960]), p. 3 describes disappointment with one of Kagawa's rather confusing lectures.

9. George B. Bikle, Jr., *The New Jerusalem: Utopianism in the Thought of Kagawa Toyohiko* (Tucson: The University of Arizona Press, 1976), p. 300, quotes a personal letter written September 7, 1966, by Tomio Muto attributing this comment to Murata.

10. Ibid., 35–44, presents an excellent discussion of this essay.

11. Ibid., p. 40.

12. Ibid.

13. Ibid., p. 42.

14. Yokoyama, op. cit., p. 31.

15. Richard H. Mitchell, *Thought Control in Prewar Japan* (Ithaca, New York: Cornell University Press, 1976); Rodger Swearingen and Paul Langer, *Red Flag in Japan: International Communism in Action, 1919–1951* (New York:

Greenwood Press, 1968); Harry Emerson Wildes, *The Press and Social Currents in Japan* (Chicago: University of Chicago Press, 1927) all give frightening glimpses of police repression and insights into the damaging effects of information control.

16. Toyohiko Kagawa, "Kagawa's Boyhood Teacher and Friend Becomes His Coworker," *Kagawa Comes Home, Friends of Jesus*, vol. 9 (June 1937), p.13.

17. Toyohiko Kagawa, *A Shooter at the Sun*, trans. T. Satchell (Kobe: Japan Chronicle Press, 1925), p. 98.

18. Yokoyama, op. cit., pp. 35–36.

19. Yoriyuki Murashima, *Kagawa Toyohiko byochu toshi* (History of Toyohiko Kagawa Fighting His Illness) (Sakai City, Osaka: Tomo Shimbunsha, 1951), pp. 34–35.

20. Axling, op. cit., p. 21.

21. Davey, op. cit., p. 26.

22. Ibid., p. 27.

23. Yokoyama, op. cit., p. 28.

24. Shiro Kuroda, *Ningen Kagawa Toyohiko* (The Human Toyohiko Kagawa) (Tokyo: Kirusuto Shimbunsha, 1970), p. 37.

25. Yokoyama, op. cit., pp. 38–39.

26. Muto, op cit., p. 59.

27. Kuroda, op. cit., p. 43.

28. Muto, op. cit., p. 72, trans. Bikle, op. cit., p. 49.

29. Yokoyama, op. cit., p. 39.

30. Emerson O. Bradshaw, *Unconquerable Kagawa* (St. Paul: MacAlester Park Publishing Co, 1952), pp. 82–83.

31. Ibid., p. 83.

32. Toyohiko Kagawa, *Before the Dawn*, trans. I. Fukumoto and T. Satchell (New York: George H. Doran, 1924), p. 260.

33. Yoshitaka Kumano, "Poetic Christianity: Toyohiko Kagawa and Takeshi Fujii," trans. Akira Demura, *Japan Christian Quarterly*, vol. 32 (Fall 1966), pp. 235–245.

34. Murashima, op. cit., pp. 46–48.

35. Ibid., pp. 50–51.

36. Yokoyama, op. cit., pp. 46–47.

37. From a copy of translation in possession of the author.

38. Donald Keene, *Dawn to the West: Japanese Literature of the Modern Era: Poetry, Drama, Criticism* (New York: Holt, Rinehart and Winston, 1984), p. 551.

39. Kagawa, *A Shooter at the Sun*, p. 84.

40. Toyohiko Kagawa, *Koya Nikki* (Hut Diary), *Kagawa Toyohiko zenshu* (The Collected Works of Toyohiko Kagawa), 24 vols., ed. Tomio Muto (Tokyo: Kirisuto Shimbunsha, 1964), vol. 22, p. 143. Hereafter cited as *Kagawa zenshu*.

41. Yokoyama, op. cit., p. 42.

42. Ibid., p. 46.

43. Murashima, op. cit., p. 53.

44. Yokoyama, op. cit., pp. 47–48.

45. Bradshaw, op. cit., p. 84.

46. Yokoyama, op. cit., p. 49.

47. Axling, op. cit., p. 24.

48. Ibid.

49. Yokoyama, op. cit., p. 52, trans. Willie Tsunetaka Nagai, *A Christian Labor Leader: Kagawa Toyohiko (1888–1960)* (Doctoral thesis, University of Colorado, 1976), pp. 100–101.

50. Ibid.

51. Ibid., pp. 53–54, trans. Nagai, pp. 101–102.

52. Toyohiko Kagawa, *Mu no tetsugaku* (Philosophy of Nothingness), trans. Nagai, p. 104, *Kagawa zenshu*, vol. 24, pp. 368–369.

53. Axling, op. cit., p. ix. Axling's *Kagawa* was perhaps most responsible for the idealized depiction of Kagawa's conversion, writing about his being "born again" when he first read the Sermon on the Mount in 1904. As a longtime friend of Kagawa, Axling was tempted to present his hero as a sterling example of the power of Christianity. His own introductory guideline cited: "There are two Kagawas. There is the Kagawa who has been aureoled and idealized by the fervent devotion of his friends and followers. There is also Kagawa, the man of human clay fighting his way toward the heights." Despite this cautionary statement, Axling glossed over the second Kagawa.

Chapter 3.

1. Haruichi Yokoyama, *Kagawa Toyohiko den* (Biography of Toyokiko Kagawa) (Kirisuto Shimbunsha, 1951), pp. 58–60 provides many of the details of Kagawa's first days in the slums which are presented here.

2. Hyogo Prefecture Exhibitors' Association, *Hyogo Prefecture and City of Kobe* (Kobe, Japan: Panama-Pacific International Exposition, 1915), pp. 4–5.

3. For some first-hand accounts of the dismal situation of the peasantry, the urban proletariat and the relations between them see Mikiso Hane, *Peasants, Rebels, and Outcastes: The Underside of Modern Japan* (New York: Pantheon Books, 1982).

4. Toyohiko Kagawa, *Chikaku o yabutte* (Breaking the Earth Crust), as quoted in *Japan Weekly Chronicle,* 16 June 1921, p. 842.

5. Ibid.

6. Ibid.

7. Ibid., p. 843.

8. Helen F. Topping, *Friends of Jesus,* vol. 4, no. 1, p. 25 ff. and vol. 2, no. 1, p. 23 ff. quoted in Carola D. Barth, *Taten in Gottes Kraft* (Heilbronn: Eugen Salzer Verlag, 1937), pp. 23–26.

9. Barth, ibid., and Yokoyama, op. cit., pp. 59–60.

10. Barth, ibid., pp. 27–28.

11. Kagawa, *A Shooter at the Sun,* trans. T. Satchell (Kobe: Japan Chronicle Press, 1925), pp. 6–7.

12. Ibid., pp. 7–8.

13. Ibid.

14. Kagawa, "Sechzehn Jahre Kriegsdienst für Christus in Japan," *Zeitschrift für Missionskunde und Religionswissenschaft,* vol. 41 (1926) p. 13.

15. Kagawa, *A Shooter at the Sun*, pp. 7–8.

16. H. W. Myers, "Toyohiko Kagawa, Christian Labor Leader," *The Missionary Review of the World*, vol. 46 (October 1923) pp. 807–811.

17. Robert E. Speer, "Kagawa the Man" in Toyohiko Kagawa, *The Religion of Jesus*, trans. Helen F. Topping (Philadelphia: The John C. Winston Company, 1931), pp. 12–13.

18. Kagawa, *Ningenku to ningen kenchiku* (Human Suffering and Human Architecture) in *Kagawa Toyohiko zenshu* (The Complete Works of Toyohiko Kagawa), 24 vols. (Tokyo: Kirisuto Shimbunsha, 1964), vol. 9, pp. 156–157.

19. William Axling, *Kagawa* (New York: Harper & Brothers, 1932), p. 37.

20. Kagawa, *A Shooter at the Sun*, pp. 78–79.

21. Ibid.

22. Ibid., p. 80.

23. Ibid.

24. Ibid.

25. Ibid., p. 83.

26. Ibid., p. 85.

27. Yokoyama, ibid., pp. 96–99; Kagawa, *A Shooter at the Sun*, pp. 20–21.

28. Ibid.

29. Kagawa, *A Shooter at the Sun*, pp. 22–24.

30. "Mr. Kagawa. A Few Reminiscences," *Japan Weekly Chronicle*, (27 November 1924), p. 721.

31. Ibid.

32. Kagawa, *Before the Dawn*, trans. I. Fukumoto and T. Satchell (New York: George H. Doran, 1924), pp. 369–370.

33. Ibid.

34. Michi Kawai and Ochimi Kubushiro, *Japanese Women Speak* (Boston: The Central Committee on the United Study of Foreign Missions, 1934), pp. 139–140.

35. Speer, op. cit., pp. 10–11.

36. Ibid.

37. Kagawa, *A Shooter at the Sun*, p. 91.

38. Ibid.

39. Kagawa, *A Shooter at the Sun*, pp. 93–94.

40. "Kagawa of the Slums," *Japan Weekly Chronicle* (27 November 1924), pp. 716–717.

41. Speer, op. cit., p. 11.

Chapter 4.

1. Toyohiko Kagawa, *A Shooter at the Sun*, trans. T. Satchell (Kobe: Japan Chronicle Press, 1925), p. 101.

2. These studies may have had an effect on changing the crude and bigoted attitude he expressed toward Japan's outcaste class, the buraku, in *Hinmin shinri no kenkyu* (Study of the Psychology of the Poor). Using current "scientific" concepts of eugenics which grew from Darwinism, he claimed the buraku people were genetically inferior in this work, but later changed this opinion. For a discussion of Kagawa's problematic relation to the buraku community, see Chapter Six.

3. Kagawa, op. cit., p. 102.

4. Jan Karel Van Baalen, *Kagawa the Christian* (Grand Rapids, Michigan: Wm. B. Eerdmans, 1936), pp. 14–15.

5. Ibid., p. 15.

6. Ibid., p. 20.

7. Ibid., pp. 18–19.

8. Ibid.

9. Kagawa, op. cit., describes the summer employment stint as follows: "Life at Princeton was very pleasant, but to obtain work in the summer vacation gave him great trouble. Owing to the war in Europe there was a depression in trade and there was no opening in New York, and he walked sorrowfully up and down Fifth Avenue, the splendid street of the millionaires. Luckily in the first summer he spent in America he found a position as a servant in a wealthy summer resort twenty miles from New York. The master was the son and heir of a millionaire coal-owner of Pennsylvania, but as he was a spendthrift and quite incompetent, his father had rented a house for him in that place, and made him live there. His wife was a great Society leader and moreover very frivolous. However, she was a very kind woman and treated Eiichi well. The two women servants who were employed there also treated Eiichi kindly. One of them claimed she was descended from Hamilton, the famous drafter of the American Constitution. Mrs. Hamilton was the housekeeper and had full charge of everything. She was a woman of about fifty, with many grey hairs, and used to sing to Eiichi many popular songs. The cook was a Swede of about thirty-five or six. She was a fine-looking woman of good character, fond of reading and walking. She did not look her age. The house was situated in the middle of a park and Eiichi often went to walk in the park with the cook, who was very fond of him."

10. Ibid., p. 103.

11. Haruichi Yokoyama, *Kagawa Toyohiko den* (A Biography of Toyohiko Kagawa) (Tokyo: Kirisuto Shimbunsha, 1951), p. 112.

12. Kagawa, op. cit., p. 103.

13. Ibid., p. 105.

14. Tomio Muto, *Kagawa Toyohiko* (Kirisuto Shimbunsha, 1981), pp. 163–167.

15. *Ogden Standard,* 1 September 1916, p. 4.

16. Ibid., 14 September 1916, p. 12.

17. Ibid., 9 October 1916, p. 1.

18. Ibid., 21 November 1916, p. 9.

19. Ibid., 4 January 1917, p. 5.

20. Yokoyama, op. cit., p. 115.

21. Ibid., p. 115, says that Kagawa sailed from Seattle, while the autobiographical *A Shooter at the Sun,* has him sailing from Astoria, Oregon.

22. Kagawa, op. cit., p. 105.

Chapter 5.

1. Umeko Momii interview.

2. Toyohiko Kagawa, *Seishin undo to shakai undo* (Spiritual and Social

Movements), *Kagawa Toyohiko zenshu* (The Collected Works of Toyohiko Kagawa), 24 vols. (Tokyo: Kirisuto Shimbunsha, 1973), vol. 8, p. 484, trans. Willie Tsunetaka Nagai, *A Christian Labor Leader: Kagawa Toyohiko (1888–1960)* (Doctoral thesis, University of Colorado, 1976), p. 170.

3. Kagawa, *Kagawa zenshu*, vol. 1, p. 3.

4. Edwin O. Reischauer and Albert M. Craig, *Japan: Tradition and Transformation* (Boston: Houghton Mifflin Company, 1978), p. 241.

5. Kagawa, *Meditations on the Cross*, trans. Helen Topping and Marion Draper (Chicago and New York: Willett, Clark and Co., 1935), p. 165.

6. Tomio Muto, ed., *Hyakusan nin no Kagawa den* (Biography of Kagawa by One Hundred and Three People) (Tokyo: Kirisuto Shimbunsha, 1960), p. 46.

7. Haruichi Yokoyama, *Kagawa Toyohiko den* (Biography of Toyohiko Kagawa) (Tokyo: Kirisuto Shimbunsha, 1951), pp. 123–124.

8. Kagawa, *Ningenku to ningen kenchiku* (Human Suffering and Human Architecture), *Kagawa zenshu*, vol. 9, p. 78.

9. Ushisaburo Kobayashi, *The Basic Industries and Social History of Japan, 1914–1918* (New Haven: Yale University Press, 1930), p. 278.

10. Stephen S. Large, *The Rise of Labor in Japan: The Yuaikai 1912–1919* (Tokyo: Sophia University, 1972), p. 3. Large presents a fascinating study of the Yuaikai and of some of Kagawa's contributions to it.

11. Harry Emerson Wildes, *Social Currents in Japan With Special Reference to the Press* (Chicago: The University of Chicago Press, 1927), p. 127.

12. Ibid., pp. 123–126.

13. Large, op. cit., p. 11.

14. Ibid., pp. 35–38.

15. Ibid., pp. 31–32.

16. Kagawa, *Shi daikoen shu* (Collected Lectures) *Kagawa zenshu*, vol. 10, pp. 70–71, trans. Nagai, op. cit., p. 182.

17. Kagawa, "Musansha kaikyu no shutsugen" (The Appearance of the Proletarian Class), *Shin Kobe*, 22 August 1918, p. 1, trans. Nagai, op. cit., p. 201.

18. Yokoyama, op. cit., pp. 126–127.

19. Kagawa, *Rodosha suhairon* (Treatise on the Adoration of the Laborer), *Kagawa zenshu*, vol. 10, p. 18, trans. George B. Bikle, Jr. *The New Jerusalem: Aspects of Utopianism in the Thought of Kagawa Toyohiko* (Tucson, Arizona: The University of Arizona Press, 1976), p. 102.

20. Ibid., p. 7.

21. Ibid., p. 29.

22. Ibid., p. 8, trans. Bikle, op. cit., p.103.

23. Kagawa, *Jiyu Kumiai Ron* (The Theory of Free Unions), *Kagawa zenshu*, vol. 11, pp. 159–160, trans. Nagai, op. cit., p. 190.

24. Large, op. cit., p. 123 ff.

25. Ibid., p. 126.

26. Mikio Sumiya, *Kagawa Toyohiko, jin to shiso* (Toyohiko Kagawa, the Man and His Thought) (Tokyo: Nihon Kirisuto Kyodan Shuppanbu, 1966), p. 67.

27. Sumiya, ibid., trans. Kenneth C. Hendricks (manuscript in collection of Disciples of Christ Historical Society, Nashville, Tennessee), p. 76.

28. Reischauer and Craig, op. cit., pp. 237–238.

29. Kagawa, *Kagawa zenshu*, vol. 10, p. 19, trans. Nagai, op. cit., p. 205.

30. Kagawa, *Chingen dorei no kaiho* (The Liberation of Wage Slaves) *Rodo shimbun*, 15 June 1919, p. 1.

31. Large, op. cit., p. 179.

32. Large, *Organized Workers and Socialist Politics in Interwar Japan* (Cambridge: Cambridge University Press, 1981), p. 26. This dramatically written and thorough study of the labor and political movements in Japan in the interwar years is a sequel to Large's earlier book and a key to understanding the relation of politics and labor in Japan and Kagawa's involvement.

33. Ibid.

34. Ibid.

35. Ibid., p. 42.

36. Ibid.

37. Shiro Kuroda, *Ningen Kagawa Toyohiko* (The Human Toyohiko Kagawa) (Tokyo: Kirisuto Shimbunsha, 1970), p. 12, trans. Nagai, op. cit., pp. 231–232.

38. *Japan Weekly Chronicle*, 7 October 1920, p. 473, hereafter cited as *JWC*.

39. *JWC*, 30 September 1920, p. 455.

40. *JWC*.

41. *JWC*, 7 October 1920, p. 473.

42. *JWC*, 10 February 1921, p.170.

43. Bikle, op. cit., pp. 122–123 et passim.

44. "Mr. Kagawa of Kobe: A Christian Labourite," *JWC*, 26 May 1921, p. 732.

45. Ibid.

46. Ibid.

47. Ibid.

48. Sumiya, op. cit., trans. Hendricks, op. cit., p. 116.

49. "Labor Movement," *JWC*, 7 July 1921, p. 30. The detailed account of the Kobe strikes in this chapter is drawn primarily from this publication and from Mikio Sumiya's account.

50. *JWC*, 14 July 1921, p. 62.

51. Ibid.

52. Sumiya, op. cit., trans. Hendricks, op. cit., p. 121.

53. *JWC*, 28 July 1921, p. 130.

54. "The Struggle at the Shipyards," *JWC*, 28 July 1921, pp. 136–138.

55. Ibid., p. 138.

56. Sumiya, op. cit., trans. Hendricks, p. 127.

57. William Axling, *Kagawa* (New York: Harper & Brothers, 1932), pp. 51–53 contains the complete text.

58. *JWC*, 11 August 1921, p. 208.

59. Sumiya, op. cit., trans. Bikle, op. cit., p. 136.

60. *JWC*, 1 December 1921, p. 791.

61. Bikle, op. cit., p. 95.

62. Bikle, ibid., pp. 313–314.

Chapter 6.

1. Toyohiko Kagawa, "Nihon no mura no shakai mondai" (Social Problems of Japan's Farm Villages), *Kyusai kenkyu*, January 1919, cited in George B. Bikle, Jr., *The New Jerusalem: Aspects of Utopianism in the Thought of Kagawa Toyohiko* (Tucson: The University of Arizona Press, 1976), pp. 141–142.

2. Mikio Sumiya, *Kagawa Toyohiko, jin to shiso* (Toyohiko Kagawa, the Man and His Thought) (Tokyo: Nihon Kirisuto Kyodan Shuppanbu, 1966), trans. Kenneth C. Hendricks (manuscript in Disciples of Christ Historical Society, Nashville, Tennessee), p. 141.

3. George Oakley Totten, III, *The Social Democratic Movement in Prewar Japan* (New Haven and London: Yale University Press, 1966), pp. 35–36.

4. Mikiso Hane, *Peasants Rebels and Outcastes: The Underside of Modern Japan* (New York, Pantheon Books, 1982), pp. 38–40. This book presents a few vivid examples from the numerous published accounts of the miseries of peasant life.

5. Hideo Yokota, *Noson kakumeiron* (On Rural Revolution) (Tokyo: Hakubunkan, 1914), p. 44, quoted in Thomas R.H. Havens, *Farm and Nation in Modern Japan: Agrarian Nationalism, 1870–1940* (Princeton, N.J.: Princeton University Press, 1974), pp. 123–124. Yokota also remarked on the influence the labor movement was exercising on rural Japan: "Has not the self-consciousness of the workers, stimulated by the victory of democracy, boldly given rise to the labor movement which today demands economic and spiritual liberation for the workers? . . . The tenants, who have suppressed their own class consciousness as though it were a bud of treason, have been shaken by the practical results of the labor movement which is now overwhelming the world. Are they not shedding the husk of their slave mentality day by day?" Cited in Havens, p. 130.

6. Ann Waswo, *Japanese Landlords: The Decline of a Rural Elite* (Berkeley: University of California Press, 1977), p. 7. Because of the incredibly complicated patchwork of ownership of land in tiny plots and the fact that many farmers owned some plots outright while renting others, exact figures on tenancy, absentee ownership, etc. will probably never be established.

7. Waswo, "In Search of Equity: Japanese Tenant Unions in the 1920s," in *Conflict in Modern Japanese History*, Tetsuo Najita and J. Victor Koschmann, eds. (Princeton: Princeton University Press, 1982), p. 367.

8. R. P. Dore, *Land Reform in Japan* (London: Oxford University Press, 1959), p. 72.

9. "Organizing the Working Farmers," *Japan Weekly Chronicle*, 1 March 1923, p. 304, hereafter cited as *JWC*.

10. Totten, op. cit., pp. 145–146.

11. Willie Tsunetaka Nagai, *A Christian Labor Leader: Kagawa Toyohiko (1888–1960)* (Doctoral thesis, University of Colorado, 1976), p. 242.

12. Iwao F. Ayusawa, *A History of Labor in Modern Japan* (Honolulu: East-West Center Press, 1966), pp. 162–163.

13. Tomio Muto, "Ushers to the Bible," *Japan Times* (11 August 1958), p. 3.

14. Ibid.

15. "Kobe Labor Troubles," *JWC*, 30 March 1922, p. 454.

16. "The Kawasaki Strike," *JWC*, 27 April 1922, p. 607.

17. "Kawasaki Strike," *JWC*, 25 May 1922, p. 761.

18. "Kagawa Denounces Capitalists," *JWC*, 1 June 1922, p. 792.

19. "Tenant Farmers," *JWC*, 18 May 1922, p. 712.

20. Ayusawa, op. cit., p. 165. Figures on the union's membership vary wildly. Mikio Sumiya, for example, claims a membership of 100,000 by the end of 1923. It is safe to say that the union had well over 60,000 at its peak.

21. Ibid., pp. 164–165.

22. Kagawa, *Rittai nogyo no riron to jissai* (The Theory and Practice of Three Dimensional Agriculture), *Kagawa Toyohiko Zenshu,* (The Complete Works of Toyohiko Kagawa), 24 vols. (Tokyo: Kirisuto Shimbunsha, 1964), vol. 12, p. 128, quoted in Bikle, op. cit., pp. 204–205.

23. Bikle, ibid., p. 207.

24. Ibid., p. 150.

25. Ayusawa, op. cit., pp. 163–164.

26. Lawrence Lader, *The Margaret Sanger Story and the Fight for Birth Control* (Garden City, New York: Doubleday & Company, 1955), pp. 186–196. See also *JWC*, 9 March 1922, p. 344.

27. "Mrs. Sanger," *JWC*, 6 April 1922, p. 509.

28. Ayusawa, op. cit., pp. 122–123.

29. "Mr. Kagawa on Uselessness of Geneva Meeting," *JWC*, 17 August 1922, p. 225.

30. *JWC*, 7 September 1922, p. 322.

31. George De Vos and Hiroshi Wagatsuma, *Japan's Invisible Race: Caste in Culture and Personality* (Berkeley: University of California Press, 1966) is a detailed study of the buraku minority group in Japan.

32. An example of the harshness of this bigotry can be seen in the following account by Iheiji Miyoshi, one of the leaders in the early civil rights movement, when he was sent to a non-burakumin school: "When I entered junior high school in 1883 everyone was curious. . . . I was made to sit alone behind all the children in the class . . . nobody talked to me, nor wanted to sit by me. . . . A teacher of a physiology class asked me if it was true that we burakumin did not defecate and urinate at the same time. . . . He also asked me who my ancestor was. I told him my ancestor was a general under Oya Gyobu Yoshitaka. He said that he had thought our ancestors were Koreans or Ainu. . . . I received the highest grades in my class, and when I was not present, the teacher told the class that it was to their shame to let an 'eta' boy be the top student, and that they should study harder to excel an 'eta.'" Cited in De Vos and Wagatsuma, op. cit., p. 37.

33. Motojiro Sugiyama, *Tochi to jiyu no tameni* (For Land and the Cause of Freedom) (Tokyo: Sugiyama Motojiro-Den Kankokai, 1965), pp. 205–206. Cited in Nagai, op. cit., p. 129.

34. Eiichi Kudo, *Dictionary of the Buraku Problem* (Osaka: Buraku Liberation Research Center, 1986), pp. 101–102, trans. R. G. Stieber.

35. Quoted in De Vos and Wagatsuma, op. cit., pp. 94–95.

36. Kagawa, "Christianity in Japan Today," *The Christian Century*, vol. 45 (12 January 1928), p. 50.

37. Ibid.

38. Stephen S. Large, *Organized Workers and Socialist Politics in Interwar Japan* (Cambridge: Cambridge University Press, 1981) provides some vivid

history of the confusing array of leftist organizations. Totten's *Social Democratic Movement in Prewar Japan* is an almost heroic work of scholarship documenting this complex topic.

39. Totten, op. cit., pp. 409–413 lists these "proletarian" parties in the social democratic camp.

40. Kagawa, *Love the Law of Life*, trans. J. Fullerton Gressit (Chicago: The John C. Winston Co., 1929), pp. 229–230.

Chapter 7.

1. "Going to Yokohama," *Japan Weekly Chronicle*, 13 September 1923, p. 373, hereafter cited as *JWC*.

2. Ibid., p. 374.

3. Joseph Dahlmann, *The Great Tokyo Earthquake*, trans. Victor F. Gettleman (New York: The America Press, 1924) is a vivid account of the earthquake written by an eye witness while the city was was still burning.

4. Helen F. Topping, in Toyohiko Kagawa, *Love the Law of Life*, trans. J. Fullerton Gressit (Chicago: The John C. Winston Co., 1929), pp. 13–14.

5. Ibid., p. 8.

6. *JWC*, 15 May 1924, p. 690.

7. *JWC*, 20 March 1924, p. 402.

8. Akira Demura, trans. in Yoshitaka Kumano, "Poetic Christianity: Toyohiko Kagawa and Takeshi Fujii," *Japan Christian Quarterly*, vol. 32 (Fall, 1966), p. 241.

9. Herbert A Miller, "Apostles of World Unity XXXI—Toyohiko Kagawa," *World Unity* , vol. 9 (October 1931), pp. 34–40.

10. Toyohiko Kagawa, "Facing a Crisis in Japan," *Missionary Review of the World*, vol. 57 (October 1934), pp. 465–466.

11. Mikio Sumiya, *Kagawa Toyohiko, jin to shiso* (Toyohiko Kagawa, the Man and His Thought) (Tokyo: Nihon Kirisuto Kyodan Shuppanbu, 1966), trans. Kenneth C. Hendricks (manuscript in Disciples of Christ Historical Society, Nashville, Tennessee), p. 165.

12. Umeko Momii interview.

13. *JWC*, 15 May 1924, p. 690.

14. Stephen S. Large, *Organized Workers and Socialist Politics in Interwar Japan* (Cambridge: Cambridge University Press, 1981), presents a fascinating discussion of how growing repression could be combined with social reform.

15. "Kagawa in Tokyo", *JWC*, 13 December 1923, p. 827.

16. "Japanese Criticism of America: The Exclusion Bill and the Response," *JWC*, 8 May 1924, p. 638.

17. "Conference of Coloured Races: Reactions to American Exclusion Bill," *JWC*, 1 May 1924, p. 604.

18. *JWC*, 3 July 1924, p. 32.

19. Kagawa, "Earthquake Relief," *The Christian Movement in Japan, Korea and Formosa. Twenty Second Annual Issue*, D. C. Holtom, ed. (Kobe: The Japan Chronicle Press, 1924), p. 211. This series is often referred to as *The Japan Christian Year Book*, which later became its title.

20. *JWC*, 23 October 1924, p. 567.

21. Copy of letter in possession of author.

22. Ibid.

23. Kagawa, "Sechzehn Jahre Kriegsdienst für Christus in Japan," translated by D. Dr. J. Witte, *Zeitschrift für Missionskund und Religionswissenschaft,* vol. 41 (1926), pp. 11–17.

24. Kagawa, "Christianity and Race Prejudice. A Japanese Plea," *The Friend,* vol. 65 (3 April 1925), p. 281.

25. Ibid.

26. Ibid.

27. Ibid.

28. See, for example, "Japanese Labor Friendly," *New York Times,* 12 March 1925, p. 22.

29. Kagawa, "Earthquake Relief," op. cit., p. 210.

30. Kagawa, *Love the Law of Life,* p. 57.

31. Ibid.

32. Kagawa, *Seishinundo to shakaiundo* (Spiritual and Social Movements) *Kagawa Toyohiko zenshu* (The Complete Works of Toyohiko Kagawa) 24 vols. (Tokyo: Kirisuto Shimbunsha, 1964), vol. 8, p. 418, trans. Willia Tsunetaka Nagai, *A Christian Labor Leader: Toyohiko Kagawa (1888–1960)* (Doctoral thesis, University of Colorado, 1976), p. 249.

33. George Oakley Totten III, *The Social Democratic Movement in Prewar Japan* (New Haven: Yale University Press, 1966), pp. 54–55.

34. Large, op. cit., pp. 102–104.

35. Ibid., pp. 104–105.

36. Ibid., pp. 105–106.

37. For those who are interested, the history of this frightening tangle of party disputes is presented in detail by both Totten and Large in their excellent books.

38. Kagawa, *Shimpen zakki* (Personal Notes), *Kagawa zenshu,* vol. 24 (Tokyo: Kirisuto Shimbunsha, 1964), p. 73.

39. Ibid., p. 6.

40. Sumiya, op. cit., pp. 170–171.

41. Kagawa, "One Million Christians in Japan," *The Japan Christian Quarterly,* vol. 3 (October 1928), p. 377.

42. Kagawa, "Facing a Crisis in Japan," op. cit., pp. 465–466.

43. George B. Bikle, Jr., *The New Jerusalem: Aspects of Utopianism in the Thought of Kagawa Toyohiko* (Tucson: The University of Arizona Press, 1976), p. 319.

44. Kagawa, "The Discovery of Redeeming Love," *The Japan Christian Quarterly,* vol. 12 (January 1937), p. 9.

45. Personal notes by Rev. Clyde H. Roddy, copy in possession of author.

46. Ibid.

47. Ibid.

48. Idabelle Lewis Main, "Kagawa Wins Chinese Trust," *The Christian Century,* vol. 51 (2 May, 1934), pp. 609–610, contains an account of this Shanghai visit.

49. Ibid.

50. John Gunther, *Inside Asia* (Harper & Brothers, 1942), p. 80.

Chapter 8.

1. George Yasukochi, "Japanese Co-opers to Visit Berkeley," *Co-op News*, Berkeley, February 25, 1987, p. 3. See also *For Peace and a Better Life* (Tokyo: Japanese Consumers' Co-operative Union, 1982).

2. Sadao Nakabayashi, *Kagawa sensei to seikyo* (Kagawa and the Cooperatives) in *Kagawa no seikyo* (Kagawa's Cooperative Movement) (Tokyo, n.d.), pp. 2–3.

3. Ibid.

4. Letter to George Yasukochi, 20 August 1987. Copy in possession of author.

5. T. T. Brumbaugh, "Kagawa on Cooperatives," *The Christian Century*, vol. 52, February 27, 1935, p. 267.

6. Yoshio Honiden, *Cooperative Movement in Japan*, vol. 1 (Tokyo: Maruzen, 1958), pp. 78.

7. Ibid., pp. 8–10.

8. Harold E. Fey, "Looking at Life with Kagawa," *The Christian Century*, vol. 47, (12 March, 1930), p. 331.

9. Brumbaugh, op. cit., p. 269.

10. Galen Fisher, "The Cooperative Movement in Japan," *Pacific Affairs*, vol. 11, (December 1938), pp. 478–491.

11. R.D. McCoy, "Medical Cooperatives in Japan," in *The Japan Christian Year Book*, vol. 34, Fred D. Gealy, ed. (Tokyo: Kyo Bun Kwan, 1936), pp. 183–184, 186.

12. *A Short Description of the Work of Toyohiko Kagawa* (Tokyo: Kagawa Fellowship in Japan, 1937), pp. 20–21.

13. McCoy, op. cit., pp. 181–182.

14. Ibid., p. 182.

15. Ibid., pp. 183–184.

16. Ralph A. Felton, "The Rural Church in Japan (II)," *Japan Christian Quarterly*, vol. 13, (April 1938), p. 144.

17. Yusuke Tsurumi, "Toyohiko Kagawa," *The Japan Christian Quarterly*, vol. 10, (April 1935), pp. 113–114.

18. *The Christian Century*, vol. 52, (18 August 1935), p. 1041.

19. *The Christian Century*, vol. 52, (December 18, 1935), p. 1637.

20. *The Japan Christian Quarterly*, vol. 11, (January 1936), pp. 4–5.

21. Quoted in *Christian Century*, vol. 52, (13 November, 1935), p.1443.

22. "Dr. Kagawa of Japan Held in San Francisco," *New York Times*, 20 December, 1935, p. 12.

23. *Time*, vol. 26, (30 December 1935), pp. 19–20.

24. "Roosevelt Arranges Permit for Dr. Kagawa to Enter Country Despite His Eye Disease," *New York Times*, 21 December 1935, p. 13.

25. *Time*, loc. cit.

26. Ibid.

27. "Kagawa Entry Protested," *New York Times*, 25 December 1935, p. 3.

28. "Kagawa Tells D.C. Audience War Impossible," *Washington Post*, 19 January 1936, p.6.

29. "Kagawa's Wit Tinges Views," *Detroit News*, 28 March 1936, p. 8.

30. "10,000 Hear Kagawa Urge U.S. to Dream," *Cleveland Plain Dealer*, 5 March 1936, p.1.

31. Ibid., p. 4.

32. For the complete itinerary of the tour, which Kagawa appears to have followed except for cancelations due to exhaustion or transit delays, see *The Publishers Weekly*, vol. 128 (28 December 1935), p. 2320. A careful search of the periodicals for the dates given in each location could be the basis for a fascinating study of the development of the Kagawa mystique in the United States.

33. Campbell to Yasukochi letter.

34. "Southern Cities Greet Kagawa," *The Christian Century*, vol. 53 (5 February, 1936), p. 241.

35. "Japanese here to Put Business on a Christian Basis," *Newsweek*, vol. 6 (28 December 1935), p. 22.

36. "Kagawa Captures New England," *The Christian Century*, vol. 53, (13 May 1936), p. 714.

37. "Kagawa Foresees New Depression," *The Christian Century*, vol. 53, (4 March 1936), p. 373.

38. Ibid., 13 May 1936, p. 714.

39. Toyohiko Kagawa and E. R. Bowen, *Christian Brotherhood in Theory and Practice* (Thorntown, Indiana: Friends of Jesus, 1936), p. 8.

40. Ibid., p. 15.

41. Ibid., pp. 15–16.

42. Ibid., p. 17.

43. Ibid., p. 19.

44. "Japanese Christian Starts an American Church War," *Newsweek*, vol. 7 (25 April 1936), p. 42.

45. Loc. cit.

46. Ibid.

47. Ibid.

48. "Attack Opens on Kagawa," *The Christian Century*, vol. 53 (8 April 1936), p. 523.

49. "Insurance Agents Asked to Fight Cooperatives," *The Christian Century*, vol. 53 (24 June 1936), p. 893.

50. Toyohiko Kagawa, *Brotherhood Economics* (New York: Harper & Brothers, 1936), p. 3.

51. Ibid., pp. 165–166.

52. Yet it must be admitted that his theory does have a certain integrity. To those concerned about the ability of "interest groups" to warp our political process by exercising undue influence on government officials, this system would at least be honest and publicly legitimize each interest group, rather than having them operate in the shadows of lobbies, cloakrooms of the legislatures and bars of the capital cities.

53. George Yasukochi, "Voorhis lauds Japan's co-op founder," *Co-op News* (Berkeley, California, 28 May 1984), pp. 1, 15.

54. *New York Times*, 1 July 1936, p. 1.

55. *Time*, vol. 28 (6 July 1936), p. 38. For the most recent European biography of Kagawa, see Carl van Drey, *Toyohiko Kagawa—ein Samurai Jesu Christi* (Stuttgart: Evangelischer Missionsverlag im Christlichen Verlagshaus GMBH, 1988). For an account of his 1950 visit to Germany, see ibid., pp. 109–114.

Chapter 9.

1. "Missions to Leave Japanese Empire," *The Christian Century*, vol. 58 (5 March 1941), p. 337.

2. Ibid.

3. "Kagawa Scoffs at Talk of War," *New York Times*, 25 January 1936, p. 16.

4. "Kagawa Lauds Takahashi," *New York Times*, 26 February 1936, p. 9.

5. Stephen S. Large, *Organized Workers and Socialist Politics in Interwar Japan* (Cambridge: Cambridge University Press, 1981), pp. 202–203.

6. Quoted in "Japan Gives War United Support," *The Christian Century*, vol. 54 (1 September 1937), p. 1082.

7. Galen M. Fisher, "Kagawa Returns to Japan," *The Christian Century*, vol. 54 (9 June 1937), pp. 741–742.

8. "Endowment Sought for Kagawa Projects," *The Christian Century*, vol. 54 (17 February 1937), p. 228.

9. Toyohiko Kagawa, "The Discovery of Redeeming Love," *The Japan Christian Quarterly*, vol. 12 (January 1937), pp. 7–12.

10. Ibid.

11. Hideo Horie, "Kaigai ni okeru jinja no mondai" (The Shinto Shrines Overseas), quoted in Daniel C. Holtom, "The Religious World in Japan," *Japan Christian Year Book*, 37th Issue, Charles Wheeler Iglehart, ed. (Tokyo: The Christian Literature Society [Kyo Bun Kwan], 1939), pp. 70–71.

12. Kagawa, *Christ and Japan*, William Axling, trans. (London: Student Christian Movement Press, 1934), p. 80.

13. Ibid., pp. 81–82.

14. Ibid., p. 83.

15. Ibid., pp. 82–83.

16. Quoted in Helen F. Topping, "Kagawa and the War," *The Christian Century*, vol. 55 (4 May 1938), pp. 558–560.

17. Kagawa, "A Christian Christmas Message," quoted in *The Missionary Review of the World*, vol. 61 (December 1938), p. 562.

18. Kagawa, "The Church and Present Trends," *Japan Christian Year Book*, 36th issue, Charles Wheeler Iglehart, ed. (Tokyo: The Christian Literature Society [Kyo Bun Kwan], 1938), pp. 169–174.

19. Ibid., pp. 170–171.

20. Ibid., p. 174.

21. Nobutaka Ike, *Japan's Decision for War* (Stanford, California: Stanford University Press, 1967), provides an intimate look at the Japanese policy-makers as they considered their diplomatic options before the war in the Pacific. One of the most disturbing books ever written, it is instructive in comprehending the utter depravity of the international power plays of this century, in which billions of human beings have been treated as mere abstractions by a small handful of "leaders" in various paroxysms of malice, confusion, neurosis, greed, senility and that strange form of psychosis: patriotism. A reading of this book challenges every vestige of reverence for the false gods of authority, nation, political party, capitalism, communism, religion and confirms that the only authentic stance is continued revolt

against all who would convert groups of human beings into mere abstractions and mere abstractions into potent fetishes.

22. E. Stanley Jones, "Apply Gandhi's Method to Japan," *The Christian Century*, vol. 55 (19 January 1938), pp. 75–76.

23. Kagawa, "My Wife," *Friends of Jesus*, vol. 9, (June, 1937,) p. 25.

24. Kagawa, "Musashino no mori yori," *Kagawa zenshu*, vol. 24, p. 258, quoted in Yuzo Ota "Kagawa Toyohiko: A Pacifist?" in Nobuya Bamba and John F. Howes, *Pacifism in Japan: The Christian and Socialist Tradition* (Vancouver: University of British Columbia Press, 1978), p. 186.

25. D. G. Tendulkar, *Mahatma: Life of Mohandas Karamchand Gandhi*, 8 vols. (Delhi: The Publications Division. Ministry of Information and Broadcasting. Government of India, 1962), vol. 5, pp. 20–22.

26. Isabelle MacCausland, "Introduction to Madras," *Japan Christian Quarterly*, vol. 4 (April 1939), pp. 107–112.

27. The other delegates were Howard W. Outerbridge, Edward M. Clark, Soichi Saito, Koji Suzuki, Arthur Jorgensen, Shinji Sasaki, C. W. Iglehart, Inoko Miura, Yugoro Chiba, Akira Ebisawa, Hachiro Yuasa, Takuo Matsumoto, Tsunegoro Nara, Shoichi Murao, John C. Mann, Sudejiro Hirono and Isabelle MacCausland.

28. "Madras Reports: by Missionary Delegates," *Japan Christian Quarterly*, vol. 14 (April 1939), pp. 133–134.

29. Toyohiko Kagawa, "The Need of Farmers in Japan," *The Missionary Review of the World*, vol. 62 (March 1939), p. 199.

30. Ibid.

31. Kagawa, "The Meaning of the Cross," *Meeting of the International Mission Council at Tamburam, Madras, India, Dec. 12 to 29, 1938*, 7 vols. (New York: International Missionary Council, 1939), vol. 7, pp. 21–25.

32. Mohandas Karamchand Gandhi, *The Collected Works of Mahatma Gandhi*, 90 vols. (New Delhi: The Publications Division, Ministry of Information and Broadcasting, Government of India, 1977), vol. 68, pp. 295–298.

33. "Message from Kagawa," *The Christian Century*, vol. 56 (16 August 1939), p. 990.

34. Ibid.

35. Ibid., p. 991.

36. T. T. Brumbaugh, "Kagawa Outlines Mission Program," *The Christian Century*, vol. 56 (6 December 1939), p. 1523.

37. *Kagawa Calendar 1940*, p. 16.

38. Emerson O. Bradshaw, *Unconquerable Kagawa* (St. Paul: MacAlester Park Publishing Company, 1952), p. 134.

39. "Kagawa Imprisoned on Military Code Charge," *The Christian Century*, vol. 57 (18 September 1940), pp. 1131–1132.

40. According to a report published in early April, those tentatively selected for the Japanese delegation were Kagawa, Bishop Yoshimune Abe of the Japan Methodist Church; H. Tada, former moderator of the Presbyterian-Reformed Church; Michio Kozaki, Congregational minister; Soichi Saito, National YMCA executive; Michi Kawai, woman educator and minister, and Tsunejiro Matsuyama, member of parliament and the Japanese Chrisitian Council. See *The Christian Century*, vol. 57 (9 April 1941), p. 508.

41. Other Japanese delegates were: the above mentioned Kozaki, Saito, Kawai, and Matsuyama, joined by Dr. Hachiro Yuasa, who was working with the General Council of Congregational and Christian Churches, and William Axling. The American representatives were Bishop James C. Baker, resident bishop in the California district of the Methodist Church; Albert Edward Day of Pasadena, vice president of the Federal Council of Churches; Roswell P. Barnes, associate general secretary of the Federal Council of Churches; Mrs. Robert L. Bowen, president of the Southern California Council of Church Women; Ralph E. Diffendorfer, executive secretary of the Division of Foreign Missions of the Board of Missions and Church Extension of the Methodist Church; Galen M. Fisher, vice president of the America-Japan Society of San Francisco; Douglas Horton, general secretary of the General Council of the Congregational and Christian Churches; Paul C. Johnston, minister of the Third Presbyterian Church in the United States; Kenneth Scott Latourette, professor of Missions and Oriental history at Yale University; Sarah S. Lyon, executive secretary, foreign division of the YWCA; Emory Ross, general secretary of the Foreign Missions Conference of North America; Luman J. Shafer, secretary of the Board of Foreign Missions of the Reformed Church in America; Bishop Bertrand Stevens, Protestant Episcopal bishop of Los Angeles; Mrs. Augustus Trowbridge, member of the Woman's Cooperating Commission of the Federal Council of Churches; A. L. Warnshuis, secretary of the International Missionary Council; and Abel Ross Wentz, president of the Lutheran Theological Seminary, Gettysburg.

42. Harold E. Fey, "Kagawa Revisits America," *The Christian Century*, vol. 58 (21 May 1941), pp. 684–686.

43. "Kagawa Calls for Redemptive Love," ibid., (28 May 1941), p. 729.

44. Ibid.

45. "The United Church Retreat at Kutsukake," *Japan Christian Quarterly*, vol. 16 (October 1941), pp. 329–332.

46. "An Appeal from Japan," *The Christian Century*, vol. 58 (17 September 1941), pp. 1134–1136.

47. E. Stanley Jones, *A Song of Ascents* (Nashville: Abingdon Press, 1968), pp. 194–207, gives Jones' account of his efforts to mediate between Japan and the United States.

48. Ibid., p. 198.

49. Ibid., p. 195.

Chapter 10.

1. General Headquarters/Supreme Commander for the Allied Powers Records (RG331). The National Archives of the United States, Washington National Record Center. Hereafter cited as GHQ/SCAP Memoranda.

2. Umeko Momii interview.

3. Ibid.

4. Toyohiko Kagawa, quoted in Yuzo Ota, "Kagawa Toyohiko: A Pacifist?" in Nobuya Bamba and John F. Howes, eds., *Pacifism in Japan: The Christian and Socialist Tradition* (Vancouver, B.C.: University of British Columbia Press, 1978), p. 190.

5. Kagawa, "The 2600th year of the Imperial Reign," *Kagawa Toyohiko zenshu* (The Complete Works of Toyohiko Kagawa) 24 vols. (Tokyo: Kirisuto Shimbunsha, 1964), vol. 24, pp. 398–399.

6. GHQ/SCAP Memoranda.

7. Nobutaku Ike, *Japan's Decision for War* (Stanford, California: Stanford University Press, 1967), contains interesting examples of the amount of guesswork involved in assessing military strength.

8. Barnard Rubin. "Under Christian Guise, This Jap Fostered War," *Stars and Stripes*, Pacific edition, (20 December 1945), p. 2.

9. The letter in question was on file in the U.S. District Attorney's office in Los Angeles. Dated 4 January 1941, it was purportedly written by Naotaro Nakayama, a minister residing in the Japanese Concession in Shanghai. There was no address on the letter. During the investigation, it turned out that there was a minister named Shintaro Nakayama, who was living in Shanghai at the time (the Chinese characters were misread as Naotaro). He had formerly lived in California and was married to a nisei (second generation Japanese American). According to the SCAP investigators, Nakayama denied writing the letter, though he did say he disapproved of Kagawa's involvement in politics. The SCAP investigators did not use the letter in assessing Kagawa for the purge because they could not determine its authenticity and they conjectured that it could have been written by an enemy of Kagawa to embarrass him in the United States. The letter may also have been written deliberately to destroy the reputation of Japanese Americans, because it also implicates them in espionage activities. This made it seem even less authentic to the investigators, because the authorities failed to uncover any proof whatsoever that Japanese Americans were spying in the United States. The following excerpts from the letter are in the SCAP file:

One matter for rejoicing is that during last year Toyohiko Kagawa also decided to add his strength to the Axis. As you know, for a long time Kagawa has opposed the Military Party in Japan but Foreign Minister Matsuoka and I acted as intermediaries to the result that he decided to turn over and assist the nation. While it is not known just when the war between Japan and America will open, if everything can be kept secret till it actually opens, Reverend Kagawa, a messenger of the Japanese people, will go to America and try to become an international roving power.

On the outside, Reverend Kagawa's purpose in going to America will be to cooperate with the church of the Americans for space. However, on the inside, really, it will be to collect maps, and data, with respect to oil pipelines, gas pipelines, waterworks, and establishments and electric generating plants and electrical lines. I request that all you Fresno Crisis Committee gather all the material you can and pass it over to Reverend Kagawa.

I have no doubt but that Reverend Tatsuo Sakaguchi of the Congregational Church of your place, who is my successor and a classmate of Reverend Mr. Kagawa's, will do everything that he can. . . .

It is uncertain as to when the war between Japan and America will start, but everybody supposes it will be within this year, but never fear, but rather on the surface be peaceful and with a bow of loyalty come under the protection of the Christians of America, while inwardly in secret pray for the victorious war of Japan and lead movement among the brethren who live in America. . . .

10. *Nippon Times*, 24 October 1942. Quoted in Richard Terrill Baker, *Darkness of the Sun: The Story of Christianity in the Japanese Empire* (Nashville: Abingdon-Cokesbury Press, 1947), pp. 149–150.

11. From copy of speech in possession of Rev. Umeko Momii. A version of this speech was also published in *Kirisuto Shimbun* (Christian Newspaper), 4 October 1944; cited in *Kagawa Toyohiko zenshu* (The Complete Works of Toyohiko Kagawa) 24 vols., (Tokyo: Kirisuto Shimbunsha), vol. 24, pp. 412–413.

12. Baker, loc. cit.

13. GHQ/SCAP Memoranda.

14. Quoted in Ota, op. cit., pp. 179–180.

15. Ibid., p. 191.

16. GHQ/SCAP Memoranda.

17. Toyohiko Kagawa, "Beikoku metsubo no yogen" (A Prophecy of the Fall of the United States), *Kirisuto Shimbun* (4 October 1944), reprinted in *Kagawa zenshu*, vol. 24, pp. 412–413.

18. Quoted in GHQ/SCAP Memorandum.

19. Toyohiko Kagawa, "A Word to America: Go Back to the Spirit of Abraham Lincoln," *Nippon Times*, 8 August 1945, p. 2.

20. Ibid.

21. Kagawa, *Christ and Japan*, trans. William Axling (London: Student Christian Movement Press, 1934), pp. 64–66.

22. Kagawa, *The Economic Foundation of World Peace* (N.P.: Friends of Jesus, 1932), pp. 64–65. (This text is Volume 5, no. 1 of *Friends of Jesus*, an English language periodical dedicated to Kagawa's activities which appeared at irregular intervals in the late 1920s and the 1930s).

23. *Time*, (24 September 1945), vol. 46, pp. 26–27.

24. Emerson O. Bradshaw, *Unconquerable Kagawa*, (St. Paul: MacCalester Park, 1952). p.138.

25. "I Would Rather Be Dead," *The Christian Century*, vol. 62 (26 September 1945), pp. 1088–1089.

26. Soichi Saito, "The Significance of the Japanese Christian Deputation," and William Axling, "An Adventure in Christian Fellowship," *Japan Christian Quarterly*, vol. 16 (July 1941), pp. 225–230 and pp. 231–234, and other accounts give the impression that the conference was more a religious exercise than a meaningful effort for peace. Discussions of political differences and disturbing issues, such as the war in China, appear to have been avoided. Dialogue on the major topic of the conference, the intrusion of the Japanese state into religion, masked, rather than revealed, the alarming extent of the totalitarian control of religious life in Japan. Profound contradictions between freedom of religion and the existence of a state cult were dissolved in notions of fellowship. Most of the Christian missionaries fled

Japan, and the Japanese churches offered little resistance to the regime. Axling was imprisoned during the war.

27. Bradshaw, loc. cit., says that Kagawa described the ordeal with his typical combination of religious autobiography and humor: "I prayed that the love of God would be preserved in Japan and I prayed for the many people who had been bombed out of their homes and were destitute. I nearly died. We had a terrible food shortage, and so I ate mulberry leaves, for they contain 40% protein. They feed silkworms very nicely, but I lost weight and became almost like a silkworm myself."

Chapter 11.

1. Jerry Thorp, "No Early Rebirth of Christianity in Japan—Kagawa," *Chicago Daily News* (11 September 1945), p. 4.

2. Ibid.

3. Ibid.

4. *Time*, vol. 46 (24 September 1945), pp. 26–27.

5. Ibid.

6. Ibid.

7. Thomas Mackin, "As Kagawa Sees Japan's Future," *The Christian Century*, vol. 62 (10 October 1945), p. 1154.

8. Ibid.

9. Thorpe, loc cit.

10. Mackin, loc. cit.

11. Ibid.

12. General Headquarters/Supreme Commander for the Allied Powers Records (RG331). The National Archives of the United States, Washington National Record Center, hereafter cited as GHQ/SCAP Memoranda.

13. Mackin, loc. cit.

14. Higashikuni's diary dates the meeting on August 28, while Kagawa puts it two days earlier.

15. Emerson Bradshaw, *Unconquerable Kagawa* (St. Paul: MacCalester Park, 1952), p. 139.

16. Ibid.

17. Naruhiko Higashikuni, *Higashikuni Nikki* (Higashikuni Diary), (Tokyo: Tokuma Shoten, 1968), p. 230.

18. "Higashikuni Bids U.S. Forget Dec. 7," *New York Times*, 15 September 1945, p. 4.

19. Ibid.

20. *Nippon Times*, 2 September 1945, p. 2.

21. Ibid.

22. Ibid.

23. Barnard Rubin, "Under Christian Guise, This Jap Fostered War," *Stars and Stripes*, Pacific edition (20 December 1945), p. 2.

24. "Toyohiko Kagawa Active for Welfare of Masses," *Nippon Times* (21 September 1945), p. 4.

25. Report of Interview with Toyohiko Kagawa, from T/5 Selznick to Lt. Pontius, GHQ/SCAP Memoranda.

26. *Nippon Times* (25 September 1945), p. 3.

27. Clarence W. Hall, "Unconquerable Kagawa," *Christian Advocate*, vol. 126 (4 January 1951), pp. 6–7, 23.

28. "Kagawa Supporters Uphold His Activities," *Nippon Times*, (24 May 1946), p. 3.

29. Quoted in GHQ/SCAP Memoranda.

30. Rubin, loc. cit.

31. For a detailed study of the concepts behind the purge and its implementation, see Hans H. Baerwald, *The Purge of Japanese Leaders under the Occupation* (University of California Publications in Political Science, vol. 8) (Berkeley: University of California Press, 1959).

32. GHQ/SCAP Memoranda.

33. Rubin, loc. cit.

34. "Pettus, Rubin Ruled Loyal in IG Inquiry But Removal from Newspaper Is Upheld," *Stars and Stripes*, Pacific edition, 3 March 1946, p. 1.

35. Hugh Deane, "Toyohiko Kagawa: Japan's Lost Leader," *The Christian Register*, vol. 125 (April 1946), pp. 158–159.

36. *The Christian Register*, vol. 125 (June 1946), p. 256.

37. Ibid.

38. Richard Terrill Baker, *Darkness of the Sun: The Story of Christianity in the Japanese Empire* (Abingdon-Cokesbury Press: New York-Nashville, 1947), p. 145.

39. Clarence W. Hall, op. cit., pp. 6–7, 23.

40. GHQ/SCAP Memoranda.

41. Deane's article says: "Kagawa's thinking is obviously wedded to the ideology of feudalism and ultranationalism, to the concepts the Allies are trying to root out of the Japanese mind"; the original SCAP typescript says "Kagawa's thinking is obviously wedded to the ideology of feudalism and ultranationalism; the concepts that Allied policy is committed to rooting out of the Japanese mind"; "wedded to" is crossed out and replaced with "confirmed in"; "very" is careted in before "concepts"; "Allied policy" and "rooting out of" are crossed out and replaced with "SCAP" and "eradicate from." Deane went on to write: "Allied headquarters in Tokyo have issued fundamentally sound directives to the Japanese Government, but it is no secret that their realization is still a distant prospect. They will never be realized if the leadership of Japan is bestowed on former liberals like Kagawa, men who, now masquerading as democrats, long ago fell by the political wayside." The SCAP original draft reads "Occupation policies cannot hope to be realized if the leadership of Japan is bestowed on former liberals like Kagawa, men who, now masquerading as Democrats, long ago fell by the political wayside." It was then more brutally reworded to say "pseudo-liberals like Kagawa, who exploit the trappings of democracy for political purposes."

42. Bradshaw, op. cit., p. 17.

43. Kagawa, "We have Abandoned War," *The Christian Century*, vol. 64 (3 December 1947), p. 1483.

44. "Kagawa Arrives on Revival Tour," *New York Times* (15 July 1950), p. 14.

45. Ibid.

46. Ibid.

47. Bradshaw, op. cit., p. 24.

48. Ibid., pp. 24–25.

49. "Reformation Sunday Brings a Call for 'Spirit of God' to 'Move Again,'" *New York Times* (30 October 1950), p. 24.

50. "Peace in Home Urged by Japanese Leader," *New York Times* (4 November 1950), p. 12.

51. Bradshaw, op. cit., p. 32.

52. Ibid.

53. "Rabbi Names Group to Work Out Peace," *New York Times* (11 October 1953), p. 28.

Chapter 12.

1. Charles A. Logan, "Evangelistic Opportunities in Japan," *Japan Christian Quarterly*, vol. 17 (Autumn 1951), pp. 119–121.

2. Ibid., p. 120.

3. Toyohiko Kagawa, *Ein Weizenkorn* (Basel: Basler Missionsbuchhandlung Gmbh.: 1954), p. 5.

4. For an account of the relationship with Takahashi, see Kenneth C. Hendricks, *The Shadow of His Hand: The Reiji Takahashi Story* (St. Louis: The Bethany Press, 1967).

5. Marianna Nugent Prichard, "Kagawa: A Time for Remembering," *The Christian Century*, vol. 79 (18 April, 1962), pp. 494–496.

6. Tomio Muto, "Memories of Toyohiko Kagawa," *Japan Christian Yearbook 1961* (Tokyo: Kirisuto Shimbunsha, 1961), pp. 45–46.

7. Umeko Momii interview.

8. Ibid., pp. 47–48.

9. Kagawa, "The Korean Situation and the World Police System," *Motive*, vol. 11 (November 1950), p. 7.

10. Ibid.

11. Ibid.

12. Ibid.

13. Lord Boyd-Orr, *As I Recall* (London: MacGibbon and Kee, 1966), p. 243.

14. Kagawa, "Japanese Christians and World Government," *Japan Christian Quarterly*, vol. 21 (October 1955), p. 311.

15. Ibid., p. 312.

16. Ibid., pp. 314–315.

17. Umeko Momii interview.

18. *Ecumenical Press Service*, Special Assembly Edition, No. 5, 26 August 1954, p. 4.

19. *Chicago Tribune*, 18 August 1954, p. 2.

20. "Kagawa Makes a Dollar Go a Long Way," *The Christian Century*, vol. 72 (7 December 1955), p. 1420.

21. Quoted in Haruichi Yokoyama, *Toyohiko Kagawa and His Works* (Tokyo: Friends of Jesus, 1961), p. 13.

22. Norman Cousins, *Albert Schweitzer's Mission: Healing and Peace* (New York: W. W. Norton, 1985), pp. 231–233.

23. "12,000 Attend Opening Rite of Christian Convention," *Japan Times* (7 August 1958), pp. 1–2.

24. Prichard, op. cit., p. 496.

25. Quoted in Muto, op. cit., p. 49.

26. Morris N. Kertzer, "My Visit with Kagawa," *The Christian Century,* vol. 75 (24 September 1958), p. 1076.

27. Ibid.

28. Ibid., p. 1077.

29. Ibid.

30. Ibid.

31. Ibid.

32. Carola Barth Diary, Carola Barth Collection, Frankfurt.

33. Albert Schweitzer letters in Carola Barth Collection.

34. Letter from Sverre Svanes of The Norwegian Nobel Institute to Karl Wandrey, 2 July 1987.

35. Richard H. Drummond, "Kagawa: Christian Evangelist," *The Christian Century,* vol. 77 (13 July 1960), pp. 823–825, indicated that the propaganda broadcasts were rumored to be the reason Kagawa did not receive the prize.

36. Muto, op. cit., p. 44.

37. Yokoyama, op. cit., p. 16.

38. Ibid., p. 19.

39. Hendricks, op. cit., p. 181.

Epilogue.

1. Bertram B. Fowler, *Christian Science Monitor Weekly Magazine* (17 July 1935), p. 3.

2. Yasuo Furuya, "Toyohiko Kagawa (1888–1960): Blessed Are the Poor," in H. T. Ker, ed., *Sons of the Prophets* (Princeton: Princeton University Press, 1963), pp. 192–204 discusses the question of Kagawa's reputation in Japan.

3. Yusuke Tsurumi, "Toyohiko Kagawa," *Japan Christian Quarterly,* vol. 10 (April 1935), pp. 111–112.

4. Emerson O. Bradshaw, *Unconquerable Kagawa* (St. Paul: MacCalester Park, 1952), p. 116.

5. Ibid.

Brief Chronology

1888   Born July 10 in Kobe, Japan.

1892–93   Father Junichi dies in November and mother Kame the following January, after which he moves to Awa, Tokushima, to live with stepmother.

1902–04   Meets missionaries Dr. Logan and Dr. Myers, and is baptized a Christian, February 14, 1904.

1905   Graduates from Tokushima Middle School and enrolls at Meiji Gakuin College, Tokyo.

1906   Writes first major article "World Peace" for *Tokushima Mainichi* (newspaper).

1907   Graduates from Meiji Gakuin and attends Kobe Theological Seminary after a summer as assistant pastor in Okazaki and Toyohashi. Suffers two severe illnesses and goes to Fuso to recover, where he pens first draft of *Crossing the Death Line*.

1909   Moves into the Shinkawa slums of Kobe on Christmas eve to start his mission and settlement work.

1912   Graduates from Kobe Theological Seminary. Organizes his first co-op, a restaurant called Tengokuya (Heavenly shop) and publishes his first book, *Yujo*, a fairy tale about David and Jonathan.

1913   Marries Haru Shiba on May 27 at the Kobe Presbyterian Church.

1914   Departs for USA to study at Princeton Theological Seminary as World War I is erupting in Europe.

1915   Kagawa's landmark study *The Psychology of the Poor* is published in Japan.

1916–17   Receives Bachelor of Divinity degree from Princeton and returns to Japan the following year in May.

1918   Ordained a minister of the Japanese Presbyterian Church.

1920   His autobiographical novel *Crossing the Death Line* is published and becomes a best seller. Organizes Kobe Consumers Cooperative.

1921   Leads strikers at the Kobe shipyards. Organizes the Japan Farmers' Union and the Friends of Jesus group.

1922   First child Sumimoto is born on December 26.

1923   Supervises relief work after massive earthquake in Tokyo, with special efforts in the slum area of Honjo.

1924–25   Makes his first major lecture tour to the USA and Europe. After his return, organizes the "Kingdom of God" movement and establishes the Shikanjima settlement house in Osaka. Daughter Chiyoko is born April 23, 1925.

1927   Sets up peasant "gospel schools" in Hyogo prefecture.

1928   Organizes All-Japan Anti-War League and the Nakanogo credit union and co-op pawnshop in Tokyo.

1929   Third child Umeko is born on June 20.

1931   Goes to China on speaking tour, attends World YMCA Conference in Canada, and starts co-op hospital in Tokyo. His *A Grain of Wheat* is published.

1934   Makes an evangelist trip to the Philippines.

1935–36   In December 1935, begins his celebrated six-month tour of the world, delivering the *Brotherhood Economic* lectures in Rochester, N.Y.

1938   Attends Madras convention of the World Missionary Council and meets Gandhi.

1940   Is jailed in Tokyo as leader of anti-war movement, and police suppress his *Pillar of Cloud* magazine.

1941   Visits USA in "last ditch" unsuccessful effort to avert war in the Pacific. War begins with Japanese bombing of Pearl Harbor.

1943   In police custody twice for anti-war stance.

1944   Visits China at invitation of China National Christian Council.

1945	Following Japan's surrender and beginning of Allied Occupation, is appointed advisor to Prime Minister Higashikuni. Organizes Socialist Political Party and is elected president of Japan League of Cooperative Unions.
1946	Becomes president of Japan Farmers' Union, publishes the *Christian News*, and initiates New Japan for Christ movement. Is appointed to House of Peers, but that is abolished before Kagawa receives security clearance.
1948	Serves as National Commissioner of Prison Affairs and National Social Welfare Commissioner.
1949–50	In December 1949, embarks on religious lecture tour to Europe and the United States.
1951	Chosen vice-president of Union for World Federal Government.
1952	First All-Asian Congress for World Federation at Hiroshima names Kagawa president, as does second at Tokyo in 1952, and third at Kyoto in 1957.
1954	Attends World Church Conference in Evanston, Illinois. Efforts are initiated by Carola Barth to nominate Kagawa for Nobel Peace Award.
1957	Travels to Thailand on lecture tour..
1958	Presides over Christian International Conference for World Peace in Tokyo, and goes abroad to Malaysia for Southeast Asian Conference of International Cooperative Alliance.
1960	Dies April 25 at his home in Kamikitazawa, Setagaya-ku, Tokyo.

Bibliography

BOOKS AND MONOGRAPHS:

Axling, William. *Kagawa*. New York: Harper and Brothers, 1932.

Ayusawa, Iwao F. *A History of Labor in Modern Japan*. Honolulu: East-West Center Press, 1966.

Baker, Richard Terrill. *Darkness of the Sun: The Story of Christianity in the Japanese Empire*. Nashville: Abingdon-Cokesbury Press, 1947.

Baerwald, Hans H. *The Purge of Japanese Leaders Under the Occupation*. (University of California Publications in Political Science, vol. 8.) Berkeley: University of California Press, 1959.

Bamba, Nobuya, and John F. Howes. *Pacifism in Japan: The Christian and Socialist Tradition*. Vancouver: University of British Columbia Press, 1978.

Barth, Carola D. *Taten in Gottes Kraft*. Heilbronn: Eugen Salzer Verlag, 1937.

Bikle, George B. Jr. *The New Jerusalem: Aspects of Utopianism in the Thought of Kagawa Toyohiko*. Tucson: The University of Arizona Press, 1976.

Boyd-Orr, Lord John. *As I Recall*. London: MacGibbon and Kee, 1966.

Bradshaw, Emerson O. *Unconquerable Kagawa*. St. Paul: MacCalester Park, 1952.

Cho, Kiyoko Takeda. "An Essay on Kagawa Toyohiko—the Place of Man in His Social Theory," *Asian Cultural Study*. Tokyo: International Christian University, [1960].

Cousins, Norman. *Albert Schweitzer's Mission: Healing and Peace*. New York: W. W. Norton, 1985.

Dahlmann, Joseph. *The Great Tokyo Earthquake*. Translated by Victor F. Gettleman. New York: The America Press, 1924.

Davey, Cyril J. *Kagawa of Japan*. New York: Abingdon Press, 1960.

De Vos, George, and Hiroshi Wagatsuma. *Japan's Invisible Race: Caste in Culture and Personality*. Berkeley: University of California Press, 1966.

Dore, R. P. *Land Reform in Japan*. London: Oxford University Press, 1959.

Furuya, Yasuo. "Toyohiko Kagawa (1888–1960): Blessed are the Poor," *Sons of the Prophets*, edited by T. Ker. Princeton: Princeton University Press, 1963.

Gandhi, Mohandas Karamchand. *The Collected Works of Mahatma Gandhi*. Volume 68. New Delhi: Ministry of Information and Broadcasting, Government of India, 1977.

Gunther, John. *Inside Asia*. New York: Harper and Brothers, 1942.

Hane, Mikiso. *Peasants, Rebels and Outcastes: The Underside of Modern Japan*. New York: Pantheon Books, 1982.

Havens, Thomas R. H. *Farm and Nation in Modern Japan: Agrarian Nationalism, 1870–1940*. Princeton, N.J.: Princeton University Press, 1974.

Hendricks, Kenneth C. *The Shadow of His Hand: The Reiji Takahashi Story*. St. Louis: The Bethany Press, 1967.

Higashikuni, Naruhiko. *Higashikuni Nikki*. Tokyo: Tokuma Shoten, 1968.

Honiden, Yoshio. *Cooperative Movement in Japan*. Tokyo: Maruzen, 1958.

Hunter, Allan A. *Three Trumpets Sound: Kagawa—Gandhi—Schweitzer*. New York: Association Press, 1939.

Hyogo Prefecture Exhibitors' Association. *Hyogo Prefecture and City of Kobe*. Kobe, Japan: Panama-Pacific International Exposition, 1915.

Ike, Nobutaka. *Japan's Decision for War*. Stanford: Stanford University Press, 1967.

Japanese Consumers' Co-operative Union. *For Peace and a Better Life*. Tokyo: Japanese Consumers' Co-operative Union, 1982.

Kagawa Fellowship in Japan. *A Short Description of the Work of Toyohiko Kagawa*. Tokyo: Kagawa Fellowship in Japan, 1937.

Kagawa, Toyohiko. *Before the Dawn*. Translation of *Crossing the Death Line* by I. Fukumoto and T. Satchell. New York: George H. Doran, 1924.

———. *Brotherhood Economics*. New York: Harper and Brothers, 1936.

———. *The Challenge of Redemptive Love*. Translated by Marion Draper. New York: Abingdon Press, 1940.

———. *Christ and Japan*. Translated by William Axling. New York: Friendship Press, 1934. London: Student Christian Movement Press, 1934.

———. *The Economic Foundation of World Peace*. N.P.: Friends of Jesus, 1932.

———. *Ein Weizenkorn*. Basel: Basler Missionsbuchhandlung Gmbh., 1954.

———. *A Grain of Wheat*. London: Hodder and Stoughton, 1933.

———. *Kagawa Toyohiko zenshu*. 24 volumes edited by Tomio Muto. Tokyo: Kirisuto Shimbunsha, 1964.

———. *Love the Law of Life*. Translated by J. Fullerton Gressit. Chicago: The John C. Winston Co., 1929.

———. "The Meaning of the Cross," *Meeting of the International Mission Council at Tamburam, Madras, India, Dec. 12 to 29, 1938*. Volume 7. New York: International Missionary Council, 1939

———. *Meditations on the Cross*. Translated by Helen Topping and Marion Draper. Chicago and New York: Willett, Clark and Co., 1935.

———. *A Shooter at the Sun*. Translated by T. Satchell. Kobe: Japan Chronicle Press, 1925.

———. *The Thorn in the Flesh*. London: Student Christian Movement Press, 1936.

Kagawa, Toyohiko, and E. R. Bowen. *Christian Brotherhood in Theory and Practice*. Thorntown, Indiana: Friends of Jesus, 1936.

Kawai, Michi, and Ochimi Kubushiro. *Japanese Women Speak*. Boston: The Central Committee on the United Study of Foreign Missions, 1934.

Keene, Donald. *Dawn to the West: Japanese Literature of the Modern Era: Poetry, Drama, Criticism*. New York: Holt, Rinehart and Winston, 1984.

Knudten, Arthur C. *Toyohiko Kagawa and Some Social, Economic and Religious Tendencies in Modern Japan*. University of Southern California, 1946.

Kobayashi, Ushisaburo. *The Basic Industries and Social History of Japan, 1914–1918*. New Haven: Yale University Press, 1930.

Kodansha International. *Modern Japanese Literature in Translation*. Tokyo: Kodansha International, Ltd., 1979.

Kudo, Eiichi. *Dictionary of the Buraku Problem*. Translated by R. G. Stieber. Osaka: Buraku Liberation Research Center, 1986.

Kuroda, Shiro. *Ningen Kagawa Toyohiko*. Tokyo: Kirisuto Shimbunsha, 1970.

Jones, E. Stanley. *A Song of Ascents*. Nashville: Abingdon Press, 1968.

Lader, Lawrence. *The Margaret Sanger Story and the Fight for Birth Control*. Garden City: Doubleday and Company, 1955.

Large, Stephen S. *Organized Workers and Socialist Politics in Interwar Japan*. Cambridge: Cambridge University Press, 1981.

———. *The Rise of Labor in Japan: The Yuaikai 1912–1919*. Tokyo: Sophia University, 1972.

Mitchell, Richard H. *Thought Control in Prewar Japan*. Ithaca: Cornell University Press, 1976.

Murashima, Yoriyuki. *Kagawa Toyohiko byochu toshi*. Sakai City: Tomo Shimbunsha, 1951.

Muto, Tomio. *Kagawa Toyohiko*. Tokyo: Kirisuto Shimbunsha, 1981.

Muto, Tomio, ed. *Hyakusan nin no Kagawa den*. Tokyo: Kirisuto Shimbunsha, 1960.

Nagai, Willie Tsunetaka. *A Christian Labor Leader: Kagawa Toyohiko (1888–1960)*. University of Colorado, 1976.

Nakabayashi, Sadao. "Kagawa sensei to seikyo," *Kagawa no seikyo*. Tokyo: n.d.

Nishimura, Ken. *The Idea of Redemption in the Writings of Toyohiko Kagawa*. Emory University, 1966.

Reischauer, Edwin O., and Albert M. Craig. *Japan: Tradition and Transformation*. Boston: Houghton Mifflin Company, 1978.

Rosenkranz, Gerhard. *Flammendes Herz in Gottes Hand, von der Christlichen Ritterschaft des Dr. Kagawa Toyohiko*. Stuttgart: Evangelische Missionsverlag, 1948.

Saunders, Kenneth. *Whither Asia?* New York: The MacMillan Company, 1933.

Simon, Charlie May. *A Seed Shall Serve: the Story of Toyohiko Kagawa, Spiritual Leader of Modern Japan*. New York: E. P. Dutton, 1958.

Speer, Robert E. "Kagawa, the Man," *The Religion of Jesus*, by Toyhiko Kagawa. Philadelphia: John C. Winston, Co., 1931.

Sugiyama, Motojiro. *Tochi to jiyu no tameni*. Tokyo: Sugiyama Motojiro-Den Kankokai, 1965.

Sumiya, Mikio. *Kagawa Toyohiko: jin to shiso*. Tokyo: Nihon Kirisuto Kyodan Shuppanbu, 1966.

Swearingen, Rodger, and Paul Langer. *Red Flag in Japan: International Communism in Action, 1919–1951*. New York: Greenwood Press, 1968.

Tendulkar, D. G. *Mahatma: Life of Mohandas Karamchand Gandhi*. Volume 5. Delhi: Ministry of Information and Broadcasting, Government of India, 1962.

Topping, Helen. *Introducing Kagawa*. Chicago: Willett, Clark and Company, 1935.

Totten, George Oakley III. *The Social Democratic Movement in Prewar Japan*. New Haven and London: Yale University Press, 1966.

Van Baalen, Jan Karel. *Kagawa the Christian*. Grand Rapids, Michigan: Wm. B. Eerdmans, 1936.

van Drey, Carl. *Toyohiko Kagawa—ein Samurai Jesu Christi*. Stuttgart: Evangelischer Missionsverlag im Christlichen Verlagshaus GMBH, 1988.

Yarita, Kenichi. *Nihon no yoru wa akeru*. 2 volumes. Toyohashi City: Daiichi Shoten, 1948.

Yokota, Hideo. *Noson kakumeiron*. Tokyo: Hakubunkan, 1914.

Yokoyama, Haruichi. *Kagawa Toyohiko den*. Tokyo: Kirisuto Shimbunsha, 1951.

———. *Toyohiko Kagawa and His Works*. Tokyo: Friends of Jesus, 1961.

Waswo, Ann. "In Search of Equity: Japanese Tenant Unions in the 1920s," *Conflict in Modern Japanese History*, Tetsuo Najita and J. Victor Koschmann, eds. Princeton: Princeton University Press, 1982.

———. *Japanese Landlords: The Decline of a Rural Elite*. Berkeley: University of California Press, 1977.

Wildes, Harry Emerson. *Social Currents in Japan with Special Reference to the Press*. Chicago: University of Chicago Press, 1927.

ARTICLES AND REVIEWS:

Axling, William. "An Adventure in Christian Fellowship," *Japan Christian Quarterly*, 16 (July 1941), 231–234.

Brumbaugh, T. T. "Kagawa on Cooperatives," *The Christian Century*, 52 (February 27, 1935), 267.

Deane, Hugh. "Toyohiko Kagawa: Japan's Lost Leader," *The Christian Register*, 125 (April 1946), 158–159.

Drummond, Richard H. "Kagawa: Christian Evangelist," *The Christian Century*, 77 (13 July 1960), 823–825.

Felton, Ralph A. "The Rural Church in Japan (II)," *Japan Christian Quarterly*, 13 (April 1938), 144.

Fey, Harold E. "Kagawa Revisits America," *The Christian Century*, 58 (21 May 1941), 684–686.

———. "Looking at Life with Kagawa," *The Christian Century*, 47 (12 March, 1930), 331.

Fisher, Galen. "The Cooperative Movement in Japan," *Pacific Affairs*, 11 (December 1938), 478–491.

———. "Kagawa Returns to Japan," *The Christian Century*, 54 (9 June 1937), 741–742.

Fowler, Bertram B. *Christian Science Monitor Weekly Magazine*, (17 July 1935), 3.

Hall, Clarence W. "Unconquerable Kagawa," *Christian Advocate*, 126 (4 January 1951), 6–7, 23.

Holtom, Daniel C. "The Religious World in Japan," *Japan Christian Year Book*, 37 (1939), 70–71.

Jones, E. Stanley. "Apply Gandhi's Method to Japan," *The Christian Century*, 55 (19 January 1938), 75–76.

Kagawa, Masuyoshi. "Gokaini kurushimu," *Bulletin for Kagawa Toyohiko zenshu*, 23 (August 1964), 2–3.

Kagawa, Toyohiko. "Beikoku metsubo no yogen," *Kirisuto Shimbun*, (4 October 1944).

——. "Chingen dorei no kaiho," *Rodo shimbun*, (15 June 1919), 1.

——. "A Christian Christmas Message," *The Missionary Review of the World*, 61 (December 1938), 562.

——. "Christianity and Race Prejudice. A Japanese Plea," *The Friend*, 65 (3 April 1925), 281.

——. "Christianity in Japan Today," *The Christian Century*, 45 (12 January 1928), 50.

——. "The Church and Present Trends," *Japan Christian Year Book*, 36 (1938), 169–174.

——. "The Discovery of Redeeming Love," *The Japan Christian Quarterly*, 12 (January 1937), 7–12.

——. "Earthquake Relief," *The Christian Movement in Japan, Korea and Formosa*, 22 (1924) 211.

——. "Facing a Crisis in Japan," *Missionary Review of the World*, 57 (October 1934), 465–466.

——. "Japanese Christians and World Government," *Japan Christian Quarterly*, 21 (October 1955), 311.

——. "The Korean Situation and the World Police System," *Motive*, 11 (November 1950), 7.

——. "Musansha kaikyu no shutsugen," *Shin Kobe*, (22 August 1918), 1.

——. "My Wife," *Friends of Jesus*, 9 (June, 1937), 25.

——. "The Need of Farmers in Japan," *The Missionary Review of the World*, 62 (March 1939), 199.

——. "Nihon no mura no shakai mondai," *Kyusai kenkyu*, (January 1919).

——. "One Million Christians in Japan," *The Japan Christian Quarterly*, 3 (October 1928), 377.

——. "Revealing Christ in Japan," *The Missionary Review of the World*, 54 (March 1931), 166.

——. "Sechzehn Jahre Kriegsdienst für Christus in Japan," *Zeitschrift für Missionskunde und Religionswissenschaft*, 41 (1926), 13.

——. "We have Abandoned War," *The Christian Century*, 64 (3 December 1947), 1483.

——. "A Word to America: Go Back to the Spirit of Abraham Lincoln," *Nippon Times*, (8 August 1945), 2.

Kazin, Alfred. "Pilgrims of Japan," *New York Times Book Review*, (9 February 1936), 6.

Kertzer, Morris N. "My Visit with Kagawa," *The Christian Century*, 75 (24 September 1958), 1076.

Kumano, Yoshitaka. "Poetic Christianity: Toyohiko Kagawa and Takeshi Fujii," *Japan Christian Quarterly*, 32 (Fall 1966), 235–245.

Logan, Charles A.. "Evangelistic Opportunities in Japan," *Japan Christian Quarterly*, 17 (Autumn 1951), 119–121.

MacCausland, Isabelle. "Introduction to Madras," *Japan Christian Quarterly*, 4 (April 1939), 107–112.

Mackin, Thomas. "As Kagawa Sees Japan's Future," *The Christian Century*, 62 (10 October 1945), 1154.

Main, Idabelle Lewis. "Kagawa Wins Chinese Trust," *The Christian Century*, 51 (2 May, 1934), 609–610.

McCoy, R. D. "Medical Cooperatives in Japan," *The Japan Christian Year Book,* 34 (1936), 183–186.

Miller, Herbert A. "Apostles of World Unity XXXI—Toyohiko Kagawa," *World Unity* , 9 (October 1931), 34–40.

Muto, Tomio. "Memories of Toyohiko Kagawa," *Japan Christian Yearbook,* (1961), 45–46.

——. "Ushers to the Bible," *Japan Times,* (11 August 1958), 3.

Myers, H. W. "Toyohiko Kagawa, Christian Labor Leader," *Missionary Review of the World,* 46 (October 1923), 807–811.

——. "Toyohiko Kagawa—Japanese Apostle to the Poor," *The Missionary Review of the World,* 54 (July 1931), 501–502.

Prichard, Marianna Nugent. "Kagawa: A Time for Remembering," *The Christian Century,* 79 (18 April, 1962), 494–496.

Rubin, Barnard. "Under Christian Guise, This Jap Fostered War," *Stars and Stripes,* Pacific edition, (20 December 1945), 2.

Saito, Soichi. "The Significance of the Japanese Christian Deputation," *Japan Christian Quarterly,* 16 (July 1941), 225–230.

Thorp, Jerry. "No Early Rebirth of Christianity in Japan—Kagawa," *Chicago Daily News,* (11 September 1945), 4.

Topping, Helen F. "Kagawa and the War," *The Christian Century,* 55 (4 May 1938), 558–560.

Tsurumi, Yusuke. "Toyohiko Kagawa," *The Japan Christian Quarterly,* 10 (April 1935), 113–114.

Yasukochi, George. "Japanese Co-opers to Visit Berkeley," *Co-op News,* [Berkeley] (25 February 1987), 3.

——. "Voorhis lauds Japan's co-op founder," *Co-op News* [Berkeley], (28 May 1984), 1, 15.

PERIODICALS:

Chicago Tribune, 1954.

Christian Advocate, 4 January 1951.

The Christian Century, 1928, 1930, 1934–1941, 1945, 1947, 1955, 1958, 1960, 1962.

The Christian Register, 1946.

Christian Science Monitor Weekly Magazine, 17 July 1935.

Cleveland Plain Dealer, 1936.

Co-op News [Berkeley, California], 1984, 1987.

Detroit News, 1936.

Friends of Jesus, 1931, 1932, 1936, 1937.

Japan Christian Quarterly, 1928, 1935, 1936, 1937, 1939, 1941, 1951, 1955, 1966.

The Japan Christian Year Book, 1924, 1936, 1938, 1939, 1961.

Japan Times, 1958, 1968.

Japan Weekly Chronicle, 1920, 1921, 1922, 1923, 1924.

Kirisuto Shimbun 4 October 1944.

The Missionary Review of the World, 1923, 1931, 1934, 1939.

New York Times, 1925, 1935, 1936, 1940, 1945, 1950, 1953.

Newsweek, 1935, 1936.

Nippon Times, 1942, 1945, 1946.
Ogden (Utah) *Standard*, 1916, 1917.
The Publishers Weekly, 28 December 1935.
Stars and Stripes, Pacific edition, 1946.
Time, 1935, 1936, 1945.
Washington Post, 1936.

UNPUBLISHED MATERIALS:

Frankfurt. Carola Barth Diary, Carola Barth Collection.
Washington, D.C. Record Group 331, General Headquarters/Supreme Commander for the Allied Powers Records. National Archives.

Index

Photo by Julia Barton

ABOUT THE AUTHOR

ROBERT SCHILDGEN was born in Lancaster, Wisconsin, into a Roman Catholic family who farmed in nearby Glen Haven township, close to the Mississippi River. He graduated from the University of Wisconsin in 1965 and completed a Masters Degree in the School of Letters at Indiana University in 1970. A writer, teacher, union and co-op activist whose articles have appeared in a variety of newspapers and periodicals, he was co-editor of the Berkeley *Co-op News* from 1978 to 1985. In 1987–88 he served as the first Co-op Scholar-in-Residence at Oberlin College. His interest in Kagawa began through involvement with cooperatives and his study of the social gospel and liberation theology in modern Christianity.